COOPER
RANGER
W9-ASF-555

McGraw-Hill Series in Political Science

Joseph P. Harris, *Consulting Editor*

Problems of American Government

McGraw-Hill Series in Political Science
JOSEPH P. HARRIS, *Consulting Editor*

BONE · American Politics and the Party System

CHASE · The United Nations in Action

FERGUSON AND McHENRY · The American Federal Government

FERGUSON AND McHENRY · The American System of Government

FERGUSON AND McHENRY · Elements of American Government

FIELD · Governments in Modern Society

FRANK · Cases on the Constitution

HARTMANN · Basic Documents of International Relations

HARTMANN · Readings in International Relations

HOLLOWAY · State and Local Government in the United States

LEONARD · International Organization

NEUMANN · European and Comparative Government

REED · Municipal Management

RIEMER · Problems of American Government

STRAUSZ-HUPÉ AND POSSONY · International Relations

WILSON · The American Political Mind

WILSON · Police Administration

PROBLEMS OF
AMERICAN GOVERNMENT

Neal Riemer
Assistant Professor of Political Science
The Pennsylvania State College

FIRST EDITION

3428

New York Toronto London
McGRAW-HILL BOOK COMPANY, INC.
1952

RANGER JUNIOR COLLEGE LIBRARY

PROBLEMS OF AMERICAN GOVERNMENT

Copyright, 1952, by the McGraw-Hill Book Company, Inc. Printed in the United States of America. All rights reserved. This book, or parts thereof, may not be reproduced in any form without permission of the publishers.

Library of Congress Catalog Card Number: 51-12945

THE MAPLE PRESS COMPANY, YORK, PA.

PREFACE

This book grew out of the need for a "problems book" of readings to be used as a supplement to a regular text in the field of American government. It grew out of the need for a well-organized book of significant readings that would raise provocative political issues in the form of meaningful questions and then present a number of stimulating articles as alternative answers or approaches to these questions or problems.

In this fashion the fundamental ideas and institutions underlying the theory and practice of American government may be treated so as to challenge the interest, imagination, and critical intelligence of the student. The conflict of alternative viewpoints may thus illuminate the logic, the facts, and the values which support the operative political ideals of the American people. Each student is provided the opportunity to work out his own stand on key problems of American political life. It is believed that only in this way can each student acquire a free, deep, and understanding commitment to liberal democracy.

Seventeen controversial problems, probing crucial areas of the American political scene, have been included. To facilitate grasp of these problems each has been prefaced by a brief introduction. Each introduction raises the general issue involved, summarizes selected approaches to the chapter's specific problem, and concludes with the exact question or questions answered by selections in each chapter.

The selections present a wide variety of political literature. They are drawn from popular newspaper and magazine articles, hard-hitting campaign speeches, pungent congressional debates, widely discussed books, carefully calculated Supreme Court decisions, and the more academic contributions of political scientists. Each selection is long enough to present clearly an answer or approach to a specific question or problem. "Classics" as well as "documents" have been utilized only when they present answers to problems posed, and not simply because of their reputation and longevity. On the other hand, some ephemeral literature has been included if representative of either a widely held or a highly controversial view on a problem or question. The choice of articles has been based on the premise that students should be prepared to criticize the facts, logic, and values of all types of arguments and positions—those they will encounter in "bull sessions," on street corners, in the daily newspaper or weekly magazine, as well as in the classroom or the learned treatise.

v

Questions at the end of each chapter have been added to enable the student to ascertain whether he has grasped the argument of each selection; sees the relationship between the several articles; and is stimulated to criticize, analyze, appraise, evaluate—and not simply to acquire facts by rote.

The select *annotated* bibliography at the conclusion of each chapter or problem is intended to refer the student to additional literature relevant to the particular problem treated. The annotations may also help to crystallize and clarify the problems themselves.

Introduction, questions, and bibliography should be of aid to the uninitiated without boring the more mature student.

The book was planned primarily to lend itself to the use of a number of tested techniques in teaching political science: classroom discussion, Socratic questioning, classroom debate, oral reports, and term papers. However, teachers and students of debate may find the book a convenient manual for debate topics.

The author wishes to express his appreciation here to those who, in different ways, have aided in the preparation of this book. Professors Ruth Silva, of The Pennsylvania State College, and Harold M. Dorr, of the University of Michigan, were helpful in formulating the "problems approach" used in the book. Professor John Ferguson, of The Pennsylvania State College, and Dean McHenry, of the University of California, contributed many useful suggestions relating to student needs. Above all, the author would like to express his debt to his wife, without whose counsel, aid, patience, and encouragement this book might well have died in embryo.

NEAL RIEMER

STATE COLLEGE, PA.
January, 1952

CONTENTS

Preface v

PART I: AMERICAN CONSTITUTIONAL PRINCIPLES

PROBLEM 1. REPRESENTATIVE GOVERNMENT: *How Should Your Congressman Vote?* 3

    Vote for the Important Home Folks First—*James M. Burns.* . . 4
    Congress Should Lead, Not Follow—*Jerry Voorhis.* 9
    Vote with the Party on Key Issues—*Henry A. Wallace.* . . 14
    Congress Should Lead and Follow Public Opinion—*George B. Galloway.* 18

PROBLEM 2. SEPARATION OF POWERS: *Can a Government Based on Separation of Powers Be Strong, Effective, and Responsible?* . 24

    Cabinet Government Is Superior to Congressional Government —*Woodrow Wilson.* 25
    Congressional Government Is Superior to Cabinet Government —*Robert Luce.* 32
    Bridge the Gap with a Joint Executive-Legislative Cabinet— *Thomas K. Finletter.* 38

PROBLEM 3. FEDERALISM: *Is Our Federal System of Government Endangered, Obsolescent, or Adequate?* 47

    We Must Guard against a Federal Police State—*1948 Platform of the States' Rights Party.* 48
    Federalism Is Obsolescent—*Harold J. Laski.* 50
    Federalism Is Still Viable—*David Fellman.* 56

PROBLEM 4. INDIVIDUAL RIGHTS: *How Fulfill the American Heritage of Liberty for All Our People?* 67

    The Federal Government Should Act Now on a Broad and Far-reaching Front—*The President's Committee on Civil Rights.* 68
    The "Civil Rights Program" Is Vicious, Unconstitutional, and Unnecessary—*Senator Clyde R. Hoey.* 82
    An Alternative Program Would Be More Sensible, Effective, and Beneficial—*Hodding Carter.* 88

PART II: INSTRUMENTS OF POPULAR CONTROL

PROBLEM 5. PRESSURE GROUPS: *Enemy or Ally of American Democracy?* 97

Special Interests versus the Public Welfare—*Stuart Chase.* . . . 99
Democracy by and for the People—*Mary E. Dillon.* 107

PROBLEM 6. PUBLIC OPINION: *How Secure a Free, Adequate, and Responsible "Press"?* 119

The Press Endangers Its Own Freedom—*Commission on Freedom of the Press.* 121
The Newspaper Press Is Fundamentally Sound—*Frank L. Mott.* 126
It Is Government Which Has Always Threatened Freedom—
Justin Miller. 131

PROBLEM 7. POLITICAL PARTIES: *Does, Should, and Can Our Two-party System Provide the Voter with a Meaningful Choice?* . . 139

The Public Interest versus the Special Interests—*Harry S. Truman.* 141
Liberty versus the Fair Deal—*Robert A. Taft.* 145
In Defense of Parties Lacking Clear-cut Differences—*John Fisher.* 147
We Need a Stronger, More Responsible Two-party System—
Committee on Political Parties of the American Political Science Association. 151

PROBLEM 8. ELECTIONS: *How Should We Elect the President of the United States?* 162

Count the State's Electoral Vote in Proportion to the Popular Vote—*Senator Henry C. Lodge.* 164
Defeat the Lodge Proposal—*Senator Homer Ferguson.* . . . 172
The Lodge Plan Will Handicap the Republicans—*Ruth C. Silva.* 177
The District System Is Preferable to Proportional Voting and the Present Electoral Setup—*Lucius Wilmerding, Jr.* 180

PART III: FEDERAL INSTITUTIONS

PROBLEM 9. CONGRESS: *Can Congress Reform Itself?* 187

The Legislative Reorganization Act Was the First Step toward Reform—*Robert M. La Follette, Jr.* 189
Congress Cannot Reform Itself—*James M. Burns.* 195

PROBLEM 10. PRESIDENT: *Presidential Power: Peril or Promise?* . . 204

Presidential Domination Ought to Be Diminished—*An Historically Minded Member of Congress (With the Aid of Edward S. Corwin).* 206

Fears of Presidential Dictatorship or Domination Are Exaggerated but Reform Is Still Necessary—*Edward S. Corwin.* . 208

The United States Needs Strong Presidential Leadership—*Harold J. Laski.* 210

Effective Management Demands a Strong Executive—*The President's (1937) Committee on Administrative Management.* . 213

Presidential Dictatorship May Save Democratic and Constitutional Government—*Clinton L. Rossiter.* 216

PROBLEM 11. FEDERAL COURTS: *Is "Judicial Review" Compatible with Democratic Rule?* 223

I. IN SUPPORT OF JUDICIAL REVIEW

Judicial Review Is the Court's Grave, Delicate, but Necessary Duty—*Justice George Sutherland.* 225

Courts Must Ensure Personal and Property Rights against Popular Action—*Justice David J. Brewer.* 226

To Safeguard Liberty the Court Must Translate an Eighteenth-century Bill of Rights into Twentieth-century Restraints—*Justice Robert H. Jackson.* 228

States' Rights Must Be Protected against Invasion by the Federal Government—*Justice George Sutherland.* . . . 229

Judicial Review Is Not Judicial Tyranny—*James M. Beck.* 231

II. IN OPPOSITION TO JUDICIAL REVIEW

Judicial Review Is Undemocratic in Theory, Untenable and Unnecessary in Practice—*Henry Steele Commager.* . . 232

PROBLEM 12. ADMINISTRATION: *Does Big Government Mean an Irresponsible, Tyrannical, and Wasteful Bureaucracy?* 242

The Attack on Big Government and Big Bureaucracy: I—*John H. Crider.* 243

The Attack on Big Government and Big Bureaucracy: II—*Ludwig Von Mises.* 245

In Defense of Big Government and Big Bureaucracy—*John A. Vieg.* 248

PART IV: PUBLIC POLICY

PROBLEM 13. FEDERAL ENTERPRISES: *How Should We Develop Our Major River Basins?* 257

The TVA Idea, Adapted Wisely, Can Be Made to Work Elsewhere—*David E. Lilienthal.*   259

The Regional Authority Is an Undesirable, Super-socialistic,
Welfare State—*Harlan I. Peyton.*   265

A Drastically Reorganized Regular Department Should Develop Our River Basins—*The Hoover Commission Task
Force on Natural Resources.*   269

PROBLEM 14. LABOR: *How Should a Free Society Handle National-
emergency Strikes or Lockouts?*   276

Inquiry, Injunction, Cooling-off, Last-offer Ballot and the Best
Conciliation Service Possible—*The Labor Management Relations Act of 1947.*   278

We Need a More Flexible and Realistic Approach than the
Taft-Hartley Act—*The Democratic Senators on the Joint
Committee on Labor-Management Relations.*   280

Temporary Government Seizure May Have to Be Our Difficult
Choice—*Charles O. Gregory.*   281

Compulsory Arbitration through Labor Courts—*Senator
Homer Ferguson.*   286

PROBLEM 15. AGRICULTURE: *What Kind of Price Support Program,
If Any, Should We Adopt?*   292

The Brannan Plan Is a Farm Policy in the Public Interest—
Charles F. Brannan.   294

The Farm Bureau Supports a Moderate, Flexible Farm Program
—*Allan B. Kline.*   301

Our Farm Price-support Program Is a Falsework of Bogus
Values—*Fortune Magazine.*   305

We Must Oppose Agricultural Subsidies of Any Kind—*H. M.
Griffith.*   308

PROBLEM 16. GOVERNMENT, THE ECONOMY, AND SOCIAL WELFARE:
The Welfare State: Reactionary Bugaboo or Socialist Menace? .   312

America Needs Democratic Socialism—*National Platform of
the United States Socialist Party.*   314

We're Rushing Headlong down the Road to Socialism—*Senator
Harry F. Byrd.*   316

Beware the Socialist Planner—*John T. Flynn.*   319

The United States Follows a Sound Constitutional Path—
Senator Paul H. Douglas.   321

PROBLEM 17. FOREIGN AFFAIRS: *How Should We Deal with the
Soviet Union?*   328

Peace with Justice through the United Nations and a Rearmed Free World—*Harry S. Truman*. 331

The United States Must Take the Offensive in the War against Communism—*James Burnham*. 337

The Quaker Alternative: Real Negotiation through the United Nations, International Disarmament, and a World Aid Program—*American Friends Service Committee*. 340

United States Naval and Air Power Will Protect Our Western Hemisphere Gibraltar—*Herbert Hoover*. 347

Peace Is the Key to Soviet Foreign Policy—*Jessica Smith*. . . 351

PART I: AMERICAN CONSTITUTIONAL PRINCIPLES

REPRESENTATIVE GOVERNMENT

How Should Your Congressman Vote?

Representation and a democratic suffrage are not necessarily Siamese twins. Representation existed before elections and before the bulk of the citizenry could participate in elections. For example, a hereditary king could claim to represent his nation. A parliament based upon a restricted franchise could assert that all, including workers and women, were represented even though all did not possess the right to vote. The framers of the Federal Constitution firmly believed in representative government but were not greatly concerned about the fact that property and religious qualifications in all the original thirteen states greatly restricted the suffrage or that women and slaves were not permitted to vote.

The elimination of voting restrictions based on property, religion, race, and sex helped us to achieve democratic representation. But this enlargement of the electorate, by increasing the number of people to whom the elected representative was theoretically responsible, complicated a problem as old as the history of the elected representative. This problem, selected as the focal point of this chapter, is summarized in the question: How should the representative vote?

In the first selection in this chapter James M. Burns describes one view of democratic representation—that of the congressman as "diplomatic agent." The typical congressman, says Burns, votes in harmony with the well-organized home folks, among whom are the local party leaders and the strategic pressure groups. Always aware of the next election, the congressman avoids or straddles national issues that seriously divide his supporters, while always protecting local rights and interests. Implicit in this very interesting account of realistic politics is the congressman's view that he *does* what he *should*.

Jerry Voorhis differs with Mr. Burns's typical congressman. Voorhis, himself a former member of Congress, believes that the congressman should have the courage to represent the best and highest long-run interests of the whole nation. The congressman should not simply mirror the views of a majority of his constituents or the latest Gallup Poll. Because of his greater access to facts and information he should provide farsighted and intelligent leadership. Such leadership, Voorhis argues, does not necessarily mean political suicide.

Henry A. Wallace advocates that the member of Congress, on penalty of loss of important committee assignments and party patronage, support certain basic policies selected by his party's leaders from the party's convention platform. Only in this way can the representative be held responsible for his actions and can the voter make an intelligent and effective choice on election day between party programs.

In the last article in this problem George B. Galloway maintains that a congressman should both lead and follow public opinion: follow public opinion in so far as it expresses the desires of the people; lead the people in formulating ways and means of accomplishing those desires. The congressman, writes Galloway, must harmonize national and local needs and ideals. He is neither purely the spineless agent of his constituents nor the godlike trustee of his own concept of the public interest. On most issues he may legitimately compromise with party or constituency. But he also reserves the right on rare occasions to follow his own conscience though the political heavens fall.

The many aspects of the complex problem of representative government may be condensed, somewhat arbitrarily, in the following questions. These questions, if adequately answered, lead into the very heart of American Democracy.

In voting, should the congressman follow the dominant political forces in his constituency? Should he lead, not follow, public opinion? Should he follow the party on the party's basic issues? Or should he both lead and follow public opinion?

VOTE FOR THE IMPORTANT HOME FOLKS FIRST

BY JAMES M. BURNS*

[Assistant Professor of Political Science at Williams College, James MacGregor Burns once acted as legislative assistant to a

* *Congress on Trial: The Legislative Process and the Administrative State* (New York: Harper, 1949), pp. 8–13. By permission of the publisher.

member of Congress. He served on the staff of the Hoover Commission and has also campaigned actively in local elections.

[The following selection is a description of what "the biologist would call a *type genus*—the member of Congress who best typifies his family. . . . He is a composite of those Senators and Representatives who year after year and despite changes in party control determine the make-up of Congress and the main direction it takes."[1] Similarly, the Ninth District is a typical congressional district and Boone Center a typical municipality in such a district. EDITOR.]

Though he may not admit it even to himself, the Congressman's chief aim is re-election. To stay in office means to gain added power and prerogatives in Congress on the basis of seniority, and to become eligible ultimately for higher office—senator, governor, judge, cabinet member. If his re-election depended on successful exploitation of key national issues, the Congressman would be compelled to run on the record of his votes on those issues. But his success at the polls hinges largely on how effectively the Congressman has served as the 9th District's representative in Washington. Here his record is almost flawless. He has rarely faltered in his protection of the sovereign interests of his locality. Against the encroachments of Big Business, Big Labor, and Big Government he has defended the rights of small business, local unions, and the average man in his district. By seeming to protect the totality of the 9th District's interests against the outside world, the Congressman contrives to avoid the basic but perilous issues of national and world policy.

But if the Congressman has little responsibility to his constituents on matters of broad public policy, he has a very definite responsibility to two groups in the 9th District. One of these consists of the local party leaders—called "bosses" by their opponents—and the other of the organized special interest groups.

The party bosses in the 9th District are concerned almost wholly with patronage and favors. They are not evil or venal men; they know that without patronage their political dominion, centered in city, courthouse, and county machines, would soon crumble. Operating at all levels of American government, they extract from Washington jobs for their followers as postmasters, federal marshals, collectors of internal revenue, judges, and the like. In state and local governments an army of petty officials makes obeisance to the machine for its jobs.

The Congressman advanced smoothly up the ladder from assistant county attorney to his present position only because he never failed to

[1] Burns, *op. cit.*, p. 1.

cooperate with his party leaders on matters of patronage. He is fully aware that he needs their support more than they need his supply of federal patronage. For in the case of falling-out and a showdown—an unthinkable occurrence for the Congressman—he could cut off only one source of their patronage; the bosses would survive to put an end to his political career in the next party primary, over which they excercise a tight grip.

The local party leaders, for the most part, have little interest in the Congressman's votes on national issues. Even when he deserts the national party platform on important legislation, it never occurs to the party leaders that they have any responsibility for that platform. Indeed, the party machine itself often has a bi-partisan slant because of unwritten covenants with the other major party over matters of patronage.

In several cases, however, the local leaders are concerned as individuals, rather than as party officials, with the Congressman's position on certain national policies. A leader of one of Boone Center's wards, for example, is a large lumber dealer, and naturally he is interested in the Congressman's votes on such matters as price control, housing, and subsidies. Two of the county leaders operate large farms and have considerable influence in the Grange; they follow the Congressman's votes on farm bills with care.

The other dominant element in the 9th District—the cluster of organized interest groups—has no concern with patronage but a deep concern with national legislation. The most important pressure groups in the district are those of business, farmers, veterans, and labor, in that order. These groups in turn are made up of individual organizations. The farmers, for example, are divided into the National Grange, the American Farm Bureau Federation, the National Cooperative Milk Producers' Federation, and the Farmers' Union. The veterans divide into the American Legion, the Veterans of Foreign Wars, and World War II organizations. Special issue groups, such as Townsendites and Prohibitionists, take an active part in politics. And there are scores of fraternal, religious, national-origin, and occupational associations.

How many votes do these groups control? The Congressman wishes he knew the answer to this question. With a sharp eye for political margins, he perceives that some organizations lay claim to large membership, like-minded on all issues, where actually the rank-and-file is small in number, divided, and irresolute. But he cannot be sure. He must feel his way cautiously. Whether or not the pressure groups deliver the votes, they are important media of communication with thousands of voters. The political apathy in his district is often so great that he is unable to "get to" the electorate. The various associations, with their meetings, newspapers, and radio programs, can help him make connections with many voters who might never attend a party rally or read ordinary campaign literature.

Naturally the Congress tries to gauge the reality of vote-power behind the facade of propaganda. But his responsiveness to the pressure groups is not a matter of votes alone. Often the Congressman makes political decisions without any evaluation of the exact line-up of the various groups back home. He truly "votes his own conscience." If his position happens to coincide with that of the organized groups in his district, it is not simply because he is controlled by them. It is because he is one of them. He is a Legionnaire; he is close to the farmers and their interests; his roots are in the business class. He knows the leaders of the various organizations, and by and large he considers them "sound."

Even the Congressman, with all his political dexterity, cannot act for every one of the groups. To some extent he must choose sides. In practice he speaks for a coalition of groups representing small business, the owners of large farms, veterans of three wars, and skilled labor. He speaks for these groups partly because they are politically effective, partly because he lives in their political world. Thus the business organizations, the Grange, the Farm Bureau, the Legion, the VFW, and the American Federation of Labor carry weight in the congressional representation of the 9th District.

Since even these interests may come into conflict, the Congressman must be able to act for one of them without seeming to flout the claims of the others. Consequently, he moves quickly to confer legislative favors on one pressure group where he can do so without injuring another. He selects his ground carefully. A bonus for veterans, subsidies and price support for farmers, high tariffs for business, the prevailing wage for AFL crafts—such measures are well adapted to the Congressman's use, for not one of them is likely to antagonize the other groups. Tariff protection for the small industries of the 9th District is an especially effective campaign argument because it appeals to both business and labor. Higher farm prices are justified as leading to more spending by farmers in Boone Center's shops. Such measures may mean a higher cost of living for the consumers of the 9th District, but consumers do not make up one of the pressure groups that the Congressman must reckon with on election day.

The Congressman reflects a sense of solidarity in the 9th District that is not wholly artificial. Not only Boone Center but the whole district is essentially a trading and producing community. The operators of big farms, employing machinery and hired hands, must be businessmen as well as farmers. On the local scale there is little disharmony between them and the businessmen of the city. The traders in Boone Center, who were originally independent and self-contained, during the past half-century have increasingly become instruments of a nation-wide commercial system. At one time free agents, Boone Center factories are now units of a national industrial order. But the myth of the autonomous and footloose community still persists, and the Congressman loses few votes in the 9th District when he attacks Wall Street and Big Business. For the dominant forces in both city and country have been steeped in the ideas of a local pecuniary society operating on its own. Militantly conservative, the substantial citizens of the district produce on the local level a gloss which partially conceals latent conflicts between large and small business, between business and industry, between workers and employer, between farm owner and hired hand, between city and country, between producer and consumer.

The most serious threat to the Congressman's strategy lies in the dramatization of epochal national questions such as often dominate the political scene during presidential campaigns. The exploitation of key issues by a Roosevelt or a Willkie, by a Wallace or a Stassen, draws unorganized voters to the polls and disrupts the united fronts assumed by pressure groups around their narrow designs. Such issues induce members of even the most tightly organized groups to forsake their petty interests and to think and vote in terms of broad national policy.

In such a juncture the Congressman assumes the politician's protective coloration—he straddles. Refusing to accept the gauge of battle on the open ground of national policy, he retires into a defensive zone of evasion, subterfuge, and recourse to "red herrings." At all costs he shifts the debate away from his position on controversial public policy and focusses attention on his fight for the 9th District and its interests. Here he is on safe ground.

Against the injection of national issues into the local campaign the Congressman's best defense is the absence of a clear-cut record on those issues. On some important votes in the House there was no record as to how the members lined up. The Congressman was not obliged to take a position on some matters because the bills died in the Senate or in committee. When other bills came before the House he may have been unavoidably detained on business in his office or district, and thus unable to vote.

The most effective way to straddle an issue, he has discovered, is to vote on both sides of the question. On one occasion the Congressman voted to kill a bill by recommitting it; half an hour after the recommittal move, he cast his ballot for the legislation. In the case of the price control act of 1942 he advocated a series of crippling amendments, some of which favored manufacturers and farmers in the 9th District, but in the end he voted for the Act. On several occasions he supported measures in Congress only to take part later in "economy drives" that would have starved the agency enforcing the laws. These subterfuges have obvious advantages. In case he is questioned back home as to his stand on these policies, the Congressman can tailor his answer to fit the views of his inquirers and he can point to the record to back up his claims.

If the Congressman were a modern Machiavelli, his advice to freshmen in Congress on "How to Stay in Office" would be: (1) vote for the home folks first, especially for those who are well organized; (2) keep on good terms with the local party bosses; (3) stress your protection of your district's interests as a whole against the outside world; (4) as far as possible do not commit yourself on the important national issues that divide your constituents. But the Congressman is not Machiavellian, and if he gave such advice he would speak in terms of the importance of following a safe and sane middle way, of the dangers of extremism and centralization, of the need for protecting local rights and interests.

CONGRESS SHOULD LEAD, NOT FOLLOW

by Jerry Voorhis*

[Horace Jerry Voorhis, a Democrat, represented the Twelfth District of California in Congress for 10 years, 1937 to 1947. He is the author of a book, *Confessions of a Congressman*, which describes his congressional service. Since 1947, he has been General Secretary of the Cooperative League of the United States. Editor.]

The United States Congress has a decisive role to play in this year of decision. How is it to act so that the best interests of the nation will be served? On what should it base its decisions? As representatives of the people should Congressmen follow the people's will or lead it? This is a dilemma as old as democracy.

The danger is that Congress will take the time-worn course of following the nation, as it does today, instead of setting such standards of courageous and farsighted leadership that all of us will be inspired to meet America's grave, new responsibilities. The danger is acute because unless Congress leads, the job America must do—at home and abroad—will not be done.

To a great many persons the phrase "representative government" means that Senators and Representatives are sent to Washington, not to use their

* "A Call to Congress to Lead, Not Follow," *The New York Times*, Jan. 25, 1948, VI, pp. 12ff. By permission of *The New York Times* and Mr. Voorhis.

own judgment and to be guided by their knowledge of the needs and problems of the nation, but rather to reflect in their votes the opinion of a majority of the people in their districts. This is the dominant attitude of Congress itself, and it is worth while examining for a moment how majority opinion is arrived at and how the vote of the average Congressman is finally determined.

To begin with, public polls, newspaper and radio commentaries and similar contemporary phenomena provide a fairly accurate picture of majority opinion; they can tell, at a given time on a given topic, what "the people" are "thinking." But these are rather loose and general appraisals, with or without specific reference to a Congressman's own district. Reports from trusted lieutenants and the views of leading citizens in one's district get closer to home and are continually utilized. There are still other means.

The mail is a familiar voice from home which Congressmen listen to and they know how to "weigh" it. It is not hard to ignore the multigraphed postal cards or the identically worded telegrams that sometimes pour in. But it is a far different matter with the letter in longhand beginning "Dear Joe" or even "Dear Congressman" and appealing to you not to "let us down" on a certain bill. It is still more impressive if the letter represents the view of a local organization, which may even have sent an emissary, or lobbyist, to Washington.

It would seem that the Senator or Representative who heeds such appeals as these—so simple, so direct, the voice of the people back home— was performing his duties in the loftiest spirit of representative government. But what shall he do when all his knowledge and convictions on a significant issue lead him to one point of view and the apparent opinion of the majority in his district directs him to the other? This is the fundamental question with respect to representative government.

The easy answer, the safe one, is that the opinion of the district should prevail. This removes, for one thing, the necessity of thought. A still easier course is for the Congressman to make an early "commitment" as to how he will vote. From then on, in legislative forum, he can argue rather than reason.

The philosophy behind such a policy—other than the view that "representation" means simply echoing what appears to be majority sentiment —lies in the realm of practical politics. After all, it is said, every Congressman was elected to office in the first place because his ideas corresponded most nearly to those of the majority in his district. If he is to remain in office to do as much as he can for the welfare of his constituency and the country at large, he must not lose sight of this basic political fact.

Is this, however, a proper standard of statesmanship? And is it the only way to endear one's self to the electorate?

To me, such a theory of representative government seems woefully inadequate and unrealistic. We are just beginning to realize that there are vast fields in which there is no real public opinion—even on crucial issues —because many voters do not have enough information about them.

To fill this vacuum a constituent may fall back on a prejudice or an old maxim. The bigger the problem is, and the more confused he becomes, the more likely he is to cling to the past; the more susceptible he is to the eloquence of special-interest pleading and the half-truths of propaganda. This is especially true when members of Congress do not supply the leadership which most constituents need and many would welcome.

The Congress of the United States does not have to be a mere echo of what "inquiring reporters" and poll-takers say the people think. It is just as possible to lead and inform public opinion as to follow it. Surely there is an obligation binding on every Senator and Representative to make his views known to his constituents, and to explain his reasons and appraise the issues honestly. Just as surely it is his duty to cast his vote in the best interests of the whole nation, as he sees them. And this even though the majority opinion among his constituents may, at the moment, be on the other side.

The truly valid concept of "representative government" holds that the people elect their representatives because they expect from those representatives better, more farsighted action than the people as a whole, with their limited access to all the facts, can provide.

It holds that the representative is supposed not so much to reflect the opinions of his constituents as to serve (or "represent") their best and highest long-run interests.

If Congress is to be nothing but a mirror one is almost tempted to conclude we could do without it. The people cannot pass judgments unless they have something to judge. Democracy cannot and does not "work"— particularly in times of crisis—unless the public opinion of the time is the result of the "pull" of concrete proposals by men daring to offer leadership to the people.

It can be done. Every successful politician worthy of that much-abused but perfectly good name knows that he owes his election, in part at least, to the organization of public opinion behind his candidacy. If this can be done to win elections it can be done to gain support for a statesman-like course of action.

In every community in America there are men and women to whom others look for guidance on public questions. They possess qualities which have given them the opportunity to help mold the opinion of that locality. Most Senators and Congressmen know who these people are.

Direct communication with them, regardless of party affiliation, should lead them to rally behind the sound position of their representatives, or else the whole theory of democratic government is questionable. It is, as a matter of fact, at least as easy to mobilize public opinion behind true leadership as it is to attempt to "gauge" the thinking of the people and then tag along behind it.

Members of Congress have access every day and every hour to information about both domestic and foreign affairs which, in the nature of the case, the average citizen cannot know. Unless, therefore, the Senators and Representatives act in the light of this information, the country is compelled to operate without any fully informed action (except, of course, that taken by the President and his Cabinet). Even if there were no other arguments for Congress leading rather than following public opinion this one would be conclusive.

To this higher concept of representative government Congress can rise, if it will. Confronted by unquestioned responsibility for the future welfare of this nation—and indeed in times like these, of the world—it is fervently to be hoped that the membership of the House and Senate will be lifted in vision and courage to the point of genuine leadership.

We have had such men in Congress. I have seen them take their political fate in their hands and vote in accordance with their mature conclusions even when they knew they were in effect telling the majority opinion in their district that it was, at the moment, mistaken. And I have seen such men—not all of them, but some—returned to office by people who, on second thought, saw that they were right.

Some of the brightest pages in the history of the Congress are those which record the career of George W. Norris of Nebraska. First as a member of the House, later as a member of the Senate, Mr. Norris consistently led the people's thinking, instead of following it. He awakened national interest in constructive reformation of the rules of the House; he led the battle for the TVA, for rural electrification, for a one-house Legislature in Nebraska, for a dozen other measures of lasting benefit to the nation.

Norris challenged the voters of his state to follow him or to defeat him. By his forthright action he gave direction to the thinking of the people, and so won their confidence that he was re-elected over and over again. At his death all America hailed him as a great man.

Less well remembered, perhaps, is the speech delivered in the Senate by Prentiss Brown, Senator from Michigan, in the mid-war debate on the OPA. For days Senators had been carrying to the Senate floor the opinions of well-knit special interest groups each of which desired concessions in the bill.

Public opinion was, without much doubt, indifferent if not hostile to a continuance of price control. Admittedly mistakes had been made and poor judgment used in some cases. Yet every informed member of the House and Senate knew how disastrous the results would be to the nation if price control was rendered ineffective at that particular time. It remained for Senator Brown to cut through the fog of half-truth and challenge the Senate to act on the larger issue that lay before it. And the Senate did.

Afterward there were those who believed he had so offended certain powerful organizations in his state that he could not be re-elected. Perhaps they were right. Brown never ran again, for he accepted the post as OPA administrator and retired from the Senate. But the re-election of Senator Brown was for one golden hour at least—and probably for longer than that—of less importance to Prentiss Brown himself than safeguarding the economy of the United States. The press and the people of the United States understood this and appreciated it.

We do not yet know the ultimate fate of the Marshall Plan for western European recovery. But we do know that specious isolationist arguments and opinions were dealt a heavy blow when Senator Vandenberg of Michigan, in defending the interim aid bill . . . gave his graphic illustration of throwing a twelve-foot rope to a drowning man fifteen feet from the pier. The Senator from Michigan had some of the most powerful figures in his own party against him. He spoke against every cliché that has hampered American foreign policy since this country came of age as a great power. But he gave public opinion a simple rallying point.

Perhaps most important of all for the future of mankind are those members of Congress, led by . . . Senator McMahon of Connecticut, who literally spent sleepless days and nights to inform the American people of the true scientific facts regarding atomic energy, to discredit the false promises of their vote-hungry opponents that America could keep "the secret" locked up somewhere in the Pentagon Building, and to pass the McMahon atomic energy control bill in the closing days of the Seventy-ninth Congress.

There are men and women of this stature in Congress today. The question is, are there enough?

If there were enough to change the course of Congress from one of following Mr. Gallup et al. to one of offering leadership to the nation based on the hard facts of the present world situation, it would spell the difference between confused forebodings and renewed hope.

The average American citizen has learned to expect a generous seasoning of partisan politics with every dish the present Congress serves to him. Suppose he learned from experience that Congress was no longer adulterating its legislative action in that way? Suppose he learned that there in Washington was a group of representatives of the people seeking with singleness of purpose to serve the long-run welfare of the nation? Then both American citizens and the other people of the world at large would know that there was a new dynamic salutary force at work around which they could rally.

VOTE WITH THE PARTY ON KEY ISSUES
BY HENRY A. WALLACE*

[Henry Agard Wallace served as Secretary of Agriculture from 1933 to 1940 and as Vice President from 1941 to 1945. He resigned as Secretary of Commerce in the first Truman administration to edit the *New Republic* and then to campaign for the Presidency in 1948 on the Progressive party ticket. He is the author of a number of books, including *The Century of the Common Man* and *Sixty Million Jobs*. EDITOR.]

. . . It is undoubtedly true that we have become somewhat cynical about party platforms and that, all too often, we have been complacent when our representatives and senators failed to support even the major policies of their party. Moreover, I have heard more than one man prominent in public life remark that only a politically naïve person would expect a congressman to support the promises in his party's platform.

I do not believe, however, that the American people are as completely cynical as this. I am certain that today the people are showing more concern over the actions of their elected representatives than at any time since the formation of our Republic. I believe that most citizens agree that we must find a way to make the people's representatives responsible for their actions—responsible to those who listen to their promises and elect them on the basis of those promises. . . .

Those back home who voted for Democratic congressmen have been dismayed at finding too many of them voting against Democratic legislation. Republicans have been equally dismayed to find Republicans voting for Democratic legislation. [A Republican leader in the Senate once] . . . expressed deep concern over the confusion in voting among Republican congressmen. He said that to elect New Dealers as Republican

* From an article entitled "Party Responsibility," June 22, 1946. By permission of Mr. Wallace.

congressmen would "only confound the present confusion and . . . betray those who entrust the future to Republican leadership."

Thus, it is not only the Democratic side that is concerned over party responsibility. Indeed, this is a problem that must concern everyone, since it involves our most cherished institution—representative government. . . .

I am writing this article not only to expand my own views, but also in the hope that it will bring forth the ideas of others so that the nation can have a beneficial debate on this vital subject. And I am dealing specifically with what should be done by the elected party. To this end, I want to present the following beliefs:

I believe that delegates should determine at a party's national convention certain major policies their candidates will go all out to support for the next four years. This platform should be drawn up—with all seriousness and after full democratic deliberation—in the knowledge that the citizens of the United States will hold the party accountable for its platform promises.

When the new Congress is organized, the leaders of the majority party in both houses—in consultation with the President and his Cabinet—should immediately select from the platform several planks that, in their opinion, concern the most important problems facing the nation. These planks would then become the test issues for determining party responsibility and party loyalty.

To amplify this point, let us select from the Democratic platform of 1944 some of the planks that could serve as test issues.

One of these test policies could be the party's pledge to promote international trade through reciprocal trade agreements. This was the policy of the Democratic Party during Franklin Roosevelt's first three terms, and the 1944 platform pledged the party to continue that policy.

Another Democratic policy that could be used as a test issue is the stated belief of the party that the federal government is responsible for using its powers to prevent economic catastrophes—such as serious inflation or deflation, and mass unemployment.

This has been the consistent policy of the party since 1933, and the co-ordination of our economy by the federal government has become firmly a fixed principle of the Democratic New Deal.

A third policy that could serve as a test of party responsibility is the party's belief in federal development and conservation of the nation's resources, through flood control, conservation of soil fertility and the building of power projects. This policy also includes the party's belief that the nation's human resources should be equally conserved and improved by the encouragement of adequate housing, health and educational programs.

I suggest these issues as typical. In making the selections, the majority party leaders of the House and Senate should discuss party policy thoroughly with the party's representatives and senators before deciding on the test issues. For this purpose, I believe most strongly that party caucuses should be held more often. . . .

Once the basic test policies of the majority party have been selected, the congressmen of that party would be required to vote with the party on bills designed to put these policies into action. But they would not have to vote with the party leadership on other party measures.

But who and what will require them to vote with the party? And what is to prevent the people from returning them to Congress in spite of their failure to live up to the party's platform promises? Here are some of the answers:

The party organization in Congress could deprive a dissident congressman of his most valuable privileges. The first result of disloyalty to party principles could be the loss of membership in Congressional committees. The dissenting congressman would still have his democratic right to speak and vote on the floor, but he could not participate in the highly important legislative decisions that are made in committee before bills reach the floor.

The constituents of a congressman without committee privileges would not long return him to Congress.

Dissident representatives or senators could also be deprived of their privilege of influencing appointments to federal offices. These appointments usually are subject to review by the National Committee of the party in power, which could discipline a congressman by completely ignoring his recommendations.

On first thought, this may seem like harsh discipline. But the demands of our time—the demands upon our democratic system—also are harsh. And we shall never have a healthy two-party system as long as a recalcitrant minority of the party in power fattens itself on party patronage and committee seniority and still flouts the party leadership that seeks to carry out a people's mandate.

Even if a congressman had shown himself a party man in name but not in deed, he would still be free to seek renomination under the party label in his own state primary or convention. If such a dissident congressman were reelected and then followed the party leadership on the test issues, party privileges would be restored to him.

I do not advocate, nor do I believe in, the direct use of the national party machinery against a dissident congressman in his own state. I was opposed to the so-called "purge" of 1938—and I told President Roosevelt so on three different occasions. However, I do believe that the President and other party leaders have the obligation to make their views known about dissident congressmen so that the voters can be fully informed. But the direct use of the national party machinery against dissidents in their own states would be an undemocratic act interfering with the people's right to choose their own representatives in free elections. . . .

In outlining my proposal, I have not attempted to answer all possible objections as I went along. I well know, however, that all manner of sincere questions will arise and I shall try to anticipate some of them.

Someone is sure to ask: "With this kind of party discipline, wouldn't a senator or representative be merely a rubber stamp?" The answer is that no congressman, as I have said, would be asked to follow the party leadership on every measure. He would be required to vote with the party only on those few basic issues that party leaders, after full consultation, decided were vital to the general welfare, from the party's own point of view.

Suppose a congressman followed the party leaderhip on some measure against his own better judgment. He would be at perfect liberty to go back to the voters at home and tell them frankly that he voted against his own wishes, that he personally was opposed to the party policy on this particular measure, and that he would work unceasingly to change this party policy. Such activities should not be cause for imposing disciplinary action.

Others will ask: "If issues develop after the platforms have been voted on by the people, will the new issues be made a test of party loyalty?" The answer is: "Yes, if they are basic to the party's position." For example, no one could have predicted, in the summer of 1944, that the control and utilization of atomic energy would become one of the most important issues before the present Congress. Certainly, the peacetime development of atomic energy should be a basic issue for testing party loyalty and party responsibility. . . .

Another question that may be asked is: "What can the people do about party platforms besides voting for or against the platforms presented to them at election time?" The people can have a great deal to say about the platforms of their parties if they become active in politics at the precinct level—and keep active.

All too often in the past we have become excited along about the end of October—only to become complacent again after the first week in November. The challenge to democracy today cannot be met by this kind of dabbling in politics.

Their national interest demands that the people constantly exercise their privileges of citizenship right down to the precinct level.

If they do this, they will find that they have a powerful voice in the selection of delegates to party conventions and, through these delegates, in making party platforms. . . .

In the decisive days ahead, the American people have definite alternatives ahead of them.

They can make an effective and intelligent choice only if our political parties stand openly and honestly for clearly defined principles—and can be counted upon to put those principles into action when the people have made their decision.

CONGRESS SHOULD LEAD AND FOLLOW PUBLIC OPINION

BY GEORGE B. GALLOWAY*

[George B. Galloway acted as Chairman of the Committee on Congress of the American Political Science Association and served as Staff Director of the Joint Congressional Committee on the Organization of Congress in 1945–1946. Author of *Postwar Planning in the U.S.* and *America's Needs and Resources*, he has been a member of the Staff Legislative Reference, Library of Congress, since 1946. EDITOR.]

It is axiomatic to say that in a democracy public opinion is the source of law. Unless legislation is sanctioned by the sense of right of the people, it becomes a dead letter on the statute books, like prohibition and the Hatch Act. But public opinion is a mercurial force; now quiescent, now vociferous, it has various moods and qualities. It reacts to events and is often vague and hard to weigh.

Nor is public opinion infallible. Most people are naturally preoccupied with their personal problems and daily affairs; national problems and legislative decisions seem complex and remote to them, despite press and radio and occasional Capitol tours. Comparatively few adults understand the technicalities of foreign loans or reciprocal trade treaties, although congressional action on these aspects of our foreign economic policy may have far-reaching effects upon our standard of living. Moreover, "men in the mass are at times prejudiced, angry, impulsive, unjust. So at times the legislator must stand up against prejudice and passion, impulse and injustice. If resistance to opinion when it is wrong proves unavailing, the legislator should yield his office rather than his judgment. Nothing short of that will bring him peace of mind."[1] . . .

* *Congress at the Crossroads* (New York: Crowell, 1946), pp. 319–322. Only direct quotations have been footnoted. By permission of the publisher.
[1] Robert Luce, *Congress: An Explanation*, p. 53.

In practice, a Congressman both leads and follows public opinion. The desires of his constituents, of his party, and of this or that pressure group all enter into his decisions on matters of major importance. The influence of these factors varies from member to member and measure to measure. Some Congressmen consider it their duty to follow closely what they think is the majority opinion of their constituents, especially just before an election. Others feel that they should make their decisions without regard to their constituents' wishes in the first place, and then try to educate and convert them afterwards. Some members are strong party men and follow more or less blindly the program of the party leaders. Except when they are very powerful in the home district, the pressure groups are more of a nuisance than a deciding influence on the average member. When a legislator is caught between the conflicting pressures of his constituents and his colleagues, he perforce compromises between them and follows his own judgment.

The average legislator discovers early in his career that certain interests or prejudices of his constituents are dangerous to trifle with. Some of these prejudices may not be of fundamental importance to the welfare of the nation, in which case he is justified in humoring them, even though he may disapprove. The difficult case occurs where the prejudice concerns some fundamental policy affecting the national welfare. A sound sense of values, the ability to discriminate between that which is of fundamental importance and that which is only superficial, is an indispensable qualification of a good legislator.

Senator Fulbright gives an interesting example of this distinction in his stand on the poll-tax issue and isolationism. "Regardless of how persuasive my colleagues or the national press may be about the evils of the poll tax, I do not see its fundamental importance, and I shall follow the views of the people of my state. Although it may be symbolic of conditions which many deplore, it is exceedingly doubtful that its abolition will cure any of our major problems. On the other hand, regardless of how strongly opposed my constituents may prove to be to the creation of, and participation in, an ever stronger United Nations Organization, I could not follow such a policy in that field unless it becomes clearly hopeless."[2]

A Two-way Job

As believers in democracy, probably most Americans would agree that it is the duty of Congressmen to follow public opinion insofar as it expresses the desires, wants, needs, aspirations, and ideals of the people.

[2] In an address on "The Legislator" delivered at the University of Chicago on February 19, 1946. *Vital Speeches*, May 15, 1946, pp. 468–472.

Most Americans probably would also consider it essential for their representatives to make as careful an appraisal of these needs and desires as they can, and to consider, in connection with such an appraisal, the ways and means of accomplishing them. Legislators have at hand more information about legal structures, economic problems, productive capacities, manpower possibilities, and the like, than the average citizen they represent. They can draw upon that information to inform and lead the people —by showing the extent to which their desires can be realized.

In other words, a true representative of the people would follow the people's desires and at the same time lead the people in formulating ways of accomplishing those desires. He would lead the people in the sense of calling to their attention the difficulties of achieving those aims and the ways to overcome the difficulties. This means also that, where necessary, he would show special interest groups or even majorities how, according to his own interpretation and his own conscience, their desires need to be tempered in the common interest or for the future good of the nation.

Thus the job of a Congressman is a two-way one. He represents his local area and interests in the national capital, and he also informs the people back home of problems arising at the seat of government and how these problems affect them. It is in the nature of the Congressman's job that he should determine, as far as he can, public opinion in his own constituency and in the whole nation, analyze it, measure it in terms of the practicability of turning it into public policy, and consider it in the light of his own knowledge, conscience, and convictions. Occasionally he may be obliged to go against public opinion, with the consequent task of educating or reeducating the people along lines that seem to him more sound. And finally, since he is a human being eager to succeed at his important job of statesmanship and politics, he is realistic enough to keep his eyes on the voters in terms of the next election. But he understands that a mere weather-vane following of majority public opinion is not always the path to reelection.

The essence of true representative government was well epitomized twenty years ago by Representative Robert Luce. "The Lawmaker is not to be purely an agent," he said, "vainly trying to decide what the majority of his principals desire. He is not to be purely a trustee, making wholly independent decisions, self-conceived and self-sustained. He is to be both agent and trustee as far as may be. He is to feel it as much his duty to try to modify in others opinions with which he disagrees, as to try to let his own opinions be modified by the advice of others. He is to deal fairly both by his constituents and by himself. Such a man deems it necessary to break with constituency or with party only on those very rare occasions when Judgment must step aside and let Conscience rule. The great mass of legislation is matter of expediency. Not once in a thousand times is it matter of what is usually thought of as right and wrong. Only when right and wrong are at stake may the legislator refuse to concede, to compromise, or to yield."[3]

QUESTIONS AND PROBLEMS

1. According to Burns, how does the typical congressman act and vote in Congress? Why does he act in this way?

2. Why do you think Burns's description is or is not an accurate picture of actual congressional behavior? Should a congressman behave as Mr. Burns says he does? Why or why not?

3. To whom back home does the congressman give most consideration? Very important people? A majority of his constituents? The majority that voted for him? What answers are suggested by Burns's typical congressman and by Voorhis's view of the "dominant" attitude toward representative government in Congress itself?

4. Why does Voorhis believe that the "dominant" attitude of Congress toward representative government is "woefully inadequate and unrealistic"? What, for Voorhis, should be the "truly valid" concept of representative government? How does Voorhis defend this concept?

5. Why does Mr. Wallace want the congressman to vote with his party on basic issues? Evaluate these reasons.

6. According to Mr. Wallace's proposal, how would basic party issues be determined? Who and what will require the congressman to vote with his party on basic party issues? Would Mr. Wallace's brand of party discipline transform the congressman into a rubber stamp? Why or why not?

7. Wherein and why do Mr. Wallace and Mr. Voorhis differ on the question of how the congressman should vote? Mr. Wallace and Mr. Burns?

8. On what grounds does Mr. Galloway conclude that Congress does or should both lead and follow public opinion?

9. Wherein and why would Mr. Wallace, Mr. Voorhis, and Mr. Burns's typical congressman agree or disagree with Mr. Galloway?

10. To what extent do you think that Congress actually does both lead and follow public opinion? Explain. What criteria would you establish to determine what the congressman should do in given instances?

SELECT BIBLIOGRAPHY

Belloc, Hilaire, and Cecil Chesterton: *The Party System* (London: Swift, Stephen, 1911). Contend that only democratic theory of representation

---

[3] Luce, *op. cit.*, pp. 52–53.

is that legislator vote as his constituents would, if consulted. Attack unprogressive and undemocratic character of British party system.

Bryce, James: *The American Commonwealth* (New York: Macmillan, 1st American ed., 1889). Especially Vol. 1, pp. 296–298, for view that United States falls short of four essentials of an excellent representative system.

Burke, Edmund: "Speech to the Electors of Bristol, November 3, 1774," *Works* (Boston: Little, Brown, 1865), Vol. II. Contains classic view that member of Parliament should not be mere mouthpiece of constituents' opinons but should represent higher and permanent interests of nation. Other writings clearly reveal greater deference to desires of constituents than careless reading of speech at Bristol indicates.

Carpenter, William Seal: *Democracy and Representation* (Princeton, N.J.: Princeton University Press, 1925), Chap. 2. Holds that United States legislature has failed to be a miniature electorate because representatives not always able or willing to reflect opinion of constituents. Contrasts United States with Britain, where representative assembly watches over and checks government.

Finer, Herman: *Theory and Practice of Modern Government* (New York: Holt, rev. ed., 1949). See pp. 219*ff.* and pp. 369–377 for treatment of problems most important in study of representative government.

Fairlie, John A.: "The Nature of Political Representation," *American Political Science Review*, Vol. 34 (April and June, 1940), pp. 236, 456. Contains analysis of evidence and criticism of views formerly held, with regard to origin, development, and characteristics of representative government.

Friedrich, Carl J.: *Constitutional Government and Democracy* (Boston: Little, Brown, 1941). Valuable for comparative study. Especially Chap. 14, "General Problems of Representation," Chap. 20, "Parliaments as Representative Assemblies," and Chap. 24, "Direct Popular Action."

Gosnell, Harold F.: *Democracy—The Threshold of Freedom* (New York: Ronald, 1948). Second part in particular. Contains best study to date of nature of representation and evolution and operation of representative government. Critically examines relation of legislator to constituents, what voter should expect of his representative, how legislature responds to political pressures, how voters may exercise control directly over legislature, and tools voter has to perform tasks of democracy.

Luce, Robert: *Congress: An Explanation* (Cambridge, Mass.: Harvard University Press, 1926). Maintains, pp. 46–53, that lawmaker is neither purely an agent nor a trustee but both, depending upon circumstances.

Hamilton, Alexander, *et al.: The Federalist* (New York: Modern Lib., 1937). Urges representative government as cure for evils of faction. Views representation as refinement of popular will. Especially Nos. 10, 35, and 71.

Mill, John Stuart: *Representative Government* (London: Oxford, 1946). Makes classic defense of representative government as ideally best form of government. Fails to take political parties into consideration.

Rice, Stuart A.: *Quantitative Methods in Politics* (New York: Knopf, 1928).

Concerned, in Chap. 14, with what is now and not with what ought to be. Investigates two hypotheses: voters tend to select men of their own kind; legislator responds to issues, on whole, in same manner as constituents.

Salter, J. T.: *The Pattern of Politics* (New York: Macmillan, 1940). An extremely readable description of the folkways of a democratic people: their talk, attitudes, opinions, politicians, leaders. Reveals in homely and realistic form the human aspects of representation.

Smith, Charles W., Jr.: *Public Opinion in a Democracy* (New York: Prentice-Hall, 1939), Chap. 16. Considers democratic representation in connection with its purpose of providing a channel through which public opinion can be tangibly expressed and made effective.

Smith, T. V.: "Should Congress Lead or Follow Public Opinion?" *Town Meeting*, Vol. 8 (July 9, 1942), pp. 3–17. Admits and defends fact that Congress does not lead but only follows. Argues that Congress is official and authoritative body commissioned by constituents to judge public opinion and time for action. Holds that will of people should prevail even over private prejudice of congressman.

Stoke, Harold W.: "The Paradox of Representative Government," in J. M. Mathews and J. Hart (eds.), *Essays in Political Science* (Baltimore: Johns Hopkins Press, 1937), pp. 77–99. Believes that representative government cannot simultaneously pursue public interest and accurately reflect the many divergent and intensely conflicting interests in society.

SEPARATION OF POWERS

Can a Government Based on Separation of Powers Be Strong, Effective, and Responsible?

Our constitutional system of separation of powers and checks and balances was designed to brake the exercise of governmental power. These principles were favored in an eighteenth-century world, many of whose citizens believed that the best government was that which governed least. The twentieth century, however, beset by such thorny problems as modern warfare, control of atomic energy, and economic depression, has a different conception of the role of government in modern society. In 1787 the objectives of a more perfect union—justice, domestic tranquillity, defense, the general welfare, and liberty—were thought to be secured by the exercise of governmental power within a relatively restricted area and by keeping government from becoming too strong, lest it endanger the liberties of the people. Today, the area of permissible governmental activity has broadened enormously. Within that area government wields greater power to secure the same objectives of 1787. In view of the changed American scene, many raise this fundamental question: Can the system of separation of powers and checks and balances, adopted for an eighteenth-century world, be reconciled with the need for strong, effective, and responsible government today?

Woodrow Wilson contended in 1885 that our system of separation of powers divides responsibility, effectiveness, and strength in proportion as it divides power. He looked with unconcealed admiration at the British parliamentary, or cabinet, system, in which power is concentrated in a cabinet which leads, and is responsible to, a strong, disciplined majority party in Parliament or—more accurately—the House of Commons. For some it was a short step from Wilson's criticism, extracted herein, to a forthright advocacy of cabinet government.

Robert Luce argues that our present system is adequate and preferable to cabinet government. He maintains that cabinet government is not fitted to the geographical, political, and sociological conditions prevailing in the United States. Separation of powers, he holds, has been justified by American experience.

In the last article in this problem Thomas K. Finletter presents the case for a compromise solution compatible with separation of powers and the American tradition. He advocates a joint executive-legislative cabinet to formulate policy, simultaneous and similar terms for President and all congressmen, and presidential power to call a general election in the event of stalemate between cabinet and Congress. Such reforms, Finletter believes, would eliminate dangerous deadlocks, secure executive-legislative cooperation without making either branch dominant, and ensure strong, effective, and responsible government.

These three positions, which clarify the meaning of separation of powers, might be phrased as follows:

If we are to secure strong, effective, and responsible government, should we move in the direction of cabinet government? Or is our present governmental system adequate and preferable to cabinet government? Or can we reach a compromise on governmental leadership by establishing a joint executive-legislative cabinet?

CABINET GOVERNMENT IS SUPERIOR TO CONGRESSIONAL GOVERNMENT

BY WOODROW WILSON*

[Woodrow Wilson (1856 to 1924) was a political scientist, President of Princeton University, Governor of New Jersey, and President of the United States (1913 to 1921). Among his separately published works are *Constitutional Government in the United States* and *The State*. The most important edition of his writings is *The Public Papers of Woodrow Wilson*. EDITOR.]

It was something more than natural that the Convention of 1787 should desire to erect a Congress which would not be subservient and an executive which could not be despotic. And it was equally to have been ex-

---

* *Congressional Government* (Boston: Houghton Mifflin, 1885), pp. 5–333 *passim*. To secure a more logical and compact argument the editor has taken the liberty of rearranging the sequence of certain passages. Only direct quotations have been footnoted.

pected that they should regard an absolute separation of these two great branches of the system as the only effectual means for the accomplishment of that much desired end. It was impossible that they could believe that executive and legislature could be brought into close relations of cooperation and mutual confidence without being tempted, nay, even bidden, to collude. How could either maintain its independence of action unless each were to have the guaranty of the Constitution that its own domain should be absolutely safe from invasion, its own prerogatives absolutely free from challange? . . . They would conquer by dividing the power they so much feared to see in any single hand. . . .

. . . Each branch of the government is fitted out with a small section of responsibility, whose limited opportunities afford to the conscience of each many easy escapes. Every suspected culprit may shift the responsibility upon his fellows. Is Congress rated for corrupt or imperfect or foolish legislation? It may urge that it has to follow hastily its Committees or do nothing at all but talk; how can it help it if a stupid Committee leads it unawares into unjust or fatuous enterprises? Does administration blunder and run itself into all sorts of straits? The Secretaries hasten to plead the unreasonable or unwise commands of Congress, and Congress falls to blaming the Secretaries. The Secretaries aver that the whole mischief might have been avoided if they had only been allowed to suggest the proper measures; and the men who framed the existing measures in their turn avow their despair of good government so long as they must entrust all their plans to the bungling incompetence of men who are appointed by and responsible to somebody else. How is the schoolmaster, the nation, to know which boy needs the whipping?

Moreover, it is impossible to deny that this division of authority and concealment of responsibility are calculated to subject the government to a very distressing paralysis in moments of emergency. There are few, if any, important steps that can be taken by any one branch of the government without the consent or cooperation of some other branch. Congress must act through the President and his Cabinet; the President and his Cabinet must wait upon the will of Congress. There is no one supreme, ultimate head—whether magistrate or representative body—which can decide at once and with conclusive authority what shall be done at those times when some decision there must be, and that immediately. Of course, this lack is of a sort to be felt at all times, in seasons of tranquil rounds of business as well as at moments of sharp crisis; but in times of sudden exigency it might prove fatal,—fatal either in breaking down the system or in failing to meet the emergency. Policy cannot be either prompt or straightforward when it must serve many masters. It must either equivocate, or hesitate, or fail altogether. It may set out with clear purpose from Congress, but get waylaid or maimed by the Executive.

If there be one principle clearer than another, it is this: that in any business, whether of government or of mere merchandising, *somebody must be trusted*, in order that when things go wrong it may be quite plain who should be punished. In order to drive trade at the speed and with the success you desire, you must confide without suspicion in your chief clerk, giving him the power to ruin you, because you thereby furnish him with a motive for serving you. His reputation, his own honor or disgrace, all his own commercial prospects, hang upon your success. And human nature is much the same in government as in the dry-goods trade. *Power and strict accountability for its use* are the essential constituents of good government. A sense of highest responsibility, a dignifying and elevating sense of being trusted, together with a consciousness of being in an official station so conspicuous that no faithful discharge of duty can go unacknowledged and unrewarded, and no breach of trust undiscovered and unpunished,—these are the influences, the only influences, which foster practical, energetic, and trustworthy statesmanship. The best rulers are always those to whom great power is intrusted in such a manner as to make them feel that they will surely be abundantly honored and recompensed for a just and patriotic use of it, and to make them know that nothing can shield them from full retribution for every abuse of it.

It is, therefore, manifestly a radical defect in our federal system that it parcels out power and confuses responsibility as it does. The main purpose of the Convention of 1787 seems to have been to accomplish this grievous mistake. The "literary theory" of checks and balances is simply a consistent account of what our constitution-makers tried to do; and those checks and balances have proved mischievous just to the extent to which they have succeeded in establishing themselves as realities. It is quite safe to say that were it possible to call together again the members of that wonderful Convention to view the work of their hands in the light of the century that has tested it, they would be the first to admit that the only fruit of dividing power had been to make it irresponsible. . . .

. . . Power is nowhere concentrated; it is rather deliberately and of set policy scattered amongst many small chiefs. It is divided up, as it were, into forty-seven seigniories, in each of which a Standing Committee is the court-baron and its chairman lord-proprietor. These petty barons, some of them not a little powerful, but none of them within reach of the full powers of rule, may at will exercise at almost despotic sway within their own shires, and may sometimes threaten to convulse even the realm itself; but both their mutual jealousies and their brief and restricted opportunities forbid their combining, and each is very far from the office of common leader. . . .

I know that to some this scheme of distributed power and disintegrated rule seems a very excellent device whereby we are enabled to escape a dangerous "one-man power" and an untoward concentration of functions; and it is very easy to see and appreciate the considerations which make this view of committee government so popular. It is based upon a very proper and salutary fear of *irresponsible* power; and those who must resolutely maintain it always fight from the position that all leadership in legislation is hard to restrain in proportion to its size and to the strength of its prerogatives, and that to divide it is to make it manageable. They aver, besides, that the less a man has to do—that is to say, the more he is confined to single departments and to definite details—the more intelligent and thorough will his work be. They like the Committees, therefore, just because they are many and weak, being quite willing to abide their being despotic within their narrow spheres.

It seems evident, however, when the question is looked at from another stand-point, that, as a matter of fact and experience, the more power is divided the more irresponsible it becomes. A mighty baron who can call half the country to arms is watched with greater jealousy, and, therefore, restrained with more vigilant care than is ever vouchsafed the feeble master of a single and solitary castle. The one cannot stir abroad upon an innocent pleasure jaunt without attracting the suspicious attention of the whole country-side; the other may vex and harry his entire neighborhood without fear of let or hindrance. It is ever the little foxes that spoil the grapes. . . .

The leaders of the House are the chairmen of the principal Standing Committees. Indeed, to be exactly accurate, the House has as many leaders as there are subjects of legislation; for there are as many Standing Committees as there are leading classes of legislation, and in the consideration of every topic of business the House is guided by a special leader in the person of the chairman of the Standing Committee, charged with the superintendence of measures of the particular class to which that topic belongs. It is this multiplicity of leaders, this many-headed leadership, which makes the organization of the House too complex to afford uninformed people and unskilled observers any easy clue to its methods of rule. For the chairmen of the Standing Committees do not constitute a cooperative body like a ministry. They do not consult and concur in the adoption of homogeneous and mutually helpful measures; there is no thought of acting in concert. Each Committee goes its own way at its own pace. It is impossible to discover any unity or method in the disconnected and therefore unsystematic, confused, and desultory action of the

House, or any common purpose in the measures which its Committees
from time to time recommend. . . .

. . . The fact that, though the Committees lead in legislation, they lead
without concert or responsibility, and lead nobody in particular, that is,
no compact and organized party force which can be made accountable
for its policy, has also a further significance with regard to the opportunities and capacities of the constituencies. The doubt and confusion of
thought which must necessarily exist in the minds of the vast majority of
voters as to the best way of exerting their will in influencing the action
of an assembly whose organization is so complex, whose acts are apparently so haphazard, and in which responsibility is spread so thin, throws
constituencies into the hands of local politicians who are more visible and
tangible than are the leaders of Congress, and generates, the while, a profound distrust of Congress as a body whose actions cannot be reckoned
beforehand by any standard of promises made at elections or any pro-
grammes announced by conventions. Constituencies can watch and understand a few banded leaders who display plain purposes and act upon
them with promptness; but they cannot watch or understand forty odd
Standing Committees, each of which goes its own way in doing what it
can without any special regard to the pledges of either of the parties from
which its membership is drawn. In short, we lack in our political life the
conditions most essential for the formation of an active and effective public opinion. "The characteristics of a nation capable of public opinion,"
says Mr. Bagehot, most sagacious of political critics, "is that . . . parties
will be *organized;* in each there will be a leader, in each there will be
some looked up to, and many who look up to them; the opinion of the
party will be formed and suggested by the few, it will be criticized and
accepted by the many."[1] And this is just the sort of party organization
which we have not. Our parties have titular leaders at the polls in the
persons of candidates, and nominal creeds in the resolutions of conventions, but no select few in whom to trust for guidance in the general
policy of legislation, or to whom to look for suggestions of opinion. What
man, what group of men, can speak for the Republican party or for the
Democratic party? When our most conspicuous and influential politicians
say anything about future legislation, no one supposes that they are
speaking for their party, as those who have authority; they are known
to speak only for themselves and their small immediate following of
colleagues and friends. . . .

It would seem to be scarcely an exaggeration to say that they [our
national parties] are homogeneous only in name. Neither of the two
principal parties is of one mind with itself. Each tolerates all sorts of

[1] *Essays on Parliamentary Reform.*

difference of creed and variety of aim within its own ranks. Each pre-
tends to the same purposes and permits among its partisans the same con-
tradictions to those purposes. They are grouped around no legislative
leaders whose capacity has been tested and to whose opinions they loyally
adhere. They are like armies without officers, engaged upon a campaign
which has no great cause at its back. Their names and traditions, not their
hopes and policy, keep them together. . . .

. . . There is no office set apart for the great party leader in our
government. The powers of the Speakership of the House of Representatives are too cramped and covert; the privileges of the chairmanships
of the chief Standing Committees are too limited in scope; the presidency
is too silent and inactive, too little like a premiership and too much like a
superintendency. [Wilson was writing before the development of the
strong, modern, popular-leader Presidency which he was to exemplify in
his own person. That he recognized the possibilities of presidential leadership is revealed by his preface to the fifteenth edition of *Congressional
Government*, written in 1900: "It may be, too, that the new leadership of
the Executive, inasmuch as it is likely to last, will have a very far-reaching effect upon our whole method of government. It may give the heads
of the executive departments a new influence upon the action of Congress. It may bring about, as a consequence, an integration which will
substitute statesmanship for government by mass meetings. It may put
this whole volume hopelessly out of date."] If there be any one man to
whom a whole party or a great national majority looks for guiding counsel, he must lead without office, as Daniel Webster did, or in spite of his
office, as Jefferson and Jackson did. There must be something in the
times or in the questions which are abroad to thrust great advocates or
great masters of purpose into a non-official leadership, which is theirs
because they represent in the greatest actions of their lives some principle
at once vital and widely loved or hated, or because they possess in their
unrivaled power of eloquent speech the ability to give voice to some such
living theme. There must be a cause to be advanced which is greater
than the trammels of governmental forms, and which, by authority of its
own imperative voice, constitutes its advocates the leaders of the nation,
though without giving them official title—without need of official title.
No one is authorized to lead by reason of any official station known
to our system. . . .

In a country which governs itself by means of a public meeting, a Congress or a Parliament, a country whose political life is representative, the
only real leadership in governmental affairs must be legislative leadership
—ascendency in the public meeting which decides everything. The leaders,
if there be any, must be those who suggest the opinions and rule the
actions of the representative body. We have in this country, therefore, no

real leadership; because no man is allowed to direct the course of Congress, and there is no way of governing the country save through Congress, which is supreme. . . .

In a word, we have no supreme executive ministry, like the great "Ministry of the Crown" over sea, in whose hands is the general management of legislation; and we have, consequently, no great prizes of leadership such as are calculated to stimulate men of strong talents to great and conspicuous public services. The Committee system is, as I have already pointed out, the very opposite of this. It makes all the prizes of leadership small, and nowhere gathers power into a few hands. It cannot be denied that this is in ordinary times, and in the absence of stirring themes, a great drawback, inasmuch as it makes legislative service unattractive to minds of the highest order, to whom the offer of really great place and power at the head of the governing assembly, the supreme council of the nation, would be of all things most attractive. If the presidency were competitive,—if it could be won by distinguished congressional service,—who can doubt that there would be a notable influx of talents into Congress and a significant elevation of tone and betterment of method in its proceedings; and yet the presidency is very far from being equal to a first-rate premiership. . . .

. . . There is, said Mr. [John Stuart] Mill, a "distinction between the function of *making* laws, for which a numerous popular assembly is radically unfit, and that of *getting good laws made*, which is its proper duty, and cannot be satisfactorily fulfilled by any other authority"; and there is, consequently, "need of a legislative commission, as a permanent part of the constitution of a free country; consisting of a small number of highly trained political minds, on whom, when parliament has determined that a law shall be made, the task of making it should be devolved; parliament retaining the power of passing or rejecting the bill when drawn up, but not of altering it otherwise than by sending proposed amendments to be dealt with by the commission."[2] [This passage, together with the following passage, makes quite clear where Wilson would place prime governmental leadership, and what function the legislature is to perform. The "legislative commission" is nothing but a British-type cabinet, which has a life dependent on, although apart from, Parliament, and which at once leads and is responsible to Parliament. The function of the legislature is not to lead the government but to debate and revise the program of the "legislative commission" or executive cabinet.]

. . . Congress spends its time working, in sections, at preparing plans, instead of confining itself to what is for a numerous assembly manifestly the much more useful and proper function of debating and revising plans prepared beforehand for its consideration by a commission of skilled men,

[2] *Autobiography*, pp. 264, 265.

old in political practice and in legislative habit, whose official life is apart from its own, though dependent upon its will. Here, in other words, is another finger pointing to Mr. Mill's question as to the best "legislative commission." Our Committees fall short of being the best form of commission, not only in being too numerous but also in being integral parts of the body which they lead, having no life apart from it. Probably the best working commission would be one which should make plans for government independently of the representative body, and in immediate contact with the practical affairs of administration, but which should in all cases look to that body for the sanctioning of those plans, and should be immediately responsible to it for their success when put into operation.
. . .

The charm of our constitutional ideal has now been long enough wound up to enable sober men who do not believe in political witchcraft to judge what it has accomplished, and is likely still to accomplish, without further winding. The Constitution is not honored by blind worship. The more open-eyed we become, as a nation, to its defects, and the prompter we grow in applying with the unhesitating courage of conviction all thoroughly-tested or well-considered expedients necessary to make self-government among us a straightforward thing of simple method, single, unstinted power, and clear responsibility, the nearer will we approach to the sound sense and practical genius of the great and honorable statesmen of 1787. And the first step towards emancipation from the timidity and false pride which have led us to seek to thrive despite the defects of our national system rather than seem to deny its perfection is a fearless criticism of that system. When we shall have examined all its parts without sentiment, and gauged all its functions by the standards of practical common sense, we shall have established anew our right to the claim of political sagacity; and it will remain only to act intelligently upon what our opened eyes have seen in order to prove again the justice of our claim to political genius.

CONGRESSIONAL GOVERNMENT IS SUPERIOR TO CABINET GOVERNMENT

BY ROBERT LUCE*

[Robert Luce (1862 to 1946), having served for twenty years as a Republican in the United States House of Representatives,

* Reprinted by permission of the publishers from Robert Luce, *Congress: An Explanation* (Cambridge, Mass.: Harvard University Press, 1926), pp. 94–110 *passim*.

spoke of Congress as an experienced observer. Among his other published works are *Legislative Procedure, Legislative Assemblies, Legislative Principles,* and *Legislative Problems.* EDITOR.]

Mankind always wants and must have leadership in government. Men cannot well function politically in the mass. They must entrust power to one or a few of their number. . . .

. . . When our Federal Constitution was framed, it had come to be accepted in England that a cabinet should ordinarily be composed of members of the same political party; should be of a party controlling a majority in the House of Commons; should resign when no longer supported by a majority; should look to the people for ultimate authority; should be responsible for all the acts of government; and should have a commanding head, the prime minister.

The next hundred years saw the wane of Parliament as an initiating body. By the middle of the nineteenth century, individual members of the House had ceased going beyond calling proposals to the attention of the government. A generation later it had become the practice for the ministry to determine upon all the important legislation before Parliament even assembled. With the passage of still another generation, the process of giving to the cabinet the monopoly of initiation was completed. Now no member of a minority, no independent member, if there be such, can hope for consideration of any proposal he may present. Indeed, the ministers have so monopolized the time that no member of the majority not in the government has more than a gambler's chance of getting so much as an insignificant measure considered. Not even by way of amendment may the private member embody his own ideas in legislation unless the government approves or permits. Discussion has dwindled in importance. Today it may be said of the English Cabinet that, besides being the chief executive and central administrative board of the nation, it is in effect the lawmaking body; that of its own initiative and upon its own responsibility it makes the laws, modified only as the criticisms of Parliament may be accepted, and subject to veto only if it loses its majority in the House of Commons; that it shapes the programme and directs the procedure of Parliament; that, save for the opportunity to criticize or vote in opposition, the member of Parliament not in the cabinet is a negligible factor; and that inasmuch as the prime minister necessarily dominates the cabinet he is virtually an autocrat, controlled by an unwritten Constitution which obliges him to act within the law, and having duration of power contingent upon the popular will.

This is the form of government commended to the American people by many academic writers as preferable to that under which we now live.

We are urged to approach it by modifying our congressional and executive practices so that we shall have one-man leadership and control. We are told by not a few publicists that this way alone does our salvation lie. From time to time steps in this direction have actually been taken.

To weigh the merit of the advice and the wisdom of the tendency, first consider how and why our radically different system came into existence.

Through a century and a half the American colonies quarrelled with their governors appointed by the Crown. More than any other one cause, these quarrels brought the Revolution. Our fathers went into the Revolutionary War embittered against executive authority. They fought it and they won it without any chief executive. As a result of their own experience, they framed their state constitutions with the deliberate intention of keeping the executive down to at least a level with the legislative. With serious, careful premeditation they devised a balance of powers. The very foundation of their frames of government was the doctrine that no one branch of the government should dominate. Measured by the results in the totality of everything that concerns the safety of the state and the welfare of its citizens, who will aver that the system worked out from the experience of the first century and a half of the American people has not, on the whole, been justified in the experience of the succeeding century and a half? . . .

The issue was brought into the forum of serious discussion by a little book called "Congressional Government," published just forty years ago and written by Woodrow Wilson, then a graduate student at Johns Hopkins University. In this vigorous volume he urged the superiority of a responsible cabinet ministry over committee government, as he called that by the Congress of the United States. The book has been read by probably most of the students of political science who have since then gone through our colleges, and its doctrine has been championed by effective writers, conspicuous among them Professor H. J. Ford of Princeton, who has taken every opportunity to press the argument that the system devised by our forefathers was unwise and that we should supplant it with the English system. Meanwhile few have wielded the cudgels in defence of the American system.

The result is that now in the scholastic world it seems to be taken for granted that the doctrine of the separation of powers is moribund if not already dead. In the legislative world, however, where practical men do the day's work, observation and experience still keep that doctrine very much alive. We who have to deal daily with the administration of government are by no means confident that our fathers were all wrong in what they did. Most of us, on the contrary, become more and more convinced that, at any rate under American conditions, it is well that the laws should not be made and executed by the same man or the same small group of men. Assuming then for the moment that the question is still open, consider the arguments.

Cabinet government is chiefly extolled because it is said to centre responsibility. By this it is meant that one man may well be held responsible for the policies and the practices of the national government, both legislative and administrative, with reward or penalty for himself or his party as may be adjudged by the voters at the following election. The theory is that the processes of election result directly in the choice of an American President, or indirectly in the choice of a British Prime Minister, who will better express and more effectively carry out the will of the majority than would Congress or Parliament left to its own devices. In support of the theory it is argued that a chief executive should be at the same time a chief legislative, because he has the more comprehensive and better proportioned conception of the interests of all the people; that he is more quickly responsive to changes in public opinion; and that he will reach decision more promptly, prudently, and bravely.

While it may be that the head of the nation, coming in contact with well-informed and judicious men from all parts of the land, will get a better perspective than any one Senator or Representative, the theory of representative government is that his knowledge will not be so comprehensive as the united knowledge of five or six hundred men chosen by states or districts, each familiar with local needs, wishes, opinions. Furthermore, it would be unreasonable to expect that in the matter of proportion a president could excel the joint acquaintance of a Congress. Inevitably he meets chiefly men from the upper walks of life. They are what we call the successful men, the dominant men. Very likely it is best that their counsel should be the loudest, but in point of proportion it would hardly be thought as representative as that of a Congress in which every stratum of society has its voice, as well as every important occupation, with every member passing some months of each year among his constituents.

As to speed in response to change of public opinion, there are arguments both ways. Unquestionably any legislative body left to itself is more conservative, more cautious, than a small group such as a cabinet would be. Congress is sluggish. Yet there are some advantages in making haste slowly. It was the tortoise who won in the race with the hare. Congress lags behind the thinkers of the nation. But the thinkers are few in comparison with the great mass of mankind, which is by nature conservative and reactionary. Much is to be said for the proposition that Congress on the whole moves as fast as the nation really wishes. Studied in detail, however, the work will be found in sundry particulars clearly and unfortunately behindhand. Were the responsibility centred in one virile, forceful man, this would doubtless be remedied.

Such a man would reach decision more promptly than Congress, and perhaps more bravely, but whether more prudently, is not so sure. It would depend on the man. Everybody is thankful that Jefferson put through the Louisiana Purchase and Roosevelt the Panama Canal, but most men will agree that the prudence of Jackson's treatment of the United States Bank, with its contribution to the panic of 1837, is gravely to be doubted. A wise despot is the best of rulers, a foolish despot the worst. The men who wrote our Constitution knew well George the Third. To be sure, the cabinet system produces prime ministers far above most hereditary monarchs in point of intellectual capacity, and so does our system of choosing presidents, but neither guarantees against the possibility of rashness in some critical juncture. It was to guard against imprudence that our fathers devised constitutions, state and federal, of checks and balances. They knew human nature, its frailties as well as its virtues. Is it certain that they erred in judgment when they sought safety in numbers?

Over against the arguments for the cabinet system are to be set certain other formidable considerations, to my mind not often squarely met by its advocates. First may be put the belief of the framers of our constitutions that the fusion of functions invites tyranny. To be sure it is an old-time belief, but a belief is not necessarily fallacious because it is old. Experience may in the past have taught mankind at least a few things that are still useful. It has been the experience of many states that when the man who makes the law also administers and adjudicates it, oppression is likely to result. Abuse of power has been a characterisic of monarchs. . . .

England itself is a compact state of small area, inhabited by a homogeneous people. Is it certain that the success of one-man government under such conditions could be duplicated in a huge country like ours, with a widely scattered population made up of the most diverse racial elements, and without any universally recognized body of tradition and precedent? . . . Does this not at least suggest that, where national interests are diverse, conflicting, and scattered, safety and success lie in a form of government whereunder the decisions are to be made by the compromises of a legislative assembly rather than by the judgment of one man or any small group of men?

Apart from such questions of basic principle, there is at least one practical consideration that seems to me of great consequence. Our system does give the opportunity for many minds to help. Every member of Congress has the chance to contribute toward good legislation. If he belong to the majority party, he is not necessarily a voting dummy as in Parliament; if he belong to the minority, he is not restricted to mere fault-finding, as Mr. Wilson wanted him to be, but in the committee room may play a most useful part in constructive effort for the public good. It should always be remembered that, anyhow, only a few big questions, if any, call for aggressive political leadership. The great mass of the business of every lawmaking body is non-partisan in nature. To sacrifice all the benefit of our parliamentary system in respect of much the larger part of the work for the sake of getting some other way of determining a very few major issues, might be a costly bargain.

Also it should be remembered that no chief executive has the time or strength to study thoroughly and to master by himself more than a few of the imporant problems of government. He must perforce rely largely on the judgment and advice of others. . . . Do the facts leave it clear that committee government in such a case is necessarily inferior to cabinet government?

But it is argued that as the President is at the centre of the administration, he is in a better position than any other one man to be informed about all of its functions and operations. Of course, that is true, but it would be the height of cruelty to demand that he take full advantage of his opportunity. He simply could not do it. The task would kill him. The 531 members of the Senate and House, divided into groups of specialists, are not fully equal to such achievement. Why expect it of one man?

The rejoinder of the moderate and judicious advocate of responsible leadership will fairly be that its principle may not justly be thus reduced to absurdity, inasmuch as only dominant leadership in broad matters of policy is really asked. Confined within such limits, the question is more debatable. Yet even here it would be hard to show that in actual results the British system works better than ours. As a matter of fact, the influence of the President is great, as it ought to be. No man reaches that high office unless he has outstanding qualities which make for leadership. The President is sure to be a man of patriotic purposes, deeply conscious of his solemn obligation to make decision with a sole view to the welfare of all the people. He is also sure to have had wide and long experience in dealing with his fellows. The circumstances of his relations with the legislative branch are such that his policies are ensured sympathetic and generous consideration. Ordinarily he prevails, though the public does not think so, because its attention is limited to the comparatively few instances in which he does not prevail. We do have effective and responsible presidential leadership to a very material degree. But Congress is not disposed to abandon entirely its share of initiative, or to abdicate, even in the broadest matters of policy, its function as the legislative branch of the government. Nor can the intelligent observer be confident that it could wisely be compelled so to do by constitutional change reorganizing our form of government on the British model.

BRIDGE THE GAP WITH A JOINT EXECUTIVE-LEGISLATIVE CABINET

BY THOMAS K. FINLETTER*

[Finletter, a lawyer by profession, lectured at the University of Pennsylvania from 1931 to 1941. Special Assistant to the Secretary of State from 1941 to 1944 and Chairman of the President's Air Policy Committee in 1947, he was appointed Secretary of Air in 1950. EDITOR.]

This conflict between the Executive and Congress is the most significant fact about the American government today. Unless something is done to cure it, it may prove to be a tragic fact. The difficulty is that the conflict is fundamentally imbedded in our system. The power of the popular leader is snatched from institutions which were intended to deny power. The President can put over his policies only by subordinating Congress. It is not like the parliamentary system where the Legislature, secure in its ultimate right to dismiss the Executive from office, can safely allow the Cabinet to run the country and even to dominate the Legislature itself. Congress cannot dismiss the President. It therefore cannot allow him to dominate it for long. For if, under the pressure of events and the need for strong government, we had a steady procession of popular-leader presidents exercising the kind of power that Wilson and Franklin Roosevelt had in the beginnings of their administrations, Congress would become a rubber stamp, and if it remained so for long, representative government and liberty would fall with it.

The alternating system is simply not good enough for the needs of the American State in the post-war period. Our new policies cannot be carried out by any such irregular apparatus. We cannot play with international peace and unemployment for a year or so and then drop them while we use up all our energy in a quarrel between the Executive and Congress. Aggressor countries will not take time out in their plans to break the peace while we play with the checks and balances. Unemploy-

---

* From *Can Representative Government Do the Job?*, pp. 17–159 *passim;* copyright, 1945, by Thomas K. Finletter. Reprinted by permission of Harcourt, Brace and Company, Inc.

ment will not cure itself while our government, torn with struggle between its two main branches, muddles incompetently.

Clearly something must be done about this, for the consequences of not doing something are unbearable. If we fail to reorganize our government so that it will be strong enough to carry out the policies the American people want, we will be faced with the choice between two very disagreeable alternatives. Either we will give up our new policies because our representative system is incapable of handling them, or we will turn to some other kind of government—which may not have the weaknesses or the liberties of the representative form—which will do what the people demand. . . .

There is, of course, another alternative which will keep our individual liberties and at the same time let us achieve the great foreign and domestic policies to which we are committed. It is to set up new procedures within our present structure of government which will make it normal for the Executive and Congress to work together instead of at cross purposes.

This is an entirely practical course. The American system of government is as capable as any of solving the problem which faces all democratic countries today—how to have a powerful Executive and at the same time a strong Legislature. Steps are already being taken in Washington which lead in this direction. The question is whether we will have the determination and wisdom to press these first steps to their goal; or whether, failing to do so, we will risk the destruction of our representative system and our individual liberties. . . .

We have reached the end of an experiment. Three strong presidents of the twentieth century [Theodore Roosevelt, Woodrow Wilson, and Franklin D. Roosevelt] have struggled to convert the American system of checks and balances into a government of steady and positive power; but the forces against them have been too great. In the battle between the fundamental purpose of the Constitution to keep down the power of government and the strong presidents who tried to convert the constitutional structure to the opposite purpose, it is the former which has prevailed for the greater part of the time. The victory of the dead hand shows itself in the great blank periods both within the strong administrations themselves and when the swings of politics put the weaker presidents in office. [For example, William H. Taft followed Theodore Roosevelt, while Warren G. Harding, Calvin Coolidge, and Herbert Hoover followed Woodrow Wilson.]

A government of fits and starts is no longer good enough for our purposes. No decent attempt toward a proper domestic policy or toward the task of stopping war can be made unless there is reasonable harmony between Congress and the Executive at all times. The conflict between the two branches must be taken out of our government so that it can devote its unshackled, even power to these appallingly difficult problems. We cannot go on with a system of bursts of legislative frenzy like the Hundred Days, followed by long periods of internal struggle and stalemate. . . .

The general line which should be taken is, I think, reasonably clear. It is to change the procedures of the federal government so as to eliminate the causes of conflict between the two branches, to centralize the affirmative powers of government in the Executive, and to do so in such a way as to preserve the authority of Congress.

This of course is easier said than done. It cannot be accomplished by making either the Executive or Congress dominant over the other. If the Executive is given sufficient power to dictate to Congress, the government will be authoritarian. If Congress dominates the Executive, the government will be weak and inadequate.

The only remaining alternative is to set up new procedures which will make it easy for the two branches to work in harmony. . . .

It is possible, I think, to eliminate the causes of this conflict between Congress and the Executive, and to substitute new techniques of collaboration between the two branches, as an orderly evolution of the American system of government. Indeed the first steps in this evolution have already been taken. . . .

A joint executive-legislative cabinet is in the direct line of evolution of our government. Practically all the many current proposals for simplification and reform of Congress and the executive branch call for the concentration of power in a small group or cabinet in Congress and a like concentration of authority on the executive side. If this were done, the next step to a combined executive-legislative cabinet would be almost inevitable. Clearly the purpose of making Congress and the Executive more effective working units is not to strengthen them to make war on each other. No seriously thought-out plan to improve the United States government can fail to arrive at the conclusion that the essential reform to which all others are subsidiary is to invent some technique which will bring the two branches together to work in harmony. . . .

A Joint Executive-Legislative Cabinet could be set up by a joint resolution of the House and Senate and by an executive order of the President. It would require no congressional legislation and no constitutional amendment.

Composed of, say, nine congressional leaders and nine members of the Executive Cabinet, with the President at its head, meeting regularly and serviced by a competent secretariat, the Joint Cabinet would soon take to itself the origination of the major policies of the government. Congress would continue to have its regular and special committees which would initiate plans for legislation, but their ideas would be funneled to the Joint Cabinet where they would be harmonized with the parallel plans of the executive side. Instead of there being an "administration bill" which Congress would fight and a counter-congressional bill which the President would veto if he felt politically strong enough, a more carefully thought-out proposal would be produced by the Joint Cabinet in the first place.

Clashes . . . would be ironed out in conference instead of being fought out by battle, as they were, in the customary manner—speeches in the House and Senate about congressional independence, talk of Congress reasserting its manhood, a presidential veto, the triumphant overriding of the veto . . . and an unsatisfactory . . . bill as the final product—all carried on with great heat in the tradition of the separation of powers.

Instead of this disorderly way of deciding on national policy, the Joint Cabinet would use the method which has proved so successful in settling differences between the House and Senate when they enact differing bills on the same subject. The conference method of settling differences of opinion between the two Houses has proved so workable that we do not realize the difficulties inherent in getting two great bodies like the House and Senate to agree to the same text of a complicated enactment of national policy. The Joint Cabinet would provide a similar meeting ground for temperate discussions of differences of opinion between the Executive and Congress. . . .

The existence of a Joint Cabinet also would do away with much of the resistance that now meets an Executive-originated bill. The members of Congress of the majority party would normally accept the judgment of their leaders in the Joint Cabinet who would have recommended the bill to them. The main cause of the suspicion which today meets a bill coming from the Executive is the fact that no member of Congress has had anything to do with preparing it. If the majority in Congress knew that its own leaders, chosen on their merits and not because of longevity of service, had helped frame the bill and favored its enactment, the traditional attitude of hostility to a new measure coming into Congress would largely disappear. Only powerful pressure from an organized group or some similar source would make the individual member of congress reject the leadership of the members of his party representing him in the Joint Cabinet. The area of conflict between the Executive and Congress would be greatly reduced. A solidarity between the Joint Cabinet and its majority of the same party in the House and Senate would grow up. They would tend to become a team working together to create constructive national policies.

A Joint Cabinet would thus be able, first, to create coherent policies and, secondly, to lessen the resistance from Congress to the programs so created. It would not interfere with the deliberative function of Congress, for the proposals of the Cabinet could always be rejected by the full Houses if they so chose. Debate in Congress would be greatly improved, for the proponents of a bill would know all about it, having taken part in preparing it, and the opposition could demand and get a full discussion of the proposal from their colleagues of the opposing party. But, most important of all, a forum would be provided where the Executive and leaders of Congress could act together to work out permanent bases for collaborative action and for the elimination of jurisdictional quarrels.

The Joint Cabinet would necessarily be partisan—that is, chosen from the majority party. Just as the party in control organizes and dominates the committees of the House and Senate now, so would they under this plan. Nonpartisan action might be necessary in time of war or other serious emergency; but the normal condition would be that which the two-party system demands. . . .

Both the Executive and Congress, as well as the people, would gain by a Joint Executive-Legislative Cabinet composed of members of the majority party. The President's position would not be weaker if such a Cabinet were a part of our government; indeed he would have a greater ability to get his policies accepted by Congress than at present. He would dominate the executive side of the Cabinet, for he would have the power of asking for the resignation of any member from the executive branch who failed to follow his leadership. He would still have the enormous prestige and power which come from the popular election.

Congress would gain because its leaders would know what was being done and what was being planned. It would have a part in policy at the important time—when it was being made. Congress would become a great factor in the constructive side of government, a role which its present . . . committees . . . will never give it under the present system.

But the big gainers would be the American people. For a Joint Cabinet would be a major step toward converting the American system of antagonistic powers into one in which the two major branches of government worked together for the common interest. . . .

. . . The most important barrier to the success of a Joint Cabinet is the system of fixed dates for elections—the rigid terms of two and six years for Congress and four years for the President.

In the first place there is the possibility that under the system of fixed terms of office one of the Houses of Congress may be of a different party than the President. This happens often enough to be a menace to our form of government. It has occurred in twenty-seven out of seventy-nine Congresses. In seven, both Houses were opposed to the President; in fourteen the House of Representatives alone was opposed; and in six the Senate. This split in party solidarity usually takes places at the congressional elections in the middle of a presidential term. It has occurred on at least three occasions within recent political history—the mid-term elections of Taft, Wilson, and Hoover.

Whenever a majority of House or Senate is of a different party than the President, the government of the United States cannot function. Of course, under such circumstances, the Joint Executive-Legislative Cabinet would be of practically no value at all. . . .

But even with the majority of both Houses of the same party as the President, the fixed terms of office would be a great barrier to the proper working of the Joint Cabinet, just as now they make collaboration between the Executive and Congress extremely difficult. The fact that the members of Congress are secure in office until the end of their fixed terms makes them independent of national party control, and therefore to some extent hostile to the President. The fact that both Congressmen and Senators are dependent for re-election more on local machines and local influences than on the national parties increases this sense of independence. Moreover, the fixed elections have made for weak national parties and thus have interfered with the growth of that party discipline which alone in representative government can constitute an effective bridge between the Executive and Congress and alone can bring them to work together harmoniously. . . .

The remedy is, I believe, to amend the Constitution so as, first, to give to the President the right to dissolve Congress and the Presidency and to call a general election of all three whenever a deadlock arises between Congress and the Joint Cabinet, and, second, to make the terms of the Senate, House, and Presidency of the same length—say six years from the date of each election (whether the election takes place as the result of a dissolution or on the expiration of the full six-year period of service). The second part of this proposal is made necessary by the first. For the main objective of the right of dissolution is to have a homogeneous Congress and Presidency and, for this purpose, to have both Houses and the President elected at the same time. This can be done only by having the fixed terms of all three of the same length. . . .

The American people are, I believe, ready to approve any change which is designed to bring our government up to date with the new demands being put upon it, and is gradualist—not revolutionary—in form. A Joint Cabinet to bridge the present gap between the Executive and Congress, fortified with the power of dissolution to make it easier for the two branches to work together, is the most immediate advance to be made. It would be only one more step in the long evolution of a form of government which has been in constant process of growth since the day it was established. . . .

Any proposal for a change in the federal government which is appropriate to the present objectives of the American state and does not destroy the objective of political liberty by subordinating wholly one of the branches of government to the others is therefore well within the limits of the doctrine of the separation of powers as it was understood by the authors of the Constitution.

QUESTIONS AND PROBLEMS

1. Do Wilson, Luce, and Finletter agree or disagree on the following points: (a) that an institutional system of separation of powers and checks and balances framed in 1787 is adequate today to secure the objectives of government found in the Preamble to the Constitution; (b) that government must be strong, effective, and responsible; (c) that separation of powers produces desirable conflict; (d) that the function of Congress is to make laws and not merely to get good laws made; (e) that suggested political changes must accord with American traditions and experience? Defend your position in each case.

2. Do you agree or disagree with Wilson's criticism of "Congressional Government"? Defend your position with documentation to substantiate or refute his specific charges that the Federal government lacks strength, promptness, wieldiness, and efficiency?

3. Do you think that developments since 1885 have weakened or strengthened Wilson's argument? What part of his argument would have to be modified in the light of subsequent developments? Can you add anything to strengthen his argument?

4. What course of action would you advocate as a logical fulfillment of Wilson's analysis? Are your suggested changes politically practical? Why or why not?

5. What arguments does Luce make in support of congressional government? What arguments does he make against cabinet government? Does Luce refute the charges made by Wilson?

6. Do you think that Luce's statement that we "do have effective and responsible presidential leadership to a very material degree" applies to the situation today? Explain.

7. Assume that we adopt the Finletter proposal for dissolution. In the light of the American electoral and party system, is there any assurance that a newly

elected Congress and a newly elected President would see eye to eye any more than they did before the dissolution?

8. To what extent are the changes advanced by Finletter dependent upon strong party government and discipline? Is strong party government a practical possibility in the near future?

9. What positive suggestions, if any, would you make for the reconciliation of separation of powers and checks and balances with strong, effective, responsible government?

SELECT BIBLIOGRAPHY

Binkley, Wilfred E.: *President and Congress* (New York: Knopf, 1947). Historical treatment of presidential-congressional relationships. Concludes that problem of executive-legislative integration has not yet been solved.

Bryce, James: *The American Commonwealth* (New York: Macmillan, 1st American ed., 1889), Vol. 1, Chaps. 20–21, and 25, pp. 271–290, 205–224, in particular. One of the classic commentaries.

Corwin, Edward S.: *The President: Office and Powers* (New York: New York University Press, 3d ed., 1948). For a summary view see his "The Presidency in Perspective," *Journal of Politics*, Vol. II (February, 1949), pp. 7–13. Sees in Constitution a struggle between view that President should always be subordinate to Congress and view that executive should be, within generous limits, autonomous and self-directing. Fears constitutional breakdown unless presidential-congressional tension, evident since 1943, is relieved.

Finer, Herman: *The Theory and Practice of Modern Government* (London: Methuen, 1932), Vol. 1, Chap. 6, "The Separation of Powers: False and True," pp. 153–180, is an historical, analytical, and comparative review.

Friedrich, Carl J.: *Constitutional Government and Democracy* (Boston: Ginn, rev. ed., 1946), Chap. 10, "The Separation of Powers," pp. 170–186. A reconsideration of conditions and forms by which separation of powers can be maintained. Essentially a defense of a reformulated separation of powers suitable to the needs of a modern industrialized society.

Galloway, George B.: *Congress at the Crossroads* (New York: Crowell, 1946). Contains, pp. 204–229, one of the best summary analyses of "Legislative-Executive Liaison." Favors devices to institutionalize liaison but is wary of Finletter's proposal for dissolution.

Hamilton, Alexander, *et al.*: *The Federalist* (New York: Modern Lib., 1937), particularly Nos. 47, 48, and 51, which present the classic exposition and defense of separation of powers. See, however, No. 70 for a justification of a vigorous executive. Hamilton and Madison never believed in an absolute separation of powers.

Hazlitt, Henry: *A New Constitution Now* (New York: McGraw-Hill, 1942). A modern argument for the adoption of cabinet government. States and refutes the objections to our adoption of cabinet government.

Herring, E. Pendleton: *Presidential Leadership* (New York: Farrar & Rinehart, 1940). Argues that President must provide governmental leadership. Recognizes necessity of congressional support if leadership is to be effective, but presents no clear-cut proposals for securing this support.

Laski, Harold: *The American Presidency* (New York: Harper, 1940). Contends that only President can provide United States with leadership it needs. Looks to nonconstitutional factors—increasing importance of Federal services and functions, development of labor's political consciousness, a rational realignment of parties—to enhance strong presidential leadership.

Price, Don K.: "The Parliamentary and Presidential Systems," *Public Administration Review*, Vol. 3 (Autumn, 1943), pp. 317–334. An illuminating comparison. Defends United States system, wherein executive provides unity and enterprise and legislature furnishes independent supervision and restraining influence of local interests. For amplification, see the Price-Laski debate in the same journal and Price's essay, "The Presidency: Its Burden and Its Promise," in *The Strengthening of American Political Institutions* (Ithaca: Cornell University Press, 1949), pp. 81–111.

Wilson, Woodrow: *Constitutional Government in the United States* (New York: Columbia University Press, 1908). Should be compared with Wilson's earlier work to understand the evolution of his thinking.

Zurcher, Arnold J.: "The Presidency, Congress and Separation of Powers: A Reappraisal," *Western Political Quarterly*, Vol. 3 (March, 1950), pp. 75–97. Explains reasons for recent increasing respect shown doctrine of separation of powers. Has aided in preservation of congressional integrity without limiting executive leadership in the legislative field.

FEDERALISM

*Is Our Federal System of Government Endangered,
Obsolescent, or Adequate?*

The framers of the Constitution adopted a form of federalism to help solve an age-old problem, the reconciliation of liberty and authority. Liberty and local self-government must be preserved against a distant and possibly oppressive central authority. Yet substantial authority must be wielded by a central government to ensure a peaceful, prosperous, well-ordered, free nation. British failure to achieve such a reconciliation precipitated the Revolutionary War. Under the Articles of Confederation, the American government, despite a few notable achievements, moved from what was considered the oppressive rule of centralized British authority to a weak and ineffective American confederation. With the writing and adopting of the Constitution a new balance was achieved which would, it was hoped, avoid both the weakened authority of confederation and the threats to liberty presented by a unitary state.

Like all balances of power, federalism has been in constant flux, responding to changing winds of economic, political, and social fortune. The thirteen colonies on the Eastern seaboard with a population of 4 million have explained from ocean to ocean to embrace a population passing 150 million. As the nation changed from a rural, agricultural commonwealth of horse and buggy, wind and steam power to an urban, industrial society of airplane, electric power, and atomic energy, so has the federal balance shifted, mainly in the direction of enhanced national power.

Many have viewed this increase of national power with alarm. The first selection in this chapter, taken from the 1948 States' Rights party platform, is a sample of opposition to expanded national power. These extracts illustrate the natural tendency of state or section to raise the states' rights banner when national action injures, or threatens to injure, what they believe are their own interests.

Harold J. Laski, writing in 1939, maintained a different position.

47

He argued that the national government does not have enough power to achieve a minimum good life for its people. Our federal form of state, he declared, is too weak to contend with the problems created in the age of giant capitalism. Only a centralized system can effectively deal with the issues facing twentieth-century America.

David Fellman, in the last article in this chapter, defends our present federal structure, hitting both at Mr. Laski's underlying arguments and at the states' righters. Fellman observes that our states are vital units of government, coping with modern problems and constantly improving their performance. Cooperation among states and between state and national governments points the way toward solutions which may remedy some of the major deficiencies of traditional federalism. Fellman emphasizes the great strength of the theory and tradition of decentralized government.

The question—whither federalism?—recurs for our generation, as it will for every generation, made new and vital by changing political, economic, and scientific conditions.

Must we protect our federal system against a dangerous march toward domestic totalitarianism? Or does the obsolescence of federalism call for a centralized system to enable us to cope with modern problems? Or is our federal system healthy and adaptable enough to operate soundly in the forseeable future?

WE MUST GUARD AGAINST A FEDERAL POLICE STATE

FROM THE 1948 PLATFORM OF THE STATES' RIGHTS PARTY*

[Rebellious Southern Democrats organized the States' Rights party in protest against the Democratic party's civil rights program. In the 1948 presidential election the 39 electoral votes of Alabama (11), Louisiana (10), Mississippi (9), South Carolina (8), and Tennessee (1) were cast for the States' Rights candidates; South Carolina's Governor James Strom Thurmond and Mississippi's Governor Fielding L. Wright. EDITOR.]

We believe that the protection of the American people against the onward march of totalitarian government requires a faithful observance of Article X of the American Bill of Rights which provides that: "The

* *The New York Times,* July 18, 1948, p. 2 *passim.*

 RANGER JUNIOR C

powers not delegated to the United States by the Constitution, nor prohibited by it to the States, are reserved to the States respectively, or to the people."

We direct attention to the fact that the first platform of the Democratic party adopted in 1840, resolved that: "Congress has no power under the Constitution to interfere with or control the domestic institutions of the several states, and that such states are the sole and proper judge of everything appertaining to their own affairs not prohibited by the Constitution."

Such pronouncement is the cornerstone of the Democratic party.

A long train of abuses and usurpations by unfaithful leaders who are alien to the Democratic parties of the states here represented has become intolerable to those who believe in the preservation of constitutional government and individual liberty in America.

The Executive Department of the government is promoting the gradual but certain growth of a totalitarian state by domination and control of a politically minded Supreme Court. As examples of the threat to our form of government, the Executive Department, with the aid of the Supreme Court, has asserted national dominion and control of submerged oil-bearing lands in California, schools in Oklahoma and Missouri, primary elections in Texas, South Carolina, and Louisiana, restrictive covenants in New York and the District of Columbia, and other jurisdictions, as well as religious instruction in Illinois. . . .

By asserting paramount Federal rights in these instances, a totalitarian concept has been promulgated which threatens the integrity of the states and basic rights of their citizens.

. . . We declare to the people of the United States as follows:

1. We believe that the Constitution of the United States is the greatest charter of human liberty ever conceived in the mind of man.

2. We oppose all efforts to invade or destroy the rights vouchsafed by it to every citizen of this republic.

3. We stand for social and economic justice, which we believe can be vouchsafed to all citizens only by a strict adherence to our Constitution and the avoidance of any invasion or destruction of the constitutional rights of the states and individuals. We oppose the totalitarian, centralized, bureaucratic government and the police state called for by the Democratic and Republican conventions.

4. We stand for the segregation of the races and the racial integrity of every race; the constitutional right to choose one's associates; to accept private employment without governmental interference, and to earn one's living in any lawful way. We oppose the elimination of segregation, employment by Federal bureaucrats called for by the misnamed civil rights

program. We favor home rule, local self-government and a minimum interference with individual rights.

5. We oppose and condemn the action of the Democratic convention in sponsoring a civil rights program for the elimination of segregation, social equality by Federal fiat, regulation of private employment practices, voting and local law enforcement.

6. We affirm that the effective enforcement of such a program would be utterly destructive of the social, economic and political life of the southern people, and of other localities in which there may be differences in race, creed or national origin in appreciable numbers.

7. We stand for the checks and balances provided by the three departments of our Government. We oppose the usurpations of legislative functions by the executive and judicial departments. We unreservedly condemn the effort to establish nation-wide a police state in this republic that would destroy the last vestige of liberty enjoyed by a citizen.

8. We demand that there be returned to the people, to whom of right they belong, those powers needed for the preservation of human rights and the discharge of our responsibility as Democrats for human welfare. We oppose a denial of those rights by political parties, a barter or sale of those rights by political convention, as well as any invasion or violation of those rights by the Federal Government.

We call upon all Democrats and upon all other loyal Americans who are opposed to totalitarianism at home and abroad to unite with us in ignominiously defeating Harry S. Truman and Thomas E. Dewey, and every other candidate for public office who would establish a police state in the United States of America.

FEDERALISM IS OBSOLESCENT

BY HAROLD J. LASKI*

[Harold J. Laski, long-time Professor of Political Science at the University of London, died in 1950. A forthright advocate of democratic socialism, he lectured in the United States, intermittently, between 1926 and 1950. Among his many published works are *A Grammar of Politics, The State in Theory and Practice, Parliamentary Government in England, The American Presidency,* and *The American Democracy.* EDITOR.]

* "The Obsolescence of Federalism," *New Republic,* Vol. 98 (May 3, 1939), pp. 367–369 *passim.* By permission of Mrs. Harold J. Laski.

No one can travel the length and breadth of the United States without the conviction of its inexpugnable variety. East and West, South and North, its regions are real and different, and each has problems real and different too. The temptation is profound to insist that here, if ever, is the classic place for a federal experiment. Union without unity—except in the Soviet Union and China, has variety ever so fully invited the implications of the famous definition? Geography, climate, culture, all of them seem to have joined their forces to insist that, wherever centralization is appropriate, here, at least, it has no meaning. Tradition demands its absence; history has prohibited its coming. The large unit, as in Lamennais' phrase would result in apoplexy at the center and anemia at the extremities. Imposed solutions from a distant Washington, blind, as it must be blind, to the subtle minutiae of local realities, cannot solve the ultimate problems that are in dispute. A creative America must be a federal America. The wider the powers exercised from Washington, the more ineffective will be the capacity for creative administration. Regional wisdom is the clue to the American future. The power to govern must go where that regional wisdom resides. So restrained, men learn by the exercise of responsibility the art of progress. They convince themselves by experiment from below. To fasten a uniformity that is not in nature upon an America destined to variety is to destroy the prospect of an ultimate salvation.

This kind of argument is familiar in a hundred forms. I believe that, more than any other philosophic pattern, it is responsible for the malaise of American democracy. My plea here is for the recognition that the federal form of state is unsuitable to the stage of economic and social development that America has reached. I infer from this postulate two conclusions: first, that the present division of powers, however liberal be the Supreme Court in its technique of interpretation, is inadequate to the needs America confronts; and, second, that any revision of those powers is one which must place in Washington, and Washington only, the power to amend that revision as circumstances change. I infer, in a word, that the epoch of federalism is over, and that only a centralized system can affectively confront the problems of a new time.

To continue with the old pattern, in the age of giant capitalism, is to strike into impotence that volume of governmental power which is necessary to deal with the issues giant capitalism has raised. Federalism, I suggest, is the appropriate governmental technique for an expanding capitalism, in which the price of local habit—which means, also, local delay—admits of compensation in the total outcome. But a contracting capitalism cannot afford the luxury of federalism. It is insufficiently

COOPER LIBRARY
RANGER COLLEGE

34 28

positive in character; it does not provide for sufficient rapidity of action; it inhibits the emergence of necessary standards of uniformity; it relies upon compacts and compromises which take insufficient account of the urgent category of time; it leaves the backward areas a restraint, at once parasitic and poisonous, on those which seek to move forward; not least, its psychological results, especially in an age of crisis, are depressing to a democracy that needs the drama of positive achievement to retain its faith. . . .

Giant capitalism has, in effect, concentrated the control of economic power in a small proportion of the American people. It has built a growing contrast between the distribution of that economic power and the capacity of the political democracy effectively to control the results of its exercise. It has transcended the political boundaries of the units in the American federation so as to make them largely ineffective as areas of independent government. Whether we take the conditions of labor, the level of taxation, the standards of education, public health, or the supply of amenities like housing and recreation, it has become clear that the true source of decision is no longer at the circumference, but at the center, of the state. For forty-eight separate units to seek to compete with the integrated power of giant capitalism is to invite defeat in every element of social life where approximate uniformity of condition is the test of the good life.

The poor state is parasitic on the body politic. It offers privileges to giant capitalism to obtain its taxable capacity, offers escape from the impositions of rich states, in order to wrest from the wealthy some poor meed of compensation for its backwardness. It dare not risk offending the great industrial empires—cotton, coal, iron and steel, tobacco—lest it lose the benefits of their patronage. Their vested interests thus begin to define the limits within which the units of the federation may venture to move. And since the division of powers limits, in its turn, the authority of the federal government to intervene—the latter being a government of limited powers—it follows that the great industrial empires can, in fact, prevent the legislation necessary to implement the purposes of a democratic society. The situation may, briefly, be summarized by saying that the Constitution inhibits the federal government from exercising the authority inherent in the idea of a democracy; while the risk to a state government of attack upon the conditions exacted by those industrial empires for their patronage is too great to permit the states to jeopardize what they have by issuing challenge. Whether, therefore, it be the hours of labor, the standards of health and housing, the effective organization of the trade unions, at every point the formal powers of the states are rarely commensurate with the actual authority they may venture to exercise. And it is the common citizen of the United States who pays the price of that margin between formal and effective power.

Political systems live by the results they can obtain for the great mass of their citizens. A democracy is not likely to survive on formal grounds merely; it will survive as it is able to convince its citizens that it adequately protects their powers to satisfy the expectations they deem their experience to warrant. In the present phase of American capitalist democracy, the central government largely lacks the power to implement the ends it is essential it should serve if its democratic context is to be maintained. It cannot obtain adequate standards of government in many of the major fields it seeks to enter. It is hamstrung, partly by the division of powers from which it derives its authority; partly because the Constitution has not enabled it to develop the instrumentalities essential to the purposes it must seek to fulfill. Its effort to obtain the proper recognition of collective bargaining may be stricken into impotence by a state law against picketing. Its effort to produce proper control of public utilities may be rendered vain by local franchises granted in a period when the recognition of the need for uniformity in this field had not dawned upon the public consciousness. So, also, with conservation; with the provision of adequate educational opportunity; with the effective prohibition (a commonplace of any well ordered state) of child labor; with the coordination of relief for unemployment; with public works, especially in the utilization of the possible sources of electric power; with public-health legislation, not least in the field of maternity and child hygiene; with a proper policy of public roads . . . ; with a proper policy in housing. I take examples only. The central point of my argument is the simple one that in every major field of social regulation, the authority of which the federal government can dispose is utterly inadequate to the issues it is expected to solve.

I do not think this argument is invalidated by the rise of cooperation between the federal government and the states, or between groups of states. That use has been carefully investigated in detail by Professor Jane Clark in an admirable and exhaustive monograph ("The Rise of a New Federalism," 1938). When all is made that can be made of the pattern she there reveals, I think it is true to say that, compared to the dimension of the problem, it amounts to very little. And set in the background of the urgent problems of time, it is, I think, clear from her account that in no fundamental matters will the pressure of political interests (behind which can be seen at every turn the hand of giant capitalism) permit the necessary uniformities to be attained by consent within the next fifty years. Not even the resiliency of American democracy can afford to wait so long. Professor Clark demonstrates admirably the inescapable interest of the federal government in a hundred subjects at every turn of which it encounters the power of the states; but she also demonstrates that the problems of dual occupancy of the same ground hinders at every turn the creative solution of the problems involved unless we conceive of those solutions in terms of geological time.

I am not arguing that the administration of government services ought to be centralized in Washington. It is true, as Professor Clark says, that "there is a line beyond which centralized administration cannot go without falling because of its own weight." My argument is the very different one: that (a) there are certain objects of administrative control now left to the states for which they are no longer suitable units of regulation. Economic centralization makes necessary at least minimum standards of uniform performance in these objects, e.g., health, education, unemployment relief; and in others, e.g., labor conditions, railroad rates, electric power, complete federal control without interference by the states; and (b) that the proper objects of federal supervision cannot any longer be dependent upon state consent. Where this dependency exists, state consent will be, in its turn, largely controlled by giant capitalism. That is why Delaware is merely a pseudonym of the du Ponts, and Montana little more than a symbol of the Anaconda Copper Corporation. That is why the people of the state of Washington, who ought long ago to have been permitted to have the advantage of the municipal electric power plant of Seattle, still suffer from the division of its potential benefits through the survival of the Puget Sound Light and Power Company.

Nor would the problem be met if, instead of the states, America were divided, as writers like Professor Howard Odum suggest, into regions more correspondent with the economic realities of the situation. If America were to consist of seven or nine regions, instead of forty-eight states, that would still leave unsolved the main issues if they operated upon the basis of the present division of powers, and if their consent were necessary to any fundamental change in that division. Once again, it must be emphasized that the unity which giant capitalism postulates in the economic sphere postulates a corresponding unity in the conference of political powers upon the federal government. There is no other way, up to a required minimum, in which the questions of taxation, labor relations and conditions, conservation, public utilities (in the widest sense), to take examples only, can be met.

At this point, of course, the relation of a federal system to the power of judicial review becomes fundamental. No one now believes Marshall's famous assertion that "courts are the mere instruments of the law, and can will nothing"; it has been obvious, above all since the Civil War, that the Supreme Court is the effective master of federal legislation. And it is clear, further, that this mastery is exercised in the main not on objective tests of constitutionality (which do not exist), but upon the accident of a temporary majority's view of what it is "reasonable" for the federal government to undertake. The Court has become a non-elective third chamber of the government which may, as in the income-tax cases, defeat for many years purposes of which its members do not happen to approve. In an epoch of rapid change, it is a grave danger to any society that the will of a federal legislature should be subject to judicial control, and more especially when, as Marshall said, the amending process is "cumbrous and unwieldy." In a phase of liberal construction the difficulties of judicial review are obscured from the public. But the years before the controversy over the President's Court plan should be a sufficient reminder of the immense dangers lurking within it.

The view here urged, of course, looks toward a fundamental reconstruction of traditional American institutions. It is not impressed by the view, associated with the great name of Mr. Justice Brandeis, that the "curse of bigness" will descend upon any serious departure from the historic contours of federalism. The small unit of government is impotent against the big unit of giant capitalism. It may be that the very power of giant capitalism is no longer of itself compatible with the maintenance of a democratic political structure in society; there is much evidence to support this view. What, at least, is certain is this: that a government the powers of which are not commensurate with its problems will not be able to cope with them. Either, therefore, it must obtain those powers, or it must yield to a form of state more able to satisfy the demands that it encounters. That is the supreme issue before the United States today; and the more closely it is scrutinized the more obviously does its resolution seem to be bound up with the obsolescence of the federal system.

For that system presents the spectacle of forty-nine governments seeking to deal with issues for many of which they are inappropriate as instrumentalities whether in the area they cover or in the authority they may invoke. They are checked and balanced upon a theory of the state completely outmoded in the traditional ends upon which its postulates are based. Giant industry requires a positive state; federalism, in its American form, is geared to vital negations which contradict the implications of positivism. Giant industry requires uniformities in the field of its major influence; American federalism is the inherent foe, both in time and space, of those necessary uniformities. Giant industry, not least, requires the opposition of a unified public will to counteract its tendency to undemocratic procedure through the abuse of power; a federal system of the American kind dissipates the unity of public opinion in those fields where it is most urgently required. And, above all, it is urgent to note that giant industry, in an age of economic contraction, is able to exploit the diversities of a federal scheme, through the delays they permit in the attainment of uniformity, to reactionary ends. Thereby, they discredit the democratic process at a time when it is least able to afford that discredit. For, thereby, the confidence of the citizen body in its power to work out democratic solutions of its problems is gravely undermined.

Men who are deprived of faith by inability to attain results they greatly desire do not long remain content with the institutions under which they live. The price of democracy is the power to satisfy living demands. American federalism, in its traditional form, cannot keep pace with the tempo of the life giant capitalism has evolved. To judge it in terms of its historic success is to misconceive the criteria by which it becomes valid for the present and the future. No political system has the privilege of immortality; and there is no moment so fitting for the consideration of its remaking as that which permits of reconstruction with the prospect of a new era of creative achievement.

FEDERALISM IS STILL VIABLE

BY DAVID FELLMAN*

[David Fellman, Professor of Poltical Science at the University of Wisconsin, is the editor of *Readings in American National Government* and *Post-war Governments of Europe* and a frequent contributor to political and legal periodicals. EDITOR.]

. . . The available evidence suggests that federalism is not yet a corpse and is not likely to become one in the predictable future.

The Continued Vitality of State Government

At the outset, it should be noted that the increase in the powers of the national government in the past few decades has not necessarily been at the expense of the states. To be sure, in some important measure national authority has invaded, by direct or devious means, the area of traditional local activity. But the expansion of that authority has proceeded largely from a more intense exploitation of powers already legitimately in the hands of the central government. While national power has been ex-

---

* By permission from *Problems of the Postwar World*, edited by T. C. T. McCormick, copyright, 1945, McGraw-Hill Book Company, Inc., pp. 183–203 *passim*. Only direct quotations have been footnoted.

panding, the same thing has been happening at the state level as well. What we have been getting in recent years is simply more government, more government at all levels of authority. The objection to centralization is, in considerable measure, an objection to government at all levels. Many who are now taking refuge in "states' rights" as a bulwark against Federal power would just as readily turn to the national government for protection against the states if the latter should seek to impose the same tax and regulatory measures.

The states are still important units of government. Although Congress legislates more today than ever before, the same holds true for the state legislatures. The President is a more powerful executive today than ever before in our history, but the governorship has also reached new heights of power and influence. Both state and national bureaucracies have grown in size and power; delegated legislation is a feature as much of state lawmaking as it is of national. The growth of the Federal commerce power has been matched by a fuller development of state control over economic life. State budgets have been enlarged through the pressure of public demand in almost the same measure as Federal budgets have responded to an insistent popular desire for more services. . . .

. . . Since about 1930 the state legislatures have been the scenes of unprecedented activity. They have all adopted comprehensive legislation establishing systems of unemployment compensation, old-age assistance, and child welfare. State public health departments have been either created or improved. Many states now have fair trade acts, labor relations acts, labor conciliation services, and laws outlawing the yellow-dog contract and restricting the issuance of court injunctions in labor cases. In the meantime, there has been a more thorough exploitation of time-honored state functions, such as those dealing with roads, education, public institutions, the regulation of agriculture and business, the conservation of natural resources, and police power regulations seeking to protect the public health, safety, and morals. If it is true that the states are dying, it may be said with some confidence that the patient will enjoy a long, lingering illness. When viewed from a standpoint that is founded upon something more modest than cosmic time, the American states seem to have a great deal of vitality left in them.

The Role of the States in the Second World War

. . . The general opinion seems to be that the state and local governments . . . participated effectively in the administration of the war program, both through cooperation with the Federal government and through independent action. . . .

Cooperative Federalism

. . . |"Cooperative federalism" has come a long way in the past century. It proceeds upon the assumption that the state and national governments are not necessarily antagonistic legal entities engaged in a perennial struggle for jurisdiction across a no-man's land policed by the Supreme Court. To the contrary, it assumes that they are public-service agencies designed to serve the same public with whatever means may be at their disposal. There are many problems which neither government is able to cope with satisfactorily without the aid of the other, and there is no insurmountable barrier standing in the way of their working together. It follows that it is in the public interest that they do work together. Experience demonstrates that a great deal of cooperation is possible on reasonably acceptable terms.|

The Federal grant-in-aid has been the most important device used for the development of this new sort of functional federalism. It has been applied to many fields of activity: education, road building, conservation, social security and public assistance, child and maternity welfare, public health, forest-fire protection, vocational rehabilitation, and housing. During 1938 Federal grants-in-aid accounted for about 6 per cent of the national budget. In this manner the national government has found a way of combining its superior fiscal resources and capacity for setting up uniform policies for the country as a whole with the flexibility of local administration. The execution of the program has required both parties to give as well as take. Out of mutual concessions has grown a valuable form of intergovernmental action in which both parties address themselves to the performance of common tasks.|

|Cooperative federalism takes many other forms, of varying degrees of significance, some formal and some informal, some persistent and some spasmodic. There is a great deal of informal cooperation between Federal and state officials by means of discussion and conference, the exchange of facilities and services, and the loan of equipment or personnel. Some Federal-state contacts are in the nature of informal agreements or formal contracts. There is a considerable amount of cooperative use of government personnel, in the field of public utility regulation, for example. The administration of many state laws depends upon Federal action and, conversely, many state activities are helped along by Federal laws. Federal tax credits, as in the cases of inheritance tax and unemployment compensation legislation, impinge directly upon state policy. A very good example of Federal-state cooperation on a tremendous scale and taking every conceivable form is found in the field of criminal law enforcement. Every Federal agency having law-enforcement functions, and there is a large number of such agencies today, works with state and local peace

officials in some measure, great or small. It is generally agreed that without this cooperation the Federal agencies could not possibly do their work effectively, at least as they are presently constituted.

It is quite likely that we shall have more and more cooperative federalism in the future. The trend is clearly marked. As the states and the national government learn how to work together at tasks requiring common effort, it may be anticipated that they will find it possible to invent new procedures which will make cooperative action an ever more effective weapon in dealing with many of the nation's general interests. It may well be that it offers the only possible solution for some of the major deficiencies of traditional federalism.

Nevertheless, it should be noted that a genuine cooperative federalism must be based upon both the ability and the willingness of the states to cooperate effectively and to maintain acceptable national standards of administration. The states must be willing to enforce impartially the provisions of the Federal Constitution and of acts of Congress, even when such provisions are locally unpopular. There has been some encouraging progress in this direction, but it would not be accurate to say that the problem no longer exists.

Furthermore, it should be recognized that this cooperation is not always freely given and that the states are not cooperating with the national government on a basis of equality. In most instances, the national government pays the fiddler and calls the tune. Important strings are always tied to grants of Federal money. The harshness of the exercise of power by the central government is mitigated, to be sure, by the participation of local agencies in its administration. The relationship here, however, is not necessarily a Federal one. It might very well exist in a unitary state, such as England, in which the tradition of local self-government is strong. If our states were to lose all vestiges of their "sovereignty," they might still be utilized in the administration of national policy. The very idea of cooperative federalism assumes two things: cooperation and federalism. It assumes that the cooperation must proceed on Federal terms.

The Possibilities of Interstate Cooperation

. . . The adoption of uniform legislation on a fairly large scale has been a particularly useful development. It has been stimulated by the tendency of the states to copy each other's statutes, by the creation of legislative reference services and legislative councils, and by private associations. Most important has been the work of the National Conference on Uniform State Laws, which was created by state statutes some 50 years ago. Increasingly, however, the impetus for the adoption of uniform legislation comes from Federal agencies, notably the Department

of Commerce, Labor, and Justice, and from such special bodies as the
Federal Deposit Insurance Corporation and the Social Security Board.
Although in a technical sense the states accept this federally inspired
legislation voluntarily, the inducement in some instances, as in the case of
unemployment compensation, is for all practical purposes irresistible.

The states have also adopted over 50 formal compacts dealing with
boundaries, rivers and harbors, public works, conservation, taxation, and
certain other social and economic problems. This method of securing
agreement among states is cumbersome and difficult to manage. There
is some reason to hope, however, that the states may yet learn how to
use it to full advantage, especially as they come to understand that it
offers a means of slowing down the further growth of national power.
There are also various forms of administrative cooperation looking toward
the adoption of uniform regulations and interpretations which help along
the cause of interstate comity. In this connection, mention should be
made of the work of the commissions on interstate cooperation. They
have been functioning since 1935 under the auspices of the Council of
State Governments and have done yeoman work in arresting the tide of
trade-barrier legislation.

The road that interstate cooperation in its various forms must travel is
long and rough, and the results that have been achieved so far are very
modest. Nevertheless, it is to be noted that the amount of such cooperation is steadily increasing and that the states are apparently learning some
of the hard lessons involved in the business of getting on together. Certainly it cannot be said that its possibilities have been exhausted; on the
contrary, the surface has scarcely been scratched.

The Improvement of State Government

. . . The legislative process has received much attention, particularly
the rules of procedure and the committee system. Aids for the legislature
have been created in many states, including bill-drafting services, legislative reference bureaus, and legislative councils. Administration has been
strengthened a great deal through the reorganization of boards and departments and through improvements in personnel administration, including the adoption in many states of some sort of merit system. Fiscal
practices have also been strengthened, notably through the widespread
adoption of the executive budget system and of better auditing practices.
The state judiciary has been improved in many ways, by experimentation
with new types of courts, such as those dealing with domestic relations,
juvenile delinquency, and small claims, and by the steady revision of civil
and criminal law procedure.

It seems clear that the states have only begun to overhaul their governmental machinery. There is no reason to be other than optimistic about the great possibilities that lie ahead in the continuation of a current trend which seems to have gathered so much momentum. The increased confidence that these reforms are engendering in the people may very likely serve as an additional bulwark against the trend toward centralization. . . .

The Strength of the Theory and Tradition of Decentralization

Finally, any assessment of the prospects of American federalism must take into account the great strength of the theory and tradition of decentralized government. Vigorous local government is among the oldest traditions of the American people. It was a central feature of a century and a half of colonial history. It has been an integral part of the American scene ever since independence was achieved. It is therefore deeply rooted in the American mind. "States' rights" is the core of an effective slogan, whatever may be the real motives of those who use it. It is advanced by people who are genuinely interested in the principle. It is used also by many as a screen for the protection of something else: white supremacy, the private ownership of public utilities, freedom from certain kinds of taxation, the support of local economic advantages or monopolies. But whatever the undisclosed major premise may be, the slogan is effective on the hustings.

Having witnessed the ravages of highly centralized dictatorship in foreign countries during the past two decades, the American people have become especially sensitive to the dangers of centralization. Many feel, rightly or wrongly, that federalism offers some additional security against a usurpation of power. The suspicion of power which has permeated American constitutions for a century and a half is expressed in part by the idea of checks and balances, one element of which is contained in the notion that the states are a counterweight to national government. It is felt by many that the concentration of all power at the center will invite the moral corruption that unchecked power breeds in those who hold it. They also believe that it may create a power system which ambitious men may too easily convert to the dictatorial pattern. In short, they believe that federalism supports so many centers of power that no single *coup d'état* can possibly be successful.

Furthermore, it is widely believed that federalism avoids many other evils of centralization, especially those associated with very large systems of administration. "The curse of bigness" is more frequently associated in this country with governmental bureaucracy than with any other aggregation of men and power. Many are convinced that the bureaucracy of the national government is already too large to be properly manageable, that it is getting bogged down in inertia, formalism, and red tape, that it is too complex, and that in its growing remoteness from the people it is becoming increasingly dehumanized and unresponsive to public opinion. . . .

Furthermore, many of the time-honored considerations in favor of federalism will in all likelihood continue to carry a great deal of weight in the future. There is a common opinion that it creates a large number of political laboratories where new ideas may be tried out without having to commit the whole country to them and without running the risk of paying too great a price for mistakes. It is felt that federalism permits the citizen to separate state and local from national issues and hence gives him a chance to vote more discriminatingly. Many also think that federalism has the merit of keeping a great deal of government close to the people, where it must be kept if it is to remain democratic, and that it therefore has considerable educational value in training the citizenry in the arts of self-government. Undeniably, federalism facilitates the adaptation of government and law to local needs and sensibilities, which vary considerably from one section of the country to another. A wide public is persuaded that only federalism can suit the needs of as large a country as ours. . . .

Paradoxically enough, however, the very sectional differences and rivalries that are commonly cited in support of federalism and states' rights may also be cited in support of a strong central government, if we are to have an effective national society at all. These very differences and rivalries made the Confederation ineffective and led to the formation of a stronger Union in 1787. If Mississippi cannot or will not support education and public health at a minimum level of adequacy; if California and the Southern states cannot be wholly trusted in the administration of their race problems; if Wisconsin insists upon imposing economic handicaps upon goods that compete with her own dairy products; if Iowa will not regulate marriages for fear that Iowa couples will go to adjoining states and spend "Iowa money" there; if Illinois will not regulate oil production in the interest of conservation, for fear that Kansas and Texas may benefit thereby; if New York is penalized for adopting legislation outlawing sweatshops by the willingness of neighboring Connecticut to accommodate them, then there will be a demand for greater and greater Federal regulation. It may be true that academic theorists and impatient reformers, in their demands for quick national solutions to social problems, do not sufficiently appreciate either the strength of the tradition of states' rights or the dangers of a highly centralized government in a country of continental proportions. It may also be true that some of the persons who resist social and economic reforms under the cloak of states' rights do not sufficiently appreciate either the implications of democracy or the institutional needs of a modern society.

The debate over centralization and decentralization is a debate that has no ending. . . .

In the last analysis, the problem of federalism cannot be solved out of hand by recourse to a purely logical construction. No simple formula will do, according to which national problems should be in the hands of the national government and local problems within the sphere of local institutions. For one thing, the formula is not at all a simple one, since there is no general agreement as to just where the line of demarcation should be drawn, and the doubtful cases are numerous and highly debatable. Furthermore, modern conditions of interdependence are such that any attempt to make national power coextensive with problems that are national in scope would mean an end to the vigorous local self-government which federalism assumes. Few indeed are the questions of contemporary life that do not in fact transcend the lines of local jurisdictions. If federalism is to be a reality, the powers of local government must necessarily be significant in the aggregate. It therefore follows that local government must be entrusted with responsibilities that with equal or even greater propriety and logic might be in the hands of the central government. McBain has written:

"The states must have real powers, and this means that they must have control over numerous matters that are from many points of view of nation-wide interest and importance. If every power for which the 'common interest' argument can be cogently put forward were to be transferred to the national government, federalism would give up the ghost. . . . If it is to live, there must be in its make-up a large amount of the artificial, the arbitrary, the illogical, the unscientific. . . . Indeed, under any genuinely federal system one might almost say of states' rights that 'whatever is is right.' "[1]

Justice Holmes once said that the life of the law has not been logic; it has been experience. The same may be said for the future of American federalism. Power will flow now in one direction, now in another, as the push of the moment dictates. No single concrete issue is likely, in our time, to put the nation in a position where it must choose sharply, once and for all, which path it will continue to tread. More likely, we shall continue to travel two roads at the same time.

QUESTIONS AND PROBLEMS

1. Why specifically has the Federal government within recent years entered into or enlarged its program in the following fields: social security, regulation of labor, support of agricultural prices, low-cost housing, insurance of banking

[1] McBain, H. L.: *The Living Constitution*, pp. 70–71, New York, 1928.

deposits, regulation of securities and exchanges, highway construction, school-lunch programs, public health, aviation?

2. What does the Federal government do in each of the above fields? Were the states not competent to deal with the problems in these fields? Did the Federal government in any case take away from the states activities which they were performing?

3. What evidence does the 1948 States' Rights party platform present to support its view that we are marching toward a totalitarian government? Explain why you agree or disagree with this states' rights argument.

4. On what grounds does Mr. Laski reach the conclusion that "the federal form of state is unsuitable to the stage of economic and social development that America has reached?" Does your examination of the American record force you to reach a similar conclusion? To what extent do Mr. Laski's socialist predilections color his interpretation of the record?

5. Mr. Laski calls for a "fundamental reconstruction of traditional institutions." Since he rejects regionalism and cooperative federalism as solutions, what kind of "reconstruction" do you think he has in mind? Evaluate this reconstruction.

6. On what grounds does Mr. Fellman reach the conclusions that "federalism is not yet a corpse and is not likely to become one in the predictable future" and that "we shall continue to travel two roads [national and state] at the same time"?

7. Evaluate the various techniques of federal-state and interstate cooperation.

8. Discuss the following much-quoted remark of Woodrow Wilson: "The question of the relation of the states to the federal government is the cardinal question of our constitutional system. It cannot be settled by the opinion of any one generation, because it is a question of growth, and every successive stage of our political and economic development gives it a new aspect, makes it a new question."

9. What have been the constitutional bases for the great expansion of national power?

10. To what extent are modern trends making for increased national power irreversible? If these trends are, in fact, irreversible, does this mean that government in the United States will be transformed from a federal into a unitary state? Explain.

11. How may the states, and the people therein, directly and indirectly, shape national interpretation of our federal system? Treat here, among other points, the composition of Congress, the election of the President, nominations to the Supreme Court, the technique of constitutional amendment.

SELECT BIBLIOGRAPHY

Anderson, William: "Federalism—Then and Now," *State Government,* Vol. 16 (May, 1943), pp. 107–112. American federalism today differs in degree and kind from the 1787 model. Opts for a "functional" federalism.

Benson, George C. S.: *The New Centralization: A Study of Intergovernmental Relationships in the United States* (New York: Farrar & Rinehart, 1941). An excellent introduction to the problem. Chapters 2 and 3 contain summary of pros and cons of a decentralized federal system. Holds readjustments at all levels of government necessary to achieve governmental efficiency and political safety.

Benson, George S. C.: "A Plea for Administrative Decentralization," *Public Administration Review,* Vol. 7 (Summer, 1947), pp. 170–178. Excellent analytical treatment of geographical decentralization. Attempts to reconcile conflicting views, pro and con. Urges administrative decentralization to avoid long-run inefficiency of top-heavy administration.

Bryce, James: *The American Commonwealth* (New York: Macmillan, 1st American ed., 1889). A late nineteenth-century view. Chaps. 27–30 (Vol. 1) although dated in spots, still provide a lucid and perspicuous appraisal of American federalism.

Clark, Jane Perry: *The Rise of a New Federalism: Federal-State Cooperation in the United States* (New York: Columbia University Press, 1938). Discusses informational cooperation; agreements and contracts; cooperative use of governmental personnel; interdependent law and administration; grants-in-aid; Federal credits for state taxation. Holds Federal-state cooperation may accomplish in many instances what neither the Federal nor the state governments could do alone. Offers such cooperation as means of reconciling centralized control with state administrative responsibility within framework of present federal system.

Council of State Governments *et al.*: *Federal-State Relations,* Senate Document 81, 81st Cong., 1st sess. (Washington: Government Printing Office, 1949). Contains six separate reports and studies. The first three—"Report on Federal-State Relations," "Outline of Study of Federal-State Relations," "Appendix to Report on Federal-State Relations"—are by the Council of State Governments, Frank Bane, Executive Director. The fourth is a "Report of Committee on Federal-State Relations," J. T. Coolidge, Chairman. The fifth is a four-page study of "State-Federal Overlapping Taxes," by Roswell Magill; and the sixth is an historical "Development of Governmental Powers in the United States," by Stanford Schewel. These documents represent results of a recent investigation made for the (Hoover) Commission on Organization of the Executive Branch of the Government. A "must" for all students of federal-state relations. Compare Bane and Coolidge reports for differing emphasis.

Drummond, Roscoe, *et al.*: "Are We Maintaining Our Federal System?" *State Government,* Special Supplement (January, 1949). Drummond's short article an excellent statement of position that trend toward centralized government is overwhelming, inevitable, and irreversible. Triumphs of F. D. R. and Truman plus Republican lack of opposition to significant reduction of national power point to popular acceptance of policies of big, centralized government. Suggests we learn to make "Big Government" function more wisely, effectively, and economically rather than futilely bemoan its existence.

Graves, W. Brooke: "The Future of the American States," *American Political Science Review*, Vol. 30 (February, 1936), pp. 24–50. Examines and rejects proposals for regionalism and city-states as alternatives to present federal structure. Alternatives undesirable, impractical, impossible, and unnecessary. Sees main hope for future of states in techniques for interstate cooperation.

Hamilton, Alexander, *et al.*: *The Federalist* (New York: Modern Lib., 1937). The great justification and rationalization of our federal union. Should be read—or reread—in view of altered scene since 1787–1788.

"Intergovernmental Relations in the United States," *Annals of the American Academy of Political and Social Science*, Vol. 207 (January, 1940). Discusses, seriatim, Federal relations with other units, interstate relations, regionalism, interrelations of local units, future considerations. With bibliography.

Koenig, Louis W.: "Federal and State Cooperation under the Constitution," *Michigan Law Review*, Vol. 36 (March, 1938), pp. 752–785. Treats sphere, problems, and promise of federal-state cooperation. Finds federal-state cooperation—despite limitations—an acceptable alternative to highly centralized government.

Lilienthal, David E.: *T.V.A.: Democracy on the March* (New York: Harper, 1944; Pocket Books, 1945). Particularly Chaps. 14 and 15 for strong argument, based on TVA's regional experience, favoring local administration of Federal functions. Holds decentralization antidote for ills of remote national control.

McGill, Ralph: "The South Must Decide," *Forum*, Vol. 105 (February, 1946), pp. 526–527. Liberal editor of *Atlanta* [Ga.] *Constitution* contends that South can't have cake (Federal aid for education, health, electricity) and eat it (decry government interference) too.

Wheare, K. C.: *Federal Government* (New York: Oxford, 1946). A comparative survey. Recognizes nationalizing tendencies in modern world, but argues federal government is worth preserving. Finds no conclusive evidence that federalism is merely a stage on relentless march toward unitary government.

INDIVIDUAL RIGHTS

How Fulfill the American Heritage of Liberty for All Our People?

Although the modern controversy over civil rights has been smoldering a long time, full-scale conflagration in the national arena did not burst out until February 2, 1948, when President Truman submitted a Civil Rights Program to Congress. This program was based on the now historic 1947 Report of the President's Committee on Civil Rights, *To Secure These Rights*.

The issue assumed major importance in the election of 1948 after a liberal wing of the Democratic party forced the adoption of a plank in the party platform expressly endorsing Mr. Truman's civil rights proposals. This led 35 delegates from Alabama and Mississippi to bolt the Convention. It resulted in the formation of a States' Rights party, which campaigned against Federal invasion of states' rights and which garnered 39 electoral votes in an unsuccessful attempt to deadlock the election of a president.

Despite Mr. Truman's unexpected triumph in November of 1948, the overwhelming majority of Southern congressmen, most of whom had supported the Democratic ticket, still opposed the Truman Civil Rights Program. When an attempt was made in the first session of the Eighty-First Congress to tighten the Senate closure (or antifilibuster) rule as a prerequisite to passing civil rights legislation, Southern senators resorted to a filibuster. Then, with the aid of some Republicans, they changed the Senate rules to make it yet more difficult to apply closure in the future.

Proponents of civil rights legislation will probably continue to press their fight, drawing arguments and moral support from the Report of the President's Committee on Civil Rights, extracted herein.

This Committee reinterprets the basic rights of all Americans. The Committee asserts that both currently acknowledged rights and those added by their broadened conception are being violated. Such rights must be secured, and can only be secured, by a comprehensive civil rights program, including legislation, education, and individual and group action. The Committee insists that the Federal government, exercising its constitutional powers, should take the leadership in such a program to protect a broad range of rights, both against the states and against private individuals.

Southerners have been the principal critics of such a far-reaching civil rights program. Senator Hoey of North Carolina, for example, contends that such a program is unconstitutional and violates states' rights. It would upset long-standing customs and feelings and destroy certain rights while attempting to create and protect others. Furthermore, he maintains, such legislation is unnecessary and uncalled for because civil rights are being adequately protected now.

Hodding Carter, a liberal Southern editor, points out, in the third and concluding article in this chapter, that specific civil rights proposals, urged by those apparently unappreciative of Southern sentiment and progress, are misdirected. If Federal action is necessary, Carter suggests the passage of alternative measures—such as Federal aid to education and slum clearance—which are better adapted to the improvement of the lot of Southern minorities.

The question of public policy involved in this continuing debate on the rights Americans possess, how such rights are protected, and how they can be secured most effectively may be posed in the following way:

In order to fulfill the American heritage of liberty for all our people, should the Federal government act now on a broad and far-reaching front? Or should we oppose such action by the Federal government as unconstitutional, unnecessary, and ill-advised?

THE FEDERAL GOVERNMENT SHOULD ACT NOW ON A BROAD AND FAR-REACHING FRONT

BY THE PRESIDENT'S COMMITTEE ON CIVIL RIGHTS*

[The Committee consisted of Charles E. Wilson (Chairman), Sadie T. Alexander, James B. Carey, John S. Dickey, Morris L. Ernst, Rabbi Roland B. Gittelsohn, Frank P. Graham, the Most Reverend Francis J. Haas, Charles Luckman, Francis P.

* *To Secure These Rights* (Washington: Government Printing Office, 1947), pp. 6–170 *passim*.

Matthews, Franklin D. Roosevelt, Jr., the Right Reverend Henry Knox Sherrill, Boris Shiskin, Dorothy Tilly, and Channing Tobias. EDITOR.]

I—THE AMERICAN HERITAGE: THE PROMISE OF FREEDOM AND EQUALITY

Four basic rights have seemed important to this Committee and have influenced its labors. We believe that each of these rights is essential to the well-being of the individual and to the progress of society.

1. *The Right to Safety and Security of the Person*

Freedom can exist only where the citizen is assured that his person is secure against bondage, lawless violence, and arbitrary arrest and punishment. Freedom from slavery in all its forms is clearly necessary if all men are to have equal opportunity to use their talents and to lead worthwhile lives. Moreover, to be free, men must be subject to discipline by society only for commission of offenses clearly defined by law and only after trial by due process of law. Where the administration of justice is discriminatory, no man can be sure of security. Where the threat of violence by private persons or mobs exists, a cruel inhibition of the sense of freedom of activity and security of the person inevitably results. Where a society permits private and arbitrary violence to be done to its members, its own integrity is inevitably corrupted. It cannot permit human beings to be imprisoned or killed in the absence of due process of law without degrading its entire fabric.

2. *The Right to Citizenship and Its Privileges*

Since it is a purpose of government in a democracy to regulate the activity of each man in the interest of all men, it follows that every mature and responsible person must be able to enjoy full citizenship and have an equal voice in his government. Because the right to participate in the political process is customarily limited to citizens there can be no denial of access to citizenship based upon race, color, creed, or national origin. Denial of citizenship for these reasons cheapens the personality of those who are confined to this inferior status and endangers the whole concept of a democratic society.

To deny qualified citizens the right to vote while others exercise it is to do violence to the principle of freedom and equality. Without the right to vote, the individual loses his voice in the group effort and is subjected to rule by a body from which he has been excluded. Likewise, the right of the individual to vote is important to the group itself. Democracy assumes that the majority is more likely as a general rule to make decisions which are wise and desirable from the point of view of the interests of the whole society than is any minority. Every time a qualified person is denied a voice in public affairs, one of the components of a potential majority is lost, and the formation of a sound public policy is endangered.

To the citizen in a democracy, freedom is a precious possession. Accordingly, all able-bodied citizens must enjoy the right to serve the nation and the cause of freedom in time of war. Any attempt to curb the right to fight in its defense can only lead the citizen to question the worth of the society in which he lives. A sense of frustration is created which is wholly alien to the normal emotions of a free man. In particular, any discrimination which, while imposing an obligation, prevents members of minority groups from rendering full military service in defense of their country is for them a peculiarly humiliating badge of inferiority. The nation also suffers a loss of manpower and is unable to marshal maximum strength at a moment when such strength is most needed.

3. The Right to Freedom of Conscience and Expression

In a free society there is faith in the ability of the people to make sound, rational judgments. But such judgments are possible only where the people have access to all relevant facts and to all prevailing interpretations of the facts. How can such judgments be formed on a sound basis if arguments, viewpoints, or opinions are arbitrarily suppressed? How can the concept of the marketplace of thought in which truth ultimately prevails retain its validity if the thought of certain individuals is denied the right of circulation? The Committee reaffirms our tradition that freedom of expression may be curbed by law only where the danger to the well-being of society is clear and present.

Our forefathers fought bloody wars and suffered torture and death for the right to worship God according to the varied dictates of conscience. Complete religious liberty has been accepted as an unquestioned personal freedom since our Bill of Rights was adopted. We have insisted only that religious freedom may not be pleaded as an excuse for criminal or clearly anti-social conduct.

4. The Right to Equality of Opportunity

It is not enough that full and equal membership in society entitles the individual to an equal voice in the control of his government; it must also give him the right to enjoy the benefits of society and to contribute to its progress. The opportunity of each individual to obtain useful employment, and to have access to services in the fields of education, housing, health, recreation and transportation, whether available free or at a price, must be provided with complete disregard for race, color, creed, and national origin. Without this equality of opportunity the individual is deprived of the chance to develop his potentialities and to share the fruits of society. The group also suffers through the loss of the contributions which might have been made by persons excluded from the main channels of social and economic activity.

The Heritage and the Reality

Our American heritage of freedom and equality has given us prestige among the nations of the world and a strong feeling of national pride at home. There is much reason for that pride. But pride is no substitute for steady and honest performance, and the record shows that at varying times in American history the gulf between ideals and practice has been wide. We have had human slavery. We have had religious persecution. We have had mob rule. We still have their ideological remnants in the unwarrantable "pride and prejudice" of some of our people and practices. From our work as a Committee, we have learned much that has shocked us, and much that has made us feel ashamed. But we have seen nothing to shake our conviction that the civil rights of the American people—all of them—can be strengthened quickly and effectively by the normal processes of democratic, constitutional government. That strengthening, we believe, will make our daily life more and more consonant with the spirit of the American heritage of freedom. But it will require as much courage, as much imagination, as much perseverance as anything which we have ever done together. The members of this Committee reaffirm their faith in the American heritage and in its promise.

II—The Record: Short of the Goal

[Part II of the *Report* examines our record with regard to the four basic rights treated in Part I. The Committee concludes that the United States has not attained its civil rights goal but makes it quite clear that there is a great deal in our record of which we can be proud—enough to warrant the belief that no other nation has ever offered more hope for the realization of the ideal of freedom and equality. The Committee pays more attention to our failures than to our accomplishments because its task was to recommend ways of strengthening the civil rights of all our people, a task which required investigation of our shortcomings.

The following excerpts illustrate some of these violations of civil rights.]

The Crime of Lynching

In 1946 at least six persons in the United States were lynched by mobs. Three of them had not been charged, either by the police or anyone else, with an offense. Of the three that had been charged, one had been accused of stealing a saddle. (The real thieves were discovered after the lynching.) Another was said to have broken into a house. A third was charged with stabbing a man. All were Negroes. During the same year, mobs were prevented from lynching 22 persons, of whom 21 were Negroes, 1 white.

On July 20, 1946, a white farmer, Loy Harrison, posted bond for the release of Roger Malcolm from the jail at Monroe, Georgia. Malcom, a young Negro, had been involved in a fight with his white employer during the course of which the latter had been stabbed. It is reported that there was talk of lynching Malcolm at the time of the incident and while he was in jail. Upon Malcolm's release, Harrison started to drive Malcolm, Malcolm's wife, and a Negro overseas veteran, George Dorsey, and his wife, out of Monroe. At a bridge along the way a large group of unmasked white men, armed with pistols and shotguns, was waiting. They stopped Harrison's car and removed Malcolm and Dorsey. As they were leading the two men away, Harrison later stated, one of the women called out the name of a member of the mob. Thereupon the lynchers returned and removed the two women from the car. Three volleys of shots were fired as if by a squad of professional executioners. The coroner's report said that at least 60 bullets were found in the scarcely recognizable bodies. Harrison consistently denied that he could identify any of the unmasked murderers. State and federal grand juries reviewed the evidence in the case, but no person has yet been indicted for the crime.

Later that summer, in Minden, Louisiana, a young Negro named John Jones was arrested on suspicion of housebreaking. Another Negro youth, Albert Harris, was arrested at about the same time, and beaten in an effort to implicate Jones. He was then released, only to be rearrested after a few days. On August 6th, early in the evening, and before there had been any trial of the charges against them, Jones and Harris were released by a deputy sheriff. Waiting in the jail yard was a group of white men. There was evidence that, with the aid of the deputy sheriff, the young men were put into a car. They were then driven into the country. Jones was beaten to death. Harris, left for dead, revived and escaped. Five persons, including two deputy sheriffs, were indicted and brought to trial in a federal court for this crime. All were acquitted.

These are two of the less brutal lynchings of the past years. The victims in these cases were not mutilated or burned. . . .

Police Brutality

The files of the Department [of Justice] abound with evidence of illegal official action in southern states. In one case, the victim was arrested on a charge of stealing a tire, taken to the courthouse, beaten by three officers with a blackjack until his head was a bloody pulp, and then dragged unconscious through the streets to the jail where he was thrown, dying, onto the floor. In another case a constable arrested a Negro against whom he bore a personal grudge, beat him brutally with a bullwhip and then forced his victim, in spite of protestations of being unable to swim, to jump into a river where he drowned. In a third case, there was evidence that officers arrested a Negro maid on a charge of stealing jewelry from her employer, took her to jail and severely beat and whipped her in an unsuccessful effort to extort a confession. All of these cases occurred within the last five years. . . .

The Right to Vote

This report cannot adequately describe the history of Negro disfranchisement. At different times, different methods have been employed. As legal devices for disfranchising the Negro have been held unconstitutional, new methods have been improvised to take their places. Intimidation and the threat of intimidation have always loomed behind these legal devices to make sure that the desired result is achieved. [The Committee then examines the white primary as one such legal device.]

In a recent case in the Department of Justice files, a Negro school teacher was disqualified under a North Carolina provision requiring an ability to read and interpret the Constitution. The registrar refused to register him on the ground that he had not read the federal Constitution in a satisfactory manner. However, in a statement to the FBI the registrar declared, "my decision not to register him was based solely on the disfranchisement of the colored people in his county rather than on his ability to read, to write and to explain the Constitution." This case was subsequently prosecuted by the Department of Justice and resulted in the conviction of the registrar.

The poll tax—another important legal obstacle to full suffrage in some southern states—limits white as well as Negro suffrage. The poll tax has frequently had an unequal racial effect, since like the "understand and explain" clauses, it has been administered in a discriminatory manner. It has been very effective as an anti-Negro device. A poll tax simply places the payment of a fee between the voter and the ballot box. In some states it is cumulative; taxes not paid in years when the voter does not go to the polls pile up and he must pay more than one year's tax before he can vote. The poll tax has curtailed the size of the entire electorate, white and Negro. Seven states—Alabama, Arkansas, Mississippi, South Carolina,

Tennessee, Texas, and Virginia—still maintain this tax as a prerequisite to voting. Since 1921 four other states have abandoned the poll tax. These are North Carolina, Louisiana, Florida, and Georgia. . . .

In addition to formal, legal methods of disfranchisement, there are the long-standing techniques of terror and intimidation, in the face of which great courage is required of the Negro who tries to vote. In the regions most characterized by generalized violence against Negroes, little more than "advice" is often necessary to frighten them away from the polls. They have learned, through the years, to discover threats in mood and atmosphere. In one case in a deep southern state, a middle-class Negro who had courageously attempted to vote and to complain to the Department of Justice when he was refused access to the polls, subsequently became so afraid of reprisal that he indicated uncertainty whether he would be willing to testify in court. He asked, if he should decide to testify, to be given ample notice of the date so that he could first move his family out of the region.

The Right to Education

Discrimination in Public Schools. The failure to give Negroes equal educational opportunities is naturally most acute in the South, where approximately 10 million Negroes live. The South is one of the poorer sections of the country and has at best only limited funds to spend on its schools. With 34.5 percent of the country's population, 17 southern states and the District of Columbia have 39.4 percent of our school children. Yet the South has only one-fifth of the taxpaying wealth of the nation. Actually, on a percentage basis, the South spends a greater share of its income on education than do the wealthier states in other parts of the country. For example, Mississippi, which has the lowest expenditure per school child of any state, is ninth in percentage of income devoted to education. A recent study showed Mississippi spending 3.41 percent of its income for education as against New York's figure of only 2.61 percent. But this meant $400 per classroom unit in Mississippi, and $4,100 in New York. Negro and white school children both suffer because of the South's basic inability to match the level of educational opportunity provided in other sections of the nation.

But it is the South's segregated school system which most directly discriminates against the Negro. This segregation is found today in 17 southern states and the District of Columbia. Poverty-stricken though it was after the close of the Civil War, the South chose to maintain two sets of public schools, one for whites and one for Negroes. With respect to education, as well as to other public services, the Committee believes that the "separate but equal" rule has not been obeyed in practice. There is a marked difference in quality between the educational opportunities offered white children and Negro children in the separate schools. Whatever test is used—expenditure per pupil, teachers' salaries, the number of pupils per teacher, transportation of students, adequacy of school buildings and educational equipment, length of school term, extent of curriculum—Negro students are invariably at a disadvantage. Opportunities for Negroes in public institutions of higher education in the South—particularly at the professional graduate school level—are severely limited. . . .

The Right to Housing

Discrimination in housing results primarily from business practices. These practices may arise from special interests of business groups, such as the profits to be derived from confining minorities to slum areas, or they may reflect community prejudice. One of the most common practices is the policy of landlords and real estate agents to prevent Negroes from renting outside of designated areas. Again, it is "good business" to develop exclusive "restricted" suburban developments which are barred to all but white gentiles. When Negro veterans seek "GI" loans in order to build homes, they are likely to find that credit from private banks, without whose services there is no possibility of taking advantage of the GI Bill of Rights, is less freely available to members of their race. Private builders show a tendency not to construct new homes except for white occupancy. These interlocking business customs and devices form the core of our discriminatory policy. But community prejudice also finds expression in open public agitation against construction of public housing projects for Negroes, and by violence against Negroes who seek to occupy public housing projects or to build in "white" sections. . . .

Segregation Reconsidered

The "Separate but Equal" Failure. Mention has already been made of the "separate but equal" policy of the southern states by which Negroes are said to be entitled to the same public service as whites but on a strictly segregated basis. The theory behind this policy is complex. On the one hand, it recognizes Negroes as citizens and as intelligent human beings entitled to enjoy the status accorded the individual in our American heritage of freedom. It theoretically gives them access to all the rights, privileges, and services of a civilized, democratic society. On the other hand, it brands the Negro with the mark of inferiority and asserts that he is not fit to associate with white people.

Legally enforced segregation has been followed throughout the South since the close of the Reconstruction era. In these states it is generally illegal for Negroes to attend the same schools as whites; attend theaters patronized by whites; visit parks where whites relax; eat, sleep or meet in hotels, restaurants, or public halls frequented by whites. This is only a partial enumeration—legally imposed separation of races has become highly refined. In the eyes of the law, it is also an offense for whites to attend "Negro" schools, theaters and similar places. The result has been the familiar system of racial segregation in both public and private institutions which cuts across the daily lives of southern citizens from the cradle to the grave.

Legally-enforced segregation has been largely limited to the South. But segregation is also widely prevalent in the North, particularly in housing, and in hotel and restaurant accommodations. Segregation has not been enforced by states alone. The federal government has tolerated it even where it has full authority to eliminate it. . . .

Civil Rights in the Nation's Capital

We have seen how, throughout the country, our practice lags behind the American tradition of freedom and equality. A single community—the nation's capital—illustrates dramatically the shortcomings in our record and the need for change. The District of Columbia should symbolize to our own citizens and to the people of all countries our great tradition of civil liberty. Instead, it is a graphic illustration of a failure of democracy. As the seat of our federal government under the authority of Congress, the failure of the District is a failure of all the people.

For Negro Americans, Washington is not just the nation's capital. It is the point at which all public transportation into the South becomes "Jim Crow." If he stops in Washington, a Negro may dine like other men in the Union Station, but as soon as he steps out into the capital, he leaves such democratic practices behind. With very few exceptions, he is refused service at downtown restaurants, he may not attend a downtown movie or play, and he has to go into the poorer section of the city to find a night's lodging. The Negro who decides to settle in the District must often find a home in an overcrowded, substandard area. He must often take a job below the level of his ability. He must send his children to the inferior public schools set aside for Negroes and entrust his family's health to medical agencies which give inferior service. In addition, he must endure the countless daily humiliations that the system of segregation imposes upon the one-third of Washington that is Negro. . . .

III—Government's Responsibility: Securing the Rights

The National Government of the United States must take the lead in safeguarding the civil rights of all Americans. We believe that this is one of the most important observations that can be made about the civil

rights problem in our country today. We agree with words used by . . .
President [Truman], in an address at the Lincoln Memorial in Washington in June, 1947: "We must make the Federal Government a friendly,
vigilant defender of the rights and equalities of all Americans. . . . Our
National Government must show the way."

It is essential that our rights be preserved against the tyrannical actions
of public officers. Our forefathers saw the need for such protection when
they gave us the Bill of Rights as a safeguard against arbitrary government.
But this is not enough today. We need more than protection of our
rights against government; we need protection of our rights against private persons or groups, seeking to undermine them. In the words of . . .
President [Truman]:

"We cannot be content with a civil liberties program which emphasizes
only the need of protection against the possibility of tyranny by the
Government. . . . We must keep moving forward, with new concepts of
civil rights to safeguard our heritage. The extension of civil rights today
means not protection of the people against the Government, but protection of the people by the Government."

There are several reasons why we believe the federal government must
play a leading role in our efforts as a nation to improve our civil rights
record.

First, many of the most serious wrongs against individual rights are
committed by private persons or by local public officers. In the most
flagrant of all such wrongs—lynching—private individuals, aided upon
occasion by state or local officials, are the ones who take the law into
their own hands and deprive the victim of his life. The very fact that
these outrages continue to occur, coupled with the fact that the states
have been unable to eliminate them, points clearly to a strong need for
federal safeguards.

Second, it is a sound policy to use the idealism and prestige of our
whole people to check the wayward tendencies of a part of them. It is
true that the conscience of a nation is colored by the moral sense of its
local communities. Still, the American people have traditionally shown
high national regard for civil rights, even though the record in many
a community has been far from good. We should not fail to make use of
this in combating civil rights violations. The local community must be
encouraged to set its own house in order. But the need for leadership is
pressing. That leadership is available in the national government and it
should be used. We cannot afford to delay action until the most backward community has learned to prize civil liberty and has taken adequate
steps to safeguard the rights of every one of its citizens.

Third, our civil rights record has growing international implications.

These cannot safely be disregarded by the government at the national level which is responsible for our relations with the world, and left entirely to government at the local level for proper recognition and action. Many of man's problems, we have been learning, are capable of ultimate solution only through international cooperation and action. The subject of human rights, itself, has been made a major concern of the United Nations. It would indeed be ironical if in our own country the argument should prevail that safeguarding the rights of the individual is the exclusive, or even the primary concern of local government.

A lynching in a rural American community is not a challenge to that community's conscience alone. The repercussions of such a crime are heard not only in the locality, or indeed only in our own nation. They echo from one end of the globe to the other, and the world looks to the American national government for both an explanation of how such a shocking event can occur in a civilized country and remedial action to prevent its recurrence.

Similarly, interference with the right of a qualified citizen to vote locally cannot today remain a local problem. An American diplomat cannot forcefully argue for free elections in foreign lands without meeting the challenge that in many sections of America qualified voters do not have free access to the polls. Can it be doubted that this is a right which the national government must make secure?

Fourth, the steadily growing tendency of the American people to look to the national government for the protection of their civil rights is highly significant. This popular demand does not by itself prove the case for national government action. But the persistent and deep-felt desire of the American citizen for federal action safeguarding his civil rights is neither a request for spoils by a selfish pressure group, nor is it a short-sighted and opportunistic attempt by a temporary majority to urge the government into a dubious or unwise course of action. It is a demand rooted in the folkways of the people, sound in instinct and reason, and impossible to ignore. The American people are loyal to the institutions of local self-government, and distrust highly centralized power. But we have never hesitated to entrust power and responsibility to the national government when need for such a course of action has been demonstrated and the people themselves are convinced of that need.

Finally, the national government should assume leadership in our American civil rights program because there is much in the field of civil rights that it is squarely responsible for in its own direct dealings with millions of persons. It is the largest single employer of labor in the country. More than two million persons are on its payroll. The freedom of opinion and expression enjoyed by these people is in many ways dependent upon the attitudes and practices of the government. By not restricting this freedom beyond a point necessary to ensure the efficiency and loyalty of its workers, the government, itself, can make a very large contribution to the effort to achieve true freedom of thought in America. By scrupulously following fair employment practices, it not only sets a model for other employers to follow, but also directly protects the rights of more than two million workers to fair employment.

The same is true of the armed forces. Their policies are completely determined by the federal government. That government has the power, the opportunity and the duty to see that discrimination and prejudice are completely eliminated from the armed services, and that the American soldier or sailor enjoys as full a measure of civil liberty as is commensurate with military service.

The District of Columbia and our dependent areas are under the immediate authority of the national government. By safeguarding civil rights in these areas, it can protect several million people directly, and encourage the states and local communities throughout the country to do likewise. Finally, through its extensive public services, the national government is the largest single agency in the land endeavoring to satisfy the wants and needs of the consumer. By making certain that these services are continuously available to all persons without regard to race, color, creed or national origin, a very important step toward the elimination of discrimination in American life will have been taken.

Leadership by the federal government in safeguarding civil rights does not mean exclusive action by that government. There is much that the states and local communities can do in this field, and much that they alone can do. The Committee believes that Justice Holmes' view of the states as 48 laboratories for social and economic experimentation is still valid. The very complexity of the civil rights problem calls for much experimental, remedial action which may be better undertaken by the states than by the national government. Parallel state and local action supporting the national program is highly desirable. It is obvious that even though the federal government should take steps to stamp out the crime of lynching, the states cannot escape the responsibility to employ all of the powers and resources available to them for the same end. Or again, the enactment of a federal fair employment practice act will not render similar state legislation unnecessary.

In certain areas the states must do far more than parallel federal action. Either for constitutional or administrative reasons, they must remain the primary protectors of civil rights. This is true of governmental efforts to control or outlaw racial or religious discrimination practiced by privately supported public-service institutions such as schools and hospitals, and of places of public accommodation such as hotels, restaurants, theaters, and stores.

Furthermore, government action alone, whether federal, state, local, or all combined, cannot provide complete protection of civil rights. Everything that government does stems from and is conditioned by the state of public opinion. Civil rights in this country will never be adequately protected until the intelligent will of the American people approves and demands that protection. Great responsibility, therefore, will always rest upon private organizations and private individuals who are in a position to educate and shape public opinion. The argument is sometimes made that because prejudices and intolerance cannot be eliminated through legislation and government control we should abandon that action in favor of the long, slow, evolutionary effects of education and voluntary private efforts. We believe that this argument misses the point and that the choice it poses between legislation and education as to the means of improving civil rights is an unnecessary one. In our opinion, both approaches to the goal are valid, and are, moreover, essential to each other.

It may be impossible to overcome prejudice by law, but many of the evil discriminatory practices which are the visible manifestations of prejudice can be brought to an end through proper government controls. At the same time, it is highly desirable that efforts be made to understand more fully the causes of prejudice and to stamp them out. These efforts will necessarily occupy much time and can in many instances best be made by private organizations and individuals. . . .

The Committee rejects the argument that governmental controls are themselves necessarily threats to liberty. This statement overlooks the fact that freedom in a civilized society is always founded on law enforced by government. Freedom in the absence of law is anarchy.

Because it believes there is need for leadership by the national government, the Committee has not hesitated to recommend increased action by that government in support of our civil rights. At the same time, it has not overlooked the many possibilities for remedial action by the states, nor the benefits to be derived from private efforts in the never ending struggle to make civil liberty more secure in America. . . .

IV—A Program of Action: the Committee's Recommendations
The Time is Now

[Only a few of the Committee's recommendations have been reprinted. They are, however, the recommendations which have aroused the greatest political opposition. They indicate a broad, far-reaching program for protection of civil rights.]

The enactment by Congress of an antilynching act. The Committee believes that to be effective such a law must contain four essential ingredients. First, it should define lynching broadly. Second, the federal offense ought to cover participation of public officers in a lynching, or failure by them to use proper measures to protect a person accused of a crime against mob violence. The failure or refusal of public officers to make proper efforts to arrest members of lynch mobs and to bring them to justice should also be specified as an offense.

Action by private persons taking the law into their own hands to mete out summary punishment and private vengeance upon an accused person; action by either public officers or private persons meting out summary punishment and private vengeance upon a person because of his race, color, creed or religion—these too must be made crimes.

Third, the statute should authorize immediate federal investigation in lynching cases to discover whether a federal offense has been committed. Fourth, adequate and flexible penalties ranging up to a $10,000 fine and a 20-year prison term should be provided.

Action by the states or Congress to end poll taxes as a voting prerequisite. . . .

The enactment by Congress of a statute protecting the right of qualified persons to participate in federal primaries and elections against interference by public officers and private persons. . . .

The enactment by Congress of a statute protecting the right to qualify for, or participate in, federal or state primaries or elections against discriminatory action by state officers based on race or color, or depending on any other unreasonable classification. . . .

The enactment by Congress of legislation, followed by appropriate administrative action, to end immediately all discrimination and segregation based on race, color, creed, or national origin, in the organization and activities of all branches of the Armed Services. . . .

The elimination of segregation, based on race, color, creed, or national origin, from American life.

The separate but equal doctrine has failed in three important respects. First, it is inconsistent with the fundamental equalitarianism of the American way of life in that it marks groups with the brand of inferior status. Secondly, where it has been followed, the results have been separate and unequal facilities for minority peoples. Finally, it has kept people apart despite incontrovertible evidence that an environment favorable to civil rights is fostered whenever groups are permitted to live and work together. There is no adequate defense of segregation.

The conditioning by Congress of all federal grants-in-aid and other forms of federal assistance to public or private agencies for any purpose on the absence of discrimination and segregation based on race, color, creed, or national origin. [A minority of the Committee dissented on this point.] . . .

The enactment of a federal Fair Employment Practice Act prohibiting all forms of discrimination in private employment, based on race, color, creed, or national origin. . . .

The federal act should apply to labor unions and trade and professional associations, as well as to employers, insofar as the policies and practices of these organizations affect the employment status of workers.

The enactment by the states of similar laws. . . .

The enactment by Congress of a law prohibiting discrimination or segregation, based on race, color, creed, or national origin, in interstate transportation and all the facilities thereof, to apply against both public officers and the employees of private transportation companies.

Legislation is needed to implement and supplement the Supreme Court decision in *Morgan* v. *Virginia*. [In this case the Supreme Court held unconstitutional a Virginia statute requiring the segregation of Negroes and whites on interstate buses within Virginia because the state rule unduly burdened interstate commerce.] There is evidence that some state officers are continuing to enforce segregation laws against interstate passengers. Moreover, carriers are still free to segregate such passengers on their own initiative since the *Morgan* decision covered only segregation based on law. Congress has complete power under the Constitution to forbid all forms of segregation in interstate commerce. We believe it should make prompt use of it.

The enactment by the states of laws guaranteeing equal access to places of public accommodation, broadly defined, for persons of all races, colors, creeds, and national origins.

THE "CIVIL RIGHTS PROGRAM" IS VICIOUS, UNCONSTITUTIONAL, AND UNNECESSARY

BY SENATOR CLYDE R. HOEY*

[Senator Hoey of North Carolina was elected to the United States Senate in 1944 and reelected in 1950. In turn country editor, lawyer, member of the State House of Representatives, State Senator, and Assistant United States Attorney, Senator Hoey served as Governor of North Carolina from 1937 until 1941. EDITOR.]

* *Congressional Record*, 81st Cong., 1st sess., Vol. 95, Pt. 2 (Mar. 2, 1949), pp. 1725–1732 *passim.*

I know something about the proposals recommended by the President's Civil Rights Committee, and recommended by the President. The four proposals are known to the American people in general, but their implications are not well known, and their dangers have not been fully presented; the viciousness of the measures has not been sufficiently discussed, so that the people can understand fully just what is involved.

Let us consider, first, the poll tax, which has caused considerable comment and discussion. It is a very insignificant matter when it is analyzed. The Constitution of the United States provides that the States shall have the right to prescribe the qualifications of electors. That was one of the rights reserved by the States when the Constitution was formed. There has never been any challenge of that authority. Each state has the right to regulate and prescribe the qualifications of its electors. That is subject to one single exception, and that is that we cannot deny the voting privilege to anyone because of race, color, or previous condition of servitude. The poll tax does neither of those things. It applies to every voter. Therefore, there is nothing offensive in the payment of a poll tax as a requirement for voting, so far as race, color, and previous condition of servitude are concerned.

Presently, there are only seven States which have poll taxes as a requirement for voting. Practically all States have poll taxes levied on the citizens, but ordinarily they go to support the public-school funds. In my State a poll tax is levied from the time a man becomes 21 years of age until he is 50 years of age. The tax is levied on male citizens. For 29 years it has not been required in North Carolina that a tax be paid in order to vote, but the tax is still collected. It is from $1 to $2 a year. Yet, from the hue and cry heard regarding the discussion of the matter, it would be thought that it is a great and exorbitant tax which is being levied upon persons to deny them their right of franchise. . . .

. . . We hear a great deal said about the fact that in the Southern States only a small vote is cast in general elections, and that is attributed to the fact that the voters have to pay a poll tax, and therefore it is said many are disqualified from voting. That is not the cause at all. Why are only a small number of votes cast in many Southern States? It is because one political party is dominant in those States, and because every voter knows that every candidate for whom he would vote will be elected without regard to whether the voter goes to the polls or not. Therefore there is no incentive for a man to go to the polls. If he belongs to the minority party it is hopeless for him to go to the polls, and he does not do so.

I am supporting a joint resolution sponsored by the distinguished junior Senator from Massachusetts [Mr. Lodge] and others to provide for a constitutional amendment to abolish the electoral college, and to let each

State's vote be counted according to the proportionate number of votes cast in the State. If that amendment to the Constitution should be ratified, I think it would go a long way toward solving the very problems being discussed about the small vote in the States where one political party is predominant, because then there would be an incentive for every man, of either the majority or minority party, to cast his vote, since his vote would be effective in determining how many votes the President of the United States should receive from each State. . . .

On the question of the poll tax, three of the seven States which now have it are preparing to do away with it. In the course of another year or so that question will therefore be settled. . . .

. . . All the talk about it being an onerous burden on the taxpayer is merely a smoke screen to hide the desire to have the Federal Government assume the power to control the ballot box within the State and station an officer at every ballot box, thereby, threatening the perpetuity of our free elections and free government. . . .

The next proposition to which they give so much allegiance and which pressure groups urge so strongly is the antilynching bill. Of all the measures which have been presented to the Congress I cannot conceive of a more useless one. Even the *Washington Post*, liberal as it is in many of its inclinations—and certainly it cannot be said to be pro-South—published an editorial last year when such a measure was under consideration and said that it was ridiculous at this stage to undertake to pass a bill against lynching. We have now good antilynching laws in every one of the 48 States. These laws are the best enforced of any criminal statutes on the books.

We have 145,000,000 people in America. Last year there was only one lynching. There have not been more than six lynchings in any 1 year in the past 10. Yet last year, when there was but one lynching—and that was more of a murder than a lynching—13,000 murders, 12,000 rapes, and 1,500,000 other felonies were committed in the United States. But the people who are so anxious to protect the one person who may be lynched, have no concern for the 13,000 who were murdered and the 12,000 who were raped and the 1,500,000 who committed other felonies. They do not suggest even that the Federal Government should do anything about that. . . .

. . . Is there any virtue in passing an antilynching law? Lynching is not an interstate act. It does not have anything to do with interstate commerce. The only way it could have any connection with interstate commerce would be if one were to cross the line of one State into another State to lynch someone. Therefore there is nothing at all about the crime of lynching to make it essentially different from the crime of murder.

Every good citizen of America, white, colored, Indian, or of any other race, is definitely opposed to lynching, and every good citizen is doing all he can to stop the crime of lynching. Now why should the Federal Government, in violation of the right of a State to patrol its own internal affairs and to exercise its own police powers in the control and the punishment of crime within its borders, undertake to invade a State and say, "We take no notice of all the murders and all the rapes and all the other felonies, but we are going to take charge of this one matter of lynching, and because one person has been lynched we are going to handle the whole situation"?

The argument may be made that if there were a Federal statute on the subject there could be better enforcement of the law, but why could better enforcement of such a law be secured? The Federal court would have to try the case in the State in which the lynching occurred and would have to try it under the law with the same people as witnesses and jurors that the State court would have. The individual persons might not be identical, but they would be in the same State, living in the same atmosphere, entertaining the same ideas. How could there be any better enforcement of the law against lynching than there would be in the State court, especially since lynching has been practically eliminated?

It may be of interest to the Senate to know that in 1898, 255 lynchings occurred in the United States. One hundred of these were of white people and 155 were of either Negroes, Indians, or persons belonging to other races. This number was reduced in 1920 to 64. There has been a gradual reduction every year, until in the past 10 years no more than six have been lynched in any one year. [In 1948] . . . only one person was lynched, and that case was more of a murder than a lynching.

Therefore I pass from the consideration of the antilynching bill to another measure, namely, the antisegregation measure. What is the necessity for passing such a measure? To begin with, the Congress has nothing in the world to do with segregation within the limits of a State. The Federal Government has no power or authority to override the law of a State and say what shall happen with reference to segregation within the confines of a State, with the sole exception of transportation that may involve interstate commerce. The Supreme Court of the United States has already decided that question. The Court said that the States have no power and no authority to legislate about interstate commerce, and therefore, State segregation laws applying to interstate commerce were null and void. Now what more can be done? Why pass any more segregation laws? . . .

I come next to the fair employment practice bill, which is the pièce de résistance of the whole list. Every single one of these measures is directed against the South. Is it not rather remarkable that in this country, 80 years and more since the War Between the States closed, a great solemn legislative assembly is having its time occupied with measures sectional in character and vicious in their conception, directed against a great section of this Nation? I am wondering, if we should pass all four of these measures today what would their sponsors ask for next? When, if ever, will the South have a surcease from the assaults made upon her customs, her traditions, her social fabric, and, indeed, her life? Are all the offerings, all the loyalty, and all the blood and treasure which the South has given to the Nation to be of no avail? Has the time come, and is it now here, when there shall be a continual persecution, a continual effort to destroy the basic fabric of our civilization in order to gratify those who wish to serve some special purpose, and who have some selfish end in view? . . .

I wish to call attention specifically to the things which this bill [the Fair Employment Practices Act] would do:

First, it would deny freedom of contract.

Second, it would deny the employer the right of selective judgment in procuring his employees.

Third, it would deny to employees the right of selecting their associates.

Fourth, it would deny to labor unions the right to determine their membership or to regulate their own affairs.

Fifth, it would deny to the employer the right to hire, promote, or discharge employees upon the basis of their efficiency, merit, or faithfulness.

Sixth, it would give to a Commission the power to compel the employer to pay persons who were never in his employ, and then force him to hire them.

Seventh, it would subject the employer to investigation, harassment, fines, and penalties, to be determined by a Commission located in Washington.

Eighth, it would deny the employer the right of trial by jury, and give him no right to a review of the facts found by the Commission.

Ninth, it would compel the employer to give testimony against himself, and expose his private letters, books, and papers for the inspection and investigation of a horde of employees of the Commission.

Tenth, it would compel the employer to hire a person whom he did not wish to have in his employ, and deny him the privilege of selecting an employee of his own choice. . . .

In addition to all these nefarious things contained in the bill, the most vicious provision of all is the concluding provision, that the Commission shall have the power and authority to make rules and regulations which shall have the effect of law, and that they shall be the law unless the Congress enacts a bill to nullify them. In other words, in addition to all the power given the Commission to take charge of the business of the citizens of America and to interfere with all their internal affairs if they employ as many as 50 persons, the Commission would have power and authority to make any other rules and regulations which suited it, to enable it to harass, annoy, fine, and punish citizens. There would be no redress unless the Congress should enact a law to nullify the rules adopted by the Commission. I submit that such a measure ought not to be considered seriously by any great free legislative assembly.

I am wondering what the American businessman, the American industrialist, the American employer of labor, or anyone else in America has done to justify the idea that the Federal Government should take charge of the affairs of citizens in this fashion. We boast about free enterprise. There would be no free enterprise if this system were in effect. There could be no free enjoyment of any of the privileges and rights guaranteed by the Constitution if this bill were to be enacted. I cannot see how any businessman in America should be calm or content in the exercise of his rights and the conduct of his own business with this sort of thing hanging over him. . . .

Of course I realize that most of the discussion about discrimination is directed against the South; but let me call attention to the fact that that is not where it exists. For instance, yesterday I noticed in the newspapers a report from the mayor's committee of Minneapolis, Minn. The report said that of 525 firms in that city, only 3 had in their employ any Negroes or any Jews or any Japanese-Americans. It also said that 63 percent of the firms in that city would not employ any member of these groups. That is not a southern city, Mr. President; it is Minneapolis, Minn.

All over the north we can cite one example after another showing discrimination similar, and in greater degree than exists in the South. . . .

. . . I maintain that in the South we do not discriminate against the Negroes. I would not say that there are not some evidences and some cases of discrimination here and there, because that would happen anywhere at any time. But I am talking about the great, overall picture. . . .

I may say that in North Carolina we do not believe in race prejudices, but we undertake to cultivate and develop race pride. We do not believe in race amalgamation, but we believe in race integrity. We do not believe in social equality; but we believe in equality of opportunity; and undertaking to furnish these things in their relative fashion and form meets the requirements and the needs and the wishes of the great body of Negroes in my State . . . .

Mr. President, I would that those who cry out so loudly, so long, and so vociferously against the treatment accorded Negroes in the South might visit North Carolina and see for themselves the sort of conditions which exist, the mutual respect and concern each race has for the other, and the consideration given to each other in all walks of life. . . .

. . . We who believe in the righteousness and justice of the people of the South and are anxious to go forward to the attainment of still greater objectives in the service we render to the Negroes in our section pray that we not be disturbed in our great undertaking, and that we may have, instead of objections or interference, the cooperation, the approval, and the encouragement of people throughout the Nation. . . .

AN ALTERNATIVE PROGRAM WOULD BE MORE SENSIBLE, EFFECTIVE, AND BENEFICIAL

BY HODDING CARTER*

[Hodding Carter is editor and publisher of the *Delta-Democratic Times*, Greenville, Mississippi. A former Nieman and Guggenheim fellow, he was awarded a Pulitzer prize for editorial writing in 1946. He is the author of *Lower Mississippi* and *The Winds of Fear*. EDITOR.]

If it were possible for . . . [the] less blatant voices [of "self-examining," "questioning" "Southerners"] to be heard, they might speak with some effect to the extremists within and outside the South, and to the policy makers of both parties. They might say to the opposed elements: Let us re-examine these civil rights proposals. Let us acquaint ourselves with what the South is itself doing, as well as with what it is refusing to do. Let us investigate those other directions in which Federal action could be beneficially undertaken. And let us look ahead to the vast social-economic-political revisions inherent in the accelerated Negro migration from a South to whose changing economy they are becoming less and less vital. . . .

. . . If the specific legislation proposed is intended to insure civil rights in the South, it seems oddly misdirected. A poll tax as a voting requisite is levied in only seven states, and its approval in a majority of these is waning—or was until it became a symbol of Southern wrong-doing, or, conversely, of persecution of the South. The constitutionality of Federal action is debatable. The tax in itself does not discriminate against the

* "A Southern Liberal Looks at Civil Rights," *The New York Times*, Aug. 8, 1948, VI, pp. 10ff. *passim.* By permission of *The New York Times* and Hodding Carter.

Negro alone, nor does it provide any longer an effective device to disfranchise him. For the Negro vote in adjacent poll tax and no poll tax Southern States—Mississippi excepted—bears about the same ratio to the white vote in each.

On the other hand, what too many Southerners really object to is not the abolition of the poll tax in Federal elections, or even the usurpation of a State's right to determine voting qualifications, but the specter of Federal protection of Negroes in the exercise of their voting rights. The South itself created the atmosphere which made such protection a matter of Federal concern, but the Negro voter is in considerably less physical danger than he has ever been, and the principal hindrances to his suffrage are those successive legal devices which the Supreme Court is apparently prepared to nullify in turn.

The proposal to make lynching a Federal offense appears to most white Southerners as evidence of a gratuitous disregard for the South's own success in reducing lynchings to a nearly non-symptomatic incidence, and an amazing constriction in the definition of the crime itself. Its proponents seemingly overlook the real remaining challenge to Southerners, which is to become as successful in punishing lynchers and others who commit crimes against Negroes as they have been in reducing the incidence of those crimes.

One may reasonably assume that the transfer of jurisdiction from state to Federal courts in the South will not result in changing the attitudes of Southern witnesses or jurors. And the very transfer of authority may dull the sense of local shame and local responsibility that has contributed so markedly to the near eradication of lynching.

It is useless to argue with most Southerners that the FEPC is not a sectional thrust, aimed at the heart of the South's racial mores, but is directed instead at job discrimination anywhere and in behalf of any racial or religious group which is the victim of varying national or regional prejudices. The South has the largest concentration of a minority which is the last hired, the first fired and the least encouraged to advance.

The majority of Southern employers—and probably the majority of Southern white employees—believe that the South would be the focal area for a foredoomed testing of the thesis that the Government can and should intervene whenever a worker protests that he has been refused employment or promotion, or has been fired by reason of race or religion. They do not interpret the FEPC as an effort at economic justice, but as an attempt to put the two races in an undesirable contact whose symbolism is social rather than economic.

Neither the poll tax nor anti-lynch recommendations has aroused onetenth the spirit of resistance that this proposed extension of the doctrine of the pursuit of happiness has kindled. Its enactment will set the stage for a mass civil disobedience in the South, which, in its disregard for the law, will make the prohibition era seem a model for lawful behavior.

The extent of Southern animosity to the emphasis upon ending the segregation pattern should be made equally clear. However wrong segregation is as a theory, it is also an actuality which the white majority in the South intends to maintain in its mass aspects. In the wake of . . . Supreme Court decisions, Jim Crowism in public carriers will vanish and Negro college students will . . . be admitted to Southern universities. Southern draftees will adjust themselves to mixed platoons and battalions.

Southern reaction to this tearing away at the fringes of the pattern has not been and will not be implacably violent. But the conviction persists that these are but the beginnings of federally imposed intermingling in the South's public schools, its theatres and hospitals and hotels, its residential areas and restaurants and churches. And should such extensions be attempted, they will be resisted.

It is sometimes harsh to state the objective truth. This is the truth, admitted even by those who wish it were not. A standing army would be necessary to end general segregation in the South.

Does it follow that the South can fairly be described as a region of atavists, deaf to the voices that insist upon applied democracy in race relations? Not if the entire record is examined. But determined protagonists are not often concerned with the full record of nations or regions or individuals whose excesses have shocked them into action.

It would be more salutary, and not only for the South, if its critics were to become familiar with and publicize equally the achievements and democratic progress of a South that is hidden behind its political dinosaurs and its group insistence upon general segregation. The very intensity and one-sidedness of the anti-Southern bias, creating as it does a false sterotype, can weld and is welding the South into resentful unity.

And if Federal intervention is the proper means of hastening orderly transformations, why do not the two major parties unite behind other legislation that can more immediately and certainly as beneficially affect the progress of the least privileged section of the country? A program of Federal aid to education would help the Negro and white masses of the South toward useful citizenship far more than would Federal abolition of the poll tax in seven states.

Adoption of a real program for conservation of soil and resources would, in its individually applied ramifications, create more economic security in the South than would the passage of fair employment legislation. And certainly a national housing program with slum segregation as its target would, in the long run, work as effectively in guaranteeing human dignity for second-class citizens as does the proscription of Jim Crowism.

Finally, the honest idealists, the political opportunists and the understandably bitter Negro leadership should alike acquaint themselves with the perceptibly shifting areas of interracial challenge. The Negro is moving from the South, his departure impelled not only by despair of subhuman status but also because of stark economic displacement.

The Negro was absolutely essential to the South in the Twenties. Today he is far less essential. A changing agricultural economy, paced by mechanization and dedicated to diversification, is uprooting the rural Negro. The new industrial South favors white workers for the assembly lines.

A tragic pilgrimage is under way. And some Southerners find grim pleasure in the stories of unfamiliar tensions in Indianapolis and Los Angeles and Seattle. What of these unskilled, hopeless migrants, whose barren, suspect existences cannot be explained away by an accusing finger pointed at the South? Will their civil rights be affirmed by poll tax repeal? Will their grisly Northern ghetto become more habitable because segregation is banned? Will their untutored hands and minds be salvaged by a fair employment act?

Or did the party band wagons forget about these matters when the civil rights program became the battle hymn of the Republicans and Democrats alike?

QUESTIONS AND PROBLEMS

1. Define each of the following: "civil rights"; "moral rights"; "freedom"; "equality." Distinguish between political, economic, and social rights.

2. Do you think Senator Hoey would accept the four basic rights which the President's Committee believes essential to the well-being of the individual and the progress of society? Why? Why not?

3. Do you accept the Committee's conclusion that the United States has fallen short of its civil rights goal? Why? Why not?

4. What improvement has there been in our civil rights record since 1947? To what extent is this improvement due to Congress? President? Supreme Court? States? Private organizations?

5. How much of the "Record" would you have to examine before you would have sufficient factual basis for reaching a conclusion as to the present status of civil rights in the United States?

6. What reasons does the President's Committee advance to justify the leading role it urges the Federal government to play in the improvement of our civil rights record? How convincing are these reasons?

7. What are the reasons for Senator Hoey's opposition to the four civil rights proposals which he treats? Do you agree or disagree with his reasons? Why? Why not?

8. Summarize and then appraise Hodding Carter's reexamination of the civil rights proposals.

9. Do you approve of the recommendations of the President's Committee? Analyze and then enumerate the grounds for your position on each recommendation.

10. State and defend your own civil rights program.

SELECT BIBLIOGRAPHY

American Civil Liberties Union, 170 Fifth Ave., New York City, for current reports on civil liberty violations.

Carr, Robert K.: *Federal Protection of Civil Rights: Quest for a Sword* (Ithaca: Cornell University Press, 1947). A history of the Civil Rights Section of the Justice Department. Urges that it be given greater powers, more money, and enlarged staff. Argues that Federal government must forge sword to protect civil rights.

Congressional Record, 81st Cong., 1st sess., Vol. 95, Feb. 28, 1949, through Mar. 17, 1949, for Senate fillibuster on motion to change closure rule. Arguments against Civil Rights Program contained in time-consuming speeches which also deal with right of virtually unrestricted debate in the Senate. Arguments for Civil Rights Program also found here.

"Essential Human Rights," *Annals of the American Academy of Political and Social Sciences,* Vol. 243 (January, 1946). Deals with rights as an international problem. Two short articles relating to the United States in particular.

Fraenkel, Osmond K.: *Our Civil Liberties* (New York: Viking, 1944). Survey by counsel for American Civil Liberties Union of Bill of Rights and other sections of the Constitution guaranteeing rights to Americans.

Konvitz, Milton R.: *The Constitution and Civil Rights* (New York: Columbia University Press, 1947). Examines history of American civil rights (defined as rights of persons to employment, public accommodation, etc.) as distinct from political rights (right to vote, etc.) and civil liberties (freedom of speech, press, assembly, right to trial by jury, etc.). Looks to Federal legislation and Supreme Court's reversal of earlier precedents to secure these rights.

Screws v. United States, 325 U.S. 91, 138*ff.* (1945), dissenting opinion of Justices Roberts, Frankfurter, and Jackson. Object to stretching Federal law to bring within reach of Federal action a state official who violated state law in committing crime for which accused. Object also to possible use of Federal statute—against legislative intent—to strike at local crimes which should be handled locally. Point to possible debilitation of local responsibility as a result of such Federal action.

"Should the President's Civil Rights Program Be Adopted?" *Town Meeting*, Vol. 13 (Mar. 23, 1948). Popular debate: Senator Wayne Morse of Oregon and Attorney Roger Baldwin versus Senator John Sparkman of Alabama and Attorney Donald R. Richberg.

Southern Governors' Conference: *Committee Report*, Washington, D.C., Mar. 13, 1948. Reply to Mr. Truman's Civil Rights Program. Denies need for and stresses danger of such legislation.

Southern Regional Council, Executive Committee: "An Honest Answer in the Civil Rights Controversy," *New South*, September, 1948. Examines and criticizes Southern opposition to civil rights. Advocates a triple approach—legal, educational, economic—to secure a reasonable, workable compromise. No magic formula available.

Truman, Harry S.: Civil Rights Message to Congress, *Congressional Record*, 80th Cong., 2d sess., Vol. 94, Pt. 1 (Feb. 2, 1948), pp. 927–929.

PART II: INSTRUMENTS OF POPULAR CONTROL

PRESSURE GROUPS

Enemy or Ally of American Democracy?

Pressure groups constitute the raw materials of politics. Without an understanding of their composition, tactics, and objectives the study of politics is sterile. James Madison shared this view and, in that brilliant essay in *The Federalist*, No. 10, gave us not only a sound explanation of their origin but also a prophetic interpretation of their significance for government:

"A landed interest, a manufacturing interest, a mercantile interest, a moneyed interest, with many lesser interests, grow up of necessity in civilized nations, and divide them into different classes, actuated by different sentiments and views. The regulation of these various and interfering interests forms the principal task of modern legislation, and involves the spirit of party and faction in the necessary and ordinary operations of government."

There is a great difference of opinion concerning the legitimate role of pressure groups in a democratic society. Publicists like Stuart Chase maintain that most pressure groups are selfish minorities, utilizing undesirable methods to secure ends harmful to the general welfare. In the following article, he describes the operation of pressure groups —their slogans, tactics, and goals. He argues that they constitute special interests which, in blatant disregard of the interdependence of our modern economy, threaten to tear our economy to pieces and thus destroy our democratic society.

Mary E. Dillon writes in defense of pressure groups. She argues that they are an important means of formulating public opinion and a healthy supplement to our two-party system. They permit a new kind of popular participation in our modern legislatures and our expanded bureaucracy, giving the people a continuing interest in government. She concludes, in the second and last article herein, that pressure groups are a necessary part of American Democracy.

These two views provide some basic exploration necessary before one can develop his own view of governmental policy toward pressure groups. Some commentators view public policy as the resultant of group pressures. Government, they assert, provides the ring wherein our numerous pressure groups fight, in a general free-for-all, for recognition of their respective claims. These students contend that this is the realistic view of politics. Furthermore, they justify the compromise reached in the ring as a proper democratic technique. The government's task is not to seek an imaginary general welfare but rather to translate into public policy the desires of politically potent group interests.

Other observers hold that government is not and should not be a mere adjuster of group interests. Government is and should be more than a disinterested umpire in the political battle of pressure groups. These critics argue that there is a public interest over and above the many diverse and particular opinions formulated by pressure groups. Government should and can be far more than a reflection of the balance of power among group pressures. They maintain that government should and can possess an independent will and purpose devoted to the public interest as opposed to special interests.

A third group of critics rejects both the concept of government as a passive umpire in the pressure-group battle and the view that government should forceably and positively pursue its own vision of the public interest. These critics castigate the uncontrolled and ruthless competition of pressure groups. They repudiate dictatorial state power which some hold necessary to curb pressure groups and to achieve an abstract "general welfare." They assert that government, in a democratic manner, must establish more decent rules of the game for pressure groups. Government must more effectively temper the demands of pressure groups in the interest of the less adequately represented—consumers, unorganized workers, farmers, and businessmen. In this way, a more just accommodation among, and selection of, competing and legitimate claims may be achieved.

The extremely difficult ideological and practical details of such a program must wait, however, until the following more basic questions treated by Mr. Chase and Miss Dillon have been explored:

Do pressure groups work primarily against the public interest? Or are they a modern expression of democracy by and for the people?

PRESSURE GROUPS: SPECIAL INTERESTS VERSUS THE PUBLIC WELFARE

BY STUART CHASE*

[Stuart Chase is well known to the American reading public for such books as *Your Money's Worth; Rich Land, Poor Land; The Tyranny of Words; Idle Money, Idle Men.* A recent contribution has been his *The Proper Study of Mankind.* EDITOR.]

Time and again, the majority of Congress has lost all track of the interest of the whole community to favor the farm bloc, the Legion, the business bloc, or the labor bloc. Congressmen, pressure group leaders, administration men, the "loyal opposition," have repeatedly forsaken the clear path of what is best for the country, to follow the path of what they think is best for themselves. . . .

The need for developing a sense of the whole community does not arise alone from . . . war. We cannot operate a high-energy economy without it. As the power age advances, every man jack of us becomes more dependent on the community. Yet the community is so large that we are seldom aware of this dependence. Only when the electric power goes off in a blizzard, or the milk train breaks down, do we realize for a few minutes how the community bears us in its arms. From San Diego to Aroostook County, we are our brothers' keepers. All the Main Streets merge into one great society.

The pressure groups seem to be largely led by men who are ignorant of the fact that we are our brothers' keepers. They think such talk is Sunday School stuff. They are wrong. It is the first law of modern technology.

The self-sufficiency of the individual farmer or the small local group, which was characteristic of the handicraft age, has been sacrificed to the superior output of quantity production. Each worker, manager, establishment, now performs a single small operation in a vast national assembly line. Every citizen is dependent for his food and shelter on millions of other citizens. Nobody can go it alone any more. Your great-grandfather could get three square meals a day from his own farm, if a little salt were thrown in. Can you? Figure out where the items for a simple breakfast come from, and how many people are involved, directly and indirectly, in producing and delivering them.

---

* *Democracy under Pressure* (New York: Twentieth Century Fund, 1945), pp. 4–118 *passim.* By permission of the publisher. Only direct quotations have been footnoted.

The men who run pressure groups seem to assume that their crowd can go it alone. They act largely on the principle of Me First and the public be damned. If their special interest and the public interest happen to coincide, it is probable they did not plan it that way. If the public is at war, why so much the worse for the public. They talk tough and they act tough. I am not here arguing about their morals. My point is more serious. . . . I am arguing that such behavior can tear the whole economy to shreds, engulfing the tough babies with the rest of us.

The depression should have provided proof enough that Americans are tied together in a single organism. No group was immune as the blight spread. Even the lordly Telephone Company had to draw on its surplus account to pay dividends. Everyone went to hell in a hack—trade unionists, unorganized workers, bankers, sharecroppers, white-collar employees, architects, railroad men, teachers, writers, government employees, "widows and orphans," farmers, brokers, fishermen, artists, miners, engineers—everybody. Do you remember the empty, flyblown store windows along Main Street in 1933?

We went over like dominoes in a row without knowing what had hit us. We ought to know by this time. A high-energy society is not only inordinately productive, as Veblen used to say, it is extremely vulnerable. If the idea is every man for himself and the devil take the hindmost, the devil in no time at all works right up to the front of the line.

The pressure boys act as though they had never heard of this state of affairs. They think they can still obtain three squares a day off the old farm. They think they can kick their way through the delicate veins, nerves, tendons of an interdependent community, and get theirs. Right now they hope, most of them, if they bite hard enough in the clinches and knock over enough Congressmen, that they can claw their way up to a nice little shelf, safe from the ravages of . . . depression.

If this spirited free-for-all actually persists . . . nobody will get anything, especially the rest of us. There will be no safe little shelf for anybody. . . . There will be no peace on Main Street. . . .

Pressure groups have long been "the despair of patriots." They have been responsible for some of the darkest days in Washington. Some of them engineered the Hawley-Smoot tariff bill, which raised so high a wall that few imports could scale it, at a time when we were a creditor nation. Others put over the Silver Purchase Act which made it virtually impossible to use our great silver hoard to serve industrial wartime needs. They were responsible for the Chinese Exclusion Act. They killed bill after bill to help the consumer of drugs and foods. They have jammed through bonus grabs, and the totally inadequate tax bill of 1944. They continually pervert, twist and halt the path of progress in the Republic.
. . .

Industrial lobbies have been operating ever since the Republic was founded. The Constitution itself was in part a compromise among interest groups. Manufacturers began pressing for tariff protection while Washington was still President. Protection and free land were the two great government handouts of the 19th century. The hearts of Congressmen were torn with the plight of "infant industries," threatened with unfair competition from the "pauper labor" of Europe and Asia. The tariffs were granted. They were in effect subsidies which made big business bigger, and strengthened its monopolistic position. Once a tariff was granted, a lobby had to be maintained at Washington to see that it was never lowered—to say nothing of seeing what might be done about raising it higher.

A monopoly as such exerts economic pressure on the community, restricting output or holding up prices. When in addition it employs a lobby to look after its political interests, it becomes a full-fledged pressure group. In lobbying for tariffs, various monopolies often joined to form a super-group, the favorite vehicle being the National Association of Manufacturers. . . .

By the turn of the century, these large aggregations of capital had workers pretty well at their mercy. The time clock was on the wall; no longer did the master know all his men by their first names. Furthermore, it was harder to find a farm to bail into when times were hard. One-crop agriculture was undermining the self-sufficient farm. Free land in the West was about gone.

The industrial worker was on the spot. If he was not to become a helot, he had to organize a pressure group to offset the pressure of the "trusts." He did, in the person of Samuel Gompers. The AF of L, under Gompers' dynamic direction, shed all ideological goals and concentrated on blasting out of the hands of management exclusive control of wages, hours and working conditions. The AF of L grew up with the trusts of the '90's, though several laps behind them. The railroad brotherhoods were growing too.

In due course, when their votes could really talk, labor leaders descended on the government for their own particular line of tariffs, subsidies and benefits. They wanted the legal right to organize, to picket, to strike. They wanted minimum wage laws, maximum hours, railroad retirement pensions, workmen's compensation, full crew laws, child labor restrictions, embargoes on immigrants, the exemption of unions from taxation. . . .

. . . So the business blocs came to represent one wing of production, the owner-managers, while the labor blocs represented another wing. The interest of all of us, as consumers, had no bloc to represent it.

The farmers were still inadequately organized when . . . [World War

I] came. That war boosted agricultural income, as . . . [did World War II]. Hogs, wheat and land values went over the moon. In 1920, the whole structure collapsed. In 1921, the Farm Bureau Federation organized the Farm Bloc in Congress. Thus the third major producer interest of the country became a specific pressure group.

The farmers moved on Washington, suspicious of "Wall Street" on the one hand, and "labor agitators" on the other. Beyond their own economic strength, they had two great sources of power.

In the first place, they symbolized the ancient, homely virtues—thrift, hard work, the soil, the old well sweep, the rugged independence of the great open spaces. These virtues made excellent camouflage for the hard-boiled commercial drive behind the Bloc. In the second place, the geographical election of Congressmen gave agricultural states a big mathematical advantage, especially in the Senate. Though dirt farmers accounted for perhaps a fifth of the population, they could, when organized, swing nearly half the votes in Congress.

In the 1920's, the embattled agriculturalists got a thin line of relatively cheap government credit, some assorted tariff protection, and many fine information services from the Department of Agriculture. In the 1930's, like labor, they really went to town. They got the AAA for big farmers, the FSA for little farmers, legislation for an ever-normal granary, crop insurance, farm mortgage relief, cheaper credit, the Food Stamp Plan, and many other benefits. . . . The Farm Bloc has engineered the major crops like cotton and corn into a position where prices are pegged and output restricted under the shelter of the federal government. . . .

Big Business, Big Labor and Big Agriculture have all organized monopolies after their fashion and left the fluid play of free competitive forces far behind them. In support of their organized economic interests, each has established powerful political lobbies to bring pressure on both federal and state governments. Political action followed economic action. The organization of labor followed the organization of business. The organization of agriculture followed both. The whole process has moved with the inevitability of a Greek drama.

There are no lobbies representing the whole consumer interest. The National Consumers League has been concerned chiefly with labor legislation. The Townsend Plan represents old folks, without too much regard for the rest of us. The American Legion represents veterans, with even less regard. Special groups of consumers have lobbies in Washington, some weak, some strong; but no pressure group so far as I know is looking out for all of us. . . .

Beside the special interests which want something, usually with a dollar sign in front of it, for their crowd, there are the reformers. They put pressure on Congress too. Most of my readers at one time or another have been members of pressure groups out to improve the world. You may have contributed a few dollars to the Civil Liberties Union, or the Urban League, or the Planned Parenthood Association, or the League of Women Voters, or the People's Lobby. You may even have gone to Washington to join a parade, or to testify before a Congressional committee. Such lobbies have their ideological pitfalls, yet they are the hallmark of a dynamic democracy. They represent people who are not satisfied with the status quo, who want to make it a better country and are not interested in the pay-off for themselves. . . .

With the Big Three—business, labor, agriculture—all organized in an impressive way, the typical Congressman has his troubles. In a clash, whom will he support? Here is the Hon. Clarence Cannon of Missouri, apparently requested by William Green of the AF of L to vote for the subsidy bill. Mr. Cannon searches his heart and comes up with this classic reaction: "I have always followed Mr. Green on labor bills. But this is not a labor bill. This is a farm bill. On this bill I follow the farm leaders."[1] Just when Mr. Cannon follows the welfare of the United States is not revealed.

The rise of the Big Three as outlined above warrants two conclusions. First, the pressure groups between them have pretty well demolished the free market as Adam Smith pictured it. Second, it is clear that a state dedicated to laissez faire can remain a passive umpire only so long as organizations are small. When Big Business, Big Unions and Big Farmers moved in upon the government, the community had to develop the Big State to cope with them. E. H. Carr summarized it this way:

"Every modern state has intervened, first, to protect employers against trade unions, and later, to protect the rights of the unions. If we wish to get a correct picture of the structure of the modern world, we must think not of a number of individuals . . . but of a number of large and powerful groups, sometimes competing, sometimes cooperating, in the pursuit of their group interests, and of a state constantly impelled to increase the strength and scope of its authority in order to maintain the necessary minimum of cohesion in the social fabric. . . . The issue is whether to allow social action to depend on the haphazard outcome of a struggle between interest groups or to control and coordinate the activities of these groups in the interest of the community."[2]

This is putting the present crisis of political democracy about as flatly as it can be put. It comes down to the question of who's in charge around here? If the pressure group free-for-all holds the stage, economic break-

---

[1] Quoted by the *New York Herald Tribune* in an editorial, November 25, 1943.
[2] *Conditions of Peace*, Macmillan, 1942.

down is not far away. If the government is in charge, there is the danger of the authoritarian state. Yet if a breakdown develops, the danger of the authoritarian state immediately reappears, and in a more extreme form. . . .

My friend Richard Neuberger, a West Coast journalist, got himself elected to the Oregon legislature a few years ago. As a new member he was fair game for lobbyists. He was waited on by a group of earnest women who wanted a law passed to restrain billboards on the highways. They were reformers interested in scenery, order and safety. The bill made sense to Mr. Neuberger and he endorsed it—just as you would, or I would. It was clearly in the public interest.

Poor innocent! The advertisers' lobby began to teach him the facts of life. Here were no fine questions of public safety and order, but a vested interest threatened with pecuniary loss. The next thing Mr. Neuberger knew, the lobby had got the Signpainters' Union to denounce the measure and call him an "enemy of labor." This is a fearsome charge to levy against any legislator. Then came a torrent of letters from "widows and orphans" who would starve if rents from the beneficent billboard companies were cut off. Then telegrams rained in, and editorials in the papers.

The legislature ran to cover, and the bill was quashed. Mr. Neuberger believes that a large majority of the citizens of Oregon would support it, but citizens are not organized, and the lobby gets there fustest with the mostest. In the course of time the bill is certain to be passed, for it is on the trend curve; but not before a lot of beautiful country has been needlessly blighted, and a lot of cars needlessly wrecked.

Every state legislature is under similar pressure, while in Washington the heat often becomes fantastic. . . .

The TNEC found more than four hundred lobbies in Washington— not counting the bright boy who collected $60,000 during one session of Congress by writing big executives every time a law they liked was passed, and admitting he was solely responsible. We might roughly classify the four hundred into:

The Big Three—official business, labor and farm organizations. . . .

Specialized producers, such as cattlemen, publishers, citrus growers, broadcasting stations, telephone interests.

Professional and occupational groups, such as the bankers, insurance companies, advertisers, real-estate men, exporters and importers, doctors, teachers, lawyers.

Reformers, such as the conservationists and the birth controllers. . . .

It is interesting to tunnel under the exalted verbiage and find the simple wants which animate some of the four hundred lobbies. For instance:

Shoe manufacturers want a higher tariff.

Farmers want parity prices.

The merchant marine wants subsidies.

So do the airlines.

The silver bloc wants 71 cents an ounce, and would take $1.00.

Teachers want federal aid.

Unions want the closed shop.

Dairymen want a prohibitive tax on oleomargarine.

Railways want to weaken the waterways and the bus lines.

Cattlemen want Argentine beef plainly labeled not fit to eat.

Insurance men do not want too much social security.

Medical men want to scuttle socialized medicine.

Coal operators want hydroelectric projects halted.

Drug men would like food and drug reformers quietly chloroformed—which would not displease the publishers either.

The aluminum interests want no nonsense at all about competitors getting hold of new government plants.

One could continue the list until it became a saga. The objective behind these wants is usually a direct subsidy for the interest itself, or a hand grenade for a competitor. Practically all the labors of the economic pressure groups revolve around these twin goals. Observe, however, that such goals are often in violent conflict as among the several groups. This is no harmony chorus.

The TNEC describes a typical week of lobbying in the 1930's:

The American Legion pushes a war widows' pension bill through the House.

The Veterans of Foreign Wars, however, cannot get their bonus bill out of committee.

The National Federation of Federal Employees stops a pay cut in the House omnibus economy bill.

The American Automobile Association, after unheard-of efforts, fails to block a Senate increase in the automobile tax.

The petroleum lobby wangles a special tariff into the general tax bill.

The druggists' lobby—sometimes called the Pain and Beauty Boys—fights off a tax on cosmetics.

Pressure groups make good use of slogans. The AF of L marches to legislative battle behind "The American Standard of Living." Who would be low enough to attack that? The Chamber of Commerce runs to "Free Enterprise," and the National Association of Manufacturers to "The American System." The investors' lobby works wonders with "Widows and Orphans," while the American Publishers can get away with practically anything in the name of "Free Speech and Free Press."

When a bill is to be killed, however, the accredited method is to label it "communistic," "socialistic," "fascist-inspired," "bureaucratic," "regimented," or "controlled by politicians."

All pressure groups protest that they are concerned with the "public interest." This comes as naturally to them as for a parson to declare himself against sin. They let it be known that they are making this splendid fight for the common good at great personal sacrifice to themselves. This makes it hard for the rest of us to discuss the public interest without acute nausea. . . .

Lobbying has been going on so long that it is now almost as formal a ceremony as the tango. All the motions are known to the professional, and are endlessly repeated. Political action can take place on four fronts:

First, get the "right" Congressman elected. He will vote for our bills. This means campaigning in the field.

Second, turn the heat on Congressman already elected.

Third, influence an administrative agency to interpret bills in the "right" way. This is usually harder than influencing Congress.

Fourth, fight the constitutionality of unfavorable bills through the courts, right up to the Supreme Court. It is said that the electric power lobby used to count on an average delay of seven years after the passage of a law affecting utilities adversely, before the final decision by the Supreme Court. This gave the gentlemen quite a lot of time to turn around.

A Washington lobby normally consists of a professional agent and a staff of research workers. The agent gets up the strategy, and the research workers get up the figures. Either or both may draft the bill they want passed. Congressmen seldom prepare their own bills. The strategy is as elemental as an army's: to take more territory, and to kill off the opposition. Sometimes, as already noted, the strategy accidentally does run parallel to the public interest. The labor bloc lobbied for the Child Labor Amendment to the Constitution. It kept children from competing for union members' jobs, and at the same time it was a good thing for the children of the nation. The doctors have campaigned from time to time for pure food and drug legislation. The farmers have sometimes got behind conservation measures.

The agent's primary task is to build up a bloc of votes in Congress, to be backed with appeals from home at the psychological moment. This is known as "hearing from the people." The agent stands at the amplifier to megaphone the appeals. He also uses his professional abilities on the press, the columnists and the radio. His men in Congress can use their franking privilege to good advantage. A large part of the *Congressional Record* is free propaganda for pressure groups.

Congressmen are rarely influenced by debates on the floor. The best way to prove this is to take a look at them when a debate is on. Of the few who are present, those who are not reading the papers seem to be taking a nap. What really stings a Congressman into activity is (1) mail from home, (2) testimony at committee hearings, (3) high pressure from the agent.

The dangerous lobbies are not out in the open. They work in the half-light or in the dark. The techniques of entertainment, dinners, cocktail parties, subtle flattery, are often exquisite. Since the corruption law of 1911, there has not been much direct bribery. The crude buying of votes has given way to more subtle blandishments. Congressmen as well as administrative officials are shy of little black bags. . . .

The role of government in a democracy is to act as agent for all the citizens, superior to any special interest, and to undertake essential things which citizens cannot undertake as individuals. In our form of government the federal executive is the most logical agent. To represent the citizens effectively, the government should not only keep a tight leash on the pressure groups—a negative activity—but under power-age conditions it must act positively and aggressively in the interest of consumers, who have no pressure group to represent them.

The consumer interest is always the public interest. Every American is either a consumer, or dead.

PRESSURE GROUPS: DEMOCRACY BY AND FOR THE PEOPLE

BY MARY E. DILLON*

[Mary Earhart Dillon, Professor of Political Science and Chair-woman of the Department at Queens College, is the author of *Frances Willard: From Prayers to Politics*. She is a contributor to the *American Political Science Review*, the *Annals*, and other journals. EDITOR.]

It is a matter of significance that almost every denunciation of pressure groups fails to include a definition and classification of the institution which is condemned. This failure to define the term under discussion seems to be based on the assumption that all pressure groups are inimical to the public welfare and seems to preclude the possibility of the existence of any agencies which logically should be classed as pressure groups but

* "Pressure Groups," *American Political Science Review*, Vol. 36 (June, 1942), pp. 471–481 *passim*. By permission of the publisher. Only direct quotations have been footnoted.

which might also be viewed as beneficial elements in the democratic process. In the interest of scientific method, it should not be too much to ask that all academic discussion of pressure groups and lobbying be preceded by a definition and classification of the terms. What, then, is a pressure group? A pressure group is a non-partisan organization of a segment of the people formed to exert influence upon the legislature, the executive, or other governmental agency through public opinion for the enactment or the rejection of certain legislation, or for the adoption, modification, or discontinuance of a public policy. A pressure group is non-partisan; that is, it is not a political party, nor part of a political party. Nevertheless a pressure group has been known to exert influence at the polls by promoting the election or the defeat of certain candidates pledged to support or obstruct various public policies. If a pressure group offers candidates of its own at the polls, it becomes a political party. A pressure group may be large or small. It may represent rural or urban interests: it may be local, sectional, or national in scope. The objective sought may be merely the benefit of the particular group, as the enactment of the Soldiers' Bonus Bill sponsored in 1924 by the American Legion.

The objective may be entirely outside the particular interest of the group, such as the bitterly contested Aid to Dependent Children Bill passed by the Illinois General Assembly in 1941 under pressure of the League of Women Voters, the American Legion, and several other organizations. Better government may be the end sought, as exemplified by the number of civil service bills passed by state legislatures in the last decade under the urge of various groups, particularly the League of Women Voters. Whether the motive be private or public interest, a group seeking legislation or opposing legislation by the leverage of public opinion is a pressure group. . . .

Pressure groups are but one means of formulating public sentiment. Political parties, newspapers, public opinion polls, the radio, public forums, debates, and lectures—all contribute to the moulding of public opinion as an instrument for political action. It is futile to brand any one of these organs of public opinion as inherently evil. None of them is fundamentally bad, in spite of the invective that has assailed each of them. The test of their beneficial or evil characters must be made on the basis of their objectives and procedures, rather than on the basis of their existence in a democratic *milieu*. Indeed, in the evolution of the democratic process they have become one of the means of crystallizing public opinion and focusing this opinion upon the government. Inasmuch as the government in a democracy must rest upon the decision of the majority of the people, pragmatic agencies for the formulation and direction of public opinion are to be welcomed rather than discouraged.

Probably the least understood of the methods of formulating public opinion is the pressure group. Certainly its legitimacy is most frequently assailed. The political party has come to be recognized as an integral and necessary part of the machinery of democracy. Yet in the early days of the Republic the party was an outcast, and even President Washington flayed parties in his Farewell Address. Until recent years, the party has been maligned as corrupt, as under the control of bosses and political machines, and as characterized by stuffed ballot-boxes and stolen elections. All this has been true, but it does not stamp the party as a vicious agency of government. Corruption may creep into any system, even into the halls of Congress or perchance the White House itself. Today the pressure group stands in the same position of ill repute as did the political party in the early years of the nation. It has become, however, a necessary part of the democratic machinery, and is to be considered as a healthy accompaniment of the two-party system.

The Political Party

Pressure groups are to be distinguished from political parties. The party, under our American system, is an organized unit seeking control of the government through the peaceful means of elections. Pressure groups, defined above as non-partisan organizations, seek to influence either or both political parties. But they remain outside of the party structure. Some such groups organize for a particular purpose and then dissolve when their objective has been reached. . . . Other pressure groups are permanent organizations which create popular demands for particular bills affecting their interests, such as the Chamber of Commerce of the United States, the American Legion, and the League of Women Voters. Many of the established women's organizations are continually interested in legislation affecting women, children, or the home. The General Federation of Women's Clubs, the American Association of University Women, the Council of Women for Home Missions, the National Council of Jewish Women, and the National Congress of Parents and Teachers are some organizations of this character.

Much has been said in deprecation of the pressure group not entering the political arena and waging an open fight as a third or fourth party. Third parties arose with considerable frequency during the closing decades of the last century. This was the method adopted by the turbulent West to secure liberal, or radical, legislation in Congress. But it was a slow, uncertain, and abortive procedure. If the new party polled a strong minority vote, a major party frequently adopted its most popular plank, or adopted it to such a degree as to destroy the third party following. Hence new parties collapsed almost as suddenly as they appeared. After a series of such experiments, leaders of new parties perceived the advantage of pressure groups. Thus they could make use of the strength and organization of the major parties in order to advance their programs without the prodigious labor, expense, and continual failures of the independent party.

The advantage of the latter system is at once apparent. Reformers seeking remedial legislation were not bound by any party line, but could enlist support from the ranks of either or both parties. Thus the Anti-Saloon League secured commitments from the candidates of both parties. The Prohibition party had one of the most progressive of the party platforms in the late nineteenth century. But its emphasis upon protection of labor, and upon anti-trust laws, was adopted by the other parties. This continual undermining of progressive measures of the third party, in addition to the difficulty of tearing voters away from the Grand Old Party at national elections, doomed such experiments to defeat. What the temperance people failed to achieve through a third party, they won by use of pressure. This is confirmed by the fact that, although the Eighteenth Amendment was adopted as a war measure, more than two-thirds of the states had already accepted prohibition, and largely because of pressure by the Anti-Saloon League.

Pressure groups, of course, were not unknown in the nineteenth century. The most outstanding example in this period was Frances Willard and her legion of women known as the National Woman's Christian Temperance Union. They pressed legislatures in every state of the nation for laws on suffrage, temperance, and the protection of women. The suffrage associations, following the brilliant example of Miss Willard, adopted the same system about the beginning of the century. Even though women had not yet received the franchise, which is the very essence of pressure-power, they were able to secure sufficient votes by proxy to lend impetus and force to their pressure campaigns. One is inclined to say that it was the women who made popular the use of the pressure group. Their success in creating public opinion with which they wielded pressure upon legislators and administrators became a pattern for emulation. Henceforth the interest in third parties waned.

The Lobby

Pressure groups are to be distinguished likewise from the lobby. "Pressure" by a pressure group results from the organization of public opinion directed against some organ of government. The "lobby" is the point of attack upon one or more representatives or other officials by persons or interests without necessarily any regard to organized public opinion. The lobby is the direct effort to influence legislators by personal contact. It is difficult to find a writer who defines "lobby" apart from pressure groups. Some scholars adopt the inadequate definition laid down by Congress at the time of its "Lobby Investigation" in 1935, namely: "One who receives money for attempting to influence a member of Congress."[1] There are, however, two types of lobby: one that represents certain financial interests, as the sugar industries or the fruit-growers of California. The other kind of lobby represents a pressure group without a financial interest. Neither type of lobbying is essentially bad. Certainly industry is entitled to a hearing before legislation affecting it is passed. The reprehensible part of the process is the instances of bribery, intimidation, and undue influence. Also to be condemned is the unsocial policy sometimes pursued. There is an obligation incumbent upon every citizen that the welfare of the many shall not be sacrificed to the advantage of the few.

Lobbyists may be paid or not paid. Some of the corporations pay high salaries to their lobbyists, while on the other hand much effective lobbying is carried on by zealous persons without remuneration. The Chamber of Commerce of the United States, one of the most powerful pressure groups, has long maintained a well paid representative at the capital.

Three essential differences mark the distinction between a pressure group and the lobby. First, the lobby is one of the methods employed by a pressure group. It is the point of contact between the pressure organization and the legislator or other government official. Second, the lobby is the formal method of representation employed by a pressure group to the members of the legislature or governmental agency. Third, the lobby merely makes use of, but does not create, the backing it possesses, whether financial or public opinion. Of course, a corporation may attempt to win public approval for a particular policy, as the utility companies have done in a number of states. As a rule, however, corporations operate through political parties and the lobby, independently of public opinion. Also there are pressure groups which maintain no lobby, but depend entirely upon influencing their legislators through a mass of telegrams and letters. Thus a lobby may or may not have a pressure group supporting it; and a pressure group may or may not have a lobbyist representing it.

Propaganda

As has been pointed out, pressure groups frequently make use of the lobby as an instrument for influencing legislatures or governmental agencies. Likewise, pressure groups use propaganda as a means of influencing public opinion. But, like lobbyists, not all propagandists represent a pressure group. Propaganda has been defined as the manipulation of symbols for the influencing of public opinion. This is a broad in-

[1] See H. R. No. 6770. This bill was referred to the Judiciary Committee of the 74th Cong., 1st Sess. (1935), but was never reported back to the House.

terpretation which might well include teachers and lecturers. As propaganda is not education, the definition should be somewhat restricted. Therefore, propaganda is the manipulation of symbols for influencing public opinion to a particular point of view. . . .

Propaganda, however, as used by a pressure group for the influencing of public opinion, entails such mediums as the newspaper, radio talks, mass meetings, circulation of pamphlets, booklets, telephone calls, and even teas and public receptions. There is nothing inherently evil in propaganda. Unethical tactics may be used. Propaganda which tells no untruths, makes no falsifications, but which is honest in presenting argument, is a wholesome, democratic procedure. . . .

Therefore, propaganda which is ethical is a legitimate instrument of the pressure group for formulating public opinion. . . .

Education

Much of propaganda is education, yet the two cannot be spoken of synonymously. Education is a systematic training of the mind through study and instruction. It presupposes unbiased teaching, with a presentation of facts on both sides of debatable issues. Although propaganda is the chief instrument of pressure groups for molding public opinion, some groups also use education. . . .

The League of Women Voters has utilized the instruments both of propaganda and of education. In the field of education, it has established study classes on major issues of the day which approximate the level of college work. . . . Not until its own organization has thus carefully studied an issue does the League place it upon the agenda for legislative action. After its policy has finally been adopted . . . the League uses the tactics of propaganda, pressure, and lobbying to force governmental action. There is no other pressure group working as a national organization which so carefully educates its own constituency upon a measure before seeking public support of that measure.

Education, then, differs from propaganda. It uses a different technique, and is objective in purpose. Nevertheless it may also be used by pressure groups as an instrument for informing the public upon the facts of a given issue. It should be pointed out, however, that the method of education is rarely used by pressure groups, as it is too long-drawn-out a process and too cumbersome.

Pressure Groups as Part of the American System

The pressure group, while known to European democracies, is particularly an American institution. This is the result of a rigid constitution, and of the two-party system. The government is elected at stated intervals. But in a rapidly moving world the electorate cannot wait for the election cycle to swing round before informing its representatives of a shift in its sentiments. . . . As new issues develop, the people, now alive and sensitive to the shifting times, want to be heard. The British system is in this respect somewhat more elastic. A government which does not keep pace with public opinion may be quickly deposed; and the relationship between people and government is more fluid.

Several political parties, furthermore, cannot possibly represent the public sentiment, even within their own ranks. Of course, it would be fantastic to presume that the opinion of the nation can be classified under the leadership of two or three national parties. Thus there are many currents of public opinion upon many issues which may criss-cross party lines totally unrepresented. Major parties of necessity build platforms which will appeal to the great mass of voters, and hence they are cautious not to arouse antagonism. Therefore there can be little liberal leadership in the two dominant political parties. New ideas and reform measures cannot be adopted by them until pressure groups or independent parties have secured a degree of public support. Practically all of our liberal legislation of the past half-century has been introduced and fostered either by a minor party or by a pressure group. The eight-hour day, the income tax, workmen's compensation, sanitary factories, anti-trust laws, social security benefits, minimum wage laws, maximum hours per week, and woman suffrage have all been initiated and fostered first by a third party or a pressure organization. The New Deal of President Roosevelt, the New Freedom of Woodrow Wilson, and the Square Deal of Theodore Roosevelt were not brought about by party liberalism, but came as the result of a mandate each leader felt he had from the people. These men of wide vision and dramatic imagination garnered the liberalism of many unsuccessful pressure groups into their own policy. The fact that such a broad political program was not in the party platform brought in each instance a storm of opposition from the conservative wing. These three leaders transcended party planks to sponsor measures long demanded in some form by the masses of the people. But only a courageous man and one in close touch with public opinion would dare so to defy the party creed.

Parties, moreover, must so frame their tenets as to appeal to the New England industrialists, the Southern cotton-growers, the Western agriculturalists, and the Pacific Coast fruit-growers. Yet these areas all have special problems deserving recognition. Within these sections are various group interests ranging from welfare work to particularized special interest associations. . . . Thus there is stratification of group interest between the sections of the country and within the sections which cannot be represented by several political parties. This diversity of interests was found in the pre-war France and the pre-war Germany in the multi-party system. Such a procedure, however, has seldom permitted democracy to function smoothly, and when the stress of crisis came, this system in each of these countries crumbled easily.

Thus so far as the mechanics of our democracy go, the two-party system is sound and workable. It is not, however, readily responsive to shifting public opinion, nor widely representative of the cross-section of group interests. It is necessary, therefore, to have pressure groups as an accompaniment to the party system. Under the democratic process, legislatures must ever be responsive to the general will of the people. On the other hand, it will be admitted that the pressure groups introduce an element of irresponsibility into our political system that may be positively dangerous to representative government.

The necessity of pressure groups bespeaks a change in democracy itself. In the early days of the Republic, only about forty per cent of the people in New England could sign their names, and New England possessed the most progressive educational system in the land. Obviously, therefore, the mass of people were little interested in political issues. Furthermore, it was an agricultural society, so that political problems arose slowly and resolved themselves even more slowly. Issues remained in the platforms from election to election. But the situation in the twentieth century is entirely different. The agricultural society has been replaced by a highly industrialized life, and the present communication system has the speed of electricity. Within twenty-four hours after Germany marched into Poland in World War II, every village in America heard the news and was discussing its implications for this country. The radio and the widespread network of newspapers have brought world news almost instantaneously to every home in the land. Radio commentators have done much to dramatize the news making the masses aware of world affairs. As a result, there has been a quickening of the people's interest in government and politics.

Hence the representative type of government set up by the founding fathers has been somewhat outmoded by changing civilization. Public opinion in Washington's day included only a part of the people—the rest were too illiterate even to understand the issues. But today the great mass of the people are vitally interested in the process of government. The people at long last have been educated for democracy, as Jefferson so wisely counselled they should be. Now they want to exercise some measure of direct control in governmental policy and procedure. Unorganized public opinion is ephemeral. To be effective, it must be integrated and organized. In recent years, the public opinion polls have been effective in reflecting public sentiment upon a variety of issues. Pressure groups, indirectly, often influence these polls. But the polls lack cohesion and force to promote a special policy.

Like good propaganda and bad propaganda, there are also good and bad pressure groups. A good pressure group presents its case to the public with candor and facts. It must be honest in its statements and ethical in its methods. In exerting pressure upon the legislators, it must be wholly upon the basis of the public opinion they represent. It is assumed, however, that this mobilized public opinion is based upon the voters and not on aliens, minors, and other groups denied the ballot. Bribes, threats, champagne parties, social influence, and other such means are to be decried as unethical and dishonest; likewise all subversive groups. An awakened and alert public must be relied upon for balance and control of these groups. The people will support those issues which they deem for the public good, and will be unmoved by the fantastic schemes of fanatics and radicals. . . . However, it must be admitted that a political charlatan may temporarily sway large groups of people, as did Dr. Francis Townsend and Huey Long. Each had his day, though short. But as the prairie lawyer pointedly expressed it, "you can't fool all of the people all of the time." Of course, the public must be constantly vigilant against the stampede of any irrational movements or irresponsible leaders.

A most outstanding pressure group of recent years is the League of Women Voters. Its educational program has been unsurpassed by that of any other organization. The timing of the transfer of an issue from the educational forum to the legislative has been most skillfully achieved. Accordingly, its success has brought it much prestige among legislators and the public at large. As a case study in pressure groups, the League would take high rank. It has set a pattern of high ethics, good public policies, and effective legislation.

Pressure groups, it may be concluded, are a part of our political system. They permit a new kind of participation of the people in legislation and administration. They give the people a continuing interest in government, not only at election time but between elections. They mold public opinion into a dynamic force for the shaping of governmental policy. Pressure groups are the modern expression of democracy by the people and for the people.

QUESTIONS AND PROBLEMS

1. Why does Mr. Chase believe that the "Me First" principle of pressure groups constitutes a threat to our economy and our democracy?

2. Is Miss Dillon oblivious to the dangers of pressure groups to a representative system? Explain.

3. Does Mr. Chase believe that all pressure groups and pressure-group activities are evil? What evidence from Chase would you present to support your answer?

4. According to Miss Dillon, is there anything inherently evil about (a) pressure groups, (b) lobbying, and (c) propaganda? What are the proper standards she suggests for evaluating pressure groups, lobbying, and propaganda? Are these satisfactory standards? Why? Why not?

5. Would governmental agencies and bureaus come within Miss Dillon's definition of pressure groups? Why or why not?

6. Mr. Chase discusses the necessity for keeping a "tight leash" on pressure groups and of acting "positively and aggressively" in the interest of consumers? Miss Dillon writes of securing a balance among, and control of, pressure groups. What policy, if any, does each suggest in this connection? Evaluate these suggestions.

7. How does Miss Dillon support her conclusion that "pressure groups are the modern expression of democracy by the people and for the people"? In your answer be sure to treat the following factors: (a) a rigid constitution; (b) our two-party system; (c) geographical representation in the House and Senate; (d) lobbying, propaganda, education, and public opinion.

8. Why doesn't the pressure group enter the political arena and wage an open fight as a third or fourth party?

9. Is the method of education heavily, moderately, or rarely used by pressure groups, according to Miss Dillon? Why?

10. What *is* the role of pressure groups in a representative democracy? Is public policy wholly, in major part, in minor part, or seldom the resultant of group pressures? Support whatever position you take with factual evidence, drawn from Chase, Dillon, and other sources. What *should* the role of pressure groups be?

11. To what extent *does* the government act to ensure the public interest against selfish pressures? Support your position with factual evidence. Assuming that you have reached a conclusion as to the proper function of pressure groups in a representative democracy, what steps *should* be taken—and by whom—to ensure the performance of this function?

SELECT BIBLIOGRAPHY

Bentley, A. F.: *The Process of Government* (Chicago: University of Chicago Press, 1908). A pioneer work. Held politics only meaningful in terms of group activity. Viewed legislation as resultant of pressure-group struggles.

Blaisdell, Donald C.: "Economic Power and Political Pressure," Monograph No. 26 in United States Congress, Temporary National Economic Committee, *Investigation of Concentration of Economic Power* (Washington:

Government Printing Office, 1941). Traces pressure-group failure to promote general welfare to geographical system of representation, business control of resources, and dominant bargaining power of business.

Childs, Harwood L.: "Pressure Groups and Propaganda," in E. B. Logan, *The American Political Scene* (New York: Harper, 1936). Would avoid both ruinous consequences of pressure-group struggles and dictatorial state action by raising standards of pressure-group competition.

Crawford, Kenneth: *The Pressure Boys* (New York: Julian Messner, 1939). A Washington reporter's account of how pressure groups over-protect property interests to the detriment of a majority of dispossessed Americans.

Douglas, Paul H., with James C. Derieux: "Big Grab at Washington," *Collier's* (Feb. 11, 1950), pp. 20–21ff. Deals in part with one of our forgotten pressure groups, the Bureaucrats. A United States Senator's view that analysis, accommodation, and resistance of demands of pressure groups in the public interest may well begin with the government's own departments and agencies.

Galloway, George B.: *Congress at the Crossroads* (New York: Crowell, 1946), especially pp. 297–310. Urges frank recognition of pressure groups. Contends that opportunity for expression should be accompanied by registration and congressional standards of organization, powers, and procedure.

Herring, E. P.: *Group Representation before Congress* (Baltimore: Johns Hopkins Press, 1929). A pathfinding study of pressures on Congress. Accepts pressure groups as healthy part of our representative system.

Herring, E. P.: *Public Administration and the Public Interest* (New York: McGraw-Hill, 1936). One of the best studies of pressure politics on the administrative side of government. Holds problem for modern administration is to allow special interests to state their case and realize their ends without coercing administration or perverting the public interest.

LaFollette, Robert M.: "Some Lobbies Are Good," *The New York Times*, May 16, 1948, pp. 15ff. Argues that lobbying is pernicious or indispensable, depending upon methods and ends of lobbyists. An understanding article by the coauthor of the Legislative Reorganization Act of 1946 (Public Law 601, 79th Cong., 2d Sess.), Title III of which is a "Regulation of Lobbying Act."

Odegard, Peter H.: *Pressure Politics, The Story of the Anti-Saloon League* (New York: Columbia University Press, 1928). The now classic account of a pressure group's ability to secure a constitutional amendment—here, the Eighteenth Amendment.

McKean, Dayton D.: *Pressures on the Legislature of New Jersey* (New York: Columbia University Press, 1938). One of the standard studies of the activities of state pressure groups.

"Pressure Groups and Propaganda," *Annals of the American Academy of Political and Social Science*, Vol. 179 (May, 1935). Portrays background of group pressures in United States, describes customary methods of exerting pressure, and indicates significance of pressure groups in formulation and execution of governmental policies. Still valuable, though dated in spots.

Schattschneider, E. E.: *Party Government* (New York: Farrar & Rinehart, 1942). Especially Chap. VIII for a stimulating analysis of pressure groups *vis-à-vis* parties by our foremost exponent of strong, central party government. Argues that management of pressures is problem of political parties.

Schattschneider, E. E.: "Pressure Groups versus Political Parties," *Annals of the American Academy of Political and Social Science*, Vol. 259 (Summer, 1948), pp. 17–23. Attacks notion of public policy as resultant of blind pressures of selfish special interests. Hostile even to "good" pressure groups because they weaken political parties.

Zeller, Belle: "The Federal Regulation of Lobbying Act," *American Political Science Review*, Vol. 42 (April, 1948), pp. 239–271. A careful analysis of the lobbying act: its background, provisions, opponents, first year's administration. Offers recommendations to strengthen act. Concludes that regulation alone will not eliminate predatory lobbies or reprehensible practices of pressure groups.

Zeller, Belle: *Pressure Politics in New York* (New York: Prentice-Hall, 1937). Another standard treatment of group representation before a state legislature.

The following texts constitute a veritable mine of information:

Bone, Hugh A.: *American Politics and the Party System* (New York: McGraw-Hill, 1949).

Key, V. O. Jr.: *Politics, Parties, and Pressure Groups* (New York: Crowell, 2d ed., 1947).

Merriam, Charles E., and Harold F. Gosnell: *The American Party System* (New York: Macmillan, 4th ed., 1947).

McKean, Dayton D.: *Party and Pressure Politics* (Boston: Houghton Mifflin, 1949).

Odegard, Peter H., and E. Allen Helms: *American Politics: A Study in Political Dynamics* (New York: Harper, 2d ed., 1947).

PUBLIC OPINION

How Secure a Free, Adequate, and Responsible "Press"?

An enlightened public opinion is vital to the preservation of democracy. To a large degree, such a public opinion rests upon a free, adequate, and responsible "press"—defined broadly herein as the agencies of mass communication: newspaper, radio, motion picture, book, and magazine.

Left-wing extremists condemn the press as a monopolistic tool of Wall Street, designed to perpetuate capitalistic slavery and to drown the oppression of workers in the opiate of bourgeois morality. More genteel critics may bemoan the debauchery of American culture in the flood of sex, sports, sensationalism, and soap opera that pours forth from our newspapers, movies, and radios. Enlightenment, others may argue, is impossible so long as the news is suppressed, biased, or distorted, so long as different and conflicting points of view are not aired and debated. Other critics see the press in a different light. They warn of outright government ownership, censorship, or control. They might summarize their feelings in the following adaptation of an English wit:

> When the last free paper is printed and the
> last free voice has sighed,
> And the fearless critic is muzzled and the
> youngest complainer has died
> We shall hearken to Government spokesmen;
> we shall read only Government news,
> And no one will doubt or question, and none
> will express their views.

These divergent points of view suggest the following questions. Is the press free? Adequate? Responsible? Wherein lies the danger to freedom of the press? What can and should be done to secure a free, adequate, and responsible press?

In the first extract presented in this chapter, the Commission on Freedom of the Press concludes that the failure of the press to meet the needs of our society constitutes the greatest danger to freedom of the press. Despite its heightened importance for good or evil the press has rendered inadequate services and has indulged in undesirable practices. A questionable concentration of power has occurred in the agencies of mass communication. The number of press units has declined. The percentage of people who can express their views through the press has decreased. Although the Commission recognizes the important role of government in communications, it looks primarily to the press and to the people to secure a free and responsible press.

Frank Luther Mott, Dean of the University of Missouri's School of Journalism, concerns himself in the second selection with presenting the fuller picture of the *newspaper* press. He warns of the danger of making freedom dependent on duty. He criticizes the Commission for failing to conduct more elaborate research which might have remedied its ignorance of the weekly newspaper and its prejudice against the schools of journalism. Dean Mott suggests that the decrease in the number of newspaper units has not necessarily limited those who would speak through the press and has frequently indicated merely the demise of inadequate papers. He explains why publishers naturally oppose meddling either by the uninformed or by government. He points out that to be profitable the newspaper must be adequate and please a diverse reading public.

In the third and last article in this chapter, Justin Miller, President of the National Association of Broadcasters, defends the radio industry against attacks which he thinks are designed to subject radio to governmental control and operation. He attacks the "monopoly of the mind" argument by pointing to the many media existing for communicating ideas. He defends radio's freedom to conduct its own program (choose its own entertainment, use advertising), answering those who maintain that the Federal Communications Commission may compel radio to be reasonable and fair.

These three positions may be summed up in the following three questions:

Is freedom of the press endangered because the press itself is inadequate and irresponsible? Or do many criticisms of the adequacy and responsibility of the newspaper press overlook its fundamental soundness? Or is it true that "the real fight is, always has been, and will continue to be, against governmental control of the media of mass communication"?

THE PRESS ENDANGERS ITS OWN FREEDOM

BY THE COMMISSION ON FREEDOM OF THE PRESS*

[The Commission on Freedom of the Press was financed by grants of \$200,000 from Time, Inc., and \$15,000 from Encyclopaedia Britannica, Inc. The Chairman of the Commission was Robert Hutchins, then Chancellor of the University of Chicago. The other regular members of the Commission were as follows: Zechariah Chafee, Jr.; John M. Clark; John Dickinson; William E. Hocking; Harold D. Lasswell; Archibald MacLeish; Charles E. Merriam; Reinhold Niebuhr; Robert Redfield; Beardsley Ruml; Arthur M. Schlesinger; and George N. Shuster. EDITOR.]

At the first meeting the Commission decided to include within its scope the major agencies of mass communication: the radio, newspapers, motion pictures, magazines, and books. Wherever the word "press" is used in the publication of the Commission, it refers to all these media. . . .

The Commission set out to answer the question: Is the freedom of the press in danger? Its answer to that question is: Yes. It concludes that the freedom of the press is in danger for three reasons:

First, the importance of the press to the people has greatly increased with the development of the press as an instrument of mass communication. At the same time the development of the press as an instrument of mass communication has greatly decreased the proportion of the people who can express their opinions and ideas through the press.

Second, the few who are able to use the machinery of the press as an instrument of mass communication have not provided a service adequate to the needs of the society.

Third, those who direct the machinery of the press have engaged from time to time in practices which the society condemns and which, if continued, it will inevitably undertake to regulate or control.

When an instrument of prime importance to all the people is available to a small minority of the people only, and when it is employed by that small minority in such a way as not to supply the people with the service they require, the freedom of the minority in the employment of that instrument is in danger.

This danger, in the case of the freedom of the press, is in part the consequence of the economic structure of the press, in part the conse-

* *A Free and Responsible Press* (Chicago: University of Chicago Press, 1947), pp. v, 1–68 *passim*. By permission of the publisher.

quence of the industrial organization of modern society, and in part the result of the failure of the directors of the press to recognize the press needs of a modern nation and to estimate and accept the responsibilities which those needs impose upon them.

We do not believe that the danger to the freedom of the press is so great that that freedom will be swept away overnight. In our view the present crisis is simply a stage in the long struggle for free expression. Freedom of expression, of which freedom of the press is a part, has always been in danger. Indeed, the Commission can conceive no state of society in which it will not be in danger. The desire to suppress opinion different from one's own is inveterate and probably ineradicable.

Neither do we believe that the problem is one to which a simple solution can be found. Government ownership, government control, or government action to break up the greater agencies of mass communication might cure the ills of freedom of the press, but only at the risk of killing the freedom in the process. Although . . . government has an important part to play in communications, we look principally to the press and the people to remedy the ills which have chiefly concerned us.

But though the crisis is not unprecedented and though the cures may not be dramatic, the problem is nevertheless a problem of peculiar importance to this generation. And not in the United States alone but in England and Japan and Australia and Austria and France and Germany as well; and in Russia and in the Russian pale. The reasons are obvious. The relation of the modern press to modern society is a new and unfamiliar relation.

The modern press itself is a new phenomenon. Its typical unit is the great agency of mass communication. These agencies can facilitate thought and discussion. They can stifle it. They can advance the progress of civilization or they can thwart it. They can debase and vulgarize mankind. They can endanger the peace of the world; they can do so accidentally, in a fit of absence of mind. They can play up or down the news and its significance, foster and feed emotions, create complacent fictions and blind spots, misuse the great words, and uphold empty slogans. Their scope and power are increasing every day as new instruments become available to them. These instruments can spread lies faster and farther than our forefathers dreamed when they enshrined the freedom of the press in the First Amendment to our Constitution.

With the means of self-destruction that are now at their disposal, men must live, if they are to live at all, by self-restraint, moderation, and mutual understanding. They get their picture of one another through the press. The press can be inflammatory, sensational, and irresponsible.

If it is, it and its freedom will go down in the universal catastrophe. **On** the other hand, the press can do its duty by the new world that is struggling to be born. It can help create a world community by giving men everywhere knowledge of the world and of one another, by promoting comprehension and appreciation of the goals of a free society that shall embrace all men.

We have seen in our time a revival of the doctrine that the state is all and that the person is merely an instrument of its purposes. We cannot suppose that the military defeat of totalitarianism in its German and Italian manifestations has put an end to the influence and attractiveness of the doctrine. The necessity of finding some way through the complexities of modern life and of controlling the concentrations of power associated with modern industry will always make it look as though turning over all problems to the government would easily solve them.

This notion is a great potential danger to the freedom of the press. That freedom is the first which totalitarianism strikes down. But steps toward totalitarianism may be taken, perhaps unconsciously, because of conditions within the press itself. A technical society requires concentration of economic power. Since such concentration is a threat to democracy, democracy replies by breaking up some centers of power that are too large and too strong and by controlling, or even owning, others. Modern society requires great agencies of mass communication. They, too, are concentrations of power. But breaking up a vast network of communication is a different thing from breaking up an oil monopoly or a tobacco monopoly. If the people set out to break up a unit of communication on the theory that it is too large and strong, they may destroy a service which they require. Moreover, since action to break up an agency of communication must be taken at the instance of a department of the government, the risk is considerable that the freedom of the press will be imperiled through the application of political pressure by that department.

If modern society requires great agencies of mass communication, if these concentrations become so powerful that they are a threat to democracy, if democracy cannot solve the problem simply by breaking them up—then those agencies must control themselves or be controlled by government. If they are controlled by government, we lose our chief safeguard against totalitarianism—and at the same time take a long step toward it. . . .

Today our society needs, first, a truthful, comprehensive, and intelligent account of the day's events in a context which gives them meaning;

second, a forum for the exchange of comment and criticism; third, a means of projecting the opinions and attitudes of the groups in the society to one another; fourth, a method of presenting and clarifying the goals and values of the society; and, fifth, a way of reaching every member of the society by the currents of information, thought, and feeling which the press supplies.

The Commission has no idea that these five ideal demands can ever be completely met. All of them cannot be met by any one medium; some do not apply at all to a particular unit; nor do all apply with equal relevance to all parts of the communications industry. The Commission does not suppose that these standards will be new to the managers of the press; they are drawn largely from their professions and practices. . . .

The new instruments which technology has given the press have enormously increased the range, variety, and speed of mass communications. They have also contributed to the growth of huge business corporations. The developments of new techniques and growth in the size of units are not peculiar to the press. They have occurred in almost all industries. Moreover, the changes in the press are closely related, partly as cause and partly as effect, to the technological and industrial changes elsewhere. The technical-industrial development in other areas made possible the new machinery of mass communication which permits, and even requires, operation on a continental scale. The minutely timed reactions of the new industrial society depend, in turn, on the service supplied by the vast network of the agencies of mass communications. . . .

These technological changes have in one sense resulted in a greater diversity of communication. Information and discussion are now supplied through different channels by different managements. Television and the broadcast newspaper may introduce still further diversity of ownership and management, for it is not certain that these new instruments will become the property of those who control the old ones.

But the outstanding fact about the communications industry today is that the number of its units has declined. In many places the small press has been completely extinguished. The great cities have three or four daily newspapers each, smaller cities may have two; but most places have only one. News-gathering is concentrated in three great press associations, and features are supplied from a central source by syndicates. There are eight majors in motion pictures, four national radio networks, eight to fifteen giants among magazine publishers, five to twenty-five big book houses. Throughout the communications industry the little fellow exists on very narrow margins, and the opportunities for initiating new ventures are strictly limited. . . .

Our survey of the instruments and the organization of the communications industry leaves us with certain questions. To what extent has the reduction in the number of the units of the press reduced variety? Has the reduction in the number of units cut down the opportunity to reach an audience on the part of those who have something to say? Has the struggle for power and profit been carried to such a point in this field that the public interest has suffered? Have the units of the press, by becoming big business, lost their representative character and developed a common bias—the bias of the large investor and employer? Can the press in the present crisis rise to its reponsibility as an essential instrument for carrying on the political and social life of a nation and a world of nations seeking understanding? If not, will its irresponsibility deprive it of its freedom? . . .

Our society needs an accurate, truthful account of the day's events. We need to know what goes on in our own locality, region, and nation. We need reliable information about all other countries. We need to supply other countries with such information about ourselves. We need a market place for the exchange of comment and criticism regarding public affairs. We need to reproduce on a gigantic scale the open argument which characterized the village gathering two centuries ago. We need to project across all groups, regions, and nations a picture of the constituent elements of the modern world. We need to clarify the aims and ideals of our community and every other.

These needs are not being met. The news is twisted by the emphasis on firstness, on the novel and sensational; by the personal interests of owners; and by pressure groups. Too much of the regular output of the press consists of a miscellaneous succession of stories and images which have no relation to the typical lives of a real people anywhere. Too often the result is meaninglessness, flatness, distortion, and the perpetuation of misunderstanding among widely scattered groups whose only contact is through these media.

As we have said, the American press has great technical achievements to its credit. It has displayed remarkable ingenuity in gathering its raw material and in manufacturing and distributing its finished product. Nor would we deny that extraordinarily high quality of performance has been achieved by the leaders in each field of mass communications. When we look at the press as a whole, however, we must conclude that it is not meeting the needs of our society. The Commission believes that this failure of the press is the greatest danger to its freedom.

THE NEWSPAPER PRESS IS FUNDAMENTALLY SOUND

BY FRANK LUTHER MOTT

[This article was written especially for this book by Dean Mott. Editor, teacher, and author, Frank Luther Mott has been Dean of the School of Journalism of the University of Missouri since 1942. A Pulitzer prize winner in the field of American history, he is the author of such books as *A History of American Magazines, American Journalism: A History*, and *Jefferson and the Press*. EDITOR.]

The present writer believes *A Free and Responsible Press* to be a good monograph. Its shortcomings are obvious, some of its dicta are demonstrably mistaken, and the wisdom of certain of its conclusions is at least debatable; but the little book gives us an orderly and acceptable statement of the principles of press freedom and an admirable emphasis on the fact that great rights (such as that of freedom) bring great responsibilities. Whole sections of this discussion of principles will rank with the best things ever written about the press. Like any re-statement of long accepted truths, the Commission's essay does not seem particularly new; and one may be forgiven for perferring some of the older statements (Milton, Mill, Jefferson) to some of the newer.

The members of this Commission put together, after some deliberation, an essay which is, within its limitations, wise and thoughtful. That the tone of the report is adversely critical of the contemporary press is, on the whole, a good feature of it: these thinkers knew that a man's reach should exceed his grasp, or what's philosophy for?

However, in the interest of a truly free and responsible newspaper press it is extremely desirable to concentrate attention on the shortcomings of the Commission's report, to indicate wherein its dicta are mistaken, and to challenge the wisdom of some of its conclusions. Only in this way may the Nation have the benefit of a full and vigorous debate on this highly important subject.

It must be pointed out, for example, that the Commission's central thesis of the integration of freedom and duty is emphatically rejected by some philosophers and has, after all, no assured standing in America. In his *German Philosophy and Politics*, John Dewey, for example, attacks what he calls the "Kantian principle of Duty," which he says presents "a striking case of the reconciliation of the seemingly conflicting ideas of freedom and authority." He then shows how "the balance cannot be maintained in practice," pointing out how, in a specific case, the principle "naturally lent itself to the consecration and idealization of such specific duties as the existing national order might prescribe."[1] While duty and responsibility are high imperatives, making freedom dependent upon them is full of practical danger.

A prime criticism of the Commission is its failure to conduct elaborate research. Since members of the Commission were outside the field of study and did not have firsthand information, extensive and elaborate research would seem to have been necessary as a basis for definite or even reliable conclusions. One wishes that the Commission had made its "investigation" less academic and more practical. The British Royal Commission on the Press, which undertook a comparable examination of the newspaper press alone, had only about three-fourths of the funds which the Luce Commission had. Yet it presented an extensive, highly detailed, and illuminating study. There is something about that kind of work that is extremely convincing.

One of the problems in the American situation that seems to cry out for proper investigation—"research," with quotes, if you please—is the actual effect of newspaper consolidations on the dissemination of information. This problem requires thorough study. The Commission held that freedom of press was in danger, in part, because "the development of the press as an instrument of mass communication has greatly decreased the proportion of the people who can express their opinions and ideas through the press." The Commission set forth the well-known facts about the decreases in the number of newspapers published, without inquiring into the actual effect of those decreases. It assumed the effect to be a limitation on the right to a hearing of conflicting ideas, yet the readers in most single-newspaper cities and towns are conceivably exposed to as many winds of doctrine as those in multiple-newspaper cities and towns. Dr. Waples, of Chancellor Hutchins' faculty, has pointed out that the reading problem is far less a matter of availability than choice; with cheap books, news magazines, and the radio there is certainly wide availability. Most students of the press think there are dangers in the concentration to which the Commission once more calls our attention, but all will resent easy assumptions and facile generalizations without supporting data.

Furthermore, many observers contend that not a few of the newspapers that died deserved to die. They, not those that survived, were failing to perform a "service adequate to the needs of society." Although surviving newspapers may not all meet the standards of the *New York Times, New York Herald Tribune, Christian Science Monitor, Washington Post, Baltimore Sun, St. Louis Post-Dispatch*—to mention only a few excellent newspapers—or the standards of the Luce-Hutchins Commis-

[1] Pp. 51 and 53.

sion, they are apparently meeting the standards of the communities which they serve. And it may plausibly be argued that in a democracy the community's standards should be, if not the criterion, at least a factor in judging the adequacy of a newspaper's services.

One field in which the Commission shows amazing ignorance is that of the weekly newspaper. A rather tricky statement gives the impression that "almost all" weekly papers are users of the Western Newspaper Union's "boiler plate." Many of them never use any such "filler," and even the limited use of "ready-prints" in these days is mostly innocuous because of the wide range of choice in material. Moreover, the Comission states that "rival newspapers exist only in the large cities," thus disregarding the many towns with rival weeklies. And when it says that the investment required for a new "small-town paper" is $25,000 to $100,000, it disregards the fact that small-town weeklies can still be started on $10,000. The fact is that the authors of this report are concerned chiefly with the large metropolitan papers and know little about any others.

Though the Commission is justly critical of the frequent lack of professional attitude among journalists, it makes a sweeping condemnation of schools of journalism wholly unsupported by evidence. Chancellor Hutchins has always opposed specialized education for journalism, and on his Commission he had only one man from an institution which teaches journalism; there are three from Harvard, however, and we have a saving clause commending the Nieman fellowships for journalists at that university. The Commission made no effort whatever to look into the truth of its "findings" about the schools. The current activity of the Accreditation Committee which has gathered copious data about the schools (data which flatly contradict the statements of the Commission in most respects) was entirely neglected. It is incredible that this activity, financed by the Carnegie Foundation, the American Newspaper Publishers Association, and other organizations, was unknown to the Commission.

The Commission says that most of the schools of journalism "devote themselves to vocational training, and even here they are not so effective as they should be." If "vocational training" as used here means emphasis on the acquirement of technical skills to the exclusion of the liberal discipline in learning, the statement is demonstrably false so far as it applies to any one of the 43 accredited schools of journalism in the country. About three-fourths of the time of a graduate of one of these schools is given to courses in the liberal arts, which are carefully integrated in a program which prepares for work in one of the communication fields; and in the other one-fourth, which are labeled "journalism," it would be difficult to argue that such courses as Typography, Photo-journalism, History of Journalism, Ethics of Journalism, and others do not contain much of the liberal discipline. What these curricula do is guide, direct, and integrate the college work of students who are entering an important field of work. That they are doing so effectively is demonstrated by the thousands of graduates now working successfully on American newspapers.

But the shocking thing about this attitude on the part of the Commission is that a prejudice and a perverse unwillingness to examine evidence has led it to condemn one of the most valiant efforts to build up the professional elements of American journalism. It is generally said by students of the subject that a profession is characterized by (*a*) liberal and specialized education, (*b*) devotion to service as such, and (*c*) zeal for and loyalty to the chosen work. The best bulwarks of all these elements are the schools of journalism.

When the Commission comes to its recommendations, one is disappointed to find so little that is new. On the whole, they seem to be sound suggestions; but many of the reforms mentioned are already wholly or partially in effect. The five recommendations to Government are all of this kind, and so are the four recommendations to the press. Indeed, the only recommendation of the Commission which seems to have made a real impression on both journalists and the public is the one for "the establishment of a new and independent agency to appraise and report annually upon the performance of the press." Publishers of large newspapers have not received this suggestion with any perceptible enthusiasm; they are nearly all against it, but the Amercian Society of Newspaper Editors has recently taken a more favorable position toward it.

If such a program were properly organized to dig into the really fundamental questions of modern communications, it might be of incalculable benefit. If, for example, adequate investigation were made of whether conflicting ideas are being promulgated in certain areas, and to what extent minorities and fresh voices are being heard in those cities or communities, whether from newspapers, periodicals, books, posters, radio, television, motion pictures, public speech, discussion groups, schools, churches, etc., then we might learn whether or not there exists that limitation which so alarms the Commissioners and other publicists. We ought to know about it if it exists to a dangerous degree, so we can all be alarmed about it. And we ought to know, too, to what extent newspapers without local competition actually do close their columns to the "opposition." If a properly qualified group of investigators, adequately endowed, and including journalists in its membership, could make such investigations over a series of years, their work should be of the utmost value. But if such a "new and independent agency" is to be merely a gadfly, criticizing superficially, there would be nothing gained over the present free-lance criticism.

We cannot too much blame the publishers who mistrust the setting up of any body to criticize their work. Very naturally they fear the meddling of persons unfamiliar with the operations of the industry, on the one hand, and of government agencies on the other. We have to realize that the profession of journalism is founded on the industry of producing and distributing an expensive product. And we have to realize also—and if we are conscious of the situation of the world press we do realize—that there is always the threat of government controls. Indeed it may well be pointed out that what "liberty of the press" originally meant, and what it means in most parts of the world today, is freedom from government. Except where government is truly and completely democratic, it is the natural enemy of press freedom; and the old issue is not dead even in this country, and never will be.

Yet a body of investigators might well be set up which could avoid both the meddling of the uninformed and the threat of governmental influence. The Royal Commission made a similar recommendation, more detailed and considered than that of the American group for an English "General Council on the Press," to be organized by the press itself. Why should not such a task be undertaken in the United States, leader in the world's journalism?

A just appraisal of the American press would appreciate that the average newspaper, like many other businesses, combines service to the community with the pursuit of profit. The newspaper must do both if it is to stay in business and remain free and responsible. If the paper does not serve the community responsibly, it will, sooner or later, cease to function. Its readers will look elsewhere for accurate news and divergent points of view. A nongovernmental source of revenue is necessary if the newspaper is to remain free of governmental control. Hence certain concessions to more profitable sales must be made. The comic strip is an example of such a concession. Newspapers, like individuals, make mistakes. If democracy is to be meaningful, the newspaper must have the right occasionally to be wrong. A free press is meaningful only if honest and unintentional error is permitted. The newspaper must have the right to voice all points of view, as it sees fit: capital and labor, the political "ins" and the political "outs," the dominant minority as well as the oppressed minority. Finally, critics of the press should never forget that, on the whole, the practices of Twentieth-century journalism are immensely superior to that of any preceding century in our history.

News reporting is more objective, coverage of domestic and foreign affairs is more complete, and presentation of differing points of view is more widespread.

IT IS GOVERNMENT WHICH HAS ALWAYS THREATENED FREEDOM

BY JUSTIN MILLER*

[Justin Miller, who has been President of the National Association of Broadcasters since 1945, brings to his post a wide background as lawyer, law-school dean, judge, and author. He was Chairman of a UNESCO committee on the media of mass communication. EDITOR.]

. . . The essential character and validity of our American concept [is] . . . that government shall not abridge, or interfere with, or censor, the free flow of information. . . . A considerable number of our people—who should have known better—have been flirting with the other concept, that government should interfere—benignly, of course—in order to make the flow freer, cleaner, more effective; in order to safeguard the national safety; to improve the tastes and attitudes of the people. . . .

. . . Let us hope that we may discover how important it is to *stand*, at home, as well as abroad, in support of the proposition that it is *government* which has always threatened freedom; however much it may have disguised its actions and pretended they were for the common good. Fortunately for us, whatever we may think of our government, we have been able to keep it our servant, rather than our master, to a greater extent than have the people of the rest of the world. . . .

The argument which is being used to break us to government control is not limited to radio broadcasting. It is simply stated by Morris Ernst, in the following terms: "With a tradition of the bill of rights, our real fight is not against governmental controls, but against economic bottlenecks which are resulting in increasing lack of diversity of thought in the mass media channels of communication. The basis of our religion of freedom of thought has shifted from the right to utter, to the right to read, to see and to hear. If the monopolies of the mind of man continue in the hands of a few score owners of radio, press and movies, I

---

* *Attacks on Freedom of Communication* (Washington: National Association of Broadcasters, 1949), pp. 4–22 *passim*. These excerpts are from an address originally delivered before the American Society of Newspaper Editors.

am fearful that the American Marxists will persuade our people to allow the government to take over these instruments."

This is the essence which underlies the discussions and recommendations of the Hutchins Commission Reports and of several books based upon them. It is the essence of Federal Communications Commission arguments in favor of program control of radio broadcasting. The idea has been picked up and given stature in dicta which has appeared in opinions of Mr. Justice Frankfurter. It is repeated over and over again by many people with diverse motives. Essentially, what they seek is to make "public common carriers" of the several media. This would move one step toward the government control—and eventual government operation—which they seek; and which already exists in most other parts of the world. This is the ultimate end and purpose of the argument.

But the argument is grossly false, in fact as well as in logic. The monopoly which is assumed to exist, now, because of chain ownership of some newspapers and network affiliation of some broadcasting stations, is as nothing compared to limited ownership and circulation of mass media in the days when the First Amendment was adopted, and in the years which followed. . . . Today, in contrast, there are thousands of media—newspapers, magazines, trade journals, independent, unaffiliated radio stations, publications of associations, labor unions, schools, church organizations and occasional pamphlets, bulletins and services—which reflect every possible point of view. Only a very ignorant or designing person could conjure up a spectre of monopolistically controlled communication in this country today; in contrast to the situation which existed in this country from 1770 to 1830, the formative stage of American constitutional theory; when the price of newsprint was as high as fifteen cents a pound; and when our people held steadfast to the proposition that the real fight is, always has been, and will continue to be, against governmental controls of mass media of communication. . . .

The extent to which present governmental officials are adopting this philosophy is revealed by the following contrast: First, Benjamin Franklin, one of the framers of the Constitution, who said: "Abuses of the freedom of speech ought to be repressed, but to whom dare we commit the power of doing it?"; and second, Wayne Coy, Chairman of the Federal Communications Commission, who, in a recent address, rejuvenated the *Mayflower* case decision in which the FCC had forbidden all broadcast licensees to editorialize. Mr. Coy's statements are significant, both in assuming, boldly, that such power has been delegated to the FCC and indicating his apparent agreement that something of the same kind should be done to the press. I have selected from his address the following comments which will illustrate the point:

First: "No amount of dispassionate analysis, no number of court decisions will, I suppose, be sufficient to put to rest the charge that the Commission, in its insistence on *fairness* and the fullest use of radio for the benefit of all the people, is impairing the licensee's freedom. But I, at least, propose to take every opportunity and make every effort to curtail the freedom of radio station licensees to be unfair. . . . The test must of necessity be one of reasonableness and of overall fairness."

Second: "With that mighty instrument of mass communication, the motion picture, given over to escapist entertainment, and the newspaper field representing the anomaly of an almost exclusively one-party press in a two-party nation, the media of broadcasting has a unique opportunity to serve as our greatest forum and thereby win a more secure place in the hearts of the American people."

Now go back to the first Coy statement. To one engaged in an academic discussion, it would, perhaps, seem the very essence of sweet reasonableness that everyone should be "fair." It would, perhaps, be conceded, also, that it is undesirable—if true—for the newspaper field to be "an almost exclusively one party press." But what a distance we have come in official thinking when a man charged with the duty of regulating broadcasting in interstate commerce—in order to prevent electrical interference and to secure efficient broadcasting—is proud to declare that he will compel broadcasters to be "fair."

It is not necessary to tell this body that nothing in the First Amendment contemplates power in government to compel "fairness" in speech or press. Exactly the contrary is true, as has been pointed out on many occasions by the Supreme Court. For example, (1) "One of the prerogatives of American citizenship is the right to criticize public men and measures—and that means not only informed and responsible criticism but the freedom to speak foolishly and without moderation"; (2) "In the realm of religious faith, and in that of political belief, sharp differences arise. In both fields the tenets of one man may seem the rankest error to his neighbor. To persuade others to his own point of view, the pleader, as we know, at times, resorts to exaggeration, to vilification of men who have been, or are, prominent in church or state, and even to false statement. But the people of this nation have ordained in the light of history, that in spite of the probability of excesses and abuses, these liberties are, in the long view, essential to enlightened opinion and right conduct on the part of the citizens of a democracy."

Is it necessary for me to tell you,

1. That the First Amendment applies equally to radio broadcasting as to the press;

2. That the power of Congress and of the Federal Communications

Commission to regulate broadcasting arises under the Commerce Clause; which is, in turn, limited by the First Amendment;

3. That if anything in the Communications Act attempts to give greater power, it violates the First Amendment;

4. That there is no magic in such words as "public interest, convenience or necessity" or in the fact of licensing, or scarcity of frequencies, to take broadcasting out of the protection of the First Amendment;

5. That if the FCC Chairman can make his proposition stick and compel broadcasters to be "fair"; inexorable logic requires the conclusion that the same thing can be done to the press, newspapers, magazines, books and all the varied forms of printed publications?

It seems incongruous, not to say fantastic, that some representatives of the press are carrying on a last-ditch, bitter battle against any form of government encroachment or control over the content, the gathering or the distribution of information, and at the same time, conceding—even urging—the propriety of government control with respect to other media which are vital in the very process of news gathering and news distribution. . . .

Some base their arguments upon a fantastic distinction between entertainment, opinion, information and education. Surely, no one from the editorial side of the press could father such a proposition. Is drama entertainment? It is the subject of education in many schools and colleges. Is fiction, or poetry, entertainment? In the days when men were afraid to criticize government, openly, in prose non-fiction, much of the political writing was done in satiric verse and fiction, as well as in description of Utopias, remote from the king and country whose government required criticism. Is art entertainment? Then what of the proverb, "One picture is worth a thousand words"? What of the political cartoon? What of the sales work for national and community causes which is done in comic strips and by radio performers? Must education, opinion and information be dull and lacking in qualities of entertainment in order to be education? God forbid! A little study in semantics will reveal the very close relationship between these various forms of communication. Shall we allow the clever, strong-government boys to divide us on such an issue, or, worse still, give them editorial ammunition with which to fight? The proposition reduces itself to absurdity when we remember that a trade journal may concern itself solely with "entertainment," motion pictures, show business or radio broadcasting and still be conceded the privilege of a free press; while the very subject upon which it lives—radio broadcasting or motion pictures—can be stifled by government, with the approval of some editorial writers.

Some people, including some editors, rely upon the argument that scarcity of broadcasting frequencies requires abandonment of the First Amendment as applied to radio. If you will put your researchers to work, you will discover that in many parts of the radio spectrum frequencies are now going begging; and, more important, that such scarcity as ever existed was caused by government itself; the very government which now proposes to make broadcasters be "fair." If the FCC would spend its appropriations and its energies, both internationally and domestically, in the fields of engineering, experimentation, negotiation and regulation—scientific in character—instead of attempting to regulate the thoughts, habits and diet of the American people in the fields of religion, economics, sociology, education, information and entertainment, it would perform its real function; it would relieve the present shocking inadequacy of American statecraft in this field of communications and it would get itself back onto the track, with respect to the constitutional guarantees.

Some undiscriminating editors rely upon the contention that because broadcasters are "licensed," the First Amendment does not apply to them. Have they forgotten that the press was licensed for a hundred years in England, and controlled by stamp taxes for another hundred years? Have they forgotten that one of the causative factors leading to the adoption of the First Amendment was the control which government exercised over the press in England and America through administrative licensing and taxing? Do they doubt that the resourceful strong-government boys can find reasons for licensing you under the authority of the Commerce Clause and of the Post Office Clause? . . . If licensing, in order to prevent chaos in the engineering of broadcasting, warrants assertion of governmental power to prevent editorializing and to control program content of radio stations, licensing to control distribution of newsprint to properly qualified persons "in the public interest" can accomplish the same end with respect to the press.

Some persons rely upon the contention that broadcasters enjoy a subsidy from government; hence, that as to them, the First Amendment has been properly scuttled. If editors support this contention, then they are definitely digging a grave for the free press. Broadcasters enjoy no subsidy. They have licenses to transport in interstate commerce over channels which, legally speaking, resemble the channels of navigable streams. But the Supreme Court has said that the *press* enjoys a real subsidy in the second class mail privilege. Whether you agree or not, the point is that if and when the strong-government boys move in on you, they can cite chapter and verse from Supreme Court decisions and from your own editorial statements to support the proposition that subsidization justifies a controlled press. . . .

Another argument upon which Chairman Coy relied, in his . . .

speech, was a statement by Zechariah Chafee that, "The First Amendment was not adopted to protect vehicles of advertising and entertainment." The Supreme Court has rejected both phases of this statement. In the *Grosjean* case, it pointed out that a tax on advertising might destroy the independence—hence the freedom—of a newspaper and consequently, struck down an act of the Louisiana legislature. In the *Winters* case, it rejected a distinction between "entertainment" and "information." But decisions of the Supreme Court, as I have pointed out, are apparently of little concern to those who have undertaken to change the First Amendment and make it read: "It shall be the duty of Congress to make laws (1) compelling speech and press to be fair and reasonable; (2) forbidding editorializing and (3) requiring that all persons be permitted to use all media, including all newspapers, all radio and television stations, and all motion picture productions; to voice, expound and display their views, upon all subjects."

We have conceded far too much to our critics even respecting advertising. Not only is it the life blood of a free press and a free radio, but is, itself, a highly valuable source of information concerning our economy and our standard of living. Is it wasteful? Perhaps. But if wastefulness is sufficient to justify destruction, how long would our government last? The socialistic government of England has eliminated waste, *perhaps*, but has it raised the standard of living? Nature wastes prolifically as any biologist can tell us. How much less wasteful it would be for the trees to keep their leaves from year to year! The laboratory scientist expends vast quantities of material in the process of experimentation and invention. Only a static world can avoid waste.

But the important consideration is that we are all in the same boat with respect to advertising as with respect to these many other things. Remember that—according to FCC standards—newspapers are 100% commercial. Are you so well off financially that you would welcome a government agency telling you what quantity of advertising you should carry; what the income on your investment should be; how you should balance the contents of your paper between news, sports, comics, serials, advertising, editorials, contributions from readers?

QUESTIONS AND PROBLEMS

1. State and then, if possible, document the reasons advanced by the Commission on Freedom of the Press in support of its conclusion that freedom of the agencies of mass communication is in danger.

2. Discuss the Commission's view of the needs of society for which, the Commission charges, an adequate service has not been provided by the agencies of mass communication.

3. What questions does the Commission raise after surveying the instruments and the organization of the communications industry? How would you answer these questions?

4. What shortcomings, mistaken data, and dubious conclusions does Dean Mott find in *A Free and Responsible Press* as they apply to the newspaper press?

5. How does Dean Mott criticize the three reasons advanced by the Commission on Freedom of the Press in support of its conclusion that the press is in danger?

6. What alternative proposals does Mott suggest in order to secure a free and responsible press?

7. How does Miller answer the arguments of those who, he alleges, desire to "break us to government control"?

8. Does Miller come to grips with the points raised by the Commission on Freedom of the Press? All? Most? Many? A few? Appraise their respective arguments when they do come to grips and then state your own position on the points at issue.

9. According to Miller, what should be done to preserve freedom and responsibility in mass communication media?

10. State and then defend your own view of the policy that should be followed if we are to have a free, adequate, and responsible press.

SELECT BIBLIOGRAPHY

Chafee, Zechariah, Jr.: *Government and Mass Communication* (Chicago: University of Chicago Press, 1947), 2 vols. A searching study by the author of *Free Speech in the United States* for Commission on Freedom of the Press. Deals with use of governmental power to limit or suppress discussion; affirmative governmental action to encourage better and more extensive communication; and government as a party to communication.

Commager, Henry S.: "Monopolies of the Mind," *Nation*, Vol. 162 (June 15, 1946), pp. 723–724. A critical review of Morris Ernst's *The First Freedom*. Concludes that we may heed Ernst's warnings and facts without accepting in full his assumptions or conclusions or interpretations of fact.

"Communication and Social Action," *Annals of the American Academy of Political and Social Science*, Vol. 250 (March, 1947). An attempt on part of students in several fields to understand the nature, significance, and difficulties of communication in the modern world.

"Dangers to Press Freedom," *Fortune*, Vol. 35 (April, 1947), pp. 2–5. An editorial on *A Free and Responsible Press* in magazine published by Henry R. Luce, the primary sponsor of the Commission on Freedom of the Press. In part, adversely critical of what it calls an important, balanced, meaty and difficult document.

Editor and Publisher, Vol. 80 (Mar. 29, 1947). Has ten pages of news, comment, and criticism on *A Free and Responsible Press*.

Ernst, Morris: *The First Freedom* (New York: Macmillan, 1946). Deals primarily with danger to democracy posed by concentration in media of mass communication. Urges Congress to reverse tide of concentration and increase diversity.

Great Britain, Royal Commission on the Press: *Report* (London: H.M. Stationery Office, 1949), Cmd. 7700. Reported no sign of monopoly in British press but warned against further concentration of ownership. Rejected state control. Recommended that press form general council as permanent body to improve standards.

Hocking, William Ernest: *Freedom of the Press: A Framework of Principle* (Chicago: University of Chicago Press, 1947). An attempt by one of the members of the Commission on Freedom of the Press to rethink the principles of freedom of the press in the light of modern conditions and developments.

Hughes, Frank: *Prejudice and the Press* (New York: Devin-Adair, 1950). An adversely critical examination of Commission on Freedom of the Press: its personnel, philosophy, and failure to conduct adequate research.

Inglis, Ruth A.: *Freedom of the Movies* (Chicago: University of Chicago Press, 1947). A report on Hollywood's self-regulation written for Commission on Freedom of the Press.

Lasch, Robert: "For a Free Press," *Atlantic Monthly*, Vol. 174 (July, 1944), pp. 39–44. Contends that newspaper press needs ownership that will give up prerogatives of absolutism and function as a trustee recognizing direct responsibility to the people. Treats such factors as yellow journalism, comics, bias, concentration of ownership, and owners' interest in status quo.

Miller, Justin: *The Blue Book, An Analysis* (Washington: National Association of Broadcasters, 1947). An attack by the President of the N.A.B. on the Federal Communications Commission's Blue Book of March 7, 1946, entitled "Public Service Responsibility of Broadcast Licensees." Defends freedom of speech on the radio.

"The Motion Picture Industry," *Annals of the American Academy of Political and Social Science*, Vol. 254 (November, 1947). Contains essays dealing with development of motion picture industry, its business and financial aspects, effects of motion pictures, relationship to public, censorship and self-regulation, and areas of research.

Tourtellot, Arthur Vernon: "In Defense of the Press," *Atlantic Monthly*, Vol. 174 (August, 1944), pp. 83–87. Argues that burden of a better press rests with education of the people. Maintains that people must act as censor on well-informed grounds.

White, Llwellyn: *The American Radio* (Chicago: University of Chicago Press, 1947). A report on the broadcasting industry in the United States for the Commission on Freedom of the Press.

White, Llwellyn, and Robert D. Leigh: *Peoples Speaking to Peoples* (Chicago: University of Chicago Press, 1946). An analysis of international mass communication for Commission on Freedom of the Press.

PROBLEM 7

POLITICAL PARTIES

*Does, Should, and Can Our Two-party System
Provide the Voter with a Meaningful Choice?*

In 1948 Henry A. Wallace bolted the Democratic party to run for
President as the candidate of the Progressive party. He justified his
action by arguing that both major parties had ceased to present the
voters with a real choice on election day. The Democratic and Republican parties, he pointed out, had become like two peas in the same
pod, no further apart on basic issues than "twiddle-de-dum" and
"twiddle-de-dee." Wallace contended not only that both parties were
identical bottles with different labels but that the contents of both
party bottles—their program—contained similar poisons. Wallace
urged his fellow Americans to save America by supporting the Progressive party, which would then become one of our two major
parties.

Wallace might have bolstered his defense of the third party by
citing the conclusion of a famous American historian, John D. Hicks,
in 1933:

"The chronic supporter of third party tickets need not worry,
therefore, when he is told, as he surely will be told, that he is 'throwing his vote away.' [A] backward glance through American history
would seem to indicate that his kind of vote is after all probably the
most powerful vote that has ever been cast."

President Harry S. Truman, the Democratic candidate to succeed
himself in 1948, refused to accept Mr. Wallace's charges or the poll-
sters' forecasts of political defeat. Instead, he proceeded to conduct
one of the most vigorous and radical presidential campaigns in United
States history. In his now famous "whistle stop" campaign, Mr.
Truman made it quite clear that he thought there was a considerable
difference between the Democratic party and the Republican party.
Repeatedly he called the Democratic party the "party of the people,"
emphasizing what it had done and would do for international peace
and for worker, farmer, businessman, and consumer on the home

front. He berated the "Do Nothing Republican Eightieth Congress." He saw the people's choice as one between the "special interests" (read Republican party) and the "public interest" (read Democratic party). In this chapter brief excerpts from Mr. Truman's broadsides in his victorious 1948 campaign introduce his speech of May 15, 1950, which set the Democratic stage for the congressional elections of 1950.

Many Republicans, after pondering Governor Thomas E. Dewey's miraculous ability in 1948 to "snatch defeat out of the jaws of victory," concluded that the American people wanted a political contest in which party differences, in both foreign and domestic affairs, would be emphatically stressed and vigorously debated. The remarks of Senator Robert A. Taft, key Republican spokesman, in a speech in 1951 after his own impressive senatorial victory in Ohio, reflect this point of view. As can be gleaned from his remarks condensed herein the domestic issue for Taft is "Liberty versus Socialism"; the touchstone in foreign affairs is "Democratic Catastrophe."

The editor presents this campaign literature to enable the reader to judge whether he agrees with party spokesmen who saw, and still see, a real choice facing the American electorate. The mature and critical student may also judge the merits of the arguments contained herein.

Mr. Wallace, President Truman, Governor Dewey, and Senator Robert Taft might all agree that our party system *should* present the voter with a meaningful choice. Other observers, however, justify the lack of a really clear-cut program. Mr. John Fisher, in the following article, argues that our two-party system does not, should not, and cannot give the voter a real choice, especially as Mr. Wallace would define "real choice." Fisher contends that clear-cut, coherent, disciplined parties can never win elections. This is so because their program has only a limited political appeal. The broadly based party, however, with its general, vague, and often conflicting programmatic platitudes, wins elections by offering all kinds of political "bait" to all kinds of political "fish." Such parties—the Democratic and Republican parties—not only win elections but also moderate political conflicts and achieve a respectable amount of progress.

The American Political Science Association's Committee on Political Parties is less complacent about the operation of our two-party system. The Committee sees it vitiated by a basic weakness. The Committee seeks a stronger, more responsible and effective two-party system, a system which will present the voter with a meaningful choice between coherent national programs to which the parties are committed and which they can carry out. Extracts relating to this thesis constitute the last selection in this chapter.

The pertinent question for the American voter will be the same in 1952 and 1956 as it was in 1948 and 1950. It is this: *Does, should, and can our two-party system provide the voter with a meaningful and effective choice between national political programs?*

THE PUBLIC INTEREST VERSUS THE SPECIAL INTERESTS

BY HARRY S. TRUMAN

Victory has become a habit of our party. . . .

The reason is that the people know that the Democratic party is the people's party and the Republican party is the party of special interests and it always has been and always will be. . . .

The Republican party . . . favors the privileged few and not the common everyday man. Ever since its inception that party has been under the control of special privilege. . . . [The Republican Party] concretely proved . . . [this] in the Eightieth Congress. . . .[1]

Why is it that the farmer and the worker and the small businessman suffer under Republican administrations and gain under Democratic administrations?

I'll tell you why. It is the result of a basic difference in the attitude between the Democratic and Republican parties!

The Democratic party represents the people. It is pledged to work for agriculture. It is pledged to work for labor. It is pledged to work for the small business man and the white-collar worker.

The Democratic party puts human rights and human welfare first.

But the attitude of the Republican gluttons of privilege is very different. The big-money Republican looks on agriculture and labor merely as expense items in his business venture. He tries to push their share of the national income down as low as possible and increase his own profits. And he looks upon the Government as a tool to accomplish this purpose. . . .

Our intentions are made clear by our deeds. In this Twentieth Century,

[1] From President Truman's extemporaneous speech at Philadelphia, July 14, 1948, accepting the Democratic nomination for President. The full text of this speech may be found in *The New York Times*, July 15, 1948, p. 4.

every great step forward has come during Democratic administrations of the national Government. Every movement backward has come under Republican auspices; and it is the people who have paid dearly for these reactionary moves. . . .[2]

. . . It is up to you, the people of this great nation, to decide what kind of government you want—whether you want government for all the people or government for just the privileged few. . . .[3]

In Jefferson's time the American people created the Democratic party to free themselves from the control of the privileged few. Since then, from time to time, the American people have chosen our party as their instrument to create the kind of nation that Jefferson dreamed of, a land of opportunity and justice for all. . . .

The Democratic party, today, is the party of the main stream of American life. It is the party of progressive liberalism.

We do not share the delusions of the extreme Left. We reject the Godless theories of communism. We believe in the free will of man, and in the democratic exercise of his rights as a human being.

We do not share the prejudices of the extreme Right. We do not share their fear of change, or their delusions that we can go back to the past. We believe in progress. We know that you cannot get along in the atomic age with . . . horse and buggy ideas. . . .

. . . We in the Democratic party are more than dreamers. We know that it takes hard work to make dreams come true.

The Democratic party has never tried to tell the American people that they could make their dreams come true simply by sitting still and wishing.

Right now, the two biggest jobs this nation faces are to assure an increased standard of living for our people and to achieve peace in the world. To do those jobs is going to take the hardest kind of work.

To achieve peace, we must cooperate with other free nations in maintaining a strong common defense against aggression. To achieve peace, we must cooperate with other free nations in building a prosperous world. To achieve peace, we must cooperate with other countries in strengthening and improving the United Nations.

These tasks are all difficult, long and expensive. But we will not shrink from them, for they are the way to peace. They are the way to create a community of nations, at peace with one another, working for the good of all men. And that is one of our greatest dreams.

[2] From speech at Dexter, Iowa, Sept. 18, 1948; text in *The New York Times*, Sept. 19, 1948, pp. 3–4.

[3] From Mr. Truman's final address to voters, Independence, Missouri, Nov. 1, 1948; text in *The New York Times*, Nov. 2, 1948, p. 10.

To assure an ever-expanding standard of living for the American people, we must have better farms and better factories, more businesses and more jobs. We must have better health, education, security and recreation for all the people.

We in the Democratic party know that these things will come about only through progressive action and hard work. But we know they can come about—that we can make our dreams come true. We know that because of the progress we have already made.

Look at the progress that business has made already.

You often hear it said that the Democratic party is unfair to business, is taxing it to death and has taken all incentives away from private enterprise. A great deal of propaganda is issued to try to make you believe that private initiative and private profit are on the last mile to extinction.

But what are the facts?

In 1949, corporate profits, after taxes, were double what they were ten years ago. In 1949, industrial production was 60 per cent more than it was in 1939. In 1949, new investment in plant and equipment for business purposes was more than double what it was ten years ago. These increases are in terms of real income, not just dollars. . . .

Business was never so productive, vital and energetic as it is today. All this talk about weakening private enterprise is sheer political bunk.

One of the reasons why business is strong and prosperous is that the income of the average American family has greatly increased in recent years.

Since 1939, the real income of the typical wage-earner's family has gone up 50 per cent.

The same kind of progress has been made by farm families. Their real incomes have risen as much as those of wage earners.

All groups in the economy have made progress together: business men, wage-earners and farmers have been moving steadily forward. We have all shared in the economic progress of the nation. . . .

The Democratic party . . . [has] a program—a definite, positive program—for increasing our national welfare. We propose to build upon the experience of the last seventeen years and strengthen the measures that have so thoroughly proved their worth during that period.

Our program is founded firmly upon the proposition that it is the duty of Government to serve all the people—not just the privileged few. . . .

In trying to get this program through the Congress, we have met strong opposition from various oddly assorted groups. In many cases we have successfully overcome this opposition. In others, we have not—at least, not yet. But we will keep up the fight, and I think we will be successful before long. . . .

We will carry on the fight . . . because we are a party that is not afraid to dream and plan and work for a better future.

We will carry on the fight for international cooperation and against a return to isolationism.

We will carry on the fight to repeal the Taft-Hartley Act and replace it with a law that is fair to both management and labor.

We will carry on the fight for improved Social Security laws.

We will carry on the fight for Federal aid to education, to help the states remedy the disgraceful conditions that exist in many schools.

We will carry on the fight for a program to assist low-income families and middle-income families to obtain better housing.

We will carry on the fight for a program to improve the nation's health.

We will carry on the fight to conserve and develop our natural resources for the benefit of all the people and not the privileged few.

We will carry on the fight for an improved farm law that is fair to producers and consumers alike.

We will carry on the fight for a program of aid to small business.

We will carry on the fight for laws that will guarantee all our citizens equal rights and equal opportunities, and will lessen discrimination based on religion, color or national origin.

All these measures will help to keep this nation strong and prosperous and to make it possible for us to meet our responsibilities in the world.

We must meet these responsibilities if we are to have peace and preserve our freedom. The strength of the United States is the bulwark of the free world today. Our cooperation with other free nations is essential to forestall Communist aggression.

The Democratic party is dedicated to the cause of peace and cooperation with other nations. We do not regard this as a partisan matter. We have worked—and will continue to work—with like-minded men of both political parties, in Congress and out, in the interest of world peace. But honest cooperation does not require the Democratic party to sacrifice its basic principles.

The Democratic party will remain firm in the faith upon which it was founded.

We will continue to fight undemocratic elements in our society, whether of the Left or of the Right.

We will continue to seek progress through practical measures that are for the benefit of all the people.[4]

[4] From talk at Chicago rally, May 15, 1950; text in *The New York Times*, May 16, 1950, p. 4.

LIBERTY VERSUS THE FAIR DEAL

BY ROBERT A. TAFT*

[Robert A. Taft, senior Senator from Ohio, has served in the
Senate continuously since 1938. Often referred to as "Mr. Republican" because of his chairmanship of the Senate Republican
Policy Committee and his leading role in opposing the Truman
administration, he has been a prominent Republican contender
for the Presidency. EDITOR.]

Now is the time for all Republicans to begin to plan the campaign of
1952 and the best way to start is to find the reasons for some of the huge
majorities in many States in 1950.
. . . It seems to me clear that the people responded and will respond
to a straightforward appeal for progress under the basic principles of
American freedom which are the foundation of the Republican Party.
I believe if that appeal is presented in behalf of liberty, justice, and
equality at home and independence and peace abroad, they will respond
to that appeal more than to any socialistic promises and programs. The
issues in the recent election [of November, 1950] included the Brannan
plan supposed to appeal to the farmer, socialized medicine supposed to
appeal to the millions of middle-income and lower-income families, and
the repeal of the Taft-Hartley law supposed to appeal to the members of
the labor unions. If those suppositions had been correct, the Republicans
would have lost by large majorities, because most of the candidates took
a head-on position against all of these three programs. They did not lose.
New Deal victories in recent years had created the impression that you
couldn't beat Santa Claus. They had created the impression that a man
can successfully promise the farmer high prices and the consumer low
prices at the same time; that people can have free medical service and
many other free benefits without paying any increased taxes; that government could give the people something for nothing. Now we know that
the American people need not be fooled by that kind of philosophy. . . .
Every program presented by our friends or our opponents should be
analyzed and tested on the basis of whether it promotes liberty in the
long run or destroys liberty; whether it favors special interests or special
groups, or whether it holds the scales of justice evenly and impartially

* Congressional Record (daily), 82d Cong., 1st Sess., Vol. 97, No. 20 (Feb. 1, 1951),
pp. A526–A527 passim. Senator Taft made this speech on Jan. 29, 1951, before the
Republican Club of the District of Columbia.

as government should do. The Republicans present a program of progress in increased production, in standards of living, better education, public works that are worth while, sound principles of finance, but they must tell the people why their program will achieve permanent results, and why the Fair Deal proposals can only lead to inflation, socialism, and complete Government control of the lives of our people.

But I believe the decision last November [1950] was probably more affected by the concern of the people over the foreign policy of the United States, and that in 1952 also, that may well be the determining factor. . . . The interest of this Congress [the Eighty-second], and very likely that of the people in 1952, is centered on this problem of meeting the threat of Communist aggression. In the last campaign, the Republicans for the first time attacked directly the past foreign policy of the administration. We pointed out that the present ability of Russia and its ability to threaten the security of the United States arose out of that policy. . . .

They accepted the promises of Stalin that he would establish freedom in Poland and other countries, although he had never kept a promise and was as much of an aggressor in Poland as Hitler was. They set him up in control in Berlin, Prague, and Vienna, and American troops were turned back from Berlin and Prague because of the agreements made at Yalta. The administration established Stalin in Manchuria contrary to every principle of American foreign policy since the days of John Hay, and contrary to our obligation to our ally who had so long fought the Japanese. They encouraged the Chinese Communists. They tried to make Chiang Kai-shek take Communists into his Cabinet. They cut off the ammunition and supplies which he needed at the most crucial period. In effect, they notified the Communists that we would not intervene in Korea, and wholly failed to arm the South Koreans, except with small arms, for fear apparently that they might attack the Communists in North Korea.

They intervened in Korea without even consulting Congress on the call of the United Nations, knowing well that Russia would veto all subsequent action. In spite of the most liberal policies of assistance for 5 years, costing our taxpayers billions of dollars, the administration apparently obtained no promises from England and France that they would back us up in the east even against all-out aggression by Chinese Communists, an aggression not only against the United States but against the United Nations. It is not strange that the people suspected the influence of communism and resented the weakness of the State Department. . . .

The detailed program to be presented by the Republican Party can hardly be determined until there is more crystallization of opinion, but I believe that our policy must be based first on the maintenance of the independence of the United States, and second, on peace unless that independence is threatened. It must be based on assistance within our capacity to assist those nations which are willing and anxious to battle communism at home and abroad. It must be based on a program which maintains America as the mightly fortress of liberty, unassailable from without and strong and sound within. It must maintain the economic soundness of this country and increased production as we go, and this both for our own interest and for the interest of those who are closer to the Communist menace. We must, therefore, avoid inflation and the waste of our resources. Foreign policy is to a large extent the application of sound principles to hundreds of situations that arise from day to day. It requires sound underlying principles, but also good sense and judgment in their application. Perhaps because the present administration failed to understand the principles, they have surely lacked judgment in their day-to-day decisions.

In foreign policy as in domestic policy, we must present our case to all the possible voters of America.

IN DEFENSE OF PARTIES LACKING
CLEAR-CUT DIFFERENCES

BY JOHN FISHER*

[John Fisher, contributing editor of *Harper's Magazine*, is the author of innumerable articles on political and social problems. One of his recent books is *Why They Behave Like Russians*. EDITOR.]

. . . The basic argument for a third party always remains the same. It is a persuasive argument, especially for well-meaning people who have not had much first-hand experience in politics. It runs something like this:

"Both of the traditional American parties are outrageous frauds. Neither the Republicans nor the Democrats have any fundamental principles or ideology. They do not even have a program. In every campaign the platforms of both parties are simply collections of noble generalities, muffled in the vaguest possible language; and in each case the two platforms are very nearly identical.

* "Unwritten Rules of American Politics," *Harper's Magazine*, Vol. 197 (November, 1948), pp. 27–36 *passim*. By permission of the publisher.

"Obviously, then, both parties are merely machines for grabbing power and distributing favors. In their lust for office they are quite willing to make a deal with anybody who can deliver a sizable block of votes. As a result, each party has become an outlandish cluster of local machines and special interest groups which have nothing in common except a lecherous craving for the public trough.

"This kind of political system"—so the argument runs—"is clearly meaningless. A man of high principles can never hope to accomplish anything through the old parties, because they are not interested in principle. Moreover, the whole arrangement is so illogical that it affronts every intelligent citizen. Consequently, it is the duty of every liberal to work for a tidier and more sensible political system.

"We ought to separate the sheep from the goats—to herd all the progressives on one side of the fence and all the conservatives on the other. Then politics really will have some meaning; we will know who the enemy is and where he stands; every campaign can be fought over clearly-defined issues. The Europeans, who are more sophisticated politically than we simple Americans, discovered this long ago, and in each of their countries they have arranged a neat political spectrum running from Left to Right.

"As a first step toward such a logical scheme of politics, we need to organize a progressive party with a precise ideology and a clearly formulated program." (Nowadays the implication usually is that such a program must be more or less Marxist, whether in the Communist or Social Democratic tradition.) "Such a party will rally together the labor movement, the farmers, and the white-collar liberals—and then it should have little trouble in defeating the reactionary business men who have long held such strategic positions in our old fashioned political system."

That, I believe, is a reasonably fair statement of the position taken by most of the supporters of Mr. Wallace [in 1948]. It is much the same as that once taken by the followers of Theodore Roosevelt and old Bob LaFollette, and a similar case has been argued in season and out by most of the splinter groups of the American left.

It sounds so plausible—at least on the surface—that it is hard to see why it has never made much headway. . . .

. . . [However,] maybe there is something wrong with the idea itself. Maybe it never gets to first base, not because the American voter is a hopeless dullard, but simply because he rejects instinctively a notion which doesn't make sense in terms of his own experience. . . .

The purpose of European parties is, of course, to divide men of different ideologies into coherent and disciplined organizations. The historic role of the American party, on the other hand, is not to divide but to unite. That task was imposed by simple necessity. If a division into ideological parties had been attempted, in addition to all the other centrifugal forces in this country, it very probably would have proved impossible to hold the nation together. The Founding Fathers understood this thoroughly; hence Washington's warning against "factions."

Indeed, on the one occasion when we did develop two ideological parties, squarely opposing each other on an issue of principle, the result was civil war. Fortunately, that was our last large-scale experiment with a third party formed on an ideological basis—for in its early days that is just what the Republican party was.

Its radical wing, led by such men as Thaddeus Stevens, Seward, and Chase, made a determined and skillful effort to substitute principles for interests as the foundations of American political life. Even within their own party, however, they were opposed by such practical politicians as Lincoln and Johnson—men who distrusted fanaticism in any form—and by the end of the Reconstruction period the experiment had been abandoned. American politics then swung back into its normal path and has never veered far away from it since. . . .

The result is that the American party has no permanent program and no fixed aim, except to win elections. Its one purpose is to unite the largest possible number of divergent interest groups in the pursuit of power. Its unity is one of compromise, not of dogma. It must—if it hopes to succeed—appeal to considerable numbers on both the left and the right, to rich and poor, Protestant and Catholic, farmer and industrial worker, native and foreign born.

It must be ready to bid for the support of any group that can deliver a sizable chunk of votes, accepting that group's program with whatever modifications may be necessary to reconcile the other members of the party. If sun worship, or Existentialism, or the nationalization of industry should ever attract any significant following in this country, you can be sure that both parties would soon whip up a plank designed to win it over.

This ability to absorb new ideas (along with the enthusiasts behind them) and to mold them into a shape acceptable to the party's standpatters is, perhaps, the chief measure of vitality in the party's leadership. Such ideas almost never germinate within the party itself. They are stolen —very often from third parties.

Indeed, the historic function of third parties has been to sprout new issues, nurse them along until they have gathered a body of supporters worth stealing, and then to turn them over (often reluctantly) to the major parties. A glance at the old platforms of the Populists, the Bull Moosers, and the Socialists will show what an astonishingly high percentage of their once-radical notions have been purloined by both Republicans and Democrats—and enacted into law. Thus the income tax, child-labor laws, minimum wages, regulation of railroads and utilities, and old-age pensions have all become part of the American Way of Life. In similar fashion, Mr. Wallace . . . forced both . . . old parties to pay a good deal more attention to such matters as civil rights than they ever would have done on their own initiative. He . . . compelled them to bid —and to bid high—for a handsome block of Negro votes.

While each major party must always stand alert to grab a promising new issue, it also must be careful never to scare off any of the big, established interest groups. For as soon as it alienates any one of them, it finds itself in a state of crisis.

. . . [In the 1930's and 1940's] the Republicans lost much of their standing as a truly national party because they had made themselves unacceptable to labor. Similarly, the Democrats, during the middle stage of the New Deal, incurred the wrath of the business interests. . . . [When] Mr. Truman was plumped into the White House, the Democratic leadership . . . struggled desperately—though rather ineptly—to regain the confidence of business men without at the same time driving organized labor out of the ranks. It probably would be safe to predict that if the Republican party is to regain a long period of health, it must . . . make . . . [a] vigorous effort to win back the confidence of labor. For the permanent veto of any major element in American society means political death—as the ghosts of the Federalists and Whigs can testify. . . .

Because we have been so preoccupied with trying to patch up the flaws in our system, we have often overlooked its unique elements of strength. The chief of these is its ability to minimize conflict—not by suppressing the conflicting forces, but by absorbing and utilizing them. The result is a society which is both free and reasonably stable—a government which is as strong and effective as most dictatorships, but which can still adapt itself to social change.

The way in which the American political organism tames down the extremists of both the left and right is always fascinating to watch. Either party normally is willing to embrace any group or movement which can deliver votes—but in return it requires these groups to adjust their programs to fit the traditions, beliefs, and prejudices of the majority of the people. The fanatics, the implacable radicals cannot hope to get to first base in American politics until they abandon their fanaticism and learn the habits of conciliation. As a consequence, it is almost impossible for political movements here to become entirely irresponsible and to draw strength from the kind of demagogic obstruction which has nurtured both Communist and Fascist movements abroad.

RANGER JUNIOR COLLEGE LIBRARY

The same process which gentles down the extremists also prods along the political laggards. As long as it is in a state of health, each American party has a conservative and a liberal wing. Sometimes one is dominant, sometimes the other—but even when the conservative element is most powerful, it must reckon with the left-wingers in its own family. . . . The Republican party . . . [has its share of conservatives]; yet it [also] contains such men as Senators Morse, Aiken, Flanders, Tobey . . . who are at least as progressive as most of the old New Dealers. They, and their counterparts in the Democratic party, exert a steady tug to the left which prevents either party from lapsing into complete reaction.

The strength of this tug is indicated by the fact that the major New Deal reforms have now been almost universally accepted. . . . [In the 1930's] the leading Republicans, plus many conservative Democrats, were hell-bent on wiping out social security, TVA, SEC, minimum-wage laws, rural electrification, and all the other dread innovations of the New Deal. Today no Presidential aspirant would dare suggest the repeal of a single one of them. In this country there simply is no place for a hard core of irreconcilable reactionaries, comparable to those political groups in France which have never yet accepted the reforms of the French Revolution.

This American tendency to push extremists of both the left and right toward a middle position has enabled us, so far, to escape class warfare. This is no small achievement for any political system; for class warfare cannot be tolerated by a modern industrial society. If it seriously threatens, it is bound to be suppressed by some form of totalitarianism, as it has been in Germany, Spain, Italy, Russia, and most of Eastern Europe.

WE NEED A STRONGER, MORE RESPONSIBLE TWO-PARTY SYSTEM

BY THE COMMITTEE ON POLITICAL PARTIES OF THE
AMERICAN POLITICAL SCIENCE ASSOCIATION*

[This Committee was composed of the following persons: E. E. Schattschneider, Wesleyan University, Chairman; Thomas S. Barclay, Stanford University; Clarence A. Berdahl, University of Illinois; Hugh A. Bone, University of Washington;

* "Toward a More Responsible Two-party System," *American Political Science Reveiw*, Vol. 44 (September, 1950), No. 3, Pt. 2 (Supplement), Foreword, pp. 1–96 *passim*. By permission of the publisher.

Franklin L. Burdette, University of Maryland; Paul T. David, Brookings Institution; Merle Fainsod, Harvard University; Bertram M. Gross, Council of Economic Advisers; E. Allen Helms, Ohio State University; E. M. Kirkpatrick, Department of State; John W. Lederle, University of Michigan; Fritz Morstein Marx, American University; Louise Overacker, Wellesley College; Howard Penniman, Department of State; Kirk H. Porter, State Universty of Iowa; and J. B. Shannon, University of Kentucky. EDITOR.]

The *purpose* of this publication is to bring about fuller appreciation of a basic weakness in the American two-party system. . . .

Of course, if the American two-party system suffers from a basic weakness, the most important thing is effective remedy. Remedy requires not only understanding of the ailment but also willingness to try a likely cure. Both understanding and willingness, in turn, must be fairly widespread. It is not enough for a few people to know about ailment and cure. Before action has a chance, knowledge must first become sufficiently common. The character of this publication is explained by the conviction of its authors that the weakness of the American two-party system can be overcome. Hence it is essential to reach the ears of many citizens.

And the *thesis* [of this report]? It can be put quite briefly. Historical and other factors have caused the American two-party system to operate as two loose associations of state and local organizations, with very little national machinery and very little national cohesion. As a result, either major party, when in power, is ill-equipped to organize its members in the legislative and the executive branches into a government held together and guided by the party program. Party responsibility at the polls thus tends to vanish. This is a very serious matter, for it affects the very heartbeat of American democracy. It also poses grave problems of domestic and foreign policy in an era when it is no longer safe for the nation to deal piecemeal with issues that can be disposed of only on the basis of coherent programs. . . .

Throughout this report political parties are treated as indispensable instruments of government. That is to say, we proceed on the proposition that *popular government in a nation of more than 150 million people requires political parties which provide the electorate with a proper range of choice between alternatives of action.* The party system thus serves as the main device for bringing into continuing relationship those ideas about liberty, majority rule and leadership which Americans are largely taking for granted.

For the great majority of Americans, the most valuable opportunity to influence the course of public affairs is the choice they are able to make between the parties in the principal elections. While in an election the party alternative necessarily takes the form of a choice between candidates, putting a particular candidate into office is not an end in itself. The concern of the parties with candidates, elections and appointments is misunderstood if it is assumed that parties can afford to bring forth aspirants for office without regard to the views of those so selected. Actually, the party struggle is concerned with the direction of public affairs. . . .

This is not to ignore that in the past the American two-party system has shown little propensity for evolving original or creative ideas about public policy; that it has even been rather sluggish in responding to such ideas in the public interest; that it reflects in an enlarged way those differences throughout the country which are expressed in the operation of the federal structure of government; and that in all political organizations a considerable measure of irrationality manifests itself.

Giving due weight to each of these factors, we are nevertheless led to conclude that the choices provided by the two-party system are valuable to the American people in proportion to their definition in terms of public policy. . . .

There is little point to talking about the American party system in terms of its deficiencies and potentialities except against a picture of what the parties ought to be. . . .

In brief, our view is this: *The party system that is needed must be democratic, responsible and effective*—a system that is accountable to the public, respects and expresses differences of opinion, and is able to cope with the great problems of modern government. . . .

In an era beset with problems of unprecedented magnitude at home and abroad, it is dangerous to drift without a party system that helps the nation to set a general course of policy for the government as a whole. In a two-party system, when both parties are weakened or confused by internal divisions or ineffective organization it is the nation that suffers. When the parties are unable to reach and pursue responsible decisions, difficulties accumulate and cynicism about all democratic institutions grows.

An effective party system requires, first, that the parties are able to bring forth programs to which they commit themselves and, second, that the parties possess sufficient internal cohesion to carry out these programs. In such a system, the party program becomes the work program of the party, so recognized by the party leaders in and out of government, by the party body as a whole, and by the public. This condition is unattainable unless party institutions have been created through which agreement can be reached about the general position of the party. . . .

The argument for a stronger party system cannot be divorced from measures designed to make the parties more fully accountable to the public. *The fundamental requirement of such accountability is a two-party system in which the opposition party acts as the critic of the party in power, developing, defining and presenting the policy alternatives which are necessary for a true choice in reaching public decisions.*

Beyond that, the case for the American two-party system need not be restated here. The two-party system is so strongly rooted in the political traditions of this country and public preference for it so well established that consideration of other possibilities seem entirely academic. When we speak of the parties without further qualification, we mean throughout our report the two major parties. The inference is not that we consider third or minor parties undesirable or ineffectual within their limited orbit. Rather, we feel that the minor parties in the longer run have failed to leave a lasting imprint upon both the two-party system and the basic processes of American government.

In spite of the fact that the two-party system is part of the American political tradition, it cannot be said that the role of the opposition party is well understood. This is unfortunate because democratic government is greatly influenced by the character of the opposition party. The measures proposed elsewhere in our report to help the party in power to clarify its policies are equally applicable to the opposition.

The opposition most conducive to responsible government is an organized party opposition, produced by the organic operation of the two-party system. When there are two parties identifiable by the kinds of action they propose, the voters have an actual choice. On the other hand, the sort of opposition presented by a coalition that cuts across party lines, as a regular thing, tends to deprive the public of a meaningful alternative. When such coalitions are formed after the elections are over, the public usually finds it difficult to understand the new situation and to reconcile it with the purpose of the ballot. Moreover, on that basis it is next to impossible to hold either party responsible for its political record. This is a serious source of public discontent. . . .

A stronger party system is less likely to give cause for the deterioration and confusion of purposes which sometimes passes for compromise but is really an unjustifiable surrender to narrow interests. *Compromise among interests is compatible with the aims of a free society only when the terms of reference reflect an openly acknowledged concept of the public interest.* There is every reason to insist that the parties be held accountable to the public for the compromises they accept.

It is here not suggested, of course, that the parties should disagree about everything. Parties do not, and need not, take a position on all questions that allow for controversy. The proper function of the parties is to develop and define policy alternatives on matters likely to be of interest to the whole country, on issues related to the responsibility of the parties for the conduct of either the government or the opposition.

Needed clarification of party policy in itself *will not cause the parties to differ more fundamentally or more sharply than they have in the past.* The contrary is much more likely to be the case. The clarification of party policy may be expected to produce a more reasonable discussion of public affairs, more closely related to the political performance of the parties in their actions rather than their words. *Nor is it to be assumed that increasing concern with their programs will cause the parties to erect between themselves an ideological wall.* There is no real ideological division in the American electorate, and hence programs of action presented by responsible parties for the voter's support could hardly be expected to reflect or strive toward such division. . . .

Party responsibility means the responsibility of both parties to the general public, as enforced in elections.

Responsibility of the party in power centers on the conduct of the government, usually in terms of policies. The party in power has a responsibility, broadly defined, for the general management of the government, for its manner of getting results, for the results achieved, for the consequences of inaction as well as action, for the intended and unintended outcome of its conduct of public affairs, for all that it plans to do, for all that it might have foreseen, for the leadership it provides, for the acts of all of its agents, and for what it says as well as for what it does.

Party responsibility includes the responsibility of the opposition party, also broadly defined, for the conduct of its opposition, for the management of public discussion, for the development of alternative policies and programs, for the bipartisan policies which it supports, for its failures and successes in developing the issues of public policy, and for its leadership of public opinion. The opposition is as responsible for its record in Congress as is the party in power. It is important that the opposition party be effective but it is equally important that it be responsible, for an irresponsible opposition is dangerous to the whole political system.

Party responsibility to the public, enforced in elections, implies that there be more than one party, for the public can hold a party responsible only if it has a choice. Again, unless the parties identify themselves with programs, the public is unable to make an intelligent choice between them. The public can understand the general management of the government only in terms of policies. When the parties lack the capacity to define their actions in terms of policies, they turn irresponsible because the electoral choice between the parties becomes devoid of meaning. . . .

The vagueness of formal leadership that prevails at the top has its counterpart in the vagueness of formal membership at the bottom. *No understandings or rules or criteria exist with regard to membership in a party*. The general situation was well put by Senator Borah in a statement made in 1923:

"Any man who can carry a Republican primary is a Republican. He might believe in free trade, in unconditional membership in the League of Nations, in states' rights, and in every policy that the Democratic party ever advocated; yet, if he carried his Republican primary, he would be a Republican. He might go to the other extreme and believe in the communist state, in the dictatorship of the proletariat, in the abolition of private property, and the extermination of the bourgeoisie; yet, if he carried his Republican primary, he would still be a Republican."

It is obviously difficult, if not impossible, to secure anything like harmony of policy and action within political parties so loosely organized as this. On the other hand, it is easy to see that the voter's political choice when confined to candidates without a common bond in terms of program amounts to no more than taking a chance with an individual candidate. *Those who suggest that elections should deal with personalities but not with programs suggest at the same time that party membership should mean nothing at all.* . . .

The growing importance of national issues in American politics puts weight into the formulation of general statements of party policy. Of course, no single statement of party policy can express the whole program of the party in all of its particulars, including questions of timing. But it is obvious that a serious attempt to define the propositions on which the parties intend to seek the voter's support would serve both party unity and party responsibility.

One of the reasons for the widespread lack of respect for party platforms is that they have seldom been used by the parties to get a mandate from the people. By and large, *alternatives between the parties are defined so badly that it is often difficult to determine what the election has decided even in broadest terms.* . . .

Party membership in this country has come to mean little in terms of allegiance to common principles or support of a national party program. It is not unusual to find less like-mindedness among those bearing the same party label than among some of these and those who fight their political battles under a different party banner.

The existing confusion was vividly underscored by former President Hoover in a recent speech: "If a man from the moon, who knew the essentials of representative government, came as a total stranger to the

United States, he would say some obvious things within the first week or two. . . . He would say that in all this ideological tumult, if there cannot be a reasonably cohesive body of opinion in each major party you are on a blind road where there is no authority in the ballot or in government." . . .[1]

Even without radical changes in the existing state primary laws, however, it is possible to move gradually in the direction of a different concept of party membership. *The existence of a national program, drafted at frequent intervals by a party convention both broadly representative and enjoying prestige, should make a great difference. It would prompt those who identify themselves as Republicans or Democrats to think in terms of support of that program, rather than in terms of personalities, patronage and local matters.* . . .

Support for needed change comes from understanding of the changes needed. If the case for change is conclusive, it makes no sense to ignore it stubbornly. In particular, it makes no sense to insist that there is always some risk in effecting changes, for the eventual outcome may not entirely conform to expectations. This result, no doubt, is possible, but it can be averted by appraising new experience while it is gained in observing the changes initiated. To magnify the risk of change out of proportion is to urge equally or more risky inertia. Doing nothing is no help when something ought to be done.

. . . Making the two parties better fitted to carry responsibility for the general line of national policy is an undertaking in which many hands must share. The motivation for sharing in this undertaking will not be exactly the same in each case. Expected benefits will differ in particulars, depending on the vantage point of each group and each individual playing a part in building a more effective party system. But one strand of reason is common to all of those participating in the effort. All will acknowledge the value of a party system that serves the basic interests of our country in its healthy domestic growth and its international security.

Today this is not a goal to be attended to at leisure, with unhurried step, as time permits. Time, on the contrary, intensifies the pressure for readjustments designed to build a stronger two-party system.

. . . What are the dangers of doing nothing? How great are the dangers? . . .

Four of these dangers warrant special emphasis. The first danger is that the inadequacy of the party system in sustaining well-considered programs and providing broad public support for them may lead to grave

[1] Speech made before the American Newspaper Publishers Association, *New York Herald Tribune*, April 28, 1950.

consequences in an explosive era. The second danger is that the American people may go too far for the safety of constitutional government in compensating for this inadequacy by shifting excessive responsibility to the President. The third danger is that with growing public cynicism and continuing proof of the ineffectiveness of the party system the nation may eventually witness the disintegration of the two major parties. The fourth danger is that the incapacity of the two parties for consistent action based on meaningful programs may rally support for extremist parties poles apart, each fanatically bent on imposing on the country its particular panacea. . . .

Orientation of the American two-party system along the lines of meaningful national programs, far from producing an unhealthy cleavage dividing the electorate, *is* actually *a significant step toward avoiding the development of such a cleavage.* It is a way of keeping differences within bounds. It is a way of reinforcing the constitutional framework within which the voter may without peril exercise his freedom of political choice.

QUESTIONS AND PROBLEMS

1. What constitutes the Democratic or Republican party? All who accept and promote the party platform? All registered Democrats or Republicans? All who vote the "straight" party ticket? All who vote for and support the party's presidential candidate? The respective conventions of each party every presidential year? The Democratic or Republican National Committee? Democratic or Republican members of Congress? The party "machines" in city and hamlet which turn out the vote and claim the spoils of victory?

2. Examine and compare the most recent national platform of the Republican party, the Democratic party, and all the significant third parties. On the basis of their platforms do you think the voter has a meaningful choice between the national Republican and Democratic platforms? Between any major party and the third parties?

3. It has been said that the differences *within* the parties are greater than the differences *between* them. Do you agree or disagree? Substantiate whatever position you take by examining the records of Democrats and Republicans in Congress on some representative but key votes.

4. What are the differences between the Democratic and Republican parties according to Mr. Truman? According to Senator Taft? Are these differences found in the realm of fact as well as in the realm of campaign literature?

5. On what grounds does Mr. Fisher refute the case that has been argued on behalf of coherent and disciplined parties which present the voter with a choice between different ideologies?

6. What is a basic weakness in the American two-party system as viewed by the Committee on Political Parties of the American Political Science Asso-

ciation? What additional evidence might be cited to support the Committee's contention?

7. After consulting the full Report of the Committee on Political Parties, state what steps it urges to remedy the weakness it sees in our two-party system.

8. Would Fisher agree with the Committee that we need and can have a more democratic, responsible, and effective party system? Why or why not?

9. Indicate *your* preference for and the feasibility of (*a*) a one-party system; (*b*) a multiparty system composed of sharply clashing ideological parties; (*c*) a definitely progressive party which would assume its place as a major party in opposition to a major, conservative party; (*d*) a more democratic, responsible, and effective two-party system, as conceived by the American Political Science Association's Committee on Political Parties; and (*e*) our party system as it now operates.

10. Comment critically on the following views expressed by Governor Dewey in a series of lectures delivered in 1950 at Princeton University on "The American Political System."

a. "The resemblance between the parties and the similarities which their party platforms show are the very heart of the strength of the American political system. We are, in truth, all members of the same family. . . . Lest anyone misunderstand, [however,] let me say that there remains a broad and inviting battle ground over which the two parties can vigorously contend."

b. "Our Party has a great tradition of sound, progressive leadership in the interests of all the people. It would be a catastrophe if it should falter now and listen to the croaking voices of reaction or isolation. Then the Party might really become what the Democrats call it."

SELECT BIBLIOGRAPHY

Bryce, James: *The American Commonwealth* (New York: Macmillan, 1st American ed., 1889), Vol. II, pp. 3–238, in particular. Points out that neither major party has genuine principles. Holds that parties will be superseded unless they adjust to new issues. An understanding appraisal by one of our greatest foreign critics.

Burns, James M.: *Congress on Trial* (New York: Harper, 1949). A critique of party impotence (Chap. 4). Calls for strong centralized parties to define and attack national problems (Chap. 11).

Congressional Digest. An independent monthly featuring controversies in Congress, pro and con.

Congressional Quarterly Almanac. Extremely valuable in checking on the activities of Congress: platforms vs. performance, party unity, voting records. Complete, succinct coverage. First published in 1945.

Congressional Record. Indispensable for checking the talking and voting behavior of Republicans and Democrats in Congress.

Herring, E. Pendleton: *The Politics of Democracy* (New York: Rinehart,

1940). A sophisticated defense of a two-party system which does not come foreward with clear-cut programs and translate such programs into public policy.

Holcombe, Arthur N.: *The Political Parties of Today* (New York: Harper, 1924). Has a great deal more to say in Chap. 1, "Empty Bottles," and Chap. 12, "The Future of the Bi-partisan Tradition," about the current scene than most of the current literature. Concludes that prospects for a more rational realignment of parties are not bright. A similar conclusion is reached in "The Changing Outlook for a Realignment of Parties," *Public Opinion Quarterly*, Vol. 10 (Winter, 1946), pp. 455–469.

Lerner, Max: "The Outlook for a Party Realignment," *The Virginia Quarterly Review*, Vol. 25 (Spring, 1949), pp. 179–193. Argues that realignment, if and when it comes, will take place within the two major parties. Believes that differences between parties are sharper and clearer since presidential election of 1948.

Nevins, Allan: "The Strength of Our Political System," *The New York Times Magazine*, July 18, 1948, pp. 5*ff.* Argues that strength of our system lies in fact that parties do not divide sharply along economic and class lines.

Rossiter, Clinton L.: "Wanted: An American Conservatism," *Fortune*, Vol. 41 (March, 1950), pp. 95*ff.* Calls for open alliance between conservative southern Democrats and conservative northern Republicans to divert turbulent forces of irresponsible conservatism into disciplined channels of political action.

Schattschneider, E. E.: *Party Government* (New York: Farrar & Rinehart, 1942). Argues in Chap. 4 that single-member-district-plus-plurality-elections is major factor explaining persistence of two-party system. Contends that defeated major party is not also wiped out because of its sectional strength and retention of monopoly of opposition. Demonstrates that two-party system produces majorities automatically and also moderate parties.

Smith, George H., and Richard P. Davis: "Do the Voters Want the Parties Changed?" *Public Opinion Quarterly*, Vol. 11 (Summer, 1947), pp. 236–243. Reveals little popular support for fundamental realignment of parties in the near future.

Thomas, Norman: "Do Left-wing Parties Belong in Our System?" *Annals of the American Academy of Political and Social Science*, Vol. 259 (September, 1948), pp. 24–29. Holds that platforms should be meaningful, should differ, and that parties should carry out promises.

Turner, Julius: "Responsible Parties: A Dissent from the Floor," *American Political Science Review*, Vol. 45 (March, 1951), pp. 143–152. A "must" for uncritical readers of report of Committee on Political Parties of American Political Science Association. Argues that committee underestimates present party responsibility—party alternatives are distinguishable; most of majority program is carried out. Contends that some committee reforms will accentuate present defects in our party system.

The following texts will be of great aid to students seeking additional information on political parties:

Bone, Hugh A.: *American Politics and the Party System* (New York: McGraw-Hill, 1949).

Key, Jr., V. O.: *Politics, Parties, and Pressure Groups* (New York: Crowell, 2d ed., 1947).

Merriam, Charles E., and Harold F. Gosnell: *The American Party System* (New York: Macmillan, 4th ed., 1947).

McKean, Dayton D.: *Party and Pressure Politics* (Boston: Houghton Mifflin, 1949).

Odegard, Peter H., and E. Allen Helms, *American Politics: A Study in Political Dynamics* (New York: Harper, 2d ed., 1947).

ELECTIONS

How Should We Elect the President of the United States?

On February 1, 1950, by a vote of 64 to 27, the Senate passed the Lodge-Gossett constitutional amendment. Senator Lodge contended that the amendment, also known as Senate Joint Resolution 2, would remedy our obsolete, unfair, and undemocratic method of electing the President and Vice President of the United States.

The amendment would abolish entirely the office of presidential elector. Voters would vote directly for President and Vice President rather than for electors, as at present. The electoral vote of each state, however, would be retained, but purely as a counting device. Secondly, the amendment would make a plurality of 40 per cent, rather than the present majority, of the electoral vote sufficient for electing a President. If no presidential candidate received at least 40 per cent of the electoral vote, the members of the House and Senate, in a joint session and *voting as individuals*, would select a President from the two leading candidates. A third reform would do away with the so-called "unit rule" of counting electoral votes. According to this rule the candidate polling the highest number of votes within a given state would receive *all* of that state's electoral votes. Under the proposed system, the electoral votes in each state would be automatically divided among the candidates in direct proportion to the candidate's popular vote.

It is the second and third of these reforms which excited most controversy. One found strange political bedfellows among the supporters and opponents of the Lodge-Gossett proposal. Progressive Republicans, like Senators Lodge, Morse, and Ives, and progressive Democrats, such as Senators Kefauver, Humphreys, and Douglas, were joined by conservative Southern Democrats in supporting the proposed amendment. Opposed were such conservative Republicans as Senators Ferguson, Taft, and Wherry; the staffs of Americans for Democratic Action and the CIO-PAC; and the leaders of the National Association for the Advancement of Colored People.

In supporting his proposal on the Senate floor, Senator Lodge contended that the present system disfranchises voters, facilitates the election of minority presidents, and unduly emphasizes the importance of heavily populated states. It also perpetuates one-party states, gives an undue influence to minority groups in pivotal states, and creates a false impression of overwhelming victory for the successful candidate. In addition to eliminating these evils, Senator Lodge argued, the proposed amendment would still preserve and protect the rights of small states, would more accurately and equitably reflect popular sentiment, and would invigorate our two-party system. Senator Lodge—whose views are expounded in the following article —denied that his proposal would produce a host of parties, introduce proportional representation, or work to the disadvantage of either major party.

Senator Ferguson, in the Senate debate, contradicted Senator Lodge on almost every point, arguing that the Lodge proposal would result in multiple parties, introduce proportional representation at the congressional level, and destroy our two-party system. Senator Ferguson declared that the amendment would adversely affect both small and large states, federalize presidential elections, and produce more, not less, minority presidents. He urged us not to amend the Constitution on the basis of dubious speculation. These points are all made in the second selection in this chapter.

Professor Ruth C. Silva lent support to the opponents of the Lodge proposal. Relying heavily on statistical analysis of past elections, she maintained that unless voting habits in the South change radically the Lodge proposal would operate to the advantage of the Democrats and to the disadvantage of the Republicans and a healthy two-party system. Her argument is also extracted herein.

Some minority and "left-wing" groups opposed the Lodge proposal on the ground that it would lessen their influence on party policy in key states, while enhancing the national strength and prestige of Southern conservatives in both Democratic and Republican circles. However, two leading journals on the "left," *Nation* and *New Republic*, both endorsed the proposed amendment in spite of its short-term disadvantages.

Although the Lodge-Gossett amendment was overwhelmingly defeated in the House of Representatives on July 17, 1950, it is probable that some variant of this proposal will again become front-page political news, largely because many of the defects of the present system are recognized by both the friends and the foes of the Lodge proposal.

Possibly another amendment—along the lines of the Coudert resolution—may seek to have the President elected on the basis of electoral districts comparable to our congressional districts. This might eliminate some of the evils Senator Lodge deplores in the present "winner take all" system without producing the ill effects adverse critics see in the Lodge-Gossett proposal. Lucius Wilmerding, Jr., states the case for the district plan in the concluding selection in this chapter.

The following query probed by the four contributors to this chapter is the central question that will face our Congress: *How should we elect the President and Vice President of the United States?*

COUNT THE STATE'S ELECTORAL VOTE IN PROPORTION TO THE POPULAR VOTE

BY SENATOR HENRY C. LODGE*

[Senator Henry Cabot Lodge, Jr., after being graduated from Harvard College, worked as a journalist and served as state representative in Massachusetts before being elected to the United States Senate in 1936. Since that date he has remained in the Senate, except for a period of military service in North Africa and Europe during World War II. EDITOR.]

[Senate Joint Resolution 2] . . . does away with the so-called unit-rule system of counting electoral votes. Under the existing system, the candidate receiving a plurality of the popular vote in any given State is credited with all the electoral votes of that State, regardless of how infinitesimal the plurality. Under the proposed system, the electoral votes in each State are automatically divided among the candidates in direct proportion to the popular vote.

Let me illustrate. Let us assume that a certain State has 12 electoral votes. Of the 2,400,000 popular votes cast in that State, R, the Republican, received 1,600,000. D, the Democrat, received 600,000. T, the third party candidate, received 200,000. Under the present system, all of the

* *Congressional Record,* 81st Cong., 2d sess., Vol. 96, Pt. 1 (Jan. 25, 1950), pp. 877–886 *passim.*

State's 12 electoral votes would go to R. Under the proposed system, the electoral vote would be divided in proportion to the popular vote as follows: Eight electoral votes for R; three electoral votes for D; and one electoral vote for T.

The electoral votes are computed to three decimal places. In the very remote, but mathematically possible, event of a tie, it is provided that the candidate receiving the most number of popular votes wins the election.

The electoral votes which each candidate receives, therefore, represent his proportional strength in the State. These votes are then taken and added to the electoral votes received in all the other States. The candidate having . . . [40 per cent (or better) of all] electoral votes wins the Presidency. Votes for the Vice-President are counted in precisely the same manner. . . .

PRINCIPLE EVILS OF THE PRESENT SYSTEM

The defects, unhealthy practices, and potential evils of the unit-rule or general ticket procedure for counting electoral votes are many and varied. Only those of particular importance will be outlined here.

A. The Disfranchisement of Voters Evil

In effect, literally millions of American voters are disfranchised in every presidential election because of the unit-rule system.

This contention is more than a figure of speech. It is an actuality. The 1948 elections furnish an excellent example of this point.

Mr. Dewey received in the 16 states which he carried a total of 8,600,000 votes. These 16 States gave him a total of 189 electoral votes. But in the 32 States which Mr. Dewey failed to carry he had a total of 13,300,000 votes. This great mass of popular votes for Mr. Dewey gave him not one single electoral vote and, therefore, counted for naught. They were of no more effect than if they had not been cast at all. . . .

B. The "Minority President" Evil

[The term "minority President" may] . . . refer to a President who was elected despite the fact that he had fewer popular votes than his leading opponent. . . .

Such a result as this is directly attributable to three characteristics of our election procedure: (a) The unit-rule method of counting electoral votes; (b) the distribution of electoral votes to States on the basis of the number of votes each State has in Congress; and (c) the fact that all save two of each State's electoral votes are awarded on the basis of population, rather than voting strength. . . .

The point which should be emphasized . . . is the fact that it is primarily the unit-rule method of counting electoral votes which contributes to such anomalous results.

. . . The electoral college has become a mere rubber stamp . . . an inaccurate rubber stamp. When a rubber stamp begins to make mistakes, the time for discarding it is at hand. A very recent example of how this rubber stamp nearly made another mistake is in the 1948 elections. Here again we came dangerously close to electing a President even though he had fewer popular votes than his opponent. A shift of approximately 17,000 votes in Illinois, 3,500 votes in Ohio, and 9,000 votes in California would have transferred 78 electoral votes from Mr. Truman to Mr. Dewey, and the latter would have been elected President in spite of the fact that his opponent would have polled 2,000,000 more popular votes. . . .

The proponents of this constitutional amendment make no claim that it will wholly abolish the possibility of minority Presidents. But because this reform eliminates one of the three—and the principal—factors which foster such results, it is believed that possibility is greatly reduced. It can never be entirely eliminated without doing away with the two-electoral-vote bonus awarded each State regardless of population and without resorting to a direct popular election of the President, thus voiding the underlying Federal principle of equality of States in the Senate which made possible the adoption of the Constitution. . . .

C. The "Doubtful State" Evil

A further charge against the unit-rule system is that it strongly tends to overemphasize the political importance of the large politically doubtful States.

. . . This has two significant effects. First, it means that presidential candidates from these States have a marked advantage over rivals from other States in the nomination struggle. Sixteen of the 26 major-party candidates since 1900–17, if Theodore Roosevelt be considered a major-party candidate in 1912—have come from New York or Ohio. . . .

The second effect of this doubtful State evil is of even greater importance. The so-called doubtful or pivotal States monopolize the attention of the candidates and the campaign-fund spenders during the canvass for popular votes, while other areas not regarded as doubtful are generally ignored. . . . [Senator Lodge then quotes the following remarks of Senator Kefauver to support his point:]

"Very important to the Nation is the fact that this new system would require the Presidential campaigns to be waged in every State. This would provide a great educational process in every section of the country. As matters now stand, there are hardly any campaigns in certain of the

Southern States or in New England. The strategists of the party get together in advance, claim some States, concede others, and wage their campaigns in the doubtful States. The pivotal States are the only ones that really enjoy the full benefits of a political campaign."

D. The "Sure State" Evil

Another charge which can be leveled against the unit-rule system is that it perpetuates so-called solid or one-party States.

Voting statistics show a high correlation between the degree of closeness of the State-wide popular vote and the amount of popular participation. In the doubtful State there is a strong incentive for the voter to vote; in States where the outcome on a State-wide basis is a foregone conclusion, there is little incentive for the voter, regardless of his political inclinations, to take the trouble to register his preference.

The striking examples of solid States, of course, lie in a dozen States in the South and a few States in New England and the North Central area. . . . [Here, Senator Lodge quotes Mr. C. S. Potts, dean emeritus of the Law School, Southern Methodist University, to support his position:]

"As it is now, the voter [in Georgia] says to himself, 'What is the use of my going to the polls in November? There is no chance that my vote will do any good, for everybody knows beforehand that Georgia will give her electoral vote to the Democratic candidate.'

"The result is that there is an enormous stay-at-home vote, alike of Republicans and Democratic voters. Not only so, but the Republican Party finds it impossible to win new recruits among the native southern population or to hold its members who move into the solid South from elsewhere. . . ."

The Brookings Institution . . . [has] summarized this whole problem in these words. . . :

"Sure States will no longer be neglected as they are at present both in nominations and campaigns because a substantial minority vote in these States will result in electoral votes for the candidate of their party. Voters opposed to the dominant party in their respective States will be encouraged to work and vote for their candidates because their work and votes may actually affect the results. Their votes will be cast and counted for the candidates of their choice and not thrown away as under the present system." . . .

E. The Pressure-group Evil

. . . One of the most serious charges against the unit-rule aspect of our present system is the undeniable fact that it not only permits but actually encourages and invites the domination of presidential campaigns by small, organized, well-disciplined minority or pressure groups within the large so-called pivotal States. These pressure groups may or may not be organized into splinter parties with candidates of their own in the field. . . .

The fact that pressure groups do hold a balance of power in States where the contest between the two major parties is close—and I call attention to the situation in New York State in the 1948 election, where Henry Wallace's party certainly exercised very great power—is an evil of the unit-rule system that has far-reaching but understandable effects. It causes both of the major parties to give undue attention to the demands and programs of relatively unimportant groups or factions. Because of the strategic position which these groups may occupy, even though in the over-all national scene the particular group may not be numerically important, they may be the vital pivot upon which a large block of electoral votes will turn. Hence, the major parties feel it necessary to make large concessions and enter strong bids for their support. . . .

In its report on the constitutional amendment proposed in Senate Joint Resolution 2, the Brookings Institution summarized this particular condition as follows . . . :

"This constitutional amendment will practically remove the chance that small minority groups can attain and exercise great power over Presidents, presidential candidates, and political parties because they hold the balance of power in certain pivotal States. These minority groups will have no power beyond that justified by their number of voters in a presidential election."

F. The "Landslide Psychology" Evil

Finally, in the list of evils of the present system which I am making, I come to what I call the "landslide psychology" evil.

Because the electoral college, through the operation of the unit-rule system, is an inaccurate rubber stamp, it grossly magnifies the victory of the winner and exaggerates the defeat of the loser. Because it fails to reflect the will of the people, it frequently gives a false impression of a sweeping triumph, coupled with an ignominious rout for the candidate placing second. This is due, of course, to the fact that the illogical unit-rule system seldom permits the electoral vote figures to correspond at all with the popular vote figures.

One of the most striking examples of this gross distortion of popular sentiment occurred in the 1936 elections. Mr. Landon received almost 39 percent of the popular vote, yet the electoral college tally credited him with only $1\frac{1}{2}$ percent of the electoral vote. . . .

Advantages of the Proposed System

Because the proposed constitutional amendment provides for the automatic division of a State's electoral votes on the basis of the popular vote, all the evils inherent in the unit-rule method of counting electoral votes are either wholly eliminated or greatly minimized.

The counting procedure would be legally uniform in all the States.

No longer would millions of voters be disfranchised and their votes appropriated to the candidate against whom they voted. No votes would be lost. Every vote for President would count.

The possibility that a President might be elected in spite of the fact that he polled fewer popular votes than his opponent would be virtually eliminated for the simple reason that the new system would bring the electoral vote and the popular vote much closer together. . . .

Presidential campaigns, campaign effort, and campaign funds would no longer be almost exclusively concentrated in the big pivotal States, to the exclusion of the smaller populated States or sure States. This method of making every vote for President count would tend to spread the campaign and any subsequent presidential activity into all the 48 States.

It would therefore, politically speaking, also tend to break up so-called solid or one-party areas.

It would discourage the prevailing tendency to nominate presidential candidates only from among the residents of those States having a large electoral vote. The danger and detriment to the general welfare is obvious when the field of presidential possibilities is so restricted. The whole Nation should be the field from which to select Presidents.

It would effectively and substantiallly reduce the undue influence which balance-of-power minority, pressure, or "splinter" factions exercise in the large pivotal States and the big cities. No longer would these groups be capable of swinging large blocks of electoral votes—and perhaps the election. These factions, if they enter the arena of presidential politics at all, would have to do so purely on the basis of their own merit. They would be no stronger than the number of votes actually cast for them. Because their numbers are small, they would in all probability receive little national attention. Their frequently assumed role of pivot in key States would no longer give them their presently exaggerated importance.

The illusion that a relatively close election was an overwhelming victory for the successful candidate and a crushing defeat for the loser would be dispelled.

Aside from these corrective advantages of the proposed procedure for election of the President, some independently affirmative benefits would result.

a. By effecting a compromise between the existing system and the idea of a direct, popular election of the President, the amendment would completely preserve and protect the rights of the small States. No State is given any greater power in electing a President than it has in passing a bill through Congress, and by retaining the distribution of electoral votes on the basis of each State's number of Congressmen and Senators, this power is in no way diminished. The rights of the small States, as effected in the so-called great compromise of the Constitutional Convention in 1787, are in no way abridged under this new arrangement.

b. The proposed system of dividing each State's electoral vote in proportion to its popular vote offers a far more accurate and equitable method of reflecting popular sentiment within that State. Under the existing procedure, were one denied access to the popular-vote totals, it would be completely impossible to tell whether a State had voted overwhelmingly in favor of the candidate carrying that State or whether he had gained all of its electoral votes in a photo-finish. Considered from that point of view, therefore, this new system enhances a State's voice in presidential politics because of the accurate barometer it furnishes of the popular will in the State.

c. Perhaps the greatest benefit which the proponents and supporters of this reform believe would result from its incorporation into the Constitution is the prospect that it would greatly enhance and invigorate the two-party system in the United States. . . .

The Senator from Tennessee [Mr. Kefauver] made the following observations regarding the effect of the proposed amendment on the two-party system. . . :

"Insofar as advantages to one party or the other are concerned, it is my impression that both would benefit. The adoption of this system would make the Republican Party a Nation-wide instead of a sectional party. The Democratic Party is already Nation-wide. But under the new system, we would have stronger party control in this Nation which is based on the strong two-party plan. A vote in Mississippi or Maine, for example, would count just as much as a vote in Pennsylvania or Ohio. All our people would have the great benefit of considering the issues, of having candidates or top-flight speakers explain the issues to them in person. This will do much toward giving us an enlightened electorate which is very desirable." . . .

Objections Considered and Answered

. . . I should like to list the objections which have been made to this proposal and to answer them briefly. . . .

The three principle criticisms were: First, that the new system would

encourage proliferation of multiple parties; second, that it would introduce the principle of proportional representation at the presidential level;
and, third, that the proposed method for counting the electoral vote
would work to the disadvantage of one or the other of the two major
political parties. . . .

[First, would the new system encourage the proliferation of multiple
parties?] Actually, as it has been stated before, this method of counting
the electoral vote so as more exactly to reflect the popular will would
have the effect of minimizing, rather than encouraging, the influence
of multiple parties and pressure factions. For example, in the 1948 elections the Wallace vote, though meager by comparison to the total vote
cast, threw two States to Mr. Dewey. Small groups in the large pivotal
States now hold an enormous bargaining power because they may add
enough votes to either party—or withhold enough votes from either
party—to swing 47 electoral votes in New York or 35 electoral votes
in Pennsylvania, one way or the other.

If the electoral votes of these and all other States were divided among
the candidates in accord with their relative standing at the polls, the influence of minority groups would be measured by their numbers or the
merits of their case, rather than on the basis of their bargaining power.
Against this prediction that the reasonable effect of this new system
would be to deflate splinter parties, the fact that some minority parties
might get a small fraction of electoral votes equivalent to its fraction of the
popular vote seems utterly insignificant.

I have heard persons say that because in the 1948 election Wallace
would have received 9.4 electoral votes, assuming that the popular vote
had been cast the same way, instead of nothing, as was the case under the
present system, a great lever would be afforded for building up a third
party. I cannot understand that argument. It seems to me it is not an
advantage at all. Certainly, it is no advantage when we compare it with
the advantage which splinter parties now have of being able to throw
the whole vote of a large State one way or the other.

The second objection relates to what is termed proportional representation. The contention was made that this new method of counting
the electoral vote for President and Vice President would introduce the
principle of proportional representation at the presidential level. . . .
This new system has no similarity to proportional representation. Proportional representation is a means of reflecting every shade of popular opinion in a legislative body. It does encourage splinter parties, of course, and
thus makes it more difficult for any dominant group to carry out a consistent policy.

In a city council or a legislature there could be a perfect rainbow of parties. That is true in some European countries. It is completely inapplicable to the election of a single official to one position such as the President of the United States. Even the cleverest surgeon cannot divide one man up—proportionally or otherwise—and expect him to live. The argument of proportional representation simply does not apply at all in the case of the election of a single official. The only place it could be applied would be in a city council or a legislature, where there are many persons elected by the people.

The third objection I label "political disadvantages." Some people say the proposed amendment would give the Republican Party a legalistic advantage over the Democratic Party, or would operate to the advantage of the Democratic Party at the expense of the Republican Party. I have heard both statements made. I categorically deny either of those contentions. It seems to me that this joint resolution removes obstacles in the way of a vigorous and healthy two-party system. The question of partisan advantage depends on the energy, imagination, and ability of American party leadership. These are qualities which cannot be created by constitutional amendment.

I think we must agree that if the present system is wrong, dangerous, and unfair—which I believe it to be—then it should be reformed regardless of party advantage. There are many people today who believe that our political parties give altogether too much thought to the political advantage which accrues to a party organization and not sufficient thought to the consideration that our parties exist to serve the people and have no other excuse for being. I think it depends on the imagination and the energy which both parties show in taking advantage of the situation. But if a reform needs to me made, let us make it.

DEFEAT THE LODGE PROPOSAL

BY SENATOR HOMER FERGUSON*

[Senator Homer Ferguson, lawyer and circuit court judge, was elected to the United States Senate in 1943 and reelected in 1948. EDITOR.]

. . . The heart of Senate Joint Resolution 2 lies in two provisions:

First. Division of a State's electoral votes among candidates on the basis of their popular vote, allowing each candidate to total up his shares

* *Congressional Record*, 81st Cong., 2d sess., Vol. 96, Pt. 1 (Jan. 30 and Feb. 1, 1950). [The exact page references to each passage quoted will follow the conclusion of the quoted passage. EDITOR.]

regardless of State lines. This substitutes a sharing system for the present unit system, but it does not provide for the popular election of the President. . . .

Second. Substitution of a plurality instead of majority requirement in the election of the President.

The Senator from Massachusetts [Mr. Lodge] and I agree on abolishing the electoral college, but we differ sharply on what are likely to be the consequences of the two radical changes I have mentioned, which he would make in our political system. My views can be stated briefly in five points.

First. Dividing up a State's electoral votes among all candidates would result in multiple parties. The present unit rule discourages the growth of minority parties. They are forced to work with either one of the two major parties. Senate Joint Resolution 2 gives them the incentive and machinery to preserve their identity, to build up their strength, as they wait for the day to take over. In time, the two-party system would be destroyed. [The Lodge proposal] . . . would foster and stimulate those people who have a single issue and desire to create a political party representing a single issue. . . .[1]

Under the present unit system, minority political groups, usually advocating extreme views, rarely attract enough votes to capture the electoral vote of a State. At most, they can swing their voting strength between the two major parties. Sponsors of the resolution deplore this nuisance value of minority parties and pressure groups. I can see considerable good in them to the two-party system. Their inability to gain electoral votes under the unit rule deprives them of incentive to remain compact and to grow as individual parties. At the same time, their limited voting strength is enough to cause ferment in the major parties which are forced to clean house, and adopt new ideas to gain the aid of minority groups. The result is to prevent fragmentation into multiple parties with all its attendant evils and to preserve and to invigorate the two-party system. Under the resolution, these minority groups will have an incentive and opportunity to grow on their own. . . .

Their share of electoral votes in each State and accumulated total across the Nation would provide a score card for their progress. The shining goal would be to divide and conquer the major parties by splintering. The resolution makes this easier and attractive because it requires only a plurality of electoral votes to win. Minorities need not bid for a majority. With enough independent factions on the voting scene, a compact minority group of 40 percent . . . [or better] in electoral votes can gain a major victory. Why do the sponsors of the resolution deny this possibility

[1] *Ibid.*, p. 1268.

when they freely admit that the sharing of electoral votes offers an incentive for the major parties to campaign in each other's strongholds, such as the Democratic South and let us say Republican Maine? What makes them think that dissatisfied voters will turn only from one major party to the other when electoral votes, essential to victory, offer them incentives? Even the existing unit rule has permitted a demonstration of what dissatisfied voters may do. When Southern voters in the 1948 election became dissatisfied with their own Democratic Party, they did not turn to the Republican Party, but set up a third independent group, the Dixicrats. . . .[2]

The South would be the first section of the country invaded by radical minorities, and the North would soon be infected. Even if Democrats are blind to this fate, Republicans cannot afford to let it happen, because multiple parties are against the national interest. . . .[3]

I only wish that I might digress here to dwell at length on the qualities of the two-party system. That system represents a vertical alinement of interests which isolates the lunatic fringes and permits the shadings at the center to move forward effectively. It represents a concentration of responsibility, where we can affirm on the one hand and deny on the other. Any break-up of party solidarity means a diffusion of responsibility which deprives the people of an opportunity to speak effectively on any issue.

It is perhaps the best commentary on the importance and durability of the two-party system that this country has known 70 political parties in its history, each of which has elected at least one Member of Congress. But each one, and in a very short time, disappeared or was absorbed in one of the two major parties. This did not happen by luck or chance. The electoral system itself had much to do with it. . . .[4]

Second. Multiple parties at the presidential level would soon build up slates at the congressional level. Eventually they would demand proportional representation in Congress, on boards and commissions, in the courts. The end result will be bloc and coalition government with all its dangers. We shall not be blind to what is happening in other countries because of coalition governments. We should be warned that a real danger would exist even here in America if we were to have coalition government.

Third. Under Senate Joint Resolution 2, States lose immediately their control over their electoral vote. Small States would be reduced to zero

[2] *Ibid.*, p. 1066.
[3] *Ibid.*, p. 1268.
[4] *Ibid.*, p. 1064.

influence, and the voice of large States would be cut in two with no recognition for their weight in population, taxation, and economic importance. . . .[5]

. . . A requirement that a State's electoral votes be broken up by proportional allocation is nothing but a surrender of the State's sovereign rights over that bloc of votes.

A sharing of electoral votes would leave the small States smaller than ever in influence, and the large States greatly reduced in proportion. Nevada's influence, for instance, would be reduced from an assured electoral vote of 3 to a minute fraction, depending on the closeness of the popular vote. In 1948, Delaware's place in the electoral vote would have been a nullity. In Michigan, a typical close popular vote would reduce the State's electoral influence from 19 to a fraction of 1. To illustrate, a popular purality of 50,000 in Michigan would result in the State's having a net influence upon the electoral result of just one-half a vote. In other words, of a total popular vote of more than 2,000,000, Michigan, having gone one way by a majority of 50,000, would in effect have a vote in the electoral college of one-half vote only. . . .[6]

Fourth. Eventually all Presidential elections would be federalized. The Constitution cannot guarantee a candidate a share in electoral votes, without following through to guarantee him the right to get on State ballots, so that he can have the means of getting those votes. Either by Supreme Court decision or by minority pressures, the States would be forced ultimately to surrender their control of elections to the Federal Government. . . .[7]

A candidate could make an unanswerable argument against any State law that would keep him off the ballot. He could say that the Constitution, as amended by Senate Joint Resolution 2, guaranteed him a share in electoral votes in proportion to his popular vote. But the election machinery of Illinois, or New York, or Mississippi is contrived to keep his name off the ballot, and thus to deprive him of his popular vote. That was done in 1949, in the case of Mr. Wallace, in the State of Illinois. This, in effect, would deprive him of his share of electoral votes which the Constitution, the highest law of the land, guarantees him. How can he be guaranteed a right by the Constitution and then be deprived of its fruits by State law? How can he be given a benefit and be deprived of the means to enjoy it? Under the present system, the States are masters in their own house. Under Senate Joint Resolution 2, State lines are wiped

[5] *Ibid.*, pp. 1268–1269.
[6] *Ibid.*, pp. 1067–1068.
[7] *Ibid.*, p. 1269.

out. Elections for President become national operations with a candidate's rights guaranteed by the Constitution. . . .[8]

Fifth. The plurality provision will result in more, not less, minority Presidents. . . . [Senator Lodge's] resolution makes minority Presidents a constant possibility on the national level. [Under the Lodge Resolution, as amended] A candidate with as low as . . . [40] percent of the vote could become President. . . .[9]

. . . Reform is one thing; radical change is quite another. To pass over from a requirement that a candidate must receive a majority of electoral votes to his election by . . . [a] plurality [of even 40 per cent] is indeed such a radical change.

The fathers of this country took special care to see that a person elected as President attained a clear majority of the total electoral vote. They knew the evils which arise when a Chief Executive assumes office, backed only by weak support of a plurality of the total electoral vote.

It is true, I know, that on 12 occasions a President of the United States has been elected without having had a majority of the popular vote. The present President [Mr. Truman] is one of those minority Presidents. But rather than improve upon that situation, the proposal to elect by plurality is almost certain to perpetuate it. The condition will be perpetuated because it is certain invitation for many parties to enter the field, if a plurality only is required. . . .

This is by no means a remote possibility. Wherever plurality decisions are provided for as in Senate Joint Resolution 2, there is an ever-present tendency toward minority control. A well-organized, compact minority may easily prevail over scattered, divided majorities. . . .[10]

As a matter of fact, it has been effectively demonstrated by opponents of Senate Joint Resolution 2 that the possibility of a minority President is a probability when the solid South is considered relative to the rest of the country. That situation cannot be changed short of a radical shift in the voting habits of the South.

To illustrate, normally solid Mississippi, with nine electoral votes, might give one party an electoral advantage of 8.5 votes, when they are counted proportionally. This margin might be gained by a popular plurality of 172,000. In Michigan, as a State which is typically more evenly divided and with a greater election turnout, it would take a popular plurality of approximately 980,000 votes for the opposite party to offest the electoral advantage in the single State of Mississippi. . . .[11]

[8] *Ibid.*, p. 1068.
[9] *Ibid.*, p. 1269.
[10] *Ibid.*, p. 1063.
[11] *Ibid.*, p. 1065.

. . . I mean no reflection upon the sincere purposes of those who sponsor Senate Joint Resolution 2, but advocates of reform suffer constantly from undernourished foresight. They are so taken with current evils and so confident they have the specific cure, that they resolutely refuse to believe the reform—or what they propose as a reform—in others words, a change—will go beyond what they plan for it. They are sure it will stop exactly where they want it to stop.

In the case of Senate Joint Resolution 2, the sponsors believe there will be no more lost votes, and no consequences if lost votes are not made completely effective by full proportional representation. They believe a plurality requirement in place of a majority electoral vote will not produce minority Presidents. They see no rise of splinter factions and minority parties, although they provide direct and powerful incentives for the growth of such groups. They naïvely believe their proposal will open up the "solid" South only to Republicans and not to many minority parties outside the major parties, and will permit only Democrats to share in Republican strongholds and not other parties. They believe that a further weakening of the Federal principle by Federal guaranties of candidates of a share in electoral votes will not lead to further Federal invasion of State election procedure. They feel that because they set up a very limited form of proportional representation, no drive to make it completely effective at the congressional and governmental level will ever materialize.

For my own part . . . I would not dream of changing the fundamental law of the land on the basis of any such optimistic speculation.[12]

THE LODGE PLAN WILL HANDICAP THE REPUBLICANS

BY RUTH C. SILVA*

[Ruth Caridad Silva, Assistant Professor of Political Science at the Pennsylvania State College, is the author of *Presidential Succession* and other articles on the electoral college and related subjects. EDITOR.]

Application of some elementary statistical methods to actual election returns indicates that . . . the Lodge-Gossett plan would operate to the advantage of the Democrats and to the disadvantage of the Republicans

[12] *Ibid.*, pp. 1068–1069.
* "The Lodge-Gossett Resolution: A Critical Analysis," *American Political Science Review*, Vol. 44 (March, 1950), pp. 92–99 *passim*. By permission of the publisher.

as long as the South remains relatively solid and southern suffrage remains limited. . . .

. . . The Lodge formula would have consistently given the Democrats a greater electoral vote and the Republicans a smaller electoral vote than they were entitled to by their percentage of the popular vote. . . . The Lodge formula would reduce the possibility of a Republican's reaching the Presidency even with a popular plurality, but would enable a Democrat to salvage victory from popular defeat. . . .

The Lodge formula would redound to the advantage of the Democrats and to the disadvantage of the Republicans because the Democratic stronghold is in the South, where a relatively few popular votes will win an electoral vote. The Republicans, on the other hand, must seek their electoral votes in the other states, where more popular votes are necessary to win an electoral vote. . . . The Democratic advantage under the Lodge formula varies directly with the solidness of the South and/or inversely with popular participation in that area. In other words, the more solid the South and the more Southerners who do not vote in the popular election, the more the Lodge formula will magnify the strength of the Democrats. . . .

The Democrats would have suffered a disadvantage under the Lodge formula only in 1892, when the Populists polled a sizeable part of a relatively large popular vote in the South, and in 1948, when the Dixiecrats invaded Southern Democracy. . . .

In those elections in which the South is more solid than it was in 1948, the Republican handicap under the Lodge formula would be much greater. In 1932, for example, if the Lodge plan had been effective, if the total popular vote had remained constant, and if the distribution of the popular vote between the two parties in the South had remained the same, Hoover could not have won the election without a popular plurality of approximately 5,417,870. That year each electoral vote in the South represented 30,381 popular votes. Under the Lodge formula, Roosevelt's popular margin of 2,250,887 in the South would have given him 103.26 electoral votes to Hoover's 19.87. In the South, Roosevelt would have had a margin of 83.39 electoral votes. In order to win 83.39 electoral votes in the other thirty-seven states, where each electoral vote represented 88,365 popular votes, Hoover would have had to poll a popular plurality of approximately 7,668,757 or an overall North-South plurality of 5,417,870. In other words, Hoover could have had a popular plurality of more than five million and been defeated in the electoral count.

Senator Lodge has stated that he does not understand how the Lodge-Gossett formula would harm the Republican Party since the formula would have given the Republican candidate more electoral votes than he actually received in 1948. Of course, the formula would also have given the Republican candidate more electoral votes in 1932, 1936, 1940, and 1944; but the significant question is not whether the Lodge formula would enlarge the electoral vote of the party which would lose the election in any event. The real question is how the Lodge plan would affect the electoral vote of the party which polled the popular plurality. . . . The [Lodge] formula would endanger a Republican electoral plurality in years when the Republican Party actually won a popular plurality. . . .

On several occasions Senator Lodge has said that it is incorrect to apply his formula to the statistics of past elections because the adoption of his plan would change America's voting habits. In particular, he thinks the South would be blessed with a Republican-Democratic-two-party system. He believes Republicans would come to the polls because their efforts would no longer be futile. And Democrats would come to the polls because their votes would no longer be superfluous. There is a possibility that this prophecy would prove true; but what is the probability? The voting pattern of the South has been remarkably uniform ever since the demise of the reconstruction regimes. Even if one compares the primary vote in the South to the general election vote in the other thirty-seven states, the number of Southerners going to the polls is relatively low. As a matter of fact, in the South as a whole participation in a *presidential* election is usually greater than participation in the largest primaries. And where will Republican votes come from in the South? To expect such miraculous results from mere electoral reform is attaching too little importance to historical, social, economic, and political factors.

The first possible source of Republican strength in the South is the uncertain number of disfranchised. The Republicans have no power in southern legislatures to enlarge the electorate. As a matter of fact, Republican popularity among the disfranchised might induce southern Democratic legislatures to tighten suffrage qualifications. In any case, southern Democracy met the Populist challenge with a program of systematic disfranchisement through literacy tests and cumulative poll taxes. That the northern states would retaliate seems unlikely; but if they did not, a northern electoral vote would continue to stand for several times as many popular votes as would be represented by a southern electoral vote. If the North did retaliate . . . one of the most unhealthy rivalries in American history would result.

The second possible source of Republican strength in the South is among those who now disfranchise themselves by staying away from the polls. Republican appeal to southern conservatives would endanger its liberal and Negro support in all forty-eight states. Appeal to southern Negroes and liberals would alienate those southern conservatives to whom

Republican economic and fiscal policy is most likely to appeal. Adoption of the Lodge-Gossett proposal would probably mean that, in years when the Republicans can win sufficient popular support outside the South to give them a national plurality in the popular vote, they would trade large blocks of electoral votes in the North for insignificant numbers in the South. This, in turn, would mean that the Republicans would have to roll up enormous popular pluralities in the North to capture the Presidency, whereas the Democrats who only placed in the popular race could win in the electoral count.

More than the fate of the Republican Party is involved. The operation of a democratic party system, in contrast to a Democratic Party system, depends on the existence of an opposition which has a reasonable chance of winning control of the executive. To make it virtually impossible for the Republicans to win the Presidency even when they poll substantial pluralities or even majorities is to render the Republican Party ineffective as a counterpoise. If the Republicans could remain sufficiently alive under such a system to win control of Congress, at least the Lodge-Gossett plan would increase the possibility that the Republican Congress would be saddled with a Democratic President.

THE DISTRICT SYSTEM IS PREFERABLE TO PROPORTIONAL VOTING AND THE PRESENT ELECTORAL SETUP

BY LUCIUS WILMERDING, JR.*

[Lucius Wilmerding, Jr., economist and political scientist, is the author of *The Spending Power*. EDITOR.]

I would suggest that the system of proportional voting be dropped from the Lodge amendment and the district system substituted. This . . . is the mode which "was mostly, if not exclusively, in view when the Constitution was framed and adopted." It is also the mode which was advocated after some experience with the Constitution by Hamilton, Jefferson, Madison, Gallatin, James A. Bayard, J. Q. Adams, Van Buren, Benton, Webster, Story, and many others. Senator Benton explained it very well in 1824:

"It would divide every State into districts, equal to the whole number

* "Reform of the Electoral System" *Political Science Quarterly*, Vol. 64 (March, 1949), pp. 9–13 *passim*. Only direct quotations have been footnoted. By permission of the publisher.

of votes to be given, and the people of each district would be governed
by its own majority, and not by a majority existing in some remote part
of the State. This would be agreeable to the rights of individuals; for, in
entering into society, and submitting to be bound by the decision of the
majority, each individual retained the right of voting for himself wherever
it was practicable, and of being governed by a majority of the vicinage,
and not by majorities brought from remote sections to overwhelm him
with their accumulated numbers. It would be agreeable to the interests
of all parts of the States; for each State may have different interests in
different parts; one part may be agricultural, another manufacturing,
another commercial; and it would be unjust that the strongest should
govern, or that two should combine and sacrifice the third. The district
system would be agreeable to the intention of our present Constitution,
which, in giving to each Elector a separate vote, instead of giving to each
State a consolidated vote, composed of all its Electoral suffrages, clearly
intended that each mass of persons entitled to one Elector, should have
the right of giving one vote, according to their own sense of their own
interests."[1]

All the objects of the Lodge amendment would be attained equally well
by the district system as by the proportional voting system. It is correct
to say with Senator Dickerson, author of what used to be called the New
Jersey plan of districting, that "upon a calculation of chances, the proba-
bilities of a fair expression of the public will are increased by dividing the
States into districts, and in the ratio of the number of districts to the
number of States."[2] But the district system is preferable to proportional
voting because it maintains the geographical constituencies and gives an
equal voice to equal units of population rather than to equal aggregations
of actual voters.

The significance of this last consideration in the distribution of a
state's electoral votes should not be overlooked. Under the district system
each group of, say, 300,000 persons residing in contiguous territory would
be entitled to cast one electoral vote, and it would cast this vote regardless
of how many of its citizens actually went to the polls. Under the proportional voting system the weight of these equal groups would vary with
the turnout. Bad weather, for instance, might give the urban communities
a fortuitous advantage over rural communities, as it does today under
the general-ticket system. Or an unusual interest in some local issue
might lead to a community's exercising a disproportionate influence in
the choice of a president. In fact, all the arguments which . . . justify

[1] 41 *Annals*, 169.
[2] 33 *Annals*, 142.

the principle of electoral voting as against nation-wide popular voting apply with equal force to the system of voting within a state—excepting only that which is based on the disproportion of the qualifications requisite for voting.

The manner of dividing a state into districts should present no special difficulties. Most of the early district system amendments provided for the establishment of as many districts in each state as that state was entitled to electors—the qualifications requisite for voting to be the same as those prescribed for congressional elections. The mode is inconvenient only in so far as it prevents the states from using the congressional district as the unit of voting. It might be better, therefore, if each state were divided by the legislature thereof into as many districts as will equal the number of representatives to which each state may be entitled in Congress. This would enable though it would not compel a state to use its congressional districts as its voting units. The two extra electoral votes to which each state is entitled under the Constitution might be given as a sort of game-winning bonus to the candidate carrying the state as a whole, or the state might be divided into two super-districts, each to cast one vote. In this connection I would point out that in Michigan in 1892 the election was by the people in districts, with the exception of two electors, one of whom was chosen by the eastern, the other by the western part of the state. Such an arrangement has the advantage of bringing into a clear view the principle of equal masses, equal votes. It also exhibits the compromise in the electoral system between the popular and federal principles.

One objection to the district system ought not to pass unnoticed. It is possible, indeed probable, that in districting a state for presidential elections the legislature thereof might resort to the iniquitous practice of gerrymandering. . . .

The solution would be, in the first place, to provide in the Constitution that the districts should be compact and contiguous territories containing, as nearly as practicable, equal numbers of inhabitants—language which appears in the act of 1911 prescribing a single-member district system for representatives. In the second place, it would be to entrust to Congress the same power to make and alter the state regulations regarding presidential elections that it now has in respect of the election of representatives. . . .

I would conclude, therefore, that, on a relative view of the merits and demerits of the district system and the proportional voting system, respectively, the palm must be awarded to the former. The district system is clearly to be preferred to the present general-ticket system.

QUESTIONS AND PROBLEMS

1. Summarize each of the arguments that Senator Lodge makes on behalf of his proposed constitutional amendment.

2. How does Senator Ferguson counter each of Senator Lodge's arguments?

3. What points does Miss Silva make against the Lodge proposal?

4. How does Senator Lodge answer the criticisms made of his proposal? How sound are his answers?

5. Is it fair to assess the operation of the Lodge proposal on the basis of past statistics and voting habits? Explain.

6. What is the "district system"? What are its merits and demerits?

7. Would the "district system" meet the objections of Senator Ferguson and Miss Silva? Why? Why not?

8. Why did most Southern Democrats support the Lodge amendment? Why did a substantial bloc of Republicans oppose it?

9. What explains the divided status of "liberals" and minority groups on the Lodge proposals?

10. State and defend your own views on (*a*) electoral reform in general; (*b*) the Lodge proposal; (*c*) the "district system"; (*d*) direct popular election of President and Vice President; (*e*) our present electoral system.

SELECT BIBLIOGRAPHY

Berdahl, Clarence A.: "Presidential Selection and Democratic Government," *Journal of Politics,* Vol. 11 (February, 1949), pp. 14–41. Examines the principal developments throughout the years in respect to presidential election. Approves the main features of the Lodge proposal.

Burns, James M.: "The Electoral College Meets—But Why?" *New York Times Magazine,* Dec. 12, 1948, pp. 14*ff.* A popular account stressing the inadequacy of the electoral college. Favors direct popular election but recognizes the greater political feasibility of the Lodge scheme.

"Congress Weighs Plan to Reform the Presidential Election Procedure," *Congressional Digest,* Vol. 29 (August–September, 1949). A brief historical and functional account of the electoral college. Contains a lengthy pro and con discussion of the 1949 proposals for reform.

Congressional Record, 81st Cong., 2d sess., Vol. 96, Pt. 1 (Jan. 25–Feb. 1, 1950). Contains the valuable Senate debate on Senate Joint Resolution 2. Affords opportunity to examine rebuttal of Lodge and Ferguson. Contains information on substitute proposals and pertinent amendments.

"Electoral College Reform," *New Republic,* Vol. 122 (Feb. 27, 1950), pp. 5–7. Concludes that reform presents many more opportunities for liberals than for conservatives to build solid majorities in every part of the nation.

Kallenbach, Joseph E.: "Presidential Election Reform," *Congressional Record,* 81st Cong., 1st sess., Vol. 95, Pt. 4 (Apr. 13, 1949), pp. 4448–4453. Indicts the present electoral-college setup. Examines current proposals for reform. Endorses the Lodge-Gossett proposal, refuting criticism made of it.

Kefauver, Estes: "Political Competition Will Help the South," *Virginia Quarterly Review*, Vol. 26 (Spring, 1950), pp. 268–276. Supports the Lodge amendment because it will strengthen the two-party system and bring about a healthy realignment of political forces in the South.

"Liberals and Electoral Reform," *Nation*, Vol. 170 (Mar. 18, 1950), pp. 244–245. Briefly sketches the political line-up on electoral reform. Recognizes disadvantages of the Lodge resolution but still favors it.

United States House of Representatives, Committee on the Judiciary, Subcommittee No. 1: *Hearings on House Joint Resolution 2, Amend the Constitution with Respect to Election of President and Vice-President*, 81st Cong., 1st sess., 1949. Contains testimony, historical data relative to electoral college, and newspaper and magazine editorials and articles.

United States House of Representatives, Committee on the Judiciary, Subcommittee No. 1: *Hearings on House Joint Resolution 11 and House Joint Resolution 19, Amend the Constitution to Abolish the Electoral College System*, 82d Cong., 1st sess., 1951. See, especially, the tentative conclusions of Miss Ruth C. Silva on Coudert, or district, system, pp. 272–273, supported by wealth of indispensable statistical material; and testimony of Lucius Wilmerding, Jr., pp. 48–67.

United States Senate, Committee on the Judiciary, *Hearings on Senate Joint Resolution 2, Election of President and Vice President*, 81st Cong., 1st sess., 1949. Includes testimony, statements by students of the problem, with majority of witnesses in favor of the proposed reform.

United States Senate, Senate Report 602, 81st Cong., 1st sess. Contains majority report (Pt. 1) and minority report (Pt. 2) on Senate Joint Resolution 2—the Lodge proposal. Summarizes the arguments on each side.

PART III: FEDERAL INSTITUTIONS

PROBLEM 9

CONGRESS

Can Congress Reform Itself?

Adverse criticism of Congress is probably one of America's favorite pastimes. According to its hostile critics, Congress is nothing more than a group of parasitic, do-nothing, rubber-stamping, unrepresentative windbags. Depending upon what "political ax" the critic is grinding, Congress is viewed as perverting the public interest in spineless surrender to a dictatorial executive, to insidious pressure groups, or to the clamor of the folks back home.

Much of this criticism, however, contains more rhetoric than fact and generates more heat than light.

The more reasonable critics insist that although not perfectly representative Congress does roughly follow public opinion. Despite the fact that Congress "has its share of crackpots, cheap publicity-seekers, shirkers, and chiselers," Senator Estes Kefauver maintains that most congressmen are honest, intelligent, and hard-working. They try conscientiously to reconcile sectional and national interests in the formation of sound public policy.

These same more fair-minded critics of Congress persist, nevertheless, in calling attention to its inefficient and obsolete legislative machinery. They highlight Congress's inability to take effective action. They underscore the difficulty of locating the responsible policy makers in Congress and of holding these formulators of policy accountable. They stress, too, the failure of Congress effectively to control the Executive and our expanded bureaucracy.

Much of this criticism—friendly and hostile—paved the way for the Legislative Reorganization Act of 1946, which provides an excellent starting point for an evaluation of the role of Congress in the modern world.

Everyone agrees that Congress must cope with tremendous problems in the years ahead. A prime problem is American leadership in securing world peace with justice. Intimately related to this problem are such issues as our strained relations with the Soviet Union,

187

the prevention of aggression, and the maintenance of military, economic, and ideological strength among free nations. Another major problem relates to the maintenance of a prosperous domestic economy. Can we provide optimum employment? Can we avoid future, catastrophic depressions? Can we sustain a high level of purchasing power for all consumer groups? A third significant problem centers around the continued fulfillment of American Democracy. This is the fight for better health, housing, and education. Involved here, too, is the endeavor to secure and preserve our civil rights. What role should Congress play in dealing with these problems?

Some view Congress as *the* policy-making organ. For them, Congress is the democratic kingpin. Congress should lead the country and not simply follow the Executive.

Others insist that Congress should merely be a representative debating society. It should debate policies submitted to it by a more adequately equipped Executive. Those in this group contend that Congress is incapable of formulating policy and that it should concern itself only with approving or rejecting a presidential program.

More realistic observers call for presidential-congressional teamwork. But what should be the respective roles of Congress and President on this team? Is Congress equipped to fulfill its designated role? If not, can Congress be equipped to fulfill this role? And by what means? Many of these questions are treated by former Senator Robert M. La Follette, Jr., in the following analysis of the achievements and shortcomings of the Legislative Reorganizaton Act of 1946.

La Follette, who was Chairman of the Joint Congressional Committee which prepared the Legislative Reorganization Act, stresses the need to complete the job started in the Act. Only in this way can Congress meet its twentieth-century responsibilities. Faith in the ability of Congress to reform itself is tempered by La Follette's recognition that the Act was only a good beginning.

In the concluding selection in this chapter James M. Burns examines the "roadblocks" to and the "boundaries" of congressional reform. The Reorganization Act, he maintains, achieved no basic reform but only a streamlining of doubtful permanence. He argues that even if Congress went on to finish the job started in 1946 fundamental reform could not be attained. Therefore Burns advances a negative answer to the focal question for this chapter: *Can Congress reform itself?*

THE LEGISLATIVE REORGANIZATION ACT WAS THE FIRST STEP TOWARD REFORM

BY ROBERT M. LA FOLLETTE, JR.*

[Former Senator Robert M. La Follette, Jr., was first elected Senator from Wisconsin in 1925 to fill the unexpired term of his famous father. "Young Bob" was reelected three times, his last term expiring January 3, 1947. A truly progressive legislator in domestic affairs, he was co-chairman of the renowned Senate Committee on Free Speech and the Rights of Labor. EDITOR.]

The Seventy-ninth Congress . . . wrestled with many knotty problems of deep significance to the American people. But none . . . [was] more fateful for its own future and the survival of democracy in America than the Legislative Reorganization Act of 1946. On June 10 [1946] the Senate upset the predictions of Capitol observers and passed this bill by a thumping three-to-one majority. And the House of Representatives followed suit on July 25. This legislative miracle was a great victory for better government.

Under our form of government Congress is supposed to be the center of political gravity in so far as it reflects and expresses the popular will in the making of national policy. In recent decades the center of gravity has been shifting to the executive branch and our national legislature has steadily declined in public esteem. Meanwhile, representative government has been eclipsed in other nations by the upsurge of dictatorship. These developments caused grave misgivings among the true friends of democracy in the United States, and gave rise to a series of independent surveys of the machinery and facilities of Congress.

Concerned lest it lose its constitutional place in the Federal scheme, and impressed with the need of self-improvement, the Seventy-eighth Congress authorized a joint committee of its own members to make a thorough study of its organization and operation. Congress . . . [, it was felt, was] neither organized nor equipped to perform adequately its main functions of determining policy, supervising the administration of the laws, controlling Federal expenditures, and representing the people. The Legislative reorganization bill . . . [was] the end-product of months and years of searching thought and hard work directed toward specific reforms and improvements [which would enable Congress to perform these main functions].

* "Congress Wins a Victory over Congress," *The New York Times*, VI (Aug. 4, 1946), pp. 11ff. By permission of the publisher and Mr. La Follette.

Determining Policy

[Prior to the passage of the Legislative Reorganization Act] Existing Congressional machinery for formulating legislative policy . . . [was] defective in several ways. Congress . . . [had] too many standing committees. For example, three Senate committees . . . [dealt] with problems of commerce and industry, five . . . [dealt] with public land problems and six with the rules and administration of the Senate. Four House committees . . . [dealt] with various public works, six with public lands and three with veterans' affairs. Responsibility for legislative action . . . [was] scattered among eighty-one little legislatures which . . . [went] their own way at their own pace and . . . [could not] act in concert.

Moreover, these standing committees in many instances . . . [had] overlapping and duplicating jurisdictions and . . . [struggled] with each other for control of proposed legislation. Their jurisdictions . . . [were] undefined in the Senate rules, while the definitions in the House rules . . . [were] the accretion of past practice rather than modern logic.

To remedy this crazy-quilt pattern the Legislative Reorganization Act will replace our jerry-built committee structure with a simplified system of . . . [fifteen committees in the Senate and nineteen in the House] corresponding with the major areas of public policy and administration. . . . The coordination of the Congressional committee system with the pattern of the administrative structure will improve the performance by Congress of its legislative and supervisory functions and provide direct channels of communication between the two branches. The spelling out in the rules of the legislative subjects to be handled by each reorganized committee should avoid jurisdictional disputes between them, such as the one in the Senate which caused the Missouri Valley Authority bill to be referred to three different committees.

Under the present committee set-up, policy-making in Congress is splintered and uncoordinated. Legislation on social security, housing, price control, and the like is developed and enacted without reference to its repercussions upon other segments of our economic life. To correct this condition the reform bill would have created majority and minority policy committees in each house to plan and coordinate the legislative program. The proposed policy committees were also designed to help crystallize the determination of party policy on major issues and to promote party responsibility for the performance of platform promises. Unfortunately, this provision was lost on the House side.

Much of the legislation now considered by Congress is so technical and complex as to render difficult a complete understanding of its subject-matter by busy legislators. Harassed by multiple committee assignments, beset by swarms of lobbyists and burdened with hundreds of constituent requests, the average Congressman has little time to study and understand all the important measures he votes on. [In addition,] Congress . . . [was] handicapped by the lack of adequate independent, technical advice necessary for wise law-making. Of its eighty-one standing committees, only half a dozen . . . [were] equipped . . . with competent professional staffs.

The Legislative Reorganization Act will improve this situation in several ways. It authorizes each standing committee to employ on merit four staff experts in its particular province to marshal the facts, plan the hearings, brief the committeemen, and prepare the reports on pending measures. The act also strengthens the legislative reference and bill drafting services of Congress, which . . . [were] seriously understaffed and underpaid. . . .

Review of Actions

Keeping a watchful eye on the administration of the laws it has enacted is another important function of our National Legislature. But Congress . . . [lacked] adequate facilities . . . for the continuous inspection and review of administrative action. The time has long since passed when we could anticipate every situation that might arise and provide for it in minute regulatory legislation.

With the expansion of Federal functions during the twentieth century, Congress has perforce created many commissions and agencies to perform them and has delegated its rule-making power to them. But it . . . [had] failed to provide any regular arrangements for follow-up in order to assure itself that administrative rules and regulations . . . [were] in accord with the intent of the law.

Instead, we have relied in large part upon sporadic investigations by special committees which have often served a salutary purpose. Special committees . . . have rendered valuable public services. But they have lacked continuity and have not provided the members of standing committees with direct knowledge of the information gathered.

In order to strengthen Congressional oversight of administrative performance, the Legislative Reorganization Act authorizes the standing committees of both houses to keep watch over the execution of the laws by the administrative agencies within their jurisdiction. Staffed with qualified specialists, these committees will conduct a continuous review of the activities of the agencies administering laws that were originally reported by the legislative committees. This over-sight job is too big to assign to a single committee of either house or even to a joint committee. Under this arrangement, it will no longer be necessary to set up special investigating committees from time to time.

The reconstructed standing committees will roughly parallel the reorganized administrative branch of the Government. They will be utilized not only as inspectors but also as vehicles of consultation and collaboration between Congress and the Administration. If properly developed, they will help [at the departmental level] to bridge the gap between the two branches . . . [of] our inherited system of separated powers.

As a further step toward better team-work between both ends of Pennsylvania Avenue, our bill provided for the establishment of a Joint Legislative-Executive Council at the top level. This Council would be composed of the majority policy committees in Congress and of the President and his Cabinet. It would seek to avoid the periodic deadlocks between Congress and the President which have hitherto caused dangerous crises in the conduct of the Federal Government.

The Legislature and the Administration have been at loggerheads on many major issues in recent years, and the people have been the chief victims of the resulting frustration and stalemate. As Speaker Rayburn has well said, "Our highest duty is to do everything in our power to see that there is team-work between the President and the Congress in carrying out the nation's business." The proposed Joint Council is a promising step in this direction. This provision was unacceptable, however, to the House leadership and was stricken from the bill before it reached the floor of the House.

Expenditures

Although Congress is charged by the Constitution with the power of the purse, there . . . [was] no correlation between Federal income and outgo. Control of the spending power . . . [was] divided between the Senate and the House of Representatives, and within each House between its revenue and appropriating committees. Taxes . . . [were] levied and appropriations made by many separate committees. The right hand . . . [did] not know what the left hand . . . [was] doing.

To strengthen budget control, the reform act provides for report not later than Feb. 15 of each year of a Legislative Budget recommending total Federal expenditures for the next fiscal year. This budget will be based upon estimates of receipts and expenditures for the ensuing fiscal, year, jointly made by the revenue and appropriating committees of both houses. The report shall be accompanied by a concurrent resolution adopting such budget, and fixing the maximum amount to be appropriated for expenditure in such year. If the estimated expenditures exceed the estimated receipts, the resolution will express the sense of the Congress that the public debt shall be increased in the amount of the excess. Although the provisions for enforcing this Legislative Budget were deleted in the lower chamber, I consider it a promising first step toward strengthening Congressional control of Federal expenditures.

There . . . [was] also much room for improvement in appropriation procedures. The hearings on departmental estimates . . . [were] held behind closed doors. The appropriation bills . . . [reached] the floor before members . . . had an opportunity to study the hearings and reports. The appropriation committees . . . [were] not adequately staffed to make a thorough scrutiny of departmental estimates. Each committee . . . [had] only eight clerks to cover the entire expenditure front. Some appropriations . . . [were] made on a permanent rather than an annual basis. Unexpended balances . . . [were] often reappropriated; and legislative riders . . . [were] attached to appropriation bills.

To correct these conditions, at least in part, the reorganization act provides for several improvements in the legislative phase of the budget process. It calls for public hearings on appropriation bills. Printed hearings and reports will be made available hereafter to members of the House at least three calendar days before floor consideration of the bills. Each appropriations committee is authorized to appoint additional qualified staff personnel. And its subcommittees would be provided with a professional staff of four experts in its field. The reappropriation of unobligated balances would be forbidden, except for continuing public works, and riders on appropriation bills would be banned. Approval of these provisions will go far, I believe, toward revitalizing legislative control of Federal spending.

Representing the People

An important part of every Congressman's job is the two-way task of representing the people in Washington and of informing the people back home about governmental problems. Now that Congress is in almost continuous session, however, direct contacts with constituents are few and far between. In the more leisurely days of yore the Legislature used to be in session only half the year, but with the rising burden of Congressional business, the legislative job has become a full-time one. By making more efficient use of Congressional time, however, it should be possible for Congress to take a regular annual recess each summer. This would insure the return of members to their constituencies for that refreshment of contact and exchange of opinion and experience so essential to responsive representative government.

For many Congressmen from populous States and districts the representative job is tending to degenerate into mere errand running. They are handicapped by a host of routine chores for constituents which they are glad to perform, but which leave them little time for the adequate study of national legislative problems. From one-half to three-fourths of the time of the average member nowadays is consumed with running errands and knocking on departmental doors on behalf of constituents.

Our bill would have mitigated this growing burden by authorizing each Senator and Representative to employ a well-qualified administrative assistant to aid him in receiving callers and handling his departmental business. The bill would also have provided for the creation of a steno-graphic pool to help Congressional offices with their mail during busy seasons. These provisions, which were designed to enable members to make more efficient use of their time, were unfortunately rejected by the House.

The bill raises the salaries of members of Congress to $12,500 and per-mits them to participate in the Federal retirement scheme now available to other Federal employes.

Finally, Congress [was and still] is overburdened by many local and private matters which divert its attention from national policy-making and which it ought not to have to consider. It functions as a common council for the District of Columbia. It . . . [served] as a tribunal for the settlement of private claims. It . . . [spent] much time on pension bills, the building of bridges over navigable waters, and other private and local matters. As a step toward reducing the non-legislative work load, the handling of private claims, pensions, and bridge bills is delegated by the reform act to appropriate administrative and judicial agencies. These time-and-labor-saving devices will help Congress to catch up with its business and avoid legislative log-jams like that of the closing days of the Seventy-ninth Congress.

Summary

Such in sketchy outline is our program for modernizing Congress. It is not a perfect measure. It omits several widely favored reforms which were either beyond the power of the committee to recommend, or upon which the committee was unable to agree, or of which the House leadership did not approve. I believe, however, that we have made a good beginning. Enactment of the Legislative Reorganization Act will go far to increase the efficiency of Congress, clear the legislative log-jams, and renew popular faith in American democracy.

By simplifying its operations, improving its relationships with the Executive Branch, and enabling it better to meet its responsibilities under the Constitution, the reorganization of Congress will speed up the legisla-ative process, quicken the solution of our pressing post-war problems, and help the country go forward with confidence into the future.

The ultimate implications of this proposed reorganization go far beyond the shadow of the Capitol and the Government buildings in Washington. As I see it, the future history of the world will depend in large measure on the success or failure of our representative form of Government in meeting the needs and desires of the people, especially in the crucial years just ahead. It is no secret that two conflicting ideologies are striving for power and favor in the world today. To the extent that we can obtain an efficient and responsive National Legislature that will truly meet the needs of the people, we will help to preserve our own democracy, liberties and form of Government.

CONGRESS CANNOT REFORM ITSELF

BY JAMES M. BURNS*

[Assistant Professor of Political Science at Williams College, James M. Burns once acted as legislative assistant to a member of Congress. His articles on parties, "Big Government," and electoral reform have appeared in the *American Political Science Review, The New York Times Magazine,* and other journals. EDITOR.]

The Legislative Reorganization Act of 1946 followed the usual pattern of modernization without basic reform. Once again minor committees were abolished and others consolidated. Expert advice was provided for the lawmakers, and committee powers were defined. Congressional salaries and expense accounts were increased. Touching a broad range of legislative activity, the act made other important repairs of creaking congressional machinery. Yet the filibuster, the seniority rule, the unrepresentative character of some of the committees, the power of the Rules Committee, were left unchanged. Even those who most warmly hailed this major streamlining of Congress knew that the worst problems remained.

Roadblocks to Reform

The men who rule Congress have a deep vested interest in the established way of life. Any attempt at major reform of House and Senate inevitably will mobilize the powerful opposition of the Representatives and Senators who benefit from the seniority rule, the Rules Committee, the power to filibuster, and other undemocratic devices in Congress.

* *Congress on Trial: The Legislative Process and the Administrative State* (New York: Harper, 1949), pp. 135–143. All footnotes, except citations for direct quotations, have been omitted. By permission of the publisher.

Who are the beneficiaries of the present system? They are the chairmen, the ranking majority members, and the ranking minority members of the committees, who owe their privileges and powers to the seniority rule. They are the Senators who use the filibuster—or the threat of a filibuster—to obstruct majority rule and to gain concessions for their states or sections. They are the Representatives who advance local and regional ends through the agency of the Rules Committee. They are the pressure politicians who find it easier to serve special interests as a result of the unrepresentative make-up of committees. Acting for various groups and belonging to either of the major parties, these Congressmen have a common talent for achieving minority rule by means of the present legislative machinery, under the guise of protecting minority rights. Together they bulwark the legislative status quo.

It is ironic that the devices in Congress which must be the targets of any major reform will be the very instruments most useful for preventing that reform. An attempt to abolish the filibuster would probably set off the longest and noisiest filibuster in history. Even taking the most quixotic view of the members of the Rules Committee, one can still hardly imagine their regarding favorably the trimming of their remaining powers. Nor is it likely that chairmen and ranking members of committees would use their supremacy over policy in Congress to aid those who would modify the seniority rule. The legislative journey of any real reform bill would be rough indeed.

The perils facing even a limited attempt to improve Congress were well demonstrated in the treatment of the Legislative Reorganization bill. Many factors in 1946 seemed to favor the chances of effective reform. There was wide popular support for congressional reorganization. The press almost unanimously favored it, and even among the experts, ranging from efficiency engineers to political scientists, united backing was found to exist. A large group of members of Congress had become only too familiar with legislative shortcomings in Washington, and they were pressing for modernization. Public opinion was so favorable that it was possible to bait the bill with lures for the legislators, such as substantial salary boosts, increased expert and clerical assistance, and longer recesses. The joint committee that was appointed to recommend legislation had such able members as Senator Elbert D. Thomas of Utah, Claude Pepper of Florida, Wallace H. White of Maine, and Representatives Mike Monroney of Oklahoma and Everett M. Dirksen of Illinois, and it enjoyed the services of George B. Galloway and other experts. The chairman of this committee and leader of the forces for reform was Senator Robert M. La Follette, Jr., of Wisconsin, an experienced parliamentarian and widely respected legislator.

But despite these advantages, and despite all the clamor for the reform and even the "reconstruction" of Congress, the bill that emerged from the joint committee was silent on the three most important matters—the Rules Committee, the filibuster, and the seniority rule. Indeed, the friends of the filibuster in the Senate had won their victory even before the battle started, for the resolution establishing the committee forbade it from making recommendations on House or Senate rules. Why the committee failed to suggest changes on seniority and the Rules Committee is not altogether clear. Senator La Follette later explained that the members could not agree upon "workable" alternatives.

Yet workable alternatives do exist. Committee chairmen could be selected by the majority party in the committee, or in the House or Senate as a whole. The tenure of office of the chairmen could be limited to a certain number of years. Or if the seniority rule was kept, it could be modified by a provision that would credit the committee member's tenure only while his party held power in Congress thus preventing him from storing up seniority simply because he came from a "safe" district or state.

Since the Reorganization Committee scorned these possibilities, one must conjecture whether they feared that a stronger bill could not pass the Congress. If such was the case, their fears were fully justified. Some Senators and Representatives raised such an outcry against even mild provisions of the reorganization bill that one wonders how they would have greeted a real effort at reform.

A section of the bill setting up a director of congressional personnel was the special target of patronage-minded Senators. "I want to bring the Government back to the people," declared Senator John L. McClellan of Arkansas. "One way to take it farther from the people is to put these little page boys under a personnel director."[1] The bill passed the Senate only after Senator LaFollette sacrificed this provision. The committee reorganization section went through the upper chamber intact despite the opposition of such Senators as the late Theodore G. Bilbo of Mississippi, who said: "I love the Republicans, but I do not like to surrender so many chairmanships while the Democratic Party is in power."[2]

The bill suffered a worse fate in the House. Among its provisions was one establishing seven-man majority and minority policy committees. It was hoped that these groups would introduce more party responsibility and coordinated policy-making into Senate and House. Since the bill did not change the seniority system and thus left control over policy largely in the hands of committee chairmen who had little interest in party responsibility, it is hard to see how this proposal would have had

[1] *Congressional Record,* June 10, 1946, p. 6556.
[2] *Ibid.,* p. 6556.

a major effect on Congress. But the speaker and the majority and minority leaders in the House regarded the proposition with suspicion. Acting, jointly, they refused to admit the reorganization bill to the House floor unless this provision, along with a section providing for a joint legislative-executive council, was struck out of the bill. Representatives Monroney and Dirksen were forced to oblige. A third proposal, permitting joint hearings of House and Senate committees on matters of common interest, was lost between the leadership and the House Rules Committee. The reorganization bill that passed the House on July 25, 1946, could be described only as a "hopeful beginning."

Passage of the reorganization measure, however, was only half the battle. The other, and perhaps more difficult, half was making it effective in operation. Assessing the results of the act a year after its passage, Representative Monroney found it to be only fifty per cent operative. Congress, he reported, had failed to follow through on what was considered one of the basic provisions of the act—the strengthening and coordinating of methods of handling fiscal matters. While faithfully carrying out the realignment of committees, it had only partially improved its staff and research facilities.

Other observers were even more critical. Both House and Senate committees set up under the new plan were censured for spawning scores of subcommittees that often took as much of the members' time as the original sprawling committee structure had done. Even major streamlining could not rid Congress of its bad habit of splitting up policymaking into fragments. And the appointment of administrative assistants, which the Senate had provided for in a separate act when the House deleted it from the reorganization bill, was dubbed "Operation Falseface" by one newspaper after most Senators had used up the $10,000 allowed not to hire administrative experts but to increase their regular secretaries' salaries.

To date the history of congressional efforts at self-improvement permits three generalizations. First, Congress has repeatedly modernized its machinery, organization, and procedure for the sake of greater efficiency, but it has largely failed to achieve basic and badly needed reforms. Second, any attempt at substantial reconstruction of Congress must cope with the opposition of the powerful elements in House and Senate that benefit from the status quo. And third, reorganization victories can be won on paper and later lost to the forces of inertia and standpattism.

Boundaries of Reform

To come to these cheerless conclusions is not, however, to offer a counsel of despair. The revolt of 1910–11 stands as a happier omen of the possibility of reform. Whatever the eventual effect of the overthrow of Cannonism, at least the rebels showed that undemocratic methods in Congress could be successfully challenged. Although the job is more formidable today than ever, the best hope for sweeping reforms of the legislative branch lies in the chance that some day a political upheaval will send to Congress a large majority of Senators and Representatives willing to abolish the undemocratic devices in each chamber. If such reform does come, it will doubtless be part of a great popular movement to achieve certain social ends, rather than an isolated effort to improve Congress.

Assuming the election of a Congress that was willing and able to carry out a sweeping self-reconstruction, to what extent would all the reforms within its power overcome the basic problems of minority rule and mal-representation in House and Senate? What are the boundaries of congressional self-improvement?

Congress can banish only those of its defects that originated in Congress. A successful house-cleaning by the legislative branch would mean alterations in the committees to make them more representative of the whole chamber. It would mean curbing the Rules Committee, abolishing the seniority system, limiting the filibuster, and changing antiquated rules of parliamentary procedure. All these were fashioned by members of Congress to achieve minority ends, or allowed to grow by default. They can be abolished by members in order to achieve majority rule.

But there are other problems that Congress cannot overcome, no matter how good its intentions or how stout its will. For these problems lie beyond its reach.

One of these difficulties beyond the range of House or Senate action is the gross inequality in the size of many congressional districts. . . . The power to determine the size of such districts is in the hands of the state legislatures. Congress has the theoretical right under the Constitution to alter state laws that permit numerical inequities in election districts, but it is highly doubtful that Congress could force the legislatures to reapportion districts fairly unless the latter were so minded. A congressional attempt to correct deliberate gerrymandering would be equally impracticable.

For unequal representation in its grandest form we must turn to the Senate, where one member may speak for over 13,000,000 persons and another for less than one-hundredth as many. Even in the unlikely event that a majority of the Senators were pledged to correct this inequity, they would be helpless to do anything about it.

Article V of the Constitution provides that no state can be deprived of equal representation in the Senate without its consent. Small but self-respecting states like Nevada and Vermont would never consent to decreased representation in the Senate. But the supreme irony here lies in the fact that even the people themselves—supposedly the source of all power in a democracy—cannot alter unequal representation in the Senate. For Article V is the amending clause of the Constitution and is itself not amendable. Even if it were amendable by the regular processes, the opposition of the thirteen smaller states would be enough to defeat it, for amendments must be ratified by conventions or legislatures in 36 states. In short, if most of the American people became aroused over mal-representation in the Senate, their only recourse would be extraconstitutional action, or revolution!

The final problem affecting Congress that is beyond its reach is the election of its members by states and districts rather than by the nation as a whole. The undue dependence of the Senator and Representative on state and locality . . . is the root evil that allows the other evils to flourish. No reorganization of Congress within the powers of that body will alter this stubborn fact. Which means also that the responsiveness of the legislators to pressure groups—a responsiveness that is due largely to the power of the special interests in states and districts—cannot be remedied by congressional action.

Recognizing this crucial dilemma, Americans have turned to hortatory attempts to induce locally elected Congressmen to act for the nation rather than for their state or district. Often, as part of their appeal, they quote the classic words of Edmund Burke, who told the electors of his district of Bristol in 1774: "Parliament is not a congress of ambassadors from different and hostile interests; which interests each must maintain, as an agent, and advocate, against other agents and advocates; but Parliament is a deliberative assembly of one nation, with one interest, that of the whole; where, not local purposes, not local prejudices, ought to guide, but the general good, resulting from the general reason of the whole. You choose a member indeed; but when you have chosen him, he is not a member of Bristol, but he is a Member of Parliament."

Unfortunately, few of our Congressmen succeed in becoming Edmund Burkes. The average member is content to play the role of "Washington representative" for his constituency. Even if he should decide to act chiefly in terms of the national interest, he would play into the hands of his political rivals at home who would remind the voters that the chief function of a representative is to protect his state or district.

As Professor Brogan has noted wryly: "The history of Congress is full of martyrs to the general welfare, but any given Congress is full of men who have had more sense than to prefer the general welfare to the local interest."[3]

The basic cause of the trouble is not the myopic legislator. It is the

[3] *The New York Times Magazine,* July 7, 1946, p. 8.

parochialism of American political life and the electoral system that fosters it. This parochialism is so intense in some areas that the best political weapon a local candidate can rig for himself is an assortment of out-of-state newspaper clippings attacking him.

The battle turns into a holy crusade against the outsiders. To be out of step with the nation as a whole becomes a badge of honor. The Rankins and Talmadges are but extreme examples of this phenomenon. Such parochialism is not a form of local independence or states' rights, but a form of the ethnocentrism that is at the root of so many of the world's ills.

The question "Can Congress reform itself?" must, then, be answered in the negative. Congress can reorganize itself, it can streamline itself, it can modernize itself. It cannot carry out the full range of needed legislative reforms. The political odds within the legislative branch, barring a political overturn of broad proportions, are against such reform, and even if Congress were able and willing to do what it could, important parts of a reform program are beyond its reach. The common saying "Only Congress can reform itself" is a glib distortion of the real situation.

This is not to say that Congress cannot be reformed, It can be. Nor is it to say that members of Congress cannot assist in the job of reform. They can and must. It is to say, however, that congressional reform can come about only as a part of far deeper changes in the organization of American politics, specifically in the party system. It is because they have recognized the partial helplessness of Congress in this respect that many students of government have turned their attention to the possibilities of a reconstruction of our whole government.

QUESTIONS AND PROBLEMS

1. According to La Follette, what are the main functions of Congress? Do you agree or disagree with this enumeration? Explain.

2. How does the Legislative Reorganization Act of 1946 enable Congress better to perform its functions?

3. What provisions, originally recommended by the Joint Committee on the Organization of Congress, were stricken from the bill before final passage? Why were these provisions deleted?

4. What problems, basic to genuine legislative reforms, were outside of the jurisdiction of the Joint Committee or were not recommended by the Committee? Why?

5. What steps might be taken to complete congressional reorganization?

6. Why does Burns believe that the Legislative Reorganization Act was merely a streamlining which did not basically alter Congress's century-old machinery?

7. What, for Burns, are the boundaries of congressional self-improvement? What facts establish these boundaries?

8. Do you agree with Burns that full-scale reform is beyond the reach of Congress? Explain.

9. Burns states that "congressional reform can come about only as a part of for deeper changes in the organization of American politics, specifically in the party system." Do you agree or disagree? Explain.

10. Some commentators argue that the Reorganization Act was a step in the wrong direction. They hold this to be true because, by strengthening Congress without building an adequate bridge to the Executive, the Act accentuates the tug-of-war that has historically existed between the White House and the other end of Pennsylvania Avenue. Analyze and criticize this argument.

SELECT BIBLIOGRAPHY

Chamberlain, Lawrence H.: *The President, Congress and Legislation* (New York: Columbia University Press, 1946). Demonstrates joint character of American legislative process. Roughly 40 per cent of 90 laws studied accredited to Congress; 30 per cent, to Congress and President jointly; 20 per cent to President; and 10 per cent to pressure groups. Congress more influential than many have thought.

Congressional Record, 79th Cong., 2d sess., Vol. 92, Pt. 5. For Senate debate on Legislative Reorganization Bill, pp. 6344–6575 *passim;* for House debate, pp. 10039–10104.

Galloway, George B.: *Congress at the Crossroads* (New York: Crowell, 1946). Analyzes evolution of essential functions of Congress since 1789, diagnoses defects, prescribes comprehensive program for reconstruction. Best single work on subject. Author was staff director of the Joint Committee on Organization of Congress.

Galloway, George B., *et al.: The Reorganization of Congress, A Report of the Committee on Congress of the American Political Science Association* (Washington: Public Affairs Press, 1945). Anticipated many recommendations of Legislative Reorganization Act. Called for constructive changes in organization and operation with view to more speed, better coordination, more efficient use of personnel, and unified leadership.

Harris, Joseph P.: "The Reorganization of Congress," *Public Administration Review*, Vol. VI (Summer, 1946), pp. 267–282. A critical review of key literature on congressional reorganization. Contends that 1946 reforms were primarily minor and not all desirable. Maintains that fundamental reforms are still needed.

Heller, Robert: *Strengthening the Congress* (Washington: National Planning Association, 1945). Analysis and recommendations of an efficiency engineer. Urged reduction of work load, emphasis on major policy, congressional-executive teamwork, fuller development of national viewpoint, and party responsibility within Congress. Advised elimination of filibuster, substitute for seniority rule, and $25,000 congressional salaries.

Kefauver, Estes: "What's to Be Done about Congress?" *The New York Times,* VI (Sept. 11, 1949), pp. 9ff. Treats Congress's fourfold troubles: (1) huge nonlegislative work load; (2) certain inefficient and undemocratic methods of work; (3) failure fully to enforce the Reform Act of 1946; (4) need to make two-party system work better. Calls for centrally strong, homogeneous parties. Author a senator from Tennessee.

Kefauver, Estes, and Jack Levin: *A Twentieth-century Congress* (New York: Duell, Sloan & Pearce, 1947). Examines present faults of Congress, analyzes its modern duties and responsibilities, and suggests specific ways to finish job of legislative reorganization.

Luce, Robert: *Congress: An Explanation* (Cambridge, Mass.: Harvard University Press, 1926). Five discriminating lectures by an experienced legislator. Source of congressional trouble is attempt to do more work than can be done well. Interesting comparison with current literature.

Smith, Thomas V.: *The Legislative Way of Life* (Chicago: University of Chicago Press, 1940). A defense by a philosopher-politician of legislative compromise. Holds tolerance and willingness to meet people halfway to be essential ingredients of the legislative way of life.

Topkis, Jay H.: "How Bad Is Congress?" *Political Science Quarterly,* Vol. 62 (December, 1947), pp. 531–551. Concerned with congressional responsiveness to public opinion during 12 years of Franklin Roosevelt's administration. Concludes that Congress, on the whole, did a rather good job.

United States Congress, Joint Committee on Organization: *Organization of Congress, Hearings,* 79th Cong., 1st sess., on House Concurrent Resolution 18, 1945. An invaluable source.

Voorhis, Jerry: *Confessions of a Congressman* (Garden City, N.Y.: Doubleday, 1947). A revealing case study, for the years 1937 to 1947, of the life of a conscientious, hard-working, and intelligent congressman.

Wilson, Woodrow: *Congressional Government* (Boston: Houghton, 1885). Written when Congress was dominant organ in American system. Criticizes divided authority and concealed responsibility.

Young, Roland: *This Is Congress* (New York: Knopf, 1943). Lucid account of Congress as a working democratic institution. Holds reorganization necessary to permit Congress to correlate and control myriad governmental activities.

PRESIDENT

Presidential Power: Peril or Promise?

"We are in the midst of a revolution, hitherto bloodless, but rapidly leading towards a total change of the pure republican character of the government and to the concentration of all power in the hands of one man." Surprisingly, the author of this statement was *not* former-president Herbert Hoover or Senator Robert A. Taft—the two outstanding critics of the New Deal and the Fair Deal. Nor was the "man" referred to the most controversial politico of our generation, Franklin D. Roosevelt. Nor was it Woodrow Wilson, nor even yet another wartime "dictator"—Abraham Lincoln. This charge was made by Henry Clay about President Andrew Jackson!

As the quotation above suggests, charges of presidential despotism have echoed and reechoed throughout the history of our nation. However, the problem of presidential power has become most critical in the present century. This is so largely because of the ever-thundering advance of the two major evil horsemen of our time: war and depression. The government has had to fight "hot wars" and wage "cold wars," prevent periodic business slumps, and raise per capita farm income. The government has also had to mitigate labor-management conflicts, check monopolistic trends, provide decent housing, education, and health facilities, and secure civil rights. These governmental efforts have literally forced a modern President to be what Woodrow Wilson called a "big man."

The Presidency, as a symbol of power for good and evil, has evoked varying responses.

In the first position advanced in this chapter, Edward S. Corwin, noted constitutional commentator, summarizes the view of those who fear presidential domination, if not dictatorship. He spells out the arresting case that could be made by an historically-minded member of Congress on behalf of the thesis that presidential power has increased, is increasing, and ought to be diminished.

Many who share this point of view warmly supported the Twenty-second Amendment to the Constitution, which limits the President to two elected terms in office. By this limitation it is hoped that the vast expansion of executive power will not lead to dictatorship and the destruction of representative democracy.

In the second extract presented herein, Corwin indicates why such fears of presidential dictatorship or domination are exaggerated. He notes the restraints on presidential power that still exist. He reminds us that public opinion has strongly demanded vigorous presidential leadership. Corwin, however, emphatically urges improved relationship between President and Congress as a possible solution to the still inadequate status of the Presidency today.

Harold Laski, in the following article, finds many blocks to the exercise of effective presidential leadership. Among these blocks are separation of powers, federalism, the party system, and the entrenched business community. Instead of fearing power, he maintains that power, equal to the function the President has to perform, and suitably criticized and controlled, should be given to the Chief Executive.

Mr. Laski endorsed the views of the President's (1937) Committee on Administrative Management which were, in general, shared by the Hoover Commission and which are strikingly pertinent today. Both groups supported administrative reorganization in the interest of a strong, energetic, unified, efficient, and responsible executive. Both groups agreed that the President must be given administrative authority commensurate with his constitutional responsibility. The Committee's views are included herein.

Clinton L. Rossiter, in the last article in this problem examines a much neglected but highly crucial problem relating to the Presidency: constitutional dictatorship. The Korean war and the tense state of American-Soviet relations heighten the meaning of his view that crises are becoming more "normal" and normality more exceptional. Rossiter urges that we recognize dictatorship as the method by which we may salvage democratic and constitutional government in the event of large-scale, atomic war or catastrophic, economic depression.

These selections deal with the peril, portent, promise, and possibility of presidential power. One should keep in mind that the points of view presented need not be mutually exclusive. The more exact questions raised are these:

Does the nation now suffer from the dangerous domination of the President? To what extent are our fears of dictatorship exaggerated? Should we increase the now restricted power of the President to advance American Democracy? Must and should we actually accept presidential dictatorship as the price for survival in a crisis-ridden world?

PRESIDENTIAL DOMINATION OUGHT TO BE DIMINISHED

BY AN HISTORICALLY MINDED MEMBER OF CONGRESS[*]

(with the aid of Edward S. Corwin)

[Edward Samuel Corwin, Emeritus Professor of Jurisprudence at Princeton since 1946, has long been an outstanding student of the American Constitution and the Presidency. Among his many publications are *The Constitution and What it Means Today*, *Constitutional Revolution Limited*, and *Total War and the Constitution*. EDITOR.]

The growth of presidential participation in legislation, and indeed the vast expansion in recent decades of the President's role in all the departments of national power, invites our attention afresh to a question which has been repeatedly raised regarding the Presidency in the past, but never with more insistency than in recent years, nor for more cogent reasons. This is the question whether the Presidency is a potential matrix of dictatorship. . . .

"Dictatorship," I hardly need to point out, is a word with a highly ambiguous connotation, so much so in fact that I propose to dismiss it at the outset in favor of a less colorful word, "domination." "A nation," it has been well said, "does not have to have a genuine dictator in order to suffer some of the evils of too great executive domination." Imagine an historically minded member of . . . Congress seeking to emulate Henry Dunning's exploit in 1781 in bringing George III's domination of Parliament to an end and with it, ultimately, British resistance to American independence. It would be the part of such a member to move a resolution declaring that "the power of the President has increased, is increasing, and ought to be diminished," and he would have little difficulty in making out an arresting case.

[*] *The President: Office and Powers* (New York: New York University Press, 3d ed. rev., 1948), pp. 353–356. By permission of the publisher.

First off, he would point out that impeachment, the weapon which the Constitution provides against presidential "high crimes and misdemeanors," is, as Jefferson early discovered, a "scarecrow," and that to galvanize this scarecrow into life would be to run the risk of reducing the Presidency to a nullity, as almost happened in 1868. Then, noting the decision in *Mississippi* v. *Johnson* shortly after the Civil War, he would assert, and quite correctly, that the President has no judicially enforcible responsibility either for nonperformance of his duties or for exceeding his powers. Congress's power of the purse, to be sure, still offers, he would concede, an obstacle to presidential usurpation which only an outright. *coup d'état* could entirely overcome. Nevertheless, as Dr. Wilmerding points out in his volume on *The Spending Power*, not only have Presidents been able repeatedly to break over statutory controls on expenditure, but such controls are usually much abated by Congress itself in times of emergency, exactly when expenditures are heaviest and presidential dominance is at its zenith. Indeed, generalizing from what happened during the Great Depression, the honorable member might urge that congressional largess in such situations, by the hold which it gives the executive branch upon millions of votes, enables the President to tighten his hold also upon Congress, and so creates a vicious circle whereby Congress pays for its own slow enslavement. And, continues our orator, when war activates the President's powers as Commander-in-Chief, the situation is still more disastrous from the point of view of opposing the power of the purse to presidential dominance. The sums which Congress is at such times under every compulsion to vote are colossal. The needs which they are designed to meet are forcefully represented, and are believed by the public, to be most urgent, while itemization is put out of the question by the demands of military secrecy; and unexpected turns in the military situation may aggravate all these difficulties. Moreover, the criticism which overworked congressional committees of varying competence can offer to the demands of the executive branch under such conditions will be haphazard in the extreme—an item of $50,000 may get more consideration, and certainly far better informed consideration than a presidential demand for billions.

Turning then to the course which constitutional interpretation has taken more and more pronouncedly in consequence of our participation in two world wars and under the stimulation of economic crisis, our fictioned Dunning will sketch a system of constitutional law which attributes to Congress a legislative power of indefinite scope, and the further power to delegate this indefinite power to the President *ad libitum*, and which attributes to the President in his own right an indefinite power to proclaim "emergencies" and thereby appropriate an indefinite "aggregate of powers" in meeting them. At the same time, he will show that the President, not without judicial encouragement, has been able to cut loose from the two most important controls which the Constitution originally imposed upon his direction of foreign policy. With our four greatest wars directly ascribable to presidential policies, the exercise by Congress of its power "to declare war" has become, he will assert, an empty formality; while by means of the executive-agreement device the President has emancipated himself from his constitutional partner in pledging the national faith.

And at this point our hypothetical member will perhaps devote a word or two to the advantages which a President today enjoys in appealing to the multitude. Propaganda, he will point out, once the casual art of a gifted few, has been within recent times converted into a skilled technique, which is supplemented by the most ingenious gadgets of mechanical science. Today the President of the United States can at any time request that the nation's broadcasting channels be cleared so that he may "chat" with the people, and the request will be granted pronto, for are not all the available frequencies allocated to companies on federal licenses which terminate every six months? Besides, every member of his administration is a propagandist and has access to the radio at will, although a first-class radio voice may not be the heaven-sent gift of all.

Finally, our orator will note certain of the consequences of the demise of the anti-third-term tradition. A third-term—*a fortiori* a fourth-term—President is bound to dominate not only his party, and Congress through it, but the executive agencies, most of whose chief personnel he will have appointed, and even the courts, a large proportion of whose judges will be his appointees. And in proportion as a President displays reluctance to quit office will the strength of the vested interests supporting his continuance in it wax greater.[1]

FEARS OF PRESIDENTIAL DICTATORSHIP OR DOMINATION ARE EXAGGERATED BUT REFORM IS STILL NECESSARY

BY EDWARD S. CORWIN*

The picture [drawn by the historically minded member of Congress, seeking to demonstrate that the power of the President has increased,

[1] Since the passage of the Twenty-second Amendment the President will have less time in which to dominate his party, Congress, the executive agencies, and the courts. EDITOR.

* *The President: Office and Powers* (New York: New York University Press, 3d ed., rev., 1948), pp. 356–358. By permission of the publisher.

is increasing, and ought to be diminished] is unquestionably overdrawn in some of its details. Thus, if it is true that impeachment is no longer to be reckoned with as an effective weapon in the arsenal of liberty, this is partly due to the fact that Presidents have in the past kept pretty clear of courses which might make people think seriously of so extreme a discipline. Again, although there is no court which is entitled to order a President to perform his duties or to enjoin him from exceeding his powers, yet the subordinates through whom he must ordinarily act do not share his immunity in this respect; and his orders are at all times subject to judicial inquiry into their validity when anybody bases on them any claim or justification whatsoever. Also, his subordinates are, ordinarily, liable at any time to be summoned before a congressional investigating committee and put to the question regarding their official conduct.

Nor is it by any means the case that Congress's control of the purse strings is ineffective as a restraint on the executive branch. To the contrary, it is potentially a highly effective restraint, which with improved machinery within the power of Congress to provide could be made actual. Again, our orator did not find it to his purpose to mention that in the "concurrent resolution" a device today exists by which sweeping delegations of power to the President can be recalled by the houses without the necessity of obtaining presidential consent; nor that ordinarily executive agreements, unlike treaties, do not have the force of law unless they have been sanctioned by Congress. And other lesser exaggerations or omissions might be indicated were it worth while.

What is more, that is a seriously contracted point of view from which presidential domination appears as solely a *menace* to democratic institutions. Why, in the face of our democratic institutions, has presidential domination attained its present proportions? Indeed, must not this development be considered as a fulfillment in a measure of those institutions, and as an answer to some demand from public opinion, on which by hypothesis they are grounded? Without doubt, such is the case, and especially as regards presidential leadership in legislation; nor is it difficult to identify this demand—it is the demand that the government assume an *active* role in matters of general concern, and especially in matters affecting the material welfare of the great masses of the people. This may eventually turn out to have been a demand impracticable of beneficial realization in the long run; but of its existence there can be no present question.

So we are not free to blame presidential leadership as such for those intrusions upon "liberty," as it has sometimes been understood, which present expanded theories of governmental functions entail. This at least must be conceded. We are free, on the other hand, to ask whether presidential leadership, as we know it, is as good an instrument of the demand which brought it into existence as conceivably it might be. Presidential leadership sets itself the task of guiding legislation; and the critics are numerous who say that it does the job badly. To make the indictment more specific, it is asserted that presidential leadership is discontinuous, not to say spasmodic; that it is too dependent on the personality of the President rather than on the authority of the office; that it is often insufficiently informed, especially as regards the all-important matter of administrative feasibility; and, finally, that the contact between the President and Congress is most faulty, being, in fact, at the mercy of either's whim. These contentions also have too much obvious validity to make it worth while to attempt to refute them or even to qualify them nicely.

In short, we are confronted, not with a *single* problem, but with *two* problems: first, the problem of bringing presidential power in *all* its reaches under some kind of institutional control; secondly, the problem of relieving presidential leadership in the legislative field of its excessive dependence on the accident of personality and the unevenness of performance which this involves. Is it possible that these two problems admit of a common solution? At least, so far as they do, it is evident what form the solution must take—*the provision, namely, of some kind of improved relationship between President and Congress.*

THE UNITED STATES NEEDS STRONG PRESIDENTIAL LEADERSHIP

BY HAROLD J. LASKI*

[Harold J. Laski, who died in 1950, was a brilliant and versatile political scientist. Although his writings are frequently colored by the point of view of British socialism, his forthright arguments clarified and popularized many of the political concepts of our time. EDITOR.]

No one who studies the proceedings of the constitutional convention can fail to see one emphasis in its construction of the presidency which has remained a living part of the traditions in which it is imbedded.

* The American Presidency (New York: Harper, 1940), pp. 12–15, 21, 24–25, 243–244, 277–278 passim. By permission of the publisher.

Fear of executive despotism is, for reasons intelligible enough in the light of American origins, evoked in the public approach to the office. . . .

[Several reasons account for the fear of and challenge to a strong executive.] Partly they lie in the constitutional position of the office itself. The president is at no point the master of the legislature. He can indicate a path of action to Congress. He can argue, bully, persuade, cajole; but he is always outside Congress and subject to a will he cannot dominate. He is, while in office, the national leader of his party; of set purpose, he is not, and cannot be, its congressional leader. Even if his party has a majority in both houses, he has to win the good will of his party in Congress; he cannot exact it. . . .

He can intiate policy; he cannot control it. The emergency of war apart, that has been the constant characteristic of his position ever since 1789. . . .

[Another] . . . reason for this suspicion of the strong executive lies, I believe, in the reasons that have led to his choice. In each case, so far, his election has been the outcome of a popular revolt, more or less conscious, against the business man's dominating influence upon the exercise of political power. Jefferson represented a revolt of the West against the narrow property interests of Eastern Federalism. Jackson embodied the nascent agrarian suspicion of Eastern banking power. Cleveland and Theodore Roosevelt were both, as it were, protest presidents—the one against corruption, and Northern domination of the South; the other against the growth of corporate power. Woodrow Wilson embodied the hostility of the little man to the trusts, his fear of being dominated by the octopus of Wall Street. Franklin Roosevelt was elected, as he himself said, by the "forgotten man," the trade unionist, the worker on relief, the little shopkeeper, the tenant-farmer, the millions, in short, who had abruptly discovered the hollowness of the permanent prosperity the Coolidge-Mellon epoch had seemed to foreshadow. . . .

[My argument] . . . assumes only that the political evaluation of the last forty years has shown that the modern state requires a strong executive, whose plans, of course suitably criticized and controlled, form the staple food of legislative digestion. . . .

My argument is . . . that a democracy needs clear direction, and that it cannot get this unless the central motive force in a political system rests in the executive's hands. He may be right or wrong; what is important is that the plan put into operation should essentially be plans for which he is willing to accept full responsibiity. . . .

America needs strong government; it needs strong leadership to attain strong government; only the president, granted its characteristics, can provide it with the leadership it requires. But against these needs must be set all the traditional impetus of the system. The Constitution makes against it partly by its separation of powers and partly by the way in which it has distributed functions between the states and the federation. It has now become of pivotal interest to the forces of privilege in the United States to maintain for their benefit both that separation and that distribution; and it must be remembered that, constitutional amendment apart, the degree to which that distribution can be effectively transcended lives precariously by the accidental composition of the Supreme Court.

The Constitution makes against it; so also . . . does the party system on its present foundations, since, except for emergencies, it enthrones the conservative forces in permanent power. These forces live by their ability to maintain weak government, for strong government, in the sense of a government with a continuously positive direction, is necessarily hostile to their interests. That can, I suggest, be seen from the intensity of their antagonism to the New Deal; they have greeted a body of legislation in general as mild as that of the Liberal government of 1906 in England as though it were inaugurating an epoch of red revolution. Since weak government is the source from which these forces draw their power in the state, their impact upon parties is always a discouragement to leadership in a positive form. And this discouragement can take many shapes. It may appear as sectionalism. It may appear through the frustration of the executive by an encouragement of opposition to its policies in the legislature. It may appear as the exploitation of the traditional American fear of strong government; there are few accusations to which the American public lends a more ready ear than to that of dictatorship, and that even when the very foundations of the system paralyze, almost a priori, any prospect of its constitutional advent. . . .

Power, no doubt, is always a dangerous thing; and the temptation to its abuse, as no generation has learned more surely than our own, the subtlest poison to which a man may succumb. Yet power is also opportunity, and to face danger with confidence is the price of its fulfilment. That is why I end with the emphasis that the president of the United States must be given the power commensurate to the function he has to perform. It must be given democratically; it must be exercised democratically; but, if he is to be a great president, let us be clear that it must be given. With all its risks, its conference is the condition upon which the American adventure may continue in that form of which its supreme exponents have most greatly dreamed. To withhold it, or to frustrate its ample operation, is to jeopardize that adventure. For great power alone makes great leadership possible; it provides the unique chance of restoring America to its people.

EFFECTIVE MANAGEMENT DEMANDS A STRONG EXECUTIVE

BY THE PRESIDENT'S COMMITTEE ON ADMINISTRATIVE MANAGEMENT*

[Two members of this 1937 Committee—its Chairman, Louis Brownlow, and Luther Gulick—are outstanding public administrators; the third member—Charles E. Merriam—is a distinguished Professor (now Emeritus) of Political Science at the University of Chicago. EDITOR.]

The need for action in realizing democracy was as great in 1789 as it is today. It was thus not by accident but by deliberate design that the founding fathers set the American Executive in the Constitution on a solid foundation. Sad experience under the Articles of Confederation, with an almost headless Government and committee management, had brought the American Republic to the edge of ruin. Our forefathers had broken away from hereditary government and pinned their faith on democratic rule, but they had not found a way to equip the new democracy for action. Consequently, there was grim purpose in resolutely providing for a Presidency which was to be a national office. The President is indeed the one and only national officer representative of the entire Nation. There was some hesitation on the part of some timid souls in providing the President with an election independent of the Congress; with a longer term than most governors of that day; with the duty of informing the Congress as to the state of the Union and of recommending to its consideration "such Measures as he shall judge necessary and expedient"; with a two-thirds veto; with a wide power of appointment; and with military and diplomatic authority. But this reluctance was overcome in the face of need and a democratic executive established.

Equipped with these broad constitutional powers, reenforced by statute, by custom, by general consent, the American Executive must be regarded as one of the very greatest contributions made by our Nation to the development of modern democracy—a unique institution the value of which is as evident in times of stress and strain as in periods of quiet.

As an instrument for carrying out the judgment and will of the people of a nation, the American Executive occupies an enviable position among the executives of the states of the world, combining as it does the elements of popular control and the means for vigorous action and leader-

* United States President's Committee on Administrative Management: *Report . . . with Studies of Administrative Management in the Federal Government* (Washington: Government Printing Office, 1937), pp. 1–3, 53 *passim.*

ship—uniting stability and flexibility. The American Executive as an institution stands across the path of those who mistakenly assert that democracy must fail because it can neither decide promptly nor act vigorously.

Our Presidency unites at least three important functions. From one point of view the President is a political leader—leader of a party, leader of the Congress, leader of the people. From another point of view he is head of the Nation in the ceremonial sense of the term, the symbol of our American national solidarity. From still another point of view the President is the Chief Executive and administrator within the Federal system and service. In many types of government these duties are divided or only in part combined, but in the United States they have always been united in one and the same person whose duty it is to perform all of these tasks.

Your Committee on Administrative Management has been asked to investigate and report particularly upon the last function; namely, that of administrative management—the organization for the performance of the duties imposed upon the President in exercising the executive power vested in him by the Constitution of the United States. . . .

Facing one of the most troubled periods in all the troubled history of mankind, we wish to set our affairs in the very best possible order to make the best use of all of our national resources and to make good our democratic claims. If America fails, the hopes and dreams of democracy over all the world go down. We shall not fail in our task and our responsibility, but we cannot live upon our laurels alone. . . .

Fortunately the foundations of effective management in public affairs, no less than in private, are well known. They have emerged universally wherever men have worked together for some common purpose, whether through the state, the church, the private association, or the commercial enterprise. They have been written into constitutions, charters, and articles of incorporation, and exist as habits of work in the daily life of all organized peoples. Stated in simple terms these canons of efficiency require the establishment of a responsible and effective chief executive as the center of energy, direction, and administrative management; the systematic organization of all activities in the hands of a qualified personnel under the direction of the chief executive; and to aid him in this, the establishment of appropriate managerial and staff agencies. There must also be provision for planning, a complete fiscal system, and means for holding the Executive accountable for his program. . . .

In the light of these canons of efficiency, what must be said of the Government of the United States today? Speaking in the broadest terms at this point . . . we find in the American Government at the present time that the effectiveness of the Chief Executive is limited and restricted, in spite of the clear intent of the Constitution to the contrary; that the work of the Executive Branch is badly organized; that the managerial agencies are weak and out of date; that the public service does not include its share of men and women of outstanding capacity and character; and that the fiscal and auditing systems are inadequate. The weaknesses are found at the center of our Government and involve the office of the Chief Executive itself. . . .

Your Committee fully appreciates that there is no magic in management alone. Management is a servant, not a master—a means, not an end, a tool in the hands and for the purposes of the Nation. Public service is the service of the common good in peace or war and will be judged by this standard. Not merely lower unit costs but higher human happiness and values are the supreme ends of our national life, and by these terms this and every other system must finally be tested. Good management will promote in the fullest measure the conservation and utilization of our national resources, and spell this out plainly in social justice, security, order, liberty, prosperity, in material benefits, and in higher values of life. The adjustments and arangements we suggest have no other purpose or justification than better public service for our people through better administrative management.

It may be said that there is danger that management itself will grow too great and forget where it came from or what it is for—in the old and recurring insolence of office. But in the judgment of your Committee, based upon broad observation of the bewildering sweep of recent events here and elsewhere, the really imminent danger now is that our democracy and perhaps others may be led by false or mistaken guides to place their trust in weak and faltering inaction, which in the bitter end runs to futility and defeat. In the late war, democracies showed vast strength and tenacity in times of strain that racked every fiber of the ship of state. And now we face and will master the critical tasks or reorganization and readjustment of many tangled parts of our national life on many new frontiers. The injustice and oppression intertwined with solid good in our American system will not always yield without a firm display of our national constitutional powers. Our national will must be expressed not merely in a brief, exultant moment of electoral decision, but in persistent, determined, competent day-by-day administration of what the Nation has decided to do.

Honesty and courage alone are not enough for victory, either in peace or in war. Intelligence, vision, fairness, firmness, and flexibility are required in an asembled, competent, strong organization of democracy. To falter at this point is fatal. A weak administration can neither advance nor retreat successfully—it can merely muddle. Those who waver at the sight of needed power are false friends of modern democracy. Strong executive leadership is essential to democratic government today. Our choice is not between power and no power, but between responsible but capable popular government and irresponsible autocracy.

The forward march of American democracy at this point of our history depends more upon effective management than upon any other single factor. The times demand better governmental organization, staffed with more competent public servants, more free to do their best, and coordinated by an Executive accountable to the Congress and fully equipped with modern tools of management. Thus the President will have effective managerial authority over the Executive Branch commensurate with his responsibility under the Constitution of the United States.

PRESIDENTIAL DICTATORSHIP MAY SAVE DEMOCRATIC AND CONSTITUTIONAL GOVERNMENT

BY CLINTON L. ROSSITER*

[Clinton Lawrence Rossiter, III, Assistant Professor of Government at Cornell University, is the author of *Documents in American Government* and numerous magazine articles on the American Presidency and party system. EDITOR.]

This is a book about dictatorship and democracy. Its treatment of these two patterns of government is not conventional. Instead of setting the one against the other, it proposes to demonstrate how the institutions and methods of dictatorship have been used by the free men of the modern democracies during periods of severe national emergency. It is written in frank recognition of a dangerous but inescapable truth: "No form of government can survive that excludes dictatorship when the life of the nation is at stake."

I can quote Lord Acton's dictum on the corrupting influence of power as approvingly as any man, and I am fully aware of the transient and long-range dangers to constitutional government inherent in this principle which I, following the lead of others, have chosen to call *constitutional dictatorship*. No person professing the democratic faith can take much delight in a study of constitutional dictatorship; the fact remains that it has been with us exactly as long as constitutional government, and has been used at all times, in all free countries, and by all free men. . . .

* *Constitutional Dictatorship* (Princeton, N.J.: Princeton University Press, 1948), pp. vii, 4–5, 7, 286–288, 306–309, 314 *passim*. By permission of the publisher.

The word *dictatorship* should be no cause for alarm. The *dictator* in Mr. Webster's dictionary is primarily "one appointed to exercise, or one exercising, absolute authority in government, esp. in a republic." Indeed, the qualifying adjective *constitutional* is almost redundant, for the historical conception of dictatorship was that it could not be other than constitutional. The original dictatorship, that of the Roman Republic, involved the legal bestowal of autocratic power on a trusted man who was to govern the state in some grave emergency, restore normal times and government, and hand back this power to the regular authorities just as soon as its purposes had been fulfilled. The phrase *constitutional dictatorship*, hyperbole though it may be in many instances, will serve as the general descriptive term for the whole gamut of emergency powers and procedures in periodical use in all constitutional countries, not excluding the United States of America.

The principle of constitutional dictatorship finds its rationale in these three fundamental facts: first, *the complex system of government of the democratic, constitutional state is essentially designed to function under normal, peaceful conditions, and is often unequal to the exigencies of a great national crisis.* . . .

Therefore, *in time of crisis a democratic, constitutional government must be temporarily altered to whatever degree is necessary to overcome the peril and restore normal conditions.* This alteration invariably involves government of a stronger character; that is, *the government will have more power and the people fewer rights.* . . .

Finally, *this strong government, which in some instances might become an outright dictatorship, can have no other purposes than the preservation of the independence of the state, the maintenance of the existing constitutional order, and the defense of the political and social liberties of the people.* . . .

. . . The United States . . . offer[s] a striking example of a potent crisis institution: the independent President. Whether or not it was planned this way makes little difference; the fact is that the Presidency today, when properly handled, is as powerful an instrument of constitutional dictatorship as the office of Prime Minister of Great Britain. Its power is the boundless grant of executive authority found in the Constitution, supplemented by broad delegations of discretionary competence from the national legislature; its limitations are the political sense of the incumbent and the patience of the American people; its effectiveness rests in the personality and energy of the President himself and the circumstances with which he has to deal. To a Van Buren, a Buchanan, or a Taft the Presidency is an instrument of government whose powers and status are virtually the same in peace, war, rebellion, or depression. To a

Lincoln, a Wilson, or a Roosevelt it becomes in time of national crisis a mighty weapon of freedom, absolute in its authority and conditioned only by its purpose: the preservation of the American constitutional system and American liberty.

Because it is so ideal a matrix for constitutional dictatorship, the Presidency does present a serious potential danger to the American people. It is for them to be eternally vigilant, to demand that this vast display of power be wielded in their behalf, as hitherto it always has been, and not against them. It is not too much to say that the destiny of this nation in the Atomic Age will rest in the capacity of the Presidency as an institution of constitutional dictatorship.

. . . Dictatorship is no sure panacea for a democratic nation's woes, especially in an economic crisis. Other things being equal, however, a great emergency in the life of a constitutional democracy will be more easily mastered by the government if dictatorial forms are to some degree substituted for democratic, and if the executive branch is empowered to take strong action without an excess of deliberation and compromise. . . .

That constitutioinal dictatorship does have a future in the United States is hardly a matter of discussion. Dismal and distressing as the prospect may be, it seems probable that in the years to come the American people will be faced with more rather than fewer national emergencies. Even if Manhattan Project had not been crowned with quite the awful success that it was, the continuing tensions of a world of sovereign nations and the irrepressible economic convulsions of the twentieth century would have made it plain that the second World War was not to be the last but only the latest of the American Republic's great national crises. The possiblity of an atomic war only establishes emergency government a little more prominently in the frightening array of this nation's problems. Not that martial law is going to save us from an atomic attack; still, it may be the only glue available when it comes time to pick up the pieces. . . .

There are two general proposals [for governmental reform] which this book has to offer. The first is not so much a reform as it is a defense of the status quo. The inherent emergency power of the President of the United States—the power used by Lincoln to blockade the South, by Wilson to arm the merchantmen, and by Roosevelt to effect the destroyer deal—should be left intact and untrammeled. Granted that the indefinite vastness of this power presents a potential threat calling for unceasing vigilance on the part of Congress and the electorate; granted that some uses of this power, for instance federal martial law and the system of "indirect sanctions" created by Wilson and Roosevelt, might at least be defined and given statutory basis; granted even the cogency of Henry C. Lockwood's anguished "Woe to that country whose destinies are involved in the fortunes of any one man, however great and pure he may be!"—still, the memorable deeds of Lincoln, Wilson, and Roosevelt are persuasive reminders that if there must be an ultimate authority in the government of the United States to take unprecedented, dictatorial, or even unconstitutional action in moments of extreme national danger, it must rest with the President. The steady increase in executive power is unquestionably a cause for worry, but so too is the steady increase in the magnitude and complexity of the problems the President has been called upon by the American people to solve in their behalf. They still have more to fear from the ravages of depression, rebellion, and especially atomic war than they do from whatever decisive actions may issue from the White House in an attempt to put any such future crises to rout. What was declared . . . [earlier] may well be repeated here: it is not too much to say that the destiny of this nation in the Atomic Age will rest in the capacity of the Presidency as an institution of constitutional dictatorship.

The second general proposal is of equal importance and even more present signficance. If Congress is to play a salutary part in future emergency governments in this country, then its functions of legislation, investigation, and control must be streamlined and strengthened. It is particularly in respect to the reorganization of Congress that the various proposals for general reform—only partially realized in the La Follette-Monroney Act of 1946—will be as beneficial to emergency government as they will be to regular government. If it is the President's duty to make emergency government more effective and dictatorial, it is Congress's to make it more responsible and constitutional. If some future strong-minded President is not to run wild in his choice of extraordinary ways and means of exercising his vast powers as constitutional dictator, then Congress is going to have to turn out legislation which will define without constricting and codify without emasculating some of the President's constitutional and statutory powers for emergency action. . . .

Constitutional dictatorship is today, and will continue to be in the stormy years before us, one of the most urgent problems to be solved by the men of the constitutional democracies. It is more than just a problem; it is compelling and anxious reality. For who in this year . . . would be so blind as to assert that the people of the United States, or of any other constitutional democracy, can afford again to be weak and divided and jealous of the power of their elected representatives? The Bomb has settled once and for all the question whether the United States can go back to being what Harold Laski has labeled (a little too contemptuously) a "negative state." You can't go home again; the positive state is here to stay, and from now on the accent will be on power, not limitations.

Power, however, does not necessarily mean despotism, and merely because we are to have a government strong enough to deal with the Atomic Age does not mean that we are henceforth to be slaves. Not at all, for if the crisis history of the modern democracies teaches us anything, it teaches us that power can be responsible, that strong government can be democratic government, that dictatorship can be constitutional. From this day forward we must cease wasting our energies in discussing whether the government of the United States is to be powerful or not. It is going to be powerful or we are going to be obliterated. Our problem is to make that power effective and responsible, to make any future dictatorship a constitutional one. No sacrifice is too great for our democracy, least of all the temporary sacrifice of democracy itself.

QUESTIONS AND PROBLEMS

1. State the "arresting case" that Professor Corwin's historically minded member of Congress makes on behalf of the thesis that presidential power ought to be diminished.

2. According to Corwin, what factors indicate that the picture of presidential dictatorship or domination is overdrawn?

3. Do *you* think the picture is overdrawn? Using recent examples document whatever answer you make.

4. How, and on what grounds, would Corwin, Laski, and the President's Committee on Administrative Management answer the following question: Is presidential leadership "as good an instrument of the demand which brought it into existence as conceivably it might be"?

5. Assuming that you accept Corwin's analysis, what kind of improved relationship between President and Congress do *you* think is necessary in order to remedy the inadequate status of the Presidency today?

6. Drawing your examples from recent history illustrate the blocks that Laski finds to the exercise of effective presidential leadership.

7. Why does Laski favor a strong executive? What is suitable criticism and control of such a strong President?

8. Discuss the relation between these two views of the President's Committee on Administrative Management: (*a*) "Strong executive leadership is essential to democratic government today"; and (*b*) "The forward march of American democracy at this point of our history depends more upon effective management than upon any other single factor."

9. According to Rossiter what is the meaning of "constitutional dictatorship"?

10. What must we do to make any future presidential dictatorship constitutional?

SELECT BIBLIOGRAPHY

Binkley, Wilfred E.: *President and Congress* (New York: Knopf, 1947). An historical analysis. Reveals forces supporting and opposing strong presidents and weak presidents.

Brownlow, Louis: *The President and the Presidency* (Chicago: Public Administration Service, 1949). Maintains President needs authority to exercise effectively power he already has.

Herring, E. Pendleton: *Presidential Leadership* (New York: Farrar & Rinehart, 1940). Asserts presidential leadership necessary but holds it must maintain confidence of nation. States that talk of dictatorship is ridiculous in view of presidential-congressional struggles.

Milton, George Fort: *The Use of Presidential Power* (Boston: Little, Brown, 1944). Focuses attention on Washington, Jefferson, Jackson, Lincoln, Cleveland, Theodore Roosevelt, Wilson, and Franklin Roosevelt. Asserts that worst periods of our history have been when presidents were weak and Congress strong.

Patterson, C. Perry: *Presidential Government in the United States* (Chapel Hill, N.C.: University of North Carolina Press, 1947). Argues that responsible cabinet government is best possible means to prevent permanent establishment of irresponsible presidential government.

Rankin, Robert S. (ed.): *The Presidency in Transition* (Gainesville, Fla.: Kallman Publishing Co., 1949). Reprinted from *Journal of Politics,* Vol. 11 (February, 1949). A competent, provocative, and up-to-date evaluation of the Presidency in relation to presidential selection, party politics, Congress, the Supreme Court, labor disputes, emergencies, powers as Commander in Chief, foreign relations, world affairs, administration, and presidential succession and inability.

Rodell, Fred: *Democracy and the Third Term* (New York: Howell, Soskin, 1940). An excellent handbook written before FDR's third-term victory. May be profitably consulted by both sides. Contends that danger of "dictatorship" is a "red herring."

Roosevelt, Theodore: *An Autobiography* (New York: Scribner, 1913). Believed in President's right and duty to do anything that needs of nation demanded, unless forbidden by Constitution or laws.

Stein, Charles W.: *The Third-term Tradition* (New York: Columbia University Press, 1943). Written after FDR smashed the no-third-term tradition. Maintains that constitutional amendment ensuring a single or double term would prevent Presidency from so easily developing into unbridled despotism.

Taft, William Howard: *Our Chief Magistrate and His Powers* (New York: Columbia University Press, 1916). Stated that the Teddy Roosevelt doctrine, ascribing undefined residuum of power to President, to be unsafe and dangerous to liberty.

United States Commission on Organization of the Executive Branch of the Government ("Hoover Commission"): *Report* . . . (Washington: Government Printing Office, 19 vols., 1949). A comprehensive, practical study. Suggests ways of securing more adequate performance in executive branch.

Wilson, Woodrow: *Constitutional Government in the United States* (New York: Columbia University Press, 1908). Asserted (Chap. 3) President at liberty, in law and conscience, to be as big a man as he can.

FEDERAL COURTS

Is "Judicial Review" Compatible with Democratic Rule?

In 1803, in the strange and strategic case of *Marbury v. Madison*, the Supreme Court of the United States, speaking through Chief Justice John Marshall, declared an act of Congress unconstitutional. It is the Court's right and duty, said the forceful and resourceful Chief Justice, to declare void "a law repugnant to the Constitution." Since that day in 1803 the Court's invalidation of congressional legislation has never failed to product storms of hostile criticism.

Jefferson, for example, was contemptuous of Marshall's "obiter dissertation" in *Marbury v. Madison*. Lincoln was severely critical of the *Dred Scott* decision, maintaining: "We propose so resisting it as to have it reversed if we can. . . . " When the majority of the Supreme Court knocked out a Federal progressive income tax in 1895, Justice Harlan, in a trenchant dissent, remarked that the court's invalidation of the income tax "impairs and cripples the just powers of the national government." Justice Holmes is credited with the comment: "I do not think the United States would come to an end if we lost our power to declare an Act of Congress void." It was Teddy Roosevelt who asserted: "I contend that . . . the courts should not be allowed to reverse the political philosophy of the people." And when the Court threw out the Agriculture Adjustment Act of 1933, Justice Stone acidly retorted that: "Courts are not the only agency of government that must be presumed to have the capacity to govern."

Defenders of judicial review of the constitutionality of Federal legislation are not slow to reply. They emphasize that judicial review safeguards fundamental civil liberties against Federal encroachment. It protects basic property rights against Federal power. It prevents the Federal government from invading states' rights and hence ending our federal system. It is exercised with care, caution, and intelligent self-restraint. Actually, they insist, judicial review ensures the safe functioning of majority rule by protecting today's minorities, who will be tomorrow's majorities; by requiring passionate and momentary majorities to reconsider hasty and ill-advised action and to muster really substantial support for extreme measures. Furthermore, it provides an elevated forum for cool, calm, objective, rational consideration for many of the basic issues confronting the nation. Judicial review aids in adjusting an eighteenth-century constitution to a twentieth-century world. These advocates of judicial review deny that the judiciary is an irresponsible, omnipotent, and tyrannical power. The courts, they conclude, have never been more than temporarily divorced from the main currents of political life. Most of these points are made in the following articles by Justices Sutherland, Brewer, Jackson, and former Solicitor-General James M. Beck, written in support of judicial review.

Henry Steele Commager, in the concluding article in this chapter, challenges the assumptions that lie behind the justification of this judicial power. He maintains that key constitutional decisions are decisions of policy—not of law. And Congress, he declares, is adequately equipped to make such policy decisions, for which special judicial learning is not prerequisite. He denies that the courts alone are independent and unbiased or possess a godlike, passionless objectivity. Furthermore, he argues that judicial review has by no means justified itself in fact as the record demonstrates. The Court's record in protecting civil liberties is not the best. Nor has the Court prevented expansion of Federal power at the expense of (alleged) property rights and states' rights. Similarly its sense of self-restraint can be challenged, as can the legitimacy of its frustration of majority rule. Finally, he contends that majorities in a democracy can be trusted: that men need no masters, not even judges.

[The very nature of American Democracy is highlighted in the fight over this exercise of judicial power. It is true that especially since 1937 the Supreme Court has approved a very generous expansion of the powers of the national government. Yet, constitutionally, the Supreme Court still possesses a potent, if latent, power in judicial review. And diverse groups—some fearful of "socialistic legislation," others alarmed by violations of civil liberties—insistently urge the Court to use its latent power to stem the drift either toward a despotic collectivism or toward the destruction of valuable individual rights by an (alleged) reactionary and hysterical Congress.]

Extremists see in this conflict a battle between majority rule and minority rights. Most observers recognize that both principles are ingredients of American Democracy. But are they really incompatible? In logic? In experience? The relationship of the Supreme Court to these vital questions is dealt with in this chapter.

The basic questions to which the following selections address themselves are these:

Is the power of the Federal courts to declare an act of Congress unconstitutional a legitimate, necessary, and desirable restriction in a democratic, federal, and constitutional government?

Or is judicial review an improper, unnecessary, and undemocratic restraint on majority rule?

I. IN SUPPORT OF JUDICIAL REVIEW

JUDICIAL REVIEW IS THE COURT'S GRAVE, DELICATE, BUT NECESSARY DUTY

BY JUSTICE GEORGE SUTHERLAND*

[Justice George Sutherland (1862 to 1942) served on the Supreme Court from 1922 to 1938. Before that he was a United States Representative and Senator from Utah. Sutherland symbolized the staunch economic conservatism that dominated the Court for most of his sixteen years. He did live to see the Supreme Court overrule the *Adkins* decision in 1937 and to treat congressional legislation more tenderly. However, although the Court has declared an act of Congress unconstitutional in few cases since March of 1937, that power still remains a potent, if little used, weapon in its armory. EDITOR.]

The judicial duty of passing upon the constitutionality of an act of Congress is one of great gravity and delicacy. The statute here in question [a Minimum Wage Act of 1918 fixing minimum wage standards for adult women in the District of Columbia] has successfully borne the scrutiny of the legislative branch of the government, which, by enacting it, has affirmed its validity; and that determination must be given great weight. This Court, by an unbroken line of decisions from Chief Justice Marshall to the present day, has steadily adhered to the rule that every

* *Adkins v. Children's Hospital,* 261 U.S. 525, 544 (1923).

possible presumption is in favor of the validity of an act of Congress until overcome beyond rational doubt. But if by clear and indubitable demonstration a statute be opposed to the Constitution we have no choice but to say so. The Constitution, by its own terms, is the supreme law of the land, emanating from the people, the repository of the ultimate sovereignty under our form of government. A congressional statute, on the other hand, is the act of an agency of this sovereign authority and if it conflict with the Constitution must fall; for that which is not supreme must yield to that which is. To hold it invalid (if it be invalid) is a plain exercise of the judicial power—that power vested in courts to enable them to administer justice according to law. From the authority to ascertain and determine the law in a given case, there necessarily results, in case of conflict, the duty to declare and enforce the rule of the supreme law and reject that of an inferior act of legislation which, transcending the Constitution, is of no effect and binding on no one. This is not the exercise of a substantive power to review and nullify acts of Congress, for no such substantive power exists. It is simply a necessary concomitant of the power to hear and dispose of a case or controversy properly before the court, to the determination of which must be brought the test and measure of the law.

COURTS MUST ENSURE PERSONAL AND PROPERTY RIGHTS AGAINST POPULAR ACTION

BY JUSTICE DAVID J. BREWER*

[Justice David J. Brewer (1837 to 1910) was an Associate Justice of the Supreme Court from 1890 to 1910. His hostility to socialism and "King Numbers" achieves new meaning in the light of current charges of "creeping socialism." His belief in a judiciary free from political pressures was later shared by millions in the country who opposed the "Court Packing" or "Court Reform" Bill of 1937. EDITOR.]

. . . But for what are written constitutions? They exist, not simply to prescribe modes of action, but because of the restraints and prohibitions they contain. Popular government may imply, generally speaking, that

* "The Nation's Safeguard," An Address before the New York Bar Association, *Proceedings of the New York Bar Association*, Vol. 16 (Jan. 17, 1893), pp. 45–47 *passim*.

the present will of the majority should be carried in effect, but this is true
in no absolute or arbitrary sense, and the limitations and checks which are
found in all our written constitutions are placed there to secure the rights
of the minority. Constitutions are generally, and ought always to be,
formed in times free from excitement. They represent the deliberate
judgment of the people as to the provisions and restraints which, firmly
and fully enforced, will secure to each citizen the greatest liberty and
utmost protection. They are rules prescribed by Philip Sober to control
Philip Drunk. When difficulties arise, when the measures and laws
framed by a majority are challenged as a violation of these rules and a
trespass upon the rights of the minority, common justice demands that
the tribunal to determine the question shall be as little under the influence
of either as is possible. . . .

It may be said that this is practically substituting government by the
judges for government by the people, and thus turning back the currents
of history. The world has seen government by chiefs, by kings and
emperors, by priests and by nobles. All have failed, and now government
by the people is on trial. Shall we abandon that and try government by
judges? But this involves a total misunderstanding of the relations of
judges to government. There is nothing in this power of the judiciary
detracting in the least from the idea of government of and by the people.
The courts hold neither purse nor sword; they cannot corrupt nor arbitrarily control. They make no laws, they establish no policy, they never
enter into the domain of popular action. They do not govern. Their
functions in relation to the State are limited to seeing that popular action
does not trespass upon right and justice as it exists in written constitutions and natural law. So it is that the utmost power of the courts and
judges works no interference with true liberty, no trespass on the fullest
and highest development of government of and by the people; it only
means security to personal rights—the inalienable rights, life, liberty and
the pursuit of happiness; it simply nails the Declaration of Independence,
like Luther's theses against indulgences upon the doors of the Wittenberg
church of human rights, and dares the anarchist, the socialist and every
other assassin of liberty to blot out a single word.

. . . Who does not see the wide unrest that fills the land? Who does
not feel that vast social changes are impending, and realize that those
changes must be guided in justice to safety and peace, or they will cul-
minate in revolution? Who does not perceive that the mere fact of numbers is beginning to assert itself? Who does not hear the old demagogic
cry, *"vox populi vox dei"* (paraphrased to-day, "the majority are always
right"), constantly invoked to justify disregard of those guarantees which

have hitherto been deemed sufficient to give protection to private property?

. . . "From him that hath shall be taken," is the watchword of a not inconsiderable . . . portion of our voters. In such a time as this the inquiry may well be, what factor in our national life speaks most emphatically for stability and justice, and how may that factor be given the greatest efficiency? Magnifying, like the apostle of old, my office, I am firmly persuaded that the salvation of the Nation, the permanence of government of and by the people, rests upon the independence and vigor of the judiciary. To stay the waves of popular feeling, to restrain the greedy hand of the many from filching from the few that which they have honestly acquired, and to protect in every man's possession and enjoyment, be he rich or poor, that which he hath, demands a tribunal as strong as is consistent with the freedom of human action and as free from all influences and suggestions other than is compassed in the thought of justice, as can be created out of the infirmities of human nature. To that end the courts exist, and for that let all the judges be put beyond the reach of political office, and all fear of losing position or compensation during good behavior.

TO SAFEGUARD LIBERTY THE COURT MUST TRANSLATE AN EIGHTEENTH-CENTURY BILL OF RIGHTS INTO TWENTIETH-CENTURY RESTRAINTS

BY JUSTICE ROBERT H. JACKSON*

[Associate Justice Robert H. Jackson was appointed to the Supreme Court in 1941 after a very successful record as Solicitor-General and Attorney General of the United States. He acted as Chief United States prosecutor at the Nuremberg trials of Nazi war criminals. Although in the *Barnette* case, extracted below, the Court overturned a state and not a Federal law, the excerpts herein apply equally to the United States government. EDITOR.]

The very purpose of a Bill of Rights was to withdraw certain subjects from the vicissitudes of political controversy, to place them beyond the reach of majorities and officials and to establish them as legal principles to be applied by the courts. One's right to life, liberty, and property, to

* *West Virginia State Board of Education v. Barnette*, 319 U.S. 624, 638, 639–640 (1942).

free speech, a free press, freedom of worship and assembly, and other fundamental rights may not be submitted to vote; they depend on the outcome of no elections. . . .

Nor does our duty to apply the Bill of Rights to assertions of official authority depend upon our possession of marked competence in the field where the invasion of rights occurs. True, the task of translating the majestic generalities of the Bill of Rights, conceived as part of the pattern of liberal government in the eighteenth century, into concrete restraints on officials dealing with the problems of the twentieth century, is one to disturb self-confidence. These principles grew in soil which also produced a philosophy that the individual was the center of society, that his liberty was attainable through mere absence of governmental restraints, and that government should be entrusted with few controls and only the mildest supervision over men's affairs. We must transplant these rights to a soil in which the *laissez-faire* concept or principle of non-interference has withered at least as to economic affairs, and social advancements are increasingly sought through closer integration of society and through expanded and strengthened governmental controls. These changed conditions often deprive precedents of reliability and cast us more than we would choose upon our own judgment. But we act in these matters not by authority of our competence but by force of our commissions. We cannot, because of modest estimates of our competence . . . withhold the judgment that history authenticates as the function of this Court when liberty is infringed.

STATES' RIGHTS MUST BE PROTECTED AGAINST INVASION BY THE FEDERAL GOVERNMENT

by JUSTICE GEORGE SUTHERLAND[*]

[Although Justice Sutherland's opinion in *Carter v. Carter Coal Co.*, excerpted below, has since been "distinguished" out of existence, it is still true to say that the Court recognizes its duty to umpire, and thus preserve, the federal system. To a great extent it umpires the federal system according to rules established by the national government. Nevertheless, even all the justices of the present Court would agree that the Court should intervene, if necessary, to protect certain state powers from Federal invasion. What "rights" or powers of the states may be legiti-

[*] *Carter v. Carter Coal Co.*, 298 U.S. 238, 294–296 *passim* (1936).

mately protected against Federal invasion is the big bone of contention.

In the *Carter* case the Court declared unconstitutional the Bituminous Coal Conservation Act of 1935. Among other things, the Act sought to control wages, hours, and working conditions of miners engaged in the production of coal and to recognize the miners' right to organize and bargain collectively. Such action, said the Court, is beyond the powers of Congress under our Federal Constitution. Such regulation invades a realm legitimately belonging to the various states. EDITOR.]

. . . While the states are not sovereign in the true sense of that term, but only *quasi*-sovereign, yet in respect of all powers reserved to them they are supreme—"as independent of the general government as that government within its sphere is independent of the States." *Collector* v. *Day*, 11 Wall. 113, 124. And since every addition to the national legislative power to some extent detracts from or invades the power of the states, it is of vital moment that, in order to preserve the fixed balance intended by the Constitution, the powers of the general government be not so extended as to embrace any not within the express terms of the several grants or the implications necessarily to be drawn therefrom. . . .

The determination of the Framers Convention and the ratifying conventions to preserve complete and unimpaired state self-government in all matters not committed to the general government is one of the plainest facts which emerge from the history of their deliberations. And adherence to that determination is incumbent equally upon the federal government and the states. State powers can neither be appropriated on the one hand nor abdicated on the other. As this court said in *Texas* v. *White*, 7 Wall. 700, 725—"the preservation of the States, and the maintenance of their governments, are as much within the design and care of the Constitution as the preservation of the Union and the maintenance of the National Government. The Constitution, in all its provisions, looks to an indestructible Union, composed of indestructable States." Every journey to a forbidden end begins with the first step; and the danger of such a step by the federal government in the direction of taking over the powers of the states is that the end of the journey may find the states so despoiled of their powers, or—what may amount to the same thing—so relieved of the responsibilities which possession of the powers necessarily enjoins, as to reduce them to little more than geographical subdivisions of the national domain. It is safe to say that if, when the Constitution was under consideration, it had been thought that any such danger lurked behind its plain words, it would never have been ratified.

JUDICIAL REVIEW IS NOT JUDICIAL TYRANNY

BY JAMES M. BECK*

[James M. Beck (1861 to 1936) was Solicitor-General of the United States, 1921 to 1925, and a Member of Congress from Pennsylvania from 1927 to 1934. Among other books he authored *The Vanishing Rights of the States* and *Our Wonderland of Bureaucracy*. EDITOR.]

. . . [An important principle] which the court adopted was that no law should be declared invalid unless its incompatibility with the Constitution was clear beyond reasonable doubt. All doubts were to be resolved in favor of the legislative act. If it admitted of two constructions—the one compatible with the Constitution and the other inconsistent —the construction favorable to its constitutionality was to be accepted. The judiciary thus sought to support the legislative will. In a democracy, no other attitude would be possible.

. . . [Another] principle was even more obvious. The court could not . . . consider the expediency of the act. The policy of the legislation was for the lawmaking body, and the only question for the court was that of legislative power, and therefore a law should be sustained by the judiciary even though in its judgment it were grossly unwise, and even immoral. This again removed from the power of the court any conflict with the popular will which might arise out of disputed questions of economics or morals. It was again the application of the Montesquieu principle of the separate functions of the legislative, executive, and judicial departments of the government. . . .

The Court has further recognized that in the discharge of legislative and executive functions by the Congress and the Executive, respectively, many questions of discretion will arise which involve the true meaning of the Constitution and yet are more political than justiciable in their nature. For example, the Constitution requires the Federal Government to guarantee to every State a "republican form of government," but what is essential to such a government and the method of enforcing such guarantee involve questions which, being political, are exclusively for Congress and not reviewable by the judiciary.

It is a mistaken idea that the Supreme Court has a plenary right to sit in judgment upon the constitutionality of the laws of Congress and the act of the Executive. It can only do so when they disclose a tangible and indisputable infringement of the Constitution. But this leaves a field of

* From: *The Constitution of the United States*. Copyright 1924 by Doubleday & Company, Inc., pp. 227, 229, 230–231. By permission of the publisher.

political discretion in which constitutional questions of a political character may arise. Nor has the Supreme Court plenary power to enforce compliance with the Constitution. . . .

All these principles and others of less importance indicate the conservatism [i.e., restraint] with which the Supreme Court has exercised its great power of holding other departments of the Government, which are more directly responsive to the public will, within the limits of their constitutional powers. . . .

The Supreme Court of the United States compels the living generation, too often swept by selfish interests and frenzied passions, to respect the immutable principles of liberty and justice. The court is thus the trustee for the unborn, for it protects their heritage from spoliation in the mad excesses of party strife of living generations. Thus, the Court must often affront the pride of power of temporary majorities.

Such has been its experience from its foundations. Continuously through its history its great decisions, when they thus defeated some momentary wish of the majority, have caused a violent but only temporary reaction against the moral power of the court.

Only a people with sufficient genius for self-restraint and willing to accept the judgments of a court as the final conscience of the nation in matters of constitutional morality, could make such an institution workable in a proud democracy, and nothing seems nobler in the history of the American republic than the fact that while each unpopular decision of the court has been followed by a temporary attack upon its powers, yet the sober second judgment of the American people has always been to accept loyally the great arbitrament. Here, however, is no judicial tyranny. Whenever the American people dislike a statement of the law as authoritatively declared by the Supreme Court, they may in turn establish a new law by the deliberate and orderly process of a constitutional amendment.

II. IN OPPOSITION TO JUDICIAL REVIEW

JUDICIAL REVIEW IS UNDEMOCRATIC IN THEORY, UNTENABLE AND UNNECESSARY IN PRACTICE

BY HENRY STEELE COMMAGER*

[Henry Steele Commager is Professor of History at Columbia University. He is author of *Theodore Parker* and *The American*

* From *Majority Rule and Minority Rights*. Copyright 1943 by Oxford University Press, Inc., pp. 38–44, 45–47, 55–56, 57–59, 60, 79–81, 82 *passim*. By permission of the publisher.

Mind, editor of *Documents in American History*, and coauthor of *Growth of the American Republic*. EDITOR.]

. . . We have come to take this institution [judicial review] so completely for granted that we have lost sight of its real nature. Few of our political institutions have been more elaborately explained and documented; none, it is safe to say, is less understood. Misunderstanding is no monopoly of conservatives who celebrate judicial review as a bulwark of republicanism; it distinguishes equally liberals who for the most part deprecate judicial intervention in the economic realm but rejoice exceedingly at judicial intervention on behalf of civil liberties. Neither group seems to appreciate the implications or the consequences of this unique institution. . . . The court reform proposal of 1937 furnished the most promising opportunity offered our generation for an analysis of the relation of judicial review to democracy, but no such analysis was vouchsafed us. . . . Indeed so general has been the failure to confront realistically the problem of judicial review that we are forced to the conclusion that it is rooted in ignorance or confusion rather than in timidity or cimcumspection.

How can it be said that the problem of judicial review is the problem of democracy? A moment's reflection on the institution will clarify the statement. The function—and effect—of judicial review is to give or deny judicial sanction to an act passed by a majority of a legislative body and approved by an executive. Every act adjudicated by the court has not only been ratified by a majority, but it has—in theory and we must suppose in fact—been subject to scrutiny in regard to its conformity with the Constitution. In support of every act, therefore, is not only a majority vote for its wisdom but a majority vote for its constitutionality.

Where the question of constitutionality is raised the judiciary subjects the act anew to scrutiny—theoretically on constitutional grounds alone, never on expediency. Where it concludes that the act involved is contrary to the Constitution, it so holds. In doing this it, of course, opposes its own opinion on constitutionality to that of the other two branches of the government. We can put the situation even more sharply: the one non-elective and non-removable element in the government rejects the conclusions on constitutionality arrived at by the two elective and removable branches.

. . . Obviously the political majorities are never aware—and would never admit—that they are violating the Constitution. There are rarely, if ever, clear-cut instances where wilful majorities deliberately ride down constitutional barriers. . . . Popular notions to the contrary notwithstanding . . . our legislative bodies, both state and national, have been throughout our history profoundly conservative and constitution-minded.

In every instance of challenged legislation we may assume that the majority reponsible for the law believed that it was legislating in harmony with the Constitution. If this should seem odd, to the lay mind, we may add that in most instances some judges have been found to agree with them! This is true of the majorities that enacted the Alien and Sedition laws, that passed Reconstruction legislation, that fabricated the New Deal; it is true equally of the majorities in state legislatures that passed workmen's compensation laws, maximum-hour and minimum-wage laws, even anti-evolution laws.

The real question, of course, is not that of blind or malicious majorities riding down constitutional guarantees, but of differing interpretations of the meaning of the Constitution. The crucial question is not so much whether an act does or does not conform to the Constitution, but who shall judge regarding its conformity? . . .

What is the argument for judicial rather than legislative or executive interpretations of the Constitution and laws? The orthodox answer is familiar enough. In the words of Marshall, "it is emphatically the province and duty of the judicial department to say what the law is." That is the essence of judicial business—to know the law and to know the Constitution, and in this the other departments cannot hope to compete. But not only are the courts peculiarly fitted to interpret the law but—and here we come to a most persuasive argument—they alone are independent and unbiased, their judgment alone is to be trusted.

These are large claims—confidently made and boldly maintained but scarcely susceptible of proof. It is possible, however, to challenge both of them; it is possible, too, to enter a demurrer— to plead that even if the claims are sound, the wisdom of judicial review in a democratic system is by no means established.

That judges—especially judges of our highest courts—are more learned in the law than legislators or executives will not be gainsaid. Is the observation relevant? Does the issue of constitutionality customarily involve legal erudition? Have acts of Congress—or of state legislatures—frequently been challenged on the basis of provisions of our constitutions so intricate that great learning is required for their comprehension? There have been examples of this, to be sure. But for the most part judicial rejection of legislative acts has not been an exercise of learning but of discretion. As Justice Holmes said back in 1896, "the true grounds of decision are considerations of policy and of social advantage, and it is vain to suppose that solutions can be attained merely by logic and the general propositions of law which nobody disputes."[1]

Indeed if we turn for simplicity to the federal scene, we shall find that

[1] *Vegelahn* v. *Guntner,* 167 Mass. 92.

acts which have encountered judicial invalidation have in every instance required the interpretation of vague and ambiguous clauses of the Constitution—clauses whose meaning is not to be determined by legal research but by "considerations of policy." Thus when the Supreme Court asserts that the Congress has not authority to regulate slavery in the Territories, to authorize legal tender, to impose a tax upon incomes, to prohibit yellow-dog contracts, to deny the channels of interstate commerce to the products of child labor, to fix minimum wages for women in the District of Columbia, to lay taxes for the purpose of regulating agricultural production—when it does all these things it is not applying clear-cut provisions of the Constitution but interpreting vague phrases like "regulation of commerce," "general welfare," "due process of law," and so forth. And when the court interprets these and similar phrases it does not so much exploit legal learning as exercise discretion.

I do not suggest that learning is not an essential quality in a judge . . . but I do submit that questions that have evoked judicial nullification of majority will have turned on considerations of policy rather than of law, and that on these questions the legal learning of the legislature and executive departments has been entirely adequate.

What of the other assumption—that judges alone, can be trusted to act independently, objectively, and dispassionately on questions of constitutionality? The assumption that legislators ever consciously permit passion or prejudice to influence their judgment where the Constitution is involved is, of course, intolerable, so what we are concerned with is unconscious bias, and the argument is that judges have less of this than legislators. The contemporary school of legal realists has dealt very harshly with the whole notion of judicial objectivity—has, perhaps, gone too far in support of the thesis that judicial opinions are largely the product of personal and environmental imponderables. But if it is an exaggeration to say that judicial opinion depends on judicial digestion, it will not be denied that the "mechanical" or "phonographic" theory of jurisprudence has been completely discredited. . . .

. . . It is interesting . . . to note that . . . [Jefferson's charges against the judiciary] have been echoed, in one form or another, by Jackson, Lincoln, Bryan, and both Roosevelts, and that from dissenting members of the court have come similar criticisms, less acrimonious but not less emphatic. It is the judges who have charged that the court indulges in "judicial legislation," warned that "fear of socialism" unduly influences decisions, protested against "a tortured construction of the Constitution." And it is difficult to read such opinions as those of Story in the Charles River Bridge Company case, Taney in the Dred Scott case, Field in the Income Tax case, Peckham in the Lochner case, Mc-

Reynolds in the Gold Clause cases—to name only a few of the more notorious—and avoid the conclusion that judges are sometimes swayed by considerations other than those of constitutional logic.

But if it cannot be shown that superior learning is an essential ingredient of judicial review or objectivity a peculiar possession of judges, what shall we say of the arguments supporting that institution? . . . Is it possible to challenge judicial review (always as a restriction on majority will rather than as a harmonizer of the federal system) on the basic ground that it has not, in fact, justified itself?

For the most part consideration of this institution has gone on in the rarefied atmosphere of theory and hypothesis, but our question is one not of theory but of fact. It is commonly taken for granted that courts decide rightly all questions of constitutional law, that they curb majority will only to protect minority rights, that their intervention has saved the Constitution from impairment or destruction. A realistic examination of the operation of judicial review in the federal field will not sustain these assumptions. It is safe to say that had there never been an instance of judicial nullification of a congressional act, our constitutional system would be essentially the same as it is today. For most of the judicial nullifications of federal legislation have been cancelled out by amendment, by new—and more acceptable—legislation, or, more frequently, by judicial reversal. It is safe to say, further, that the judicial record in the important —and controversial—field of personal liberties is practically barren—again, as far as federal legislation is concerned. In short, if we had to depend upon the courts rather than upon Congress and the President for maintaining our constitutional system and protecting personal liberties, we would be in an awkward position. The fact is, of course, that there are very few instances where the Congress has threatened the integrity of the constitutional system or the guarantee of the Bill of Rights. . . .

This is the record. It is familiar enough to students of our constitutional law; less familiar, perhaps, to the layman who, not unnaturally, supposes the court continuously intervening to protect fundamental rights of life, liberty, and property from congresional assault. It discloses not a single case, in a century and a half [prior to 1943], where the Supreme Court has protected freedom of speech, press, assembly, or petition against congressional attack. It reveals no instance (with the possible exception of the dubious Wong Wing case) where the court has intervened on behalf of the underprivileged—the Negro, the alien, women, children, workers, tenant-farmers. It reveals, on the contrary, that the court has effectively intervened again and again to defeat congressional efforts to free slaves, guarantee civil rights to Negroes, to protect workingmen, outlaw child labor, assist hard-pressed farmers, and to democratize the tax system.

From this analysis the Congress, and not the courts, emerges as the instrument for the realization of the guarantees of the bill of rights.

Our examination, then, of the theory and practice of judicial review, of congressional legislation, affords some basis for accepting the Jeffersonian rather than the Hamiltonian view of this institution. Whatever the logical support for the theory, it cannot be found in the philosophy of democracy if by democracy we mean majority rule; whatever the practical justification, it cannot be found in the defense of fundamental rights against the assaults of misguided or desperate majorities. Almost every instance of judicial nullification of congressional acts appears, now, to have been a mistaken one. In many—perhaps in most—instances the mistake has been (after a decent interval) conceded and corrected by the court itself. In other instances it has been rectified by the operation of public opinion. The conclusion is almost inevitable that judicial review in this realm has been a drag upon administrative efficiency and upon democracy. . . .

. . . What assurance do we have, if we remove the judicial restraints, that majorities will not disregard the "laws of Nature and Nature's God," destroy minority rights, and bring down upon themselves the whole fine structure of constitutionalism? What guarantee is there, in short, that the people, if conceded the right, will not do wrong?

. . . [The question, Professor Commager writes, "is a leading and a misleading one."] The judiciary is not the only check upon majority will. The supposition that the removal of the judicial check would leave our government an unlimited one is entirely erroneous, and the confusion of majority rule with despotism or even anarchy almost deliberately malicious.

Our constitutional system . . . is one of checks and balances. . . . It is sometimes forgotten that our political system is one of checks and balances too. Anyone who has followed the slow and tortuous course of a major public issue—the poll tax, for example, . . . through the arena of public opinion into the party conventions and caucuses, into the halls of Congress and the rooms of appropriate committees, knows how much of delay, of balance, of compromise, is implicit in our political machinery. A good part of our politics, indeed, seems to be concerned with reconciling majority and minority will, class hostilities, sectional differences, the divergent interests of producer and consumer, of agriculture and labor, of creditor and debtor, of city and country, of tax-payer and tax-beneficiary, of the military and the civilian. In small issues as in great, the result is generally a compromise. Democracy, in short, whether from instinct or from necessity, furnishes its own checks and balances—quite aside from such as may be provided in written constitutions. . . .

A majority rule system, then, such as ours, is not a system of unlimited government either in theory, in law, or in practice. To the formal limits of the Constitution are added the informal limits of politics. With this in mind we can return to our original question: Is there any reason to suppose that majorities so limited would invade minority rights if it were not for the obstacles interposed by the courts? Or may we advance with equal plausibility the assertion that majorities can be trusted, without judicial assistance, to govern in accordance with the law and to respect minority rights, and that—with full realization of all the risks involved—training in such governance is essential to the maturing of democracy?

[On the basis of our factual record Professor Commager tentatively concludes that the answer to the second question posed above is Yes—majority rule can be trusted.] . . .

The philosophical basis of judicial review is undemocratic. The purpose of judicial review is to restrain majorities. The assumption behind judicial review is that the people either do not understand the Constitution or will not respect it and that the courts do understand the Constitution and will respect it.

The assumptions and practices of the courts excited . . . the most passionate protests from Jefferson. He regarded judicial review as wrong in theory and dangerous in practice and prophesied that it would, in the end, imperil both democracy and the Union. He did not believe that judges were either better informed or more impartial than legislatures or executives. He was persuaded that the people were, in the long run, the safest depositories of all powers and that from errors of judgment on the part of their representatives the proper appeal was to the good sense of the mass.

An examination of the actual incidence of judicial review in the field of federal legislation would seem to support the Jeffersonian contention. It does not appear, from such an examination, that the courts are sounder in their interpretation of the Constitution or more tender of minority rights than are legislative bodies.

Nor is there any persuasive evidence from our own long and complex historical experience that majorities are given to contempt for constitutional limitation or for minority rights. Our majorities, state and federal alike, have been, to a remarkable extent, stable, law-abiding, and conservative. They have not justified any of the doleful jeremiads of Adams or Hamilton or their successors. They have not taxed wealth out of existence—there are and have long been more great fortunes here than elsewhere in the world; they have not crushed minorities; they have not set up dictatorships; they have not been hostile to education or to science. The pulpit, the press, the school, the forum, are as free here as anywhere else in the world—with the possible exception of that other great majority-rule country—Britain.

From the states, from time to time, there have been occasional departures from these high standards of constitutional integrity and, in the last quarter-century, the courts have intervened to protect victims of these lapses. From a short-range view this intervention has been desirable—it has saved individual victims and satisfied our desire that justice shall be done. From a longer perspective it may be doubted that judicial intervention has served a useful purpose. It has made for a confusion in our thinking about politics, it has supported the notion that what is constitutional is good, it has, above all, deprived democracy of its most effective training school—experience. . . .

Our own experience, I believe, justifies Jefferson's faith that men need no masters—not even judges. It justifies us, too, in believing that majority will does not imperil minority rights, either in theory or in operation. It gives us firm basis for a belief that the people themselves can be trusted to realize that the majority has a vital interest in the preservation of an alert and critical minority and that, conversely, the minority can have no rights fundamentally inimical to the commonwealth.

QUESTIONS AND PROBLEMS

1. First state and *then* criticize the logic by which Chief Justice Marshall and those who, like Justice Sutherland, follow him reach the conclusion that the Supreme Court has the right to declare an act of Congress unconstitutional.

2. Why does Justice Brewer desire a judiciary "beyond the reach of political office," without "fear of losing position or compensation during good behavior"? Explain why you do or do not share his convictions.

3. Utilizing pertinent cases, discuss the ease or difficulty of translating an eighteenth-century Bill of Rights into twentieth-century restraints on the Federal government.

4. What is the difference, if any, between personal and property rights? What dangers to both, if any, lie in the withering of the concept of *laissez faire* in the economic field and the concomitant expansion of Federal power?

5. What are the powers reserved to the states? What matters are not committed to the national government? What are the powers possessed by the national government, either by express grant or by necessary implication? Can the future powers of the national government or of the states be ascertained with exactitude or finality? In the light of the questions above discuss the Court's role in protecting the legitimate powers of the states within our federal system.

6. Why does Beck believe that judicial review is not judicial tyranny? De-

fend or attack his argument in the light of your knowledge of (a) pertinent Supreme Court decisions; (b) those factors that serve to keep the Supreme Court in line with prevailing political sentiment; (c) the ease or difficulty of "the deliberate and orderly process of constitutional amendment"; and (d) the "genius for self-restraint" of the American people.

7. According to Commager: "How can it be said that the problem of judicial review is the problem of democracy?" State the reasons for your agreement or disagreement with his answer.

8. How does Commager criticize "the argument for judicial rather than legislative or executive interpretations of the Constitution and laws"? Evaluate Commager's criticism in the light of Supreme Court history since 1940.

9. Explain why Commager is critical both of "conservatives who celebrate judicial review as a bulwark of republicanism" and of "liberals who for the most part deprecate judicial intervention in the economic realm but rejoice exceedingly at judicial intervention on behalf of civil liberties"? To what extent, and why, do you agree or disagree with this criticism?

10. "What guarantee is there . . . that the people, if conceded the right, will not do wrong?" How does Commager answer this question? How would you?

11. What proposals, if any, would you make for modifying or eliminating the Supreme Court's power to declare an act of Congress null and void? Explain the reasons for your position.

SELECT BIBLIOGRAPHY

Alfange, Dean: *The Supreme Court and the National Will* (New York: Doubleday, 1937). Maintains that, despite lags, Court has in long run reflected national will; that wise use of its power secures clearer and more lasting expression of national will.

Boudin, Louis B.: *Government by Judiciary* (New York: William Godwin, 2 vols., 1932). An "all-out" attack on judicial review by a lawyer prominent in field of civil liberties and labor law.

Cardoza, Benjamin Nathan: *The Nature of the Judicial Process* (New Haven: Yale University Press, 1921). Especially pp. 91–94 for a thoughtful, well-balanced defense of "restraining power of the judiciary" by a great liberal jurist.

Carr, Robert K.: *The Supreme Court and Judicial Review* (New York: Farrar & Rinehart, 1942). Contends, in Chap. 12, that it is difficult to establish a completely convincing case for either retention or abolition of judicial review. Observes that American people have accepted exercise of judicial review and majority pressure on Supreme Court.

Corwin, Edward S.: *Constitutional Revolution, Ltd.* (Claremont, Calif.: Claremont Colleges, 1941). Notes decline of Court's concepts, supporting *laissez faire*, which prevented national government from performing economic and social functions.

Curtis, Charles P. Jr.: *Lions under the Throne* (Boston: Houghton Mifflin, 1947). Argues that justices should exercise little or no self-restraint in protecting democratic liberties against malfunctioning or undemocratic government. Ordinarily, vis-à-vis governmental authority, Court's self-restraint should be that of great lawyer, statesman, and philosopher.

Cushman, Robert E.: "The Role of the Supreme Court in a Democratic Nation," Edmund Janes James Lecture at the University of Illinois, Mar. 9, 1938. Examines nature and growth of Supreme Court's power to invalidate laws. Concludes that Court's present (1938) "legislative" power is incompatible with democracy.

Haines, Charles Grove: *The American Doctrine of Judicial Supremacy* (Berkeley: University of California Press, 2d ed., 1932). A storehouse of adverse historical and analytical criticism of judicial supremacy. Considers, in Chap. 17, proposals to remedy defects of judicial veto of legislation. For a more recent view see his "Judicial Review of Acts of Congress and the Need for Constitutional Reform," *Yale Law Journal*, Vol. 45 (March, 1936), pp. 816–856.

Jackson, Robert: *The Struggle for Judicial Supremacy* (New York: Knopf, 1941). Contains vivid, if pro New-Deal, account of New Deal in Court. Argues that Court frustrated efforts of both nation and states to meet urgent twentieth-century needs.

McCune, Wesley: *The Nine Young Men* (New York: Harper, 1947). A readable, if not always judicious, treatment of the Court since 1937. Includes profiles of justices, thumbnail case sketches, description of Supreme Court building, atmosphere, and politics.

Pritchett, Charles Herman: *The Roosevelt Court* (New York: Macmillan, 1948). Studies judicial politics and values through Court's nonunanimous opinions. Maintains that liberal court's judicial activism is no more consistent with democracy than a conservative court's, unless limited to protection of liberty.

Selected Essays on Constitutional Law (Chicago: Foundation Press, 5 vols., 1938). The best single collection on the subject. Indispensable. Compiled and collected by a committee of the Association of American Law Schools.

United States Senate, Committee on the Judiciary: *Adverse Report on Reorganization of the Federal Judiciary*, 75th Cong., 1st sess., Senate Report 711, 1937. Contains reasons for Judiciary Committee's rejection of Court Reform Bill.

Warren, Charles: *The Supreme Court in United States History* (Boston: Little, Brown, 3 vols., 1922). One of the classic works. Presents a conservative interpretation of the Court's work.

Wright, Benjamin F.: *The Growth of American Constitutional Law* (Boston: Houghton Mifflin, 1942). Sees Court as product of American life; as umpire of federal system; as censor of personal and property rights; and as conservator of method of rational debate and justification—the only proper reliance in a constitutional system.

ADMINISTRATION

Does Big Government Mean an Irresponsible, Tyrannical, and Wasteful Bureaucracy?

"As a result of depression, war, new needs for defense, and our greater responsibilities in the foreign field, the Federal Government," declared the Hoover Commission in its 1949 report on *General Management of the Executive Branch*, "has become the most gigantic business on earth." It employs over 2,100,000 civil servants. It spends over $42,000,000,000 yearly. The conduct of its business has resulted in a national debt per average family of about $7,500.

The increase in the size and power of the national government has resulted in considerable adverse criticism of our huge bureaucracy. Charges of poor performance of accepted functions have been leveled against the bureaucrat. Similarly, bureaucracy has been taken to task for its part in the invasion of fields hitherto unoccupied by government. These attacks on bureaucracy and Big Government, however, have not gone unchallenged.

The debate on the subject of Big Bureaucracy and Big Government allows one to come to grips with the strategic role of administration in modern government, to analyze the defense and ponder the implications of Big Government, and to evaluate the differing programs of action offered for the preservation of a responsible, efficient, bureaucracy and free, sound government in the United States.

Those who, like John H. Crider in the first selection in this chapter, are adversely critical of bureaucracy stress the deplorable aspects of the bureaucrat. Crider maintains that the real problem is a permanent, deplorable bureaucracy made inevitable by an all-powerful, ever-aggrandizing, social-service state.

Ludwig Von Mises reinforces Mr. Crider's major point. In the passage herein extracted Von Mises summarizes a case against the evils of progressing bureaucratization. It is tyrannical, irresponsible, and arbitrary. It is—so he charges—antiliberal, undemocratic, and un-American. Von Mises argues, however, that the real devil is not the bureaucrat but the totalitarian political philosophy of governmental control that has produced the bureaucrat in such large numbers and given him such extensive power over the lives of our citizens.

John A. Vieg, himself a former bureaucrat, writes in defense of the species. He summarizes and then refutes the principal charges against the bureaucrats. He denies that a doctrinaire political ideology is responsible for the size and power of government. He holds that the government's power increased in response to felt needs and is necessary to preserve liberty and welfare in the modern world. Bureaucrats, he holds, are—generally speaking—productive, relatively efficient, responsible, "American," intelligent, fair, and responsive to true national needs.

The basic question to which all three address their remarks and to which Crider and Von Mises answer "Yes" and Vieg "No" is this:

Does Big Government mean an irresponsible, tyrannical, inefficient, wasteful bureaucracy and the destruction of free, sound government in the United States?

THE ATTACK ON BIG GOVERNMENT AND BIG BUREAUCRACY: I

BY JOHN H. CRIDER*

[John H. Crider learned about Washington, D.C., as a correspondent of *The New York Times*. From 1946 to 1951 he was Editor in Chief of the *Boston Herald*. EDITOR.]

. . . We can hardly hope to play a leading role in a world dedicated to freedom and democracy unless we set an example of freedom and democracy at home. It is here that the issue of *The Bureaucrat* becomes acute. For it is not the swollen bureaucracy of wartime which should be our great concern—it will deflate to some extent in any event when victory comes—but the more serious problem of permanent bureaucracy. We must be aware of how far we have come along the road to centralized government, to the social service state, and getting into the habit of letting Washington solve our problems for us. And, we must understand that the bureaucrat, like the bureaucracy of which he is a part, did not invent himself. He is the creature of a system—the result of a philosophy

* *The Bureaucrat* (Philadelphia: Lippincott, 1944), pp. 10, 26–28, 39 *passim*. By permission of Mr. Crider.

of government which, as it may later appear, has enveloped us while we hardly knew what was happening. . . .

The bureaucrat defies precise definition. The encyclopedias, limiting their definitions to the traditional type of bureaucrat, say he is the official of a department or bureau of government who loves red tape, worships routine, and is scared to death of new ideas.

This ancient definition would include the fellow at the license bureau who slammed down the window precisely at quitting time in the face of a young woman who had been waiting in line an hour and a half, taking time out from her job to get her license. He is the Cambridge, Mass., police officer who explained there was not anything the police could do about the many thefts from parked cars because the department was denied the new patrol cars it had asked for, and had to use vehicles that were two years old. Horrors! He is the supervisor of garbage collectors in the District of Columbia who, personalizing what he said was a local rule, refused to let his men empty garbage cans if they contained any paper whatsoever. She is the woman bureaucrat who refused to open the door of a Maryland license bureau a few minutes before 9 A.M. to let five shivering citizens stand inside to wait instead of out in a cutting February wind. And he is the fellow who prepared that questionnaire with sixteen questions, which had to be sworn to in the presence of a notary before a civilian employee at Fort Monmouth, N.J., could get a refund of a nickel lost in a vending machine. In short, he or she is anybody in government who is (1) obnoxious, and (2), forgets that they are working for the people, and not the people for them.

But while the American public has been irked by the traditional type of bureaucrat during recent years of swollen wartime bureaucracy, it is another, new variety of the species, which has concerned us most of all. This is the heaven-sent bureaucratic zealot who enters the government service conscious of the great mission to which he has been called. He was first observed during the New Deal Thirties as the bright young man who burned the midnight oil thinking up new "services" for the public, and buzzed around government offices all day obtaining support for the products of his brain.

. . . Like the idea men of a great corporation's promotion department, the new kind of bureaucrat sat up many a night devising ways to sell his product—reform, and to achieve the bureaucrat's greatest objective in life —extension of the government's sphere of activity. . . .

This new kind of bureaucrat proved quite the opposite from the traditional variety. Instead of spinning red tape and observing regulations to the point of nausea, they disregarded any rule that seemed to get in their way and were always cutting corners. Instead of too much lost motion, they were usually guilty of two much motion, getting into the hair of the traditional bureaucrats, as well as that of the public. Masters of the bureaucratic jargon, they were always recommending issuance of "directives," insisting that this or that problem was being handled on the "wrong level," demanding that a new regulation be "implemented" by a dozen more, and urging that such-and-such a situation be "frozen" if the limits of bureaucratic zeal had been about reached which, more often than not, meant overstepped.

Then, of course, there is that rare bird known as the true public servant. He is what all bureaucrats become when they die. The best place to find out about them is in the obituary columns. In the bureaucratic heaven there are no bureaucrats, only true public servants. . . .

The bureaucrat, then, is a composite of all things known of the species. He is, for our purposes, unless otherwise indicated, an abstraction. The term includes the bulk of all, male and female, who feed from the public trough, thereby obtaining a degree of authority of which they remind us in various ways. The abstraction is necessarily weighted on the side of the more offensive aspects of the bureaucrat which, unhappily, predominate. He (the abstraction) is distinguished from the true public servant, an obscure and usually deceased form of the species, by his authoritarian manner, his proficiency at soldiering on the job to wait out his retirement age, his constant entanglement in red tape, and general disregard for economy. Or, if the new kind of bureaucrat, he wears out the public and himself by his dizziness. The bureaucrat, most conspicuously, is more concerned with solidifying his position and extending his authority than in performing a public service. Indeed, to the true bureaucrat, public service becomes merely an object of exploitation. And, if you fail to find him any other way, you can surely spot the bureaucrat as the fellow who always knows what is best for you and me.

THE ATTACK ON BIG GOVERNMENT AND BIG BUREAUCRACY: II

BY LUDWIG VON MISES*

[Ludwig Von Mises, Austrian economist, is one of the outstanding advocates of laissez-faire capitalism. He has taught in Vienna, Geneva, London, and New York. Now Professor of Economics at New York University, he is the author of *Om-*

* *Bureaucracy* (New Haven: Yale University Press, 1944), pp. 1, 2–4, 7, 9 *passim*. By permission of the publisher.

nipotent Government and *Human Action: A Treatise on Economics.* EDITOR.]

The terms *bureaucrat, bureaucratic,* and *bureaucracy* are clearly invectives. Nobody calls himself a bureaucrat or his own methods of management bureaucratic. These words are always applied with an opprobrious connotation. They always imply a disparaging criticism of persons, institutions, or procedures. Nobody doubts that bureaucracy is thoroughly bad and that it should not exist in a perfect world. . . .

An American, asked to specify his complaints about the evils of progressing bureaucratization, might say something like this:

"Our traditional American system of government was based on the separation of the legislative, the executive, and the judicial powers and on a fair division of jurisdiction between the Union and the States. The legislators, the most important executives, and many of the judges were chosen by election. Thus the people, the voters, were supreme. Moreover, none of the three arms of the government had the right to interfere with the private affairs of the citizens. The law-abiding citizen was a free man.

"But now, for many years and especially since the appearance of the New Deal, powerful forces are on the point of substituting for this old and well-tried democratic system the tyrannical rule of an irresponsible and arbitrary bureaucracy. The bureaucrat does not come into office by election of the voters but by appointment of another bureaucrat. He has arrogated a good deal of the legislative power. Government commissions and bureaus issue decrees and regulations undertaking the management and direction of every aspect of the citizens' lives. Not only do they regulate matters which hitherto have been left to the discretion of the individual; they do not shrink from decreeing what is virtually a repeal of duly enacted laws. By means of this quasi-legislation the bureaus usurp the power to decide many important matters according to their own judgment of the merits of each case, that is, quite arbitrarily. The rulings and judgments of the bureaus are enforced by Federal officials. The purported judicial review is in fact illusory. Every day the bureaucrats assume more power; pretty soon they will run the whole country.

"There cannot be any doubt that this bureaucratic system is essentially antiliberal, undemocratic, and un-American, that it is contrary to the spirit and to the letter of the Constitution, and that it is a replica of the totalitarian methods of Stalin and Hitler. It is imbued with a fanatical hostility to free enterprise and private property. It paralyzes the conduct of business and lowers the productivity of labor. By heedless spending it squanders the nation's wealth. It is inefficient and wasteful. Although it styles what it does planning, it has no definite plans and aims. It lacks unity and uniformity; the various bureaus and agencies work at cross-purposes. The outcome is a disintegration of the whole social apparatus of production and distribution. Poverty and distress are bound to follow."

This vehement indictment of bureaucracy is, by and large, an adequate although emotional description of present-day trends in American government. But it misses the point as it makes bureaucracy and the bureaucrats responsible for an evolution the causes of which must be sought for elsewhere. Bureaucracy is but a consequence and a symptom of things and changes much more deeply rooted.

The characteristic feature of present-day policies is the trend toward a substitution of government control for free enterprise. Powerful political parties and pressure groups are fervently asking for public control of all economic activities, for thorough government planning, and for the nationalization of business. They aim at full government control of education and at the socialization of the medical profession. There is no sphere of human activity that they would not be prepared to subordinate to regimentation by the authorities. In their eyes, state control is the panacea for all ills. . . .

Those who criticize bureaucracy make the mistake of directing their attacks against a symptom only and not against the seat of the evil. It makes no difference whether the innumerable decrees regimenting every aspect of the citizen's economic activities are issued directly by a law, duly passed by Congress, or by a commission or government agency to which power has been given by a law and by the allocation of money. What people are really complaining about is the fact that the government has embarked upon such totalitarian policies, not the technical procedures applied in their establishment. It would make little difference if Congress had not endowed these agencies with quasi-legislative functions and had reserved to itself the right to issue all decrees required for the conduct of their functions. . . .

It is quite correct, as the opponents of the trend toward totalitarianism say, that the bureaucrats are free to decide according to their own discretion questions of vital importance for the individual citizen's life. It is true that the office-holders are no longer the servants of the citizenry but irresponsible and arbitrary masters and tyrants. But this is not the fault of bureaucracy. It is the outcome of the new system of government which restricts the individual's freedom to manage his own affairs and assigns more and more tasks to the government. The culprit is not the bureaucrat but the political system. And the sovereign people is still free to discard this system.

IN DEFENSE OF BIG GOVERNMENT AND BIG BUREAUCRACY

BY JOHN A. VIEG*

[John Albert Vieg has mingled college research and teaching with government service with the U.S. Bureau of the Budget and other agencies. Mr. Vieg is now Professor of Government and Department Chairman at Pomona College. He is coauthor of *The Future of Government in America* and *Elements of Public Administration*. EDITOR.]

The term "bureaucracy" is used in several different ways. These fall, however, into two main categories. Either the word is used in a neutral and technical sense to denote the body of officials which executes the policies and effectuates the programs of government, or it is used in a symbolic and unneutral sense to connote the worst features of administrative personnel and procedures in all large organizations, private as well as public, but especially public. Ordinarily, one has no difficulty in deciding from the context which meaning is intended.

Popular usage accords generally with the latter definition. That this should be the case is perhaps a sad commentary, whether on the competence of governmental officialdom in the United States or on the intelligence of the American people, or both. But it is a fact. In our own time, to be sure, many millions, particularly among those with low incomes, have come to regard government as their friend and its employees more or less as friends and helpers. Yet other millions, including some of our most influential citizens, continue to hold attitudes toward the state and toward civil service personnel which comport hardly at all with the benefits they receive from government.

The development and maintenance of a competent and responsible bureaucracy is one of the most basic public problems of our age. The future of free government, upon which all else chiefly depends, will depend upon our ability to build such a public service more than upon any other thing, excepting only our success in generating enlightened public opinion and translating that opinion into sound legislation. Although this proposition is absolutely clear, it can be useful as it is necessary to examine and investigate the various charges and indictments leveled against the public service in the big democracy which is the United States today.

These accusations and indictments vary greatly in content and severity.

* "Democracy and Bureaucracy," *Public Administration Review*, Vol. 4 (Summer, 1944), pp. 248–250, 252 *passim*. By permission of the publisher.

While they do not lend themselves to neat and easy classification, they may for convenience be grouped into eight main categories. To summarize their faults, the trouble with the bureaucrats is: (1) that "there are too damned many of them"; (2) that "they are worse than useless, they are parasitical"; (3) that they are woefully inefficient and so bound up in red tape that they either never get anything done or, if they do, succeed only at execessive cost of time, money, or both; (4) that they are officious, contemptuous of the citizen, and arrogant toward his representatives in Congress, in the state legislatures, and in municipal councils; (5) that they are zealots and reformers endeavoring through their positions to remake the world according to the blueprints of their dreams; (6) that they are timid, ignorant, and unimaginative, functioning more or less like robots; (7) that they are arbitrary and capricious and inclined to indulge in favoritism in the distribution of appointments and emoluments within their control; (8) that those in the employ of the national government are so hungry for power that they have gradually taken over more and more of the functions of the states, cities, and counties, with the result that local government has been undermined and the federal system is being destroyed. . . .

[Vieg recognizes that "Our American bureaucracy has grown to prodigious absolute size. On that point there can be neither doubt nor dispute." Hence, he concerns himself with the reasons for and implications of this size.]

Of all the factors which account for the growth of government to its present size, ideology is of the least importance. Both of the major parties operate more on the basis of expediency than of philosophy. Our bureaucracy has expanded under Republican as well as under Democratic administrations. The reason for this is the pragmatism of the American people in matters of politics: they want their government to do whatever needs to be done by government. They have no systematic doctrines by which they insist that all questions relating to the range of governmental action be settled. Neither does either of the dominant parties. Government has taken on new functions under Republican leadership despite the conservatism and rugged individualism within the Grand Old Party. So has it under Democratic auspices—but not because the New Dealers are united by a well-wrought philosophy of liberalism or robust collectivism.

The principal problem for the American people is not the size of their bureaucracy or, to put the same point in different language, the power of their government, but its accountability. Today no nation lacking a big bureaucracy and a powerful government has the means of insuring either its liberty or its welfare. This proposition is so plain that it should not need to be labored. . . . The history of Liberty is a history of the limitation of the arbitrary use of governmental power, not of the limitation of governmental power itself.

If it were true, by far the most serious accusation with which bureaucrats are wont to be indicted is the accusation that they are parasites, that their activities are not only not productive but a drain and burden on the production of others. But the statement is not true. It is so false that it is high time it is challenged flatly and openly, notwithstanding the fact that it is very commonly made and that even some very high governmental officials have said things which too easily lend credence and circulation to the charge. . . .

All work is creative which is essential to building and sustaining the good society; it is all productive. . . . The production of economic stability is no less creative than the production of a piece of machinery or a bushel of wheat—and it may be far more difficult.

To judge by the frequency and intensity with which bureaucrats are berated for inefficiency, one would gather that, in public as well as in business administration, efficiency is universally accepted as the greatest of all goods. In a sense, but only in a very limited one, that is true. The misleading thing is the assumption that aims and ends in government are indentical with those in business. Efficiency is a term that has for its connotation the atmosphere of the market place. The objective of business is simple—to make money. Success in business can, therefore, be very easily measured. But that is not the case in government. There are, of course, some fields of public administration in which the objectives sought resemble those in a commercial undertaking but these are the exception rather than the rule. By its very nature, government has objectives more complex and more intangible than those in business.

Men look to government for justice, law, peace, and order; for the maintenance of liberty, equality, and opportunity; for impartiality in the enforcement of economic regulations and even-handedness in the administration of economic assistance; for service that is safe and sure rather than swift and cheap. They want their government to be efficient, certainly, but only in so far as being "efficient" is consistent with satisfying these other and more basic expectations. They do not run their government to make money. They run it in order to establish and preserve an environment in which they themselves can make money. They do not expect the government to show a profit on its operations at the end of the year because they purposely reserve to private enterprise the areas appropriate and safe for profit-making. . . .

Space will not permit anything like a detailed analysis of the other common indictments against the bureaucrats. Some of them may admittedly be officious in their attitude toward the citizen and occasionally careless, even contemptuous, of his rights, but that this is anything like their general inclination is belied by the experience of every citizen who still retains his wits. As for the accusation that they are arrogant toward the political representatives of the American people, all that need be said is that, by and large, their attitude is more likely to be one not only of respect but of deference.

It is hard to take seriously the charge that, as a whole, they are zealots, radicals, and reformers. No sound or substantial evidence has ever been adduced to show that they are anything in political philosophy except a typical cross-section of the American people. Indeed, the thinness of this charge is proved by the fact that it is often made in the breath preceding or following the accusation that governmental employees are as a class timid, ignorant, and unimaginative to the point where they act more or less like robots. For both of these charges to be true would be impossible. Neither of them can, in fact, be sustained. The most that can be said is that each represents a caricature of a very small minority of public employees. . . .

As for the charge that bureaucrats are arbitrary, capricious, and inclined to favoritism in the distribution of appointments and emoluments among their brethren, it all depends upon the standard of comparison whether one can get excited about it or not. Certainly there is some of it, and some is too much when measured by the standards of perfection. But as compared with the situation in our commercial bureaucracy—that is, in private business—governmental bureaucracy is relatively free from these faults.

Finally, as for the accusation that because of their lust for power the bureaucrats in Washington have taken over so many of the functions of our states, cities, and counties that local government has been undermined and the federal character of our government vitiated, it simply will not hold water. If, as is true, the national government has grown in size more rapidly than the governments of our states and localities, that is mainly owing not to deliberate national encroachment upon the states and the localities but, on the one hand, to the fact that more and more of our public problems have become national in their scope and incidence and, on the other, to the fact that when the states and localities have failed or defaulted in meeting their own responsibilities, the people have insisted that the national government step in and either take over the load or help them to carry it.

In the years following . . . the United States will need a competent and responsible bureaucracy more than ever before. . . . The improvement of the public service must for this reason be placed high and kept high on the agenda of American democracy. Thanks, however, to the marked advances made in public administration during the last half-century, the betterment of our bureaucracy does not constitute our foremost problem in government. . . . The crucial question is not whether its public administration will be adequate and efficient, but whether its public policies will be sound and enlightened.

QUESTIONS AND PROBLEMS

1. Which of the following should be regarded as bureaucrats? A public-school teacher, a city policeman, a health-department nurse, a fireman, a meteorologist in the weather bureau, a clerk in the treasury department, a forester in the state forestry service, a highway engineer, a playground director, a garbage collector?

2. How do Crider, Von Mises, and Vieg define "the bureaucrat"? How would you define "bureaucrat" and "bureaucracy"?

3. Summarize in some detail the case against the "evils of progressing bureaucratization" that Von Mises' American makes? What would you add to this case, if anything? How much of this case do you accept or reject and why?

4. How does Vieg answer Von Mises' case against bureaucracy? How would you bolster Vieg's defense, if at all? How much of Vieg's defense of bureaucracy do you accept or reject and why?

5. First state and then evaluate the controls *at hand* to keep bureaucracy responsible.

6. What reforms, if any, might be made to ensure more effective administrative responsibility in the future?

7. Von Mises charges that "Bureaucracy is but a consequence and a symptom of things and changes much more deeply rooted." What are these "things" and "changes"? Explain why you agree or disagree with Von Mises' analysis.

8. State why the findings and recommendations of the Hoover Commission lend weight to the position of (*a*) Crider and Von Mises or (*b*) Vieg or (*c*) Crider, Von Mises, and Vieg or (*d*) none of these men.

9. In the light of the current tension in international affairs does it appear likely that our "swollen bureaucracy" will deflate appreciably? Explain.

10. In 1945 Leonard D. White, an outstanding student of public administration, contended that in the future administrators would need greater (not less) freedom, can be trusted, and must be held accountable for results. Discuss this contention in the light of your over-all knowledge of administration.

SELECT BIBLIOGRAPHY

Appleby, Paul H.: *Big Democracy* (New York: Knopf, 1945). A sympathetic but not uncritical account by an experienced administrator who thinks in terms of government as active effort to satisfy popularly felt necessities of the time.

Appleby, Paul H.: *Policy and Administration* (University, Ala.: University of Alabama Press, 1949). Attempts to sketch full-dimensional picture of public administration viewed as only one of a number of basic political processes by which a democratic people govern.

Bureau of National Affairs: *Administrative Procedure Act* (Washington: Bureau of National Affairs, 1946). A history and section-by-section analysis of act which was designed to secure observance of "rule of law" in administrative agencies. Contains full text of act.

Dickinson, John: "The Perennial Cry of Bureaucracy," *Yale Review*, Vol. 24 (March, 1935), pp. 448–463. Although somewhat dated, still one of the ablest defenses of bureaucracy against its hostile critics.

Finer, Herman: "Administrative Responsibility in a Democratic Government." *Public Administration Review*, Vol. 1 (Summer, 1941), pp. 335–350 Emphasizes importance of "external controls" on administration in comparison with "inner check" advocated by such men as Carl J. Friedrich in *Public Policy* (Cambridge, Mass.: Harvard University Press, 1940), Vol. 1, pp. 3–24.

Frank, Jerome: *If Men Were Angels* (New York: Harper, 1942). Argues for government of laws well administered by men with faith in democracy and ability to make it efficient.

Gaus, John M.: *Reflections on Public Administration* (University, Ala.: University of Alabama Press, 1947). Concludes that administration is intermingled with entire process of government and with environment in which people affected by government exist.

Gervasi, Frank: *Big Government* (New York: McGraw-Hill, 1949). Examines meaning and purpose of Hoover Commission Report. Asserts bigness not evil per se but executive modernization still imperative if we are to discharge properly twentieth-century domestic and international responsibilities.

Herring, E. Pendleton: *Public Administration and the Public Interest* (New York: McGraw-Hill, 1936). Concerned with difficult and illusive pursuit of public interest in great administrative machine made necessary by modern democratic state.

Hyneman, Charles S.: *Bureaucracy in a Democracy* (New York: Harper, 1950). Interested in effective democratic direction and control of governmental officials. Recommends unification of direction and control through device of central council or executive-legislative liason committee.

Pusey, Merlo J.: *Big Government: Can We Control It?* (New York: Harper, 1945). Traces and assesses significance of modern governmental trends produced by impact of depression, war, and technocracy. Suggests reforms to help in reconciling big government with constitutional democracy.

Rosenfarb, Joseph: *Freedom and the Administrative State* (New York: Harper, 1948). Argues that we can preserve and advance freedom and democracy in the administrative state. Sees administrators playing major role in running managed economy, founded on private enterprise, but democratically controlled and oriented.

Sullivan, Lawrence: *Bureaucracy Runs Amuck* (Indianapolis: Bobbs-Merrill, 1944). The latest edition in Mr. Sullivan's series of vitriolic castigations of bureaucracy.

United States Commission on Organization of the Executive Branch of the Government ("Hoover Commission"): *Reports* (Washington: Government Printing Office, 19 vols., 1949). Most recent and exhaustive treatment of subject. Provides indispensable factual basis for assessing present status and future possibilities of responsible, manageable, economic administration.

Waldo, Dwight: *The Administrative State* (New York: Ronald, 1948). A critical study of political theory of American public administration. Presents development of public administration as chapter in history of American political thought.

White, Leonard D.: "Legislative Responsibility for the Public," *New Horizons in Public Administration* (University, Ala.: University of Alabama Press, 1945). Argues that administrators need greater freedom, can be trusted, and must then be held accountable for their actions.

PART IV: PUBLIC POLICY

FEDERAL ENTERPRISES

How Should We Develop Our Major River Basins?

On April 10, 1933, a new President provided a twentieth-century answer to this perplexing problem. Said Franklin D. Roosevelt:

"I . . . suggest to the Congress legislation to create a Tennessee Valley Authority—a corporation clothed with the power of Government but possessed of the flexibility and initiative of a private enterprise. It should be charged with the broadest duty of planning for the proper use, conservation, and development of the natural resources of the Tennessee River drainage basin and its adjoining territory for the general social and economic welfare of the nation."

In the closing paragraph of his message to Congress, President Roosevelt declared: "If we are successful here we can march on, step by step, in a like development of other great natural territorial units within our borders."

By May 18, 1933, Mr. Roosevelt's suggestion for a TVA had become law. Our first integrated, multipurpose, river-development project had been launched!

The success of this experiment is now generally conceded, but the wisdom of its application to other river basins is still being vigorously debated.

David E. Lilienthal, former Chairman of the Tennessee Valley Authority, contends that the "TVA idea," with wise adaptation, can be made to work in other river basins. He emphasizes that intelligent adaptation requires adherence to the essential characteristics of the "TVA idea." (1) Natural resources must be developed in a really unified way by a flexible, enterprising, and responsible government corporation. (2) Private activity, investment, initiative, and profit in manufacturing, commerce, farming, transportation, forestry, and other fields must be stimulated and encouraged. (3) Administration of the river basin must be decentralized, with state, local, and private agencies and citizens participating in accomplishing the authority's broad objectives. (4) Politics must be kept out of the Valley Authority and the Valley Authority must be kept out of politics.

Harlan I. Peyton, Spokane businessman and a Director of the United States Chamber of Commerce, opposes the creation of regional authorities. In the second selection in this chapter he argues that regional authorities violate states' rights and threaten our federal system. He holds that currently functioning agencies, working in coordination according to a democratic master plan of unified river development, are doing a competent job. Progress is satisfactory. In particular, he asserts that a Columbia Valley Administration would be unnecessary, autocratic, irresponsible, and supersocialistic.

The Hoover Commission Task Force on Natural Resources stresses the difficulties of applying TVA's experience to other areas. The Task Force opposes the extension of the "valley authority type" to other river basins at this time. It urges instead the establishment of a Water Development Service within the regular departmental hierarchy. The Service would consolidate the functions of presently conflicting agencies and achieve truly unified development. The Service would have a broad basin-wide responsibility in given river areas although its powers would not have to be so broad as that of TVA. The Water Development Service would combine the best, and avoid the worst, features of the regular department and the regional authority.

The proper development of our river basins is not a problem relating merely to Federal enterprises. It touches problems in the fields of federalism, public opinion, pressure groups, legislative-executive relations, Federal powers, administration, civil service, public finance, national defense, aid to general business, regulation of utilities, labor, education and welfare, agriculture, and conservation of natural resources.

Although the proposed Missouri Valley Authority and Columbia Valley Administration have received the lion's share of attention, other projects have beeen suggested for other river areas. Despite the fact that adverse committee action was taken on an MVA in 1945 and no favorable action on President Truman's proposal for a CVA in 1949, recurrent flood and drought, soil erosion, power shortages, expensive "pork-barrel" legislation, plus conflict among related agencies in the field, will keep the issue of valley authorities alive.

The basic questions of public policy are these:

Should we develop a program similar to TVA for the major undeveloped river basins of the country? Or should we oppose the creation of regional authorities of any name, scope, or form? Or should we oppose extension of regional authorities while entrusting major development to drastically reorganized, regular, departments of governments?

THE TVA IDEA, ADAPTED WISELY, CAN BE MADE TO WORK ELSEWHERE

BY DAVID E. LILIENTHAL*

[David E. Lilienthal was Director of TVA from 1933 to 1941 and its Chairman from 1941 to 1946. He was Chairman of the Atomic Energy Commission from 1946 until his resignation in 1950. He is the author of *TVA: Democracy on the March, This I Do Believe*, and one of the coauthors of "A Report on the International Control of Atomic Energy." EDITOR.]

During its far from tranquil existence since June, 1933, a good many words have been used to characterize the TVA. Some have been sulphuric, some extravagantly enthusiastic. But the expression most commonly applied has been "experiment."

Congress and the President did launch the TVA as an experiment, and from the outset we have administered it in that spirit. The chief importance of the TVA, it seems to me, is as a demonstration of a new and distinctive way for a people to develop their natural resources of rivers and waters, land and minerals and forests. After a decade the TVA is now able to throw the light of actual experience—not just theories or talk—upon a fundamental problem of universal concern.

The stakes of such an experiment, in a new way to perform an old task are high. For not only in the Tennessee Valley, but in a thousand valleys the world over the hopes and aspirations of all peoples rest upon their natural resources, the universal foundation stones of economic life.

What have TVA's new methods demonstrated? What lessons are there in TVA's story that other valleys and natural regions may profit by? More specifically, does the record of this pilot plant in the Tennessee Valley bespeak the creation of more TVA's?

* "More TVA's?" *The New York Times Magazine*, Jan. 7, 1945, pp. 10ff. *passim.* By permission of *The New York Times* and Mr. Lilienthal.

A substantial body of American opinion seems to think so. . . .
. . . Should there be more TVA's?

Without bothering to examine the evidence, the dogmatists of both "left" and "right" have entered a confident verdict of "no." Everyone else will want to appraise the demonstration before reaching a conclusion. An adequate statement, such as I endeavored to make in . . . [my] book, "TVA—Democracy on the March," is of course quite beyond the limits of this article. But for those interested in results rather than abstract doctrine, in judging whether the TVA idea should be and can be adapted elsewhere, I would invite scrutiny and consideration of the following four distinctive and essential characteristics of this undertaking:

I. Development of Natural Resources in a Unified Way

The TVA idea represents a departure in American national policy in this, that one Federal agency, the TVA, not a dozen or so (as is customary) is responsible for the unified, not the divided, development of resources in a natural region.

These new principles of unity of resources and unity of responsibility for their development are now . . . written into the very landscape and the life of a resurgent region.

As one concrete result of this new way of doing things, a major river has been made to do what it is told to do, by a unique control of its waters for the benefit of men.

America for over a century has puttered at the job of developing her rivers; the work has lagged far behind our proud technical standards in almost every other field. . . . When the largest of the TVA's new structures [as of 1945]—Fontana Dam and Kentucky Dam—went into service, modern unified river control became an accomplished fact on an American river—the first river in the world of which this can be said. I venture the assertion that it will not be the last.

The Tennessee River System has been dealt with by TVA as a comprehensive whole, not as a series of unrelated sites for dams. Each dam was seen as a part of that whole, made to yield all of its potential value—not a navigation channel alone, or flood control only, or power as a separate asset, or re-creation. The series of TVA dams—the largest job of engineering and construction undertaken by one organization in American history—has made all those assets available from each dam.

By this system of dams, designed and operated almost as if they were one dam, the waters of the Tennessee River system can now be turned on and off from the TVA's central water dispatchers office with almost the same precision with which you handle vessels of liquid in a laboratory.

When rainfall is heavy and floods threaten, the reservoirs hold back the excess till the crisis is past—and that crisis may be at Cairo on the Ohio River, hundreds of miles away. When the dry season comes in the fall and the water is needed to keep deep-water navigation moving, enough water can be let down to maintain a nine-foot channel. (We have ample rainfall in this valley, so irrigation is not one of the multiple uses made of the water; it could be, if that were needed.)

As water is released from behind the dams, it turns water wheels that produce electric power in great quantities. TVA is today the largest electricity-producing system in the United States, the "paying partner" of the enterprise with an annual gross revenue of over $35,000,000 from sales of electricity, that (through 130 locally owned and operated distribution systems) serves 550,000 homes, farms and factories in five States. At the levels of the past five years it will take only thirty years to repay Uncle Sam the total power investment, with net income remaining after operating expenses, depreciation, taxes to local agencies and other costs.

The success of the idea of unified development is written not only on the river but on the changed face of the land of the region, and in the forests and woodlots. The land was not dealt with separately from the river, the customary method. In nature land and streams are a unity. Everyone knows that what farmers do on their land affects the flow of waters both on the land and in the rivers. Minerals affect the fertility and hence the waterholding ability of land; the same is true of forests.

The TVA principle required that the same unity of resources that in fact exists in nature should be reflected in the way men develop those resources.

The results of the new method are to be seen on every hand, as one travels through the region. Farmers, many thousands of them, work on their own acres, with the aid of science, to restore the fertility and security of the soil of their farms and the growth of their timber. They are consciously paying heed to the oneness, in nature, of land and river, of forests and minerals.

A half-dozen or more different Government agencies, having separate responsibilities and policies and different sources of authority, could hardly perform such a unified task. In any event, they never have done so. Congress had to create a new kind of Government tool, the TVA. This regional development corporation was to have "the flexibility and initiative of a private enterprise"; so it was not put within any of the old-line Washington departments and bureaus. It was to function under a Congressional charter explicitly defining its duties and prescribing the policies its administrators were to follow.

That charter fixed responsibility for results squarely upon TVA for an entire undertaking of many parts, all interrelated. This was, and still is, almost a revolution in Government administration, though to a manager it seems the plainest sense. In the development of the river, not flood control alone, or navigation or power, but all the water's uses, together, were made the responsibility of one public agency, the TVA. Not water resources in one compartment of government, dealt with separately from soil or forests, nor farming separately from industry, not industry separate from transport and electricity.

The TVA has responsibility to see that things happen—but no powers of compulsion. We were given no power in 1933 and we want no power . . . to issue orders to farmers, owners of forest land, business men—citizens generally—or to local or State Governments. Coercion will not do a democratic job.

The fact is that the changes one sees in this valley are chiefly due to TVA's record in successfully enlisting the active participation of the people, their private enterprises and their local and State public institutions. That federation of interests was achieved and is held together by a common understanding, one that is growing in this valley—and to me this is more impressive than the massive dams or even the new green-clad slopes. That understanding is this: that our natural resources are the region's entire capital, and their development must be in accordance with the unity of those resources in the plan of nature.

II. THE INCREASE OF INDEPENDENT ACTIVITY AND ENTERPRISE BY PRIVATE CITIZENS

In the early days of the TVA a notable adversary said over and again that private business would decline in the Tennessee Valley because business men and investors would fear and avoid a region where Government played so important an economic role.

The contrary has been the case. What TVA has accomplished in stimulating and encouraging private undertakings in manufacturing, commerce, farming, transportation, forestry and other fields is now widely known. As *The Baltimore Sun* said editorially on Nov. 16, 1944, "Far from withering private enterprise, TVA has afforded the means for a variety of new businesses to spring up in the valley."

By the presence of abundant low-cost electricity and a new 650-mile waterway, by industrial research in new uses of the region's raw materials in private industry, by protection from floods that damage business and by making available facts about resources in a form that business men require for their decisions, there has developed in this region a unique relation between TVA and small and large business. This has been expressed in large private investments and plans for continued expansion.

Since TVA was created, the figures show that private enterprise in this region has made greater progress than in the United States as a whole during the same period—whether the measure of progress be increase in retail sales, number of new manufacturing establishments, bank deposits, value added by manufacture and persons engaged therein, or any other index. *The New York Times* summarized the matter in accordance with the facts when it said editorially recently: "There is abundant evidence in big as well as little businesses in the Tennessee Valley that private initiative has been encouraged, not stamped out."

That Government activity can nourish and encourage the expansion of industry, commerce and agriculture is no new idea, of course. But in the Tennessee Valley the demonstration affects so many varied kinds of business activity and has resulted in such huge permanent private investment that with the fair-minded it should lay to rest any notion that public investment and public technical leadership necessarily exclude private investment and initiative.

The important question is: what kind of public activity? It is now clear to most observers that the TVA is the kind that helps and multiplies private activity, investment, initiative and profit.

III. A Method of Achieving Genuine Decentralization of the Federal Government's Role in Resource Development

Congress and the President created TVA as an autonomous corporation rooted in a region rather than as a remote bureau of a Washington department. This is the first major exception in more than fifty years to the trend toward centralized administration of Federal functions.

TVA's administrators, engineers and technicians were selected from all parts of the country. But they live and work in the Tennessee Valley. That is where the problems of the people are; that is where the decisions are made. Local delegations don't have to go to Washington to get an answer where the TVA is involved. The men they want to see are right in the valley.

This experiment in government in the open air has developed a body of experience of general usefulness. The TVA has shown, under none too easy circumstances that, in the field of resource development, there is an alternative to ever larger departments in Washington and to cumbersome, top-heavy, over-centralized government.

This decentralization from Washington has made it possible for TVA in turn to decentralize within the region. To that end we have entered into scores of contracts with State and local agencies and private groups. As a consequence of this deliberate policy, most of the changes wrought in this valley are not affected directly by TVA at all.

They result from the combined efforts of hundreds of local, State and private agencies, such as farmers' associations, State universities, rural electric cooperatives and city power boards, State and community planning boards, State and local conservation agencies. It is this aspect of the TVA, this citizen partnership and participation, that strongly impresses visitors who are, wisely, fearful of "bureaucratic domination."

IV. A Demonstration That Politics Can Be Kept out of the Administration of an Important Public Enterprise

Congress itself, in a rare provision of law, prohibited politics in the administration of TVA. We took that direction literally. Furthermore, we have observed the corollary—that we of TVA keep strictly out of politics.

No technical enterprise can possibly succeed on any other basis. It is more than a matter of "patronage"; the integrity of every decision on a technical or business question would be in doubt were any other rule observed.

The significant thing in the TVA's experience is that the public has fought off any attempt to tamper with TVA's uncompromising position on this matter of politics. Whenever someone, however powerful, seeks to inject political considerations into TVA's operations, there are widespread public expressions of protest from almost every quarter. The people understand the issue: TVA's broad policies are matters for Congress and political institutions; but they don't want political administration of their business.

The general assumption of public apathy concerning the conduct of public business we have not found to be true; quite the contrary.

It will be apparent that all TVA's accomplishments are due to the distinctive methods it has employed. It is coming to be recognized in many parts of the world that it is these methods that embody what is known as "the TVA idea."

After eleven and a half years of observation it is my opinion that these methods, adapted wisely to the variety of circumstances in a thousand regions of the world, can be made to work elsewhere.

It is obvious, of course, that the TVA pattern is no cooky cutter, not something to be copied. The TVA idea will be useful elsewhere by the process of intelligent adaptation.

The results in the Tennessee Valley led *The Wall Street Journal* to observe a few days ago: "President Roosevelt's proposal for 'TVA's' in every important watershed in the country has a certain logical foundation —no doubt about that. If TVA has been a 'good thing' for the Tennessee River region it should be a good thing for every other river region."

Similar developments elsewhere will be a "good thing" only if it is clearly recognized that the distinguishing features of TVA that I have here summarized are essential: one agency doing a unified job; that agency decentralized, adapted to stimulate private development at the grass roots and free from politics. These essential characteristics are not dependent upon the physical circumstances peculiar or distinctive to the Tennessee Valley. They can be adapted to other regions, and other problems.

THE REGIONAL AUTHORITY IS AN UNDESIRABLE, SUPERSOCIALISTIC, WELFARE STATE

BY HARLAN I. PEYTON*

[Harlan I. Peyton, prominent Spokane businessman, is a Director of the Chamber of Commerce of the United States. He is also a Republican National Committeeman for Washington. EDITOR.]

The Chamber of Commerce of the United States is opposed to the creation of regional authorities of any name, scope, or form. A long-standing policy opposes Federal regional authorities. The reasons for this objection are principally two:

1. Authorities encroach upon and displace State jurisdiction of natural resources. The extension of the regional idea to the entire country, as has been repeatedly proposed in single bills before Congress, would mean the eventual disregard of State lines and a new subdividing of the United States on a regional basis. Local and State governments would be subordinated to Federal controls, not only of their waters and others resources; but also in large degree of their whole State economy.

2. Authorities displace the regularly established agencies of the Federal Government. It is the long-standing view of the chamber, first established by referendum vote of its membership in 1937, that "the Federal Government should continue to use its regularly established agencies, operating on a national basis, for activities properly belonging to the Federal Government in relation to natural resources." . . .

The policy of the Chamber of Commerce of the United States supports the principle that what may be construed as the national interest in a natural resource, as distinguished from a State or local interest, should be dealt with on a functional basis by a single Federal agency. This was the Federal policy up until the time that TVA was created. Thus, we have

* Statement filed before United States House of Representatives, Committee on Public Works, *Hearings, Columbia Valley Administration*, 81st Cong., 1st sess., 1949, pp. 454–457 *passim*.

the Corps of Engineers handling first navigation, and later including flood control. We have the Bureau of Reclamation handling all western reclamation in the 17 Western States. We have the Forest Service handling all national forests; the Park Service handling all national parks; and so on through the Extension Service, the land-grant colleges, soil conservation, fish and wildlife, the Geological Survey, the Bureau of Mines, the Indian Bureau, and the Weather Bureau.

Our support of this functional division of the Federal interest is based on technical grounds. Each Federal interest is a speciality. The technical skills used in building revetments and dredging rivers, for example, apply to all rivers and not to the streams of a single watershed. Reclamation is a technical problem common to 17 Western States. Recently projected plans for river development in the West show clearly that the basin idea has no general application. . . .

It seems to me, gentlemen, that this regional idea is clearly overrated. The first thing the Congress should do, in my opinion, is to determine what the Federal responsibility is in resource development. The chamber's policy adheres to the conception that the Federal function is a limited function—a "delegated" function—and that the rest belongs to the States. The regional authority stands in direct conflict with this idea of Federal powers.

The Columbia Valley Administration bills and the long list of similar proposals for Federal basin corporations all seem to presume primary Federal rights, and to permit, if you please, some consultative privileges to local boards and agencies, whose advice the Administration will seek "in its discretion" and apply "as far as practicable."

Gentlemen, I do not propose to take your time in going over the Columbia Valley Administration bill (S. 1645) in detail. Taken as a whole, it provides, potentially at least, for a federally planned economy in the Columbia River Basin. Its declared policy is that the "relevant powers" of the Federal Government in this region is organized, directed, and administered so as to get "full and unified conservation, development, and use of the water, land, forest, mineral, fish and wildlife, and other resources of the region." That leaves out nothing. Provisions in the bill respecting State and local participation are expressed in such broad, general language as to be meaningless. Here is an example: "The Administration shall make arrangements for such consultation and interchange of views . . . as may be necessary or appropriate to achieve the objectives of this section." I submit that something vastly more specific is necessary if the rights of the States are to be respected.

. . . I live in the Columbia River Basin. Out there we believe deeply that use of Federal Funds toward the development of Columbia River

Basin resources, including generation of electrical power, is not an issue in evaluation of bills for creation of a Columbia Valley Authority, Administration, or Commission.

The issue here is between the established processes of the United States and a Marxist-American hybrid collectivism.

Proponents of CVA contend:

1. That river-basin development is stagnated.
2. That the present State and Federal agencies are incompetent.
3. That something new and untested will do a better job.

[Peyton maintains that none of these contentions can be substantiated.]

. . .

The famous "308 report" was made by the Corps of Army Engineers as a direct result of the repeated demands by . . . [a] Spokane group and by others in the Pacific Northwest. The "308 report" has been the bible of river-development projects since it was originally filed with Congress in 1932.

Grand Coulee and Bonneville Dams were built as a result of it. They provided power to help win the war through the construction of ocean ships and airplanes and through the reduction of aluminum and magnesium.

The revised "308 report" was completed last year by the Army. It is one of the most complete and most democratic documents of its kind ever prepared by man. It is democratic in that every major proposal was reviewed at public hearings, and several were tossed aside when it was shown they would cause undue economic or social loss.

This latest report includes among other things:

a. A comprehensive picture of undeveloped resources.

b. Evaluation of irrigation, reclamation, flood control, power, navigation, recreation, and other uses.

c. Comparisons of benefits with damage or local displacements.

d. A schedule for the development of major projects.

e. A schedule of deferred projects.

Irrigation, reclamation, soil conservation, and flood control have moved ahead at great speed in the 30 years since a drought pointed to the need. Speed was limited by the war, by shortages of materials afterward and by other factors, including the size of congressional appropriations. The individual who wants water for a particular acreage may feel that progress is slow, but anyone who views the Pacific Northwest as a whole must admit there has been no stagnation as charged by some CVA boosters.

It should be noted that the period from 1919, when the drought was seriously apparent, to 1932, when the "308 report" was filed, was given over to planning. The years since 1933 with the exception of the war years, have seen phenomenal development by private, State and Federal means in many areas of the Columbia River Basin. . . .

I want to talk a minute about the Army engineers and the Reclamation Bureau. Each of these is a specialist, and each is justifiably proud of its abilities and accomplishments. In the Columbia River Basin, the Army engineers are interested primarily in navigation and flood control while the Bureau has promoted irrigation, reclamation, and power. . . .

As we in the Pacific Northwest see it, the CVA planners now so active in high places in the national capital would like to do the following things for us:

First, they would set up a superstate; a sort of fifth wheel that would find itself in direct conflict with many of the functions now exercised by the States. It would be a superstate over which the people of the Pacific Northwest would have no more authority than they now have over the socialistic dreamings of the Bonneville Power Administration. [Several paragraphs before Peyton had written: "Bonneville has demonstrated a determination to eliminate private capital from the electrical industry. Its reports repeatedly show a desire to create a planned, socialistic economy."]

Second, there would be a gradual invasion of the fields of private enterprise. This trend is charted in the original Mitchell bill introduced in the Senate in 1945. Under that bill a CVA could have taken over about every function of public and private enterprise in the Pacific Northwest other than the armed services and the post office. That bill speaks for itself. The present proposal has been modified, but the advocates speak the same language. We of the Pacific Northwest consider this to be a very grave danger to our future.

Third, there would be a definite effort to create a controlled welfare state in which the lives of the people would be regimented to whatever extent the dictators of the hour might presume necessary to their own desires or benefits. Thinking in the direction of regimentation is shown in the Bonneville reports.

We are told that we might as well have a CVA since we already are controlled and regimented by hordes of bureaucrats. We will agree that we have had far too many Federal controls in our Pacific Northwest, but there is one difference between the multiplicity of bureaucrats and a CVA. We can hope to exert control over unrelated bureaucrats by the force of our ballots, but a CVA, once fully in the saddle, would be able to sway elections in their own favor.

In conclusion, it is our contention that the Pacific Northwest should be developed at a reasonably rapid pace by private, State, and Federal enterprise, but without the intervention of a supersocialistic welfare state.

A DRASTICALLY REORGANIZED REGULAR DEPARTMENT SHOULD DEVELOP OUR RIVER BASINS

BY THE HOOVER COMMISSION TASK FORCE ON NATURAL RESOURCES*

[The members of this Task Force included the following men: Leslie A. Miller, former Governor of Wyoming, Chairman; Horace Albright, former Director, National Park Service; John Dempsey, former Governor of New Mexico; Ralph Carr, former Governor of Colorado; Donald H. McLaughlin, President, Homestake Mining Corp.; Dr. Isaiah Bowman, President, Johns Hopkins University; Dr. Gilbert White, President, Haverford College; Professor Samuel T. Dana, Dean, School of Forestry and Conservation, University of Michigan; and a special unit of the Legislative Reference Service of the Library of Congress under direction of Ernest Griffith, Director of the Service. EDITOR.]

DIFFICULTY OF APPRAISAL

The starting point for an evaluation of the valley authority type of organization is the experience of TVA. It is essential, however, to keep in mind certain limitations on the applicability of this experience.

a. Although TVA was established 15 years ago there is still no objective comprehensive study of its experience.

b. Even where results of its operations are reasonably clear it is not easy to decide what is due to type of organization and what to other circumstances.

c. Conditions differ widely from one river basin to another, raising questions as to the extent to which TVA's experience is a safe guide for predicting the way in which similar organizations would work in other areas. Resource development problems in the Tennessee basin are complex, involving irregular flow, competing uses, undeveloped power, exploited lands, undeveloped resources, unbalanced economy, and low standards of living. This same complexity of interrelated problems is not found in all great river basins.

d. Because of the complexity of interrelated resource problems in the Tennessee basin, the legislative authority of the TVA to deal with these problems is quite broad—broader than may be required for Federal agencies operating in basins having less difficult problems.

* Appendix 4 of *Task Force Report on Natural Resources*, prepared for United States Commission on Organization of the Executive Branch of the Government ("Hoover Commission") (Washington: Government Printing Office, 1949), pp. 94–97.

e. Many proposals for valley authorities differ substantially from the TVA model.

f. Existence of a number of valley authorities raises problems on which relatively little light is shed by the experience of a single authority.

Distinctive Features of TVA

TVA had its origin in the failure to adapt our national departmental structure to the requirements of river basin development. Piecemeal, single-purpose development remained the order of the day in spite of the evidence that maximum benefit was attainable only through river basin planning and development on a comprehensive, multiple-purpose basis. TVA's charter gave it a number of significant advantages in comparison with established river development agencies.

a. It was organized to develop an entire river basin in a manner calculated to provide the maximum benefits, all purposes to be taken into consideration. It did not have to confine its efforts to specific portions of the river basin, nor did it have to give primary consideration to specific purposes.

b. It provided a focal point for leadership and responsibility in river development planning and operations. It did not have to share responsibility with other Federal agencies, but was itself authorized and directed to prepare and carry out plans for the comprehensive development of the river basin. It did not actually perform all of the related functions itself. There was a division of labor, but not of responsibility. It cooperated with other agencies, but it was responsible for getting the job done, and for taking the lead in working out methods of cooperation.

c. It provided a method for decentralizing the Federal Government's river development activities. Other agencies were organized along traditional lines, with a high degree of centralized control over field offices. In the case of TVA, decisions could be made in the region, thereby avoiding many of the delays and clearances involved in normal departmental procedure. Undoubtedly, this regional emphasis also facilitated cooperative arrangements with state and local agencies. TVA advocates place great emphasis on "grass roots" administration.

d. TVA's independence and corporate status gave it a measure of flexibility greater than that enjoyed by other water development agencies, with respect to financing, accounting, personnel policies, and other matters.

Advantages of National Departmental Organization

The committee is of the opinion that the functions of the TVA should not be consolidated with other natural resource development functions at least at this time. TVA was established as an experiment. The development of the Tennessee River Basin is not yet completed, and the committee therefore recommends that TVA be continued. The committee is, however, also opposed to the extension of the valley authority type or organization to other river basins at this time. It believes that the functions of the National Government with respect to water resource development should be entrusted to regular departments of the Government, provided drastic reorganizations are effected.

There are important values in the traditional vertical bureau and departmental type of organization that make it desirable to administer natural resource development functions through that means.

a. It provides greater assurance of similiar treatment of similar resource problems throughout the Nation than would a regional type of organization.

b. It makes possible the utilization of central services which cannot be afforded in each regional area.

c. It makes possible the development of standards by which similar programs in many river basins can be measured.

d. It operates as a restraint on sectional tendencies which might influence a regional authority to develop regional interests in a manner detrimental to the best national interest.

The committee is keenly aware of the dangers of extreme centralization, and its recommendations take full account of the desirability of decentralized administration. It recognizes further the validity of river basin areas as proper units for the decentralized administration of the natural resource functions of the National Government. At the same time, it cannot overlook the fact that there are over-riding national interests in the development of our water and other resources. The development of the potentialities of one region cannot be considered without careful regard to its effects on the economies of other regions, and that of the nation as a whole. Irrigation and land drainage, power development, and navigation improvements, for example, need to be examined in the light of their effects on the total economy, not merely on that of a particular river basin. The committee is concerned that the undesirable effects of establishing a series of regional authorities would lie not merely in the increasing friction that might develop among these authorities, but in a growing disregard of the national interest in resource development.

It has been suggested that the resolution of interregional conflicts and the protection of national interests could be left to Congress. Within limits, it is true that sectional and regional conflicts of interest always have to be adjusted by Congress, whatever the form of administrative organization. It should not be overlooked, however, that the successful resolution of sectional or regional conflicts, and the harmonizing of regional and national interests, can be greatly facilitated by proper ad-

ministrative organization. The committee has noted that one reason for
the unsatisfactory state of national water policies is the absence of a
proper organization of national functions in this area. It is idle to expect
Congress to formulate initially a detailed national water resource development program. The Congress unquestionably will, and ought to, have the
last word. The only way in which it can be expected to arrive at soundly
conceived policies, however, is for it to have adequate assistance from
the administrative branch in bringing before it the facts and viewpoints
which are most significant, and in formulating suggested policies. Such
assistance can be provided most effectively by an agency with Nation-
wide responsibility.

The committee wishes to make clear that in stressing the values of the
traditional departmental form of organization it does not mean to imply
that these values are actually being realized at the present time. The
contrary is true. Under the existing system local interests, rarely even
harmonized on a regional basis, too often predominate. The logrolling
method of distributing Federal funds is certainly not unknown in this
area. Authority for development is divided in an uneconomic and inefficient manner. Responsibility to the Executive exists in name only.
In fact, the situation has been and is so bad that sooner or later a strong
movement for valley authorities is bound to be revived unless drastic
changes are put into effect. Properly organized, the ordinary departmental system can incorporate the desirable features of regional organization, at the same time avoiding its undesirable features. The essentials
of sound departmental organization in this area may be summarized as
follows:

a. Some agency must be granted fairly broad responsibility to integrate
at least the major Federal water development functions in given river
basins. The scope of its functions need not be as broad as that of TVA,
but it must be broad enough to enable the agency to formulate a program
of water use and control taking into consideration the purposes of navigation, flood control, irrigation, power development, pollution control,
recreation, domestic and industrial water consumption, etc. [In a note
on this point the Task Force added the following: "In view of the fact
that the consumptive use of water resources of the West is governed by
water rights established by State law and by interstate and international
compacts, any Federal action should be in compliance with local, State,
and interstate rights and interests."]

b. The jurisdiction of the agency with full responsibility for water
resource development in a river basin must be coextensive with the
boundaries of that basin. It makes no sense to divide responsibility between two water development agencies operating in the same basin.

c. The agency with responsibility for water resource development within a river basin must make provision for adequate decentralization so that basic resource decisions will be made in light of conditions in the areas they affect. The advantages of "grass roots" administration should be preserved.

d. Similarly, if other bureaus and departments with related functions are to share in this development they will need to modify their programs to make possible more effective coordination than is now possible. This means a greater degree of decentralization along river basin lines; greater uniformity in a regional and field office headquarters; more even delegations of authority; and a policy of adapting national departmental programs to the pace of regional water resource development.

e. Adoption of a mechanism for interagency review and coordination on a national and regional scale, with strong presidential support.

f. Adoption of uniform legislative and administrative standards for estimating costs and benefits, determining over-all economic and engineering feasibility, requiring repayment of costs, making authorizations and appropriations for multiple-purpose projects and the several features thereof.

The strongest argument for valley authorities has been that reform in the directions indicated above has proceeded at a geologic pace, as one observer has characterized it. The committee believes that if the consolidations it has recommended are not carried into action and if the present competition among Federal resource agencies continues, the establishment of regional authorities will in all probability become necessary.

[The chief consolidation recommended was the "Establishment of a consolidated Water Development Service, to administer the present functions of the Bureau of Reclamation, the river development functions of the Corps of Engineers, the power marketing functions of the Bonneville and South Western Power Administrations and of the Division of Power in the Department of the Interior, certain river-development functions now administered by the Federal Power Commission; and certain functions of the Department of State relating to international boundary streams."]

QUESTIONS AND PROBLEMS

1. What is "the TVA idea"?
2. State and then appraise the arguments of those who propose more TVA's.
3. How are our other river basins being developed now?
4. Explain in some detail why Mr. Peyton opposes the creation of regional authorities of any name, scope, or form. Evaluate Mr. Peyton's argument.

5. What limitations on the applicability of TVA's experience must be kept in mind in evaluating the valley authority type of organization?

6. According to the Hoover Commission Task Force, what are the advantages of the traditional departmental type of organization that make it desirable to administer natural resources development through the regular department?

7. What "drastic reorganization" does the Task Force recommend? Why?

8. What are the "essentials of sound departmental organization in this area" according to the Task Force?

9. Wherein do Lilienthal, Peyton, and the Task Force agree? Disagree?

10. After surveying the operation of TVA and the agencies now handling the development of our major river basins, how do *you* propose that we continue to develop our river basins? Defend whatever position you take.

SELECT BIBLIOGRAPHY

Daniels, Walter M. (ed.): *Should We Have More TVA's?* (New York: H. W. Wilson, 1950) (Vol. 22, No. 2, of The Reference Shelf). An excellent compilation of articles on TVA, CVA, MVA, the proposed St. Lawrence Seaway, and "The Authority Idea in Perspective." Contains useful bibliography.

Espy, Willard R.: "More TVA's? The Issues Weighed," *The New York Times Magazine*, May 7, 1950, pp. 14–15*ff.* Argues that more TVA's are desirable, feasible, inevitable.

Fesler, James W. (ed.): "Government and Water Resources: A Symposium," *American Political Science Review*, Vol. 44 (September, 1950), pp. 575–649. May be read with great profit by the fully initiated student.

Lepawsky, Albert: "Water Resources and American Federalism": maintains that our States must put up or shut up.

Maass, Arthur A.: "Congress and Water Resources": a devastating critique of Congress's role in this field.

McKinley, Charles: "The Valley Authority and Its Alternatives": brushes aside extravagant charges, pro and con, and seeks to ascertain best organization for development of water resources.

White, Gilbert F.: "National Executive Organization for Water Resources": demonstrates great lag in adjustment of governmental institutions to such widely recognized needs as multiple-purpose projects, basin-wide planning, and broader regional and national outlook.

Lilienthal, David E.: *TVA: Democracy on the March* (New York: Harper, 1944; Pocket Books, 1945). Best single explanation of TVA as regional experiment and contribution to American democracy. Enunciates Lilienthal's faith, facts, and reasons.

"New 'Valley Authority' for the U.S.? Congress Studies a Long-range Policy," *Congressional Digest*, Vol. 29 (January, 1950), pp. 5–32. Contains brief background material and pro and con discussion. A good starting point.

Pacific Northwest Development Association: "Is CVA-MVA-TVA Legislation Socialistic?" *Congressional Record,* 81st Cong., 1st sess., Vol. 95, Pt. 12 (Feb. 25, 1949), pp. A1073-A1075. Attacks CVA and other valley authorities as socialistic, autocratic, undemocratic, and unnecessary.

Russell, Dean: *The TVA Idea* (Irvington-on-Hudson, N.Y.: Foundation for Economic Freedom, 1949). Alleges that TVA's electric power is subsidized, its rates "rigged" and its "yardstick" unfair, its operation expensive, and its authority excessive. Minimizes TVA's achievements. Stresses TVA's competition with private power and enterprise.

Tennessee Valley Authority: "Rebuttal of 'The TVA Idea,' " (Knoxville, Tenn.: TVA, Department of Information, 1949). Answers charges against TVA.

Terral, Rufus: *The Missouri Valley: Land of Drouth, Flood, and Promise* (New Haven: Yale University Press, 1947). Readable account of the history and problems of the Missouri Valley. Criticizes Pick-Sloan Plan, advocates an MVA.

United States Commission on Organization of the Executive Branch of the Government ("Hoover Commission"): *Federal Business Enterprises; Task Force Report on Revolving Funds and Business Enterprises of the Federal Government* (Appendix J); *Department of the Interior; Task Force Report on Water Resources Projects* (Appendix K); *Task Force Report on Natural Resources* (Appendix L) (Washington: Government Printing Office, 1949). Cover different aspects of river-basin development. Disagree on exact way to handle river basins; substantially agree on need to eliminate present conflicts and faulty organization. Required reading for advanced students.

United States President's Water Resources Policy Commission: *A Water Policy for the American People* (Vol. 1); *Ten Rivers in America's Future* (Vol. 2); *Water Resources Law* (Vol. 3) (Washington: Government Printing Office, 1950). One of the latest studies. A mine of information. Recommends that we change the multitude of resources activities going on in all parts of nation into a series of integrated complete programs, one for each region.

United States Senate: *Bill to Establish a Columbia Valley Administration,* S. 1645, 81st Cong., 1st sess., 1949. To be consulted to ascertain exact contents of CVA bill.

United States Senate: *Bill to Establish a Missouri Valley Authority,* S. 1160, 81st Cong., 1st sess., 1949. A recent MVA bill.

United States Senate, Committee on Irrigation and Reclamation: *Senate Report 639, Missouri Valley Authority Act,* 79th Cong., 1st sess., 1945. Contains (Pt. 1) reasons for adverse action on 1945 MVA bill.

Whittington, William M.: "Address before 30th Annual Convention of the Mississippi Valley Association," *Congressional Record,* 81st Cong., 1st sess., Vol. 95, Pt. 12 (Feb. 8, 1949), pp. A614-A617. Defense of current handling of river basins by Chairman of House Public Affairs Committee.

LABOR

How Should a Free Society Handle National-emergency Strikes or Lockouts?

What happens when a strike or lockout occurs in a vital segment of our highly interdependent economy? If labor-management conflict breaks out in the coal industry the major coal pits in the nation shut down. The shortage of coal soon affects railroad locomotion and transportation, curtailing shipments of all sorts and resulting in the loss of heat and power for commercial and domestic uses. Steel is shortly affected, and then the assembly lines producing planes, guns, tanks, automobiles, and refrigerators grind to a halt. Rapidly the impact hits the innumerable smaller industries which feed and are fed by the major users of coal and steel. If the conflict remains unresolved, depression and catastrophe may quickly overwhelm the nation. And coal is only one of our many strategic industries!

The chain reaction that can be set off by one key dispute demonstrates dramatically the importance of finding a solution to avoid such national-emergency strikes or lockouts.

In a democracy we seek to mitigate, if we cannot always eliminate, labor-management conflict. In a free society, and within the framework of a largely free-enterprise economy, labor unions and business management utilize voluntary collective bargaining to settle their differences. In the large majority of cases, bargaining is peaceful and successful. The ultimate weapons of strike and lockout, although always present at bargaining talks, seldom have to be employed.

Crisis occurs, however, when bargaining breaks down and the ultimate weapons are invoked. One side or the other foregoes the use of the other's facilities, hoping that the injury resulting from a work or production stoppage will force the other side to make concessions and negotiate a satisfactory contract. Labor suffers because it is without work and wages. Management suffers because it is without production and profits. Dependent labor and management are pinched. And the affected public moans and groans at the loss of product or service.

The interdependence of our modern economy heightens the calculated risk that a free society takes when it accepts voluntary collective bargaining and the ultimate weapons that either side may employ if the battle seems to demand them. This risk is particularly grave in connection with conflicts that threaten the national health, safety, and welfare.

Ordinarily the contest is mitigated to some degree by the sense of economic, social, and political responsibility manifested by both the representatives of labor and management. The contest is not solely a callous and selfish power struggle. At times, however, the contestants ignore their responsibility to the noncontestants and to the public. It is then that voices are heard urging that "something be done." This chapter is concerned with the nature and rationale of that "something."

In what industries and under what conditions should strikes and lockouts be permitted—and for how long? When does the national health, safety, and welfare demand the settlement of the conflict and the return to work and production? What machinery—if any—should be utilized to cope with national emergency conflicts?

The present approach of our government to these questions is found in the provisions of the Labor Management Relations (Taft-Hartley) Act herein presented. The Act's essential features include a presidential board of inquiry, which, however, can make no recommendations; a cooling-off period of approximately 80 days (enforced by injunction); and a secret vote by employees on their employer's last offer of settlement. At the end of the injunctive period, the parties are free to continue their fight. The President is required to report to Congress on the whole affair. At all times the Federal Mediation and Conciliation Service stands by to assist in a voluntary settlement.

The national-emergency provisions of the Taft-Hartley Act are severely criticized by Senators Murray, Pepper, Neely, and Humphrey in the accompanying report from the Joint Committee on Labor-Management Relations. They urge a more flexible plan, featuring greater presidential discretion, a ban on the injunction, the elimination of the last-offer ballot, permission to fact-finding boards to make recommendations, and a shorter (30-day) cooling-off period.

Charles O. Gregory, in the third selection in this chapter, indicates the difficulties of finding a workable or realistic alternative to either complete license or complete repression in industrial conflicts. He tentatively advances a technique of temporary government seizure as a possible approach in certain industries. He believes that his plan for seizure would avoid compulsory arbitration, would permit production and service to continue, and would still be disliked enough by both sides to induce them to reach a voluntary settlement.

A fourth approach to the problem of the national emergency dispute is compulsory arbitration. Senator Ferguson advocates this technique in the concluding article on this problem. Labor-management disputes, he maintains, if unresolved, should be settled in labor courts on the basis of law and justice and enforced by means of stiff penalties for violation. Law and order would thus be restored to industrial relations and safety to the nation.

These approaches are only a few of the many that have been suggested in answer to the question: *How should a free society handle strikes or lockouts which threaten the national health, safety, and welfare?*

INQUIRY, INJUNCTION, COOLING-OFF, LAST OFFER BALLOT AND THE BEST CONCILIATION SERVICE POSSIBLE

FROM THE LABOR MANAGEMENT RELATIONS ACT OF 1947*

Whenever in the opinion of the President of the United States, a threatened or actual strike or lock-out affecting an entire industry or a substantial part thereof engaged in trade, commerce, transportation, transmission, or communication among the several States or with foreign nations, or engaged in the production of goods for commerce, will, if permitted to occur or to continue, imperil the national health or safety, he may appoint a board of inquiry to inquire into the issues involved in the dispute and to make a written report to him within such time as he shall prescribe. Such report shall include a statement of the facts with respect to the dispute, including each party's statement of its position but shall not contain any recommendations. The President shall file a copy of such report with the [Federal Mediation and Conciliation] Service and shall make its contents available to the public.

A board of inquiry shall be composed of a chairman and such other members as the President shall determine, and shall have power to sit and act in any place within the United States and to conduct such hear-

* 61 Stat. 155–156 (1947); Title II, secs. 206–210, 212.

ings either in public or in private, as it may deem necessary or proper, to ascertain the facts with respect to the causes and circumstances of the dispute.

Members of a board of inquiry shall receive compensation at the rate of $50 for each day actually spent by them in the work of the board, together with necessary travel and subsistence expenses.

For the purpose of any hearing or inquiry conducted by any board appointed under this . . . [Act, such board is empowered to issue subpenas for the attendance of witnesses and the production of books, papers, and documents.]

Upon receiving a report from a board of inquiry the President may direct the Attorney General to petition any district court of the United States having jurisdiction of the parties to enjoin such strike or lock-out or the continuing thereof, and if the court finds that such threatened or actual strike or lock-out—

(i) affects an entire industry or a substantial part thereof engaged in trade, commerce, transportation, transmission, or communication among the several States or with foreign nations, or engaged in the production of goods for commerce; and

(ii) if permitted to occur or to continue, will imperil the national health or safety, it *shall have jurisdiction to enjoin any such strike or lock-out*, or the continuing thereof, and to make such other orders as may be appropriate. [Italics added.]

In any case, the provisions of the . . . [Norris La Guardia Act, which limited the power of the Federal courts to grant injunctions in labor disputes] shall not be applicable.

The order or orders of the courts shall be subject to review by the appropriate circuit court of appeals and by the Supreme Court upon writ of certiorari or certification. . . .

Whenever a district court has issued an order . . . enjoining acts or practices which imperil or threaten to imperil the national health or safety, it shall be the duty of the parties to the labor dispute giving rise to such order to make every effort to adjust and settle their differences, with the assistance of the [Federal Mediation and Conciliation] Service created by this Act. Neither party shall be under any duty to accept, in whole or in part, any proposal of settlement made by the [Federal Mediation and Conciliation] Service.

Upon the issuance of such order, the President shall reconvene the board of inquiry which has previously reported with respect to the dispute. At the end of a sixty-day period (unless the dispute has been settled by that time), the board of inquiry shall report to the President the current position of the parties and the efforts which have been made for settlement, and shall include a statement by each party of its position and a statement of the employer's last offer of settlement. The President shall make such report available to the public. The National Labor Relations Board, within the succeeding fifteen days, shall take a secret ballot of the employees of each employer involved in the dispute on the question of whether they wish to accept the final offer of settlement by their employer as stated by him and shall certify the results thereof to the Attorney General within five days thereafter.

Upon the certification of the results of such ballot or upon a settlement being reached, whichever happens sooner, the Attorney General shall move the court to discharge the injunction, which motion shall then be granted and the injunction discharged. When such motion is granted, the President shall submit to the Congress a full and comprehensive report of the proceedings, including the findings of the board of inquiry and the ballot taken by the National Labor Relations Board, together with such recommendations as he may see fit to make for consideration and appropriate action. . . .

The provisions of this title shall not be applicable with respect to any matter which is subject to the provisions of the Railway Labor Act, as amended from time to time.

WE NEED A MORE FLEXIBLE AND REALISTIC APPROACH THAN THE TAFT-HARTLEY ACT

BY THE DEMOCRATIC SENATORS ON THE JOINT COMMITTEE ON LABOR-MANAGEMENT RELATIONS*

[The four Senators who signed this report were James E. Murray, Claude Pepper, Matthew M. Neely, and Hubert H. Humphrey. EDITOR.]

There has been ample evidence of the abject failure of the inflexible and artificial national-emergency strike provisions of the Taft-Hartley Act. The 80-day injunction and the last-offer vote have failed to aid in the settlement of a single dispute in which they were applied. Settlements were actually delayed in a number of instances by the knowledge that 80-day injunctions might be forthcoming. Settlements were not reached during the period of the injunction, which frequently proved to be a "heating up" period rather than a "cooling off" period. . . .

* Labor-Management Relations, Senate Report 374, 81st Cong., 1st sess., 1949, pp. 5, 39–43 passim.

We agree . . . that any approach to emergency disputes must accord with the principles of free collective bargaining. For the preservation and encouragement of collective bargaining is an essential attribute of our democracy. It is a basic characteristic of totalitarian countries that collective bargaining, together with strikes and lock-outs, are non-existent. Therefore, even in national emergency disputes we must ensure that settlement is reached between the parties themselves. The two functions of any procedure must, first, enhance the possibilities that the parties can reach settlement themselves, and, second, permit informed public opinion to aid in obtaining voluntary settlement where the interests of the community at large are vitally affected. Any other approach can only lead to governmental determination of wages and working conditions with increasing Government concern regarding the conduct of private enterprise.

We believe that any procedure to cope with national emergency disputes must permit a maximum degree of flexibility to meet the variegated patterns of labor-management disputes. The provisions of the Taft-Hartley Act, and particularly the 80-day injunction provisions, failed in this. It is significant that this was the unanimous view of those labor-relations experts who have frequently represented the public interest in emergency labor situations. . . .

These experts, with their extensive experience in national-emergency disputes, testified that the compulsive force of injunctions aggravated delicate situations. It was their unanimous view that such compulsion was undesirable, and that the parties to a dispute would readily accede to a request by the President of the United States to postpone a work stoppage where he found a national emergency existed. The following was typical of their testimony:

"I have learned by experience not to put too much faith in any particular formula as a patent remedy for any crisis. Different areas, different industries or unions, different personalities, different times and circumstances, require different treatment. I suggest that in considering how best to equip the President to handle industrial crises, you do not limit him to any one mechanism. I suggest that you provide him with the power to do the needful in the particular case by amplifying rather than restricting the power which he might otherwise possess. . . . " (Testimony of Nathan P. Feinsinger, Senate hearings on S. 249, p. 2576.). . . .

The exhaustive testimony before the standing committees, as well as the empirical results, clearly demonstrate the inadequacies and actual harmful effects of the injunctive and last-offer ballot provisions of the act. There is clear and ample evidence that the injunctive provision has thwarted collective bargaining and stalled settlement. . . .

The testimony of Theodore W. Kheel is . . . evidence of the obstacles placed in the way of settlement by the injunctive provision. As director of the New York City Division of Labor Relations, he encountered serious difficulties in aiding the parties in the tugboat industry negotiations to reach a settlement since—

"because of the uncertainty as to whether or not they would be enjoined in the event of a failure to agree, there was absolutely no collective bargaining taking place whatsoever, for the reason that if there was the possibility of an injunction, then they were not going to bargain against the December 31 dead line, but March 20. . . . They were not going to make concessions before the expiration of their contract, as they would have roughly 80 days after the contract expired. So we had a state of great uncertainty with no collective bargaining taking place." (House Committee on Education and Labor, hearings on H.R. 2032, 1949, p. 1121).

The prolonged 80-day "cooling off" period induced by the injunctive process, with its severe penalties for violation, has further thwarted the collective bargaining process by heightening animosities. . . .

We agree . . . that the last-offer ballot requirements of the Taft-Hartley Act should be eliminated, since they are "of little value.". . . [The premise, which justified the requirement of a last-offer ballot, and] which was constantly reiterated in the debates on the bill, assumed that union leaders failed to represent the views of their constituents, and that strikes were frequently caused by unreasonable demands by union leaders in disregard of the rank-and-file wishes. However, employer "last offers" were overwhelmingly rejected by the union membership in every instance where ballots were conductd. . . .

The appointment of boards of inquiry to investigate the causes of threatened work stoppages is the only phase of the Taft-Hartley Act provisions in which there is some flexibility to meet particular situations. The flexibility, however, arises out of the good judgment of the experienced labor-relations experts who have been appointed to these boards, and not from the provisions of the act. Even in this area where there is real opportunity for avoidance of work stoppages, the act's prohibition on any recommendations by boards of inquiry weakens their effectiveness.

Boards of inquiry are flexible instruments. They may be able to effectuate a settlement between the parties; where this fails, they may be able to focus public attention on the causes of the dispute through their findings and recommendations. Recommendations are essential in two ways. They suggest a solution to the parties; they also clarify the issues for the public, thus permitting the application of public pressure to obtain the settlement of the dispute.

We agree with the impartial experts whose views we have cited that both labor and management would accept a reasonable "cooling off" period at the request of the President. A 30-day period is reasonable, and experience indicates that boards of inquiry can readily complete their functions during this period.

The 80-day period established in the Taft-Hartley Act is an arbitrary and unreasonable period. . . . The 30-day period reduces to a minimum . . . [those factors complicating the process of] voluntary collective bargaining.

TEMPORARY GOVERNMENT SEIZURE MAY HAVE TO BE OUR DIFFICULT CHOICE

BY CHARLES O. GREGORY*

[Charles O. Gregory, Professor of Law at the University of of Chicago, served with the U.S. Department of Labor and as a public member of many World War II Labor Board panels. He has also served as permanent arbitrator between Swift and Company and its union employees. He is coauthor of *Labor Law: Cases Materials and Comments.* EDITOR.]

. . . When strikes do result in crippling the economy and in imposing general inconvenience, many people would no doubt say that the thing to do is simply to "outlaw" such strikes. But that sort of talk is ridiculous, since it is impossible just to repress strikes by making them illegal; and it would be a dangerous and foolish thing to do, even if it were possible. It is true that Congress has adopted a policy of repression, pure and simple, with respect to strikes of government employees—and in that restricted area the policy may work. However, a policy of repression—without more—is like sealing up a sore that hasn't healed. It will continue to fester until it causes far more harm in the long run than if it had been properly treated or even left entirely alone. Indeed, the general enactment of such a policy into law would result eventually in a process of nullification which would exceed the disregard for law manifested during the prohibition era. Furthermore, the very desire simply to repress strikes, or the possibility of doing so, has most unwholesome political implications, for it signifies the kind of anti-democratic authoritarianism which would destroy all of our institutions based on freedom.

But these same people who would outlaw bargaining strikes sincerely

* *Labor and the Law* (New York: Norton, rev. and enlarged ed., 1949), pp. 475–476, 489–490, 479–481, 486, 489 *passim*. By permission of the publisher.

believe, as do several of our leading economists, that big unions have become so powerful that there is not much real freedom left, anyway, as far as our economic system is concerned. What third alternative is there, they may ask, to complete license or complete repression in dealing with bargaining strikes of the sort under discussion? This, of course, is the great question—the one for which nobody has a sure answer and one which most of our outstanding labor relations experts feel hesitant about answering at all. For aside from the most effective and efficient mediation and conciliation facilities possible, these experts can think of no formula which does not at some point involve one or another aspect of compulsory arbitration—the decision of a government-sponsored board which gives a solution and establishes the prevailing terms of employment. That is the last thing they want—and it seems pretty certain that the employers and unions are in complete agreement with them on this score. These experts and their supporters know what they want in a general way. They want a method of settling these socially inconvenient strikes whereby the parties themselves—the unions and employers involved—make their own terms and agreements. In such a solution they apparently see the retention of the American ideal of free enterprise and of an economy not regulated and planned by the government. At this point, however, they run up against the same question: How can this agreement be achieved without the inconvenience of strikes? Apparently they are seeking an answer in something called "improved relations between management and unions" and in "constantly increasing maturity and responsibility on the part of union and management representatives," with the ability to "see each other's point of view," etc. And the various industrial relations institutes throughout the country are working overtime trying to devise methods of bargaining out voluntary agreements without recourse to strikes and without legislative regulation of bargaining power. . . .

[Gregory recognizes the difficulties and complexities of the problem. He maintains, however, that "if anything is to be done at all, the time to decide upon a course of action is not when the country is in an emotional uproar during another nationwide strike. In view of our experience in the past, the time to make the decision is in a period of industrial peace and before the lid blows off again. This it will surely do if we don't do our thinking and prepare for these emergencies in advance." Hence, in the light of this belief and the foregoing analysis, Gregory advances the following scheme.]

. . . Suppose that bargaining has broken down between an employer and the union representing his employees in a plant whose continued operation is essential to the public convenience, and that the union is about to call a strike. Under a law enacted in accordance with this . . .

[suggested] scheme the government would forbid the strike for a stated time, during which a duly appointed commission would make an investigation and would determine a schedule of wages, salaries and other terms of employment to be in effect for the period of government seizure, as well as a fair rental of the plant premises to be paid to the owner of the plant over the same period. When these determinations had been made, the government would then formally seize the plant and assume operation of it. Naturally, the union would not be allowed to call a strike while the government was in possession.

Thenceforth, the government's agents would run the plant, presumably employing the same workers and operating managerial personnel who were there before the seizure. They would assume charge of all the ordinary business of the firm, including the purchase of materials and the marketing of its products, and would pay the help in accordance with the commission's determinations. The workers would no longer be employed in accordance with the terms of the collective agreement previously in force, except insofar as the commission saw fit to retain any terms which might be appropriate to the new setup. While concerted walkouts such as strikes would be forbidden, any individual employee would be free to leave his job at any time he wished, although it would be clearly stated that if he did so, he would have no right to come back to that job and would have forfeited any rights he might otherwise have had under prevailing labor laws, including unemployment compensation. In other words, he would be treated as a voluntary "quit." All profits of the business, over and above operating expenses (which would include the rental paid to the owners of the plant), would go into the public treasury and stay there as public funds. As for union dues, they would either be suspended entirely for the duration or, if collected, would also be put in the public treasury and stay there as public funds. In the meantime, top management and the union would be invited by the government to go off somewhere and negotiate an agreement—and not come back until it was signed, at which time they could have the plant back and resume their former relations. This would, indeed, be a real seizure, with the government becoming the *actual* employer for the duration, and not just a paper transaction for legalistic purposes like the "seizure" of the bituminous coal mines in 1946.

If this plan would work, its advantages are manifest. It provides most of the economic pressures of the strike and obviates most of the inconveniences. Thus, top management and the owners of the enterprise are anxious to get their plant back—assuming that it has always been a paying proposition and that the interim rental from the government is not too generous—while the union is anxious to resume its role in the plant and to begin getting dues again. Two of the elements of pressure normally present in strikes are absent. One usually operating in the union's favor is the deterioration of plant and business; and the other, which usually operates in the employer's favor, is the desperation experienced by the strikers and their families over a protracted period without wages. While the scales may thus be left balanced slightly in favor of the union, there is nevertheless enough pressure remaining on the parties to make an early compromise worth the effort. Certainly there would seem to be little incentive for any union in such a case to turn the government's seizure of the plants or industry in question into virtual nationalization of such units by indefinitely protracted refusal to reach an agreement. At any rate, the public is not inconvenienced by the shutdown of the plant, albeit service from the government may not be up to prior levels of efficiency; nor are the employees and their families exposed to the distressing circumstances ordinarily experienced by most workers and their dependents during strikes, albeit they might have been somewhat better off had the prior collective agreement remained in effect. Furthermore, by being kept busy, the employees are automatically removed from the possibility of participating in riots and other kinds of trouble frequently associated with strikes. . . .

[Gregory recognizes that this plan, whose basic elements were originally conceived by Eugene C. Gerhart, might "not be suitable in the large industries where multi-employer bargaining has become established on an industry-wide scale or where there may be one or two large international unions in the picture making separate agreements with different employers throughout a given industry." His proposal is not intended to be a "panacea." What Gregory has tried to do "is to show what might be considered along the lines of *making* the parties reach their own agreements without recourse to the expedient of open economic warfare so harmful to the public interest."]

COMPULSORY ARBITRATION THROUGH LABOR COURTS

BY SENATOR HOMER FERGUSON*

[Senator Homer Ferguson, lawyer and circuit court judge, was elected to the U.S. Senate in 1943 and re-elected in 1948. EDITOR.]

* "Should Basic Industries Be Subject to Compulsory Arbitration?" *Congressional Record*, 80th Cong., 1st sess., Vol. 93, Pt. 1 (Jan. 13, 1947), pp. 276–277 *passim*. Reprinted from *American Magazine*, February, 1947. By permission.

Labor disputes should be settled where all our other domestic disputes are settled—in court. When two private citizens, a landlord and tenant, for example, fall into disagreement over the terms of a lease, they are not permitted to fight it out in the public streets. If they did, they would be jailed for disturbing the peace or for disorderly conduct. Instead, they take their problem to court. And when the judge pronounces the decision they abide by it. Justice has spoken.

Why are labor-management disputes any different from tenant-landlord disputes except that the issues are bigger, more people are involved, and the economic security of the Nation is endangered?

Basically, they are the same. The difference is in the handling of the issues. Industrial disputes are still settled on the basis of economic power. Which side can outstrangle the other in a showdown? And nowadays these strangle holds cover such wide areas that the public's neck is usually included.

The time has come to settle these disputes on the basis of justice instead of on the basis of strangle holds.

I think we should subject industrial disputes, along with all other disputes, to the legal discipline of a civilized society.

After talking with representatives of both labor and management and with representatives of both major political parties I have worked out a plan to set up a system of American labor courts.

These courts would parallel our regular Federal courts, and would judge every dispute on the basis of justice. All labor contracts affecting interstate commerce would be filed with these courts, and whenever disagreements arose concerning the terms set down the judges would help the parties arrive at a settlement.

If they failed to arrive at such a settlement the court would hold public hearing[s] as in any other case, and then make a decision which would be binding on all parties to the contract. Furthermore, where basic industries or interstate public utilities were involved, and the parties were unable to reach an agreement on a contract to start with, the courts would resolve the matter and the decisions of the court would be final.

This amounts to compulsory arbitration in these basic industries. I see no other remedy when the Nation is faced with a monopoly, either of labor or of management, which can paralyze the industrial life of the country.

Such drastic penalties would be available to ensure enforcement that neither party would seriously consider defying the labor courts, just as today contestants never consider defying the decision of any of our other courts.

I believe that such a system of labor courts offers a fair, sane, and sensible solution to one of the . . . big problems facing the Nation. . . .

Strikes, like wars, have become too expensive. And just as innocent civilians are now the main victims of wars, they are the main victims of strikes.

Most people will grant that strikes once had their proper role in our economy, but that time is rapidly passing. Today, our economy is so intermeshed, and both unions and industries have grown so big, that a single strike can paralyze the Nation. . . .

We do not have to decide that either union leaders or industrialists are to "blame" for the series of strikes we have had to suffer in order to decide that we need a forum and machinery with which to settle labor disputes.

The blame rests on us as a whole for allowing unions and industries to exist in our midst as sovereign powers.

Given such sovereignity and such conflicting interests, strikes probably are inevitable, just as wars are inevitable when there are no laws that nations abide by. Both capital and labor want to get all they can, and, lacking restraints, will do so. . . .

I have heard it argued by those who oppose any change in the present "voluntary" system of handling strikes that everything will work out all right once we have an "aroused public interest." Frankly, I don't think an aroused public opinion fazes the Petrillos or the Bridgeses in the least.

Public opinion is aroused. In fact, it is close to the boiling point. Opinion is so aroused that it may force through punitive laws that may throttle labor so completely that capital will again have the upper hand.

But that is not the solution. We would start building toward the same economic war all over again. What we need is a sane program, fair to both sides, that will still give the long-suffering public a break, and let the country get on with its . . . [task]. . . .

. . . Passing . . . laws [prohibiting monopoly in labor, the closed shop, secondary boycotts, and coercion of individual workers by violence through mass picketing, although having some merit] will not get at the basic problem, which is to provide the machinery and a forum where disputes can be settled decisively short of conflict.

Such a machinery is available in the labor courts which I suggest.

The appealing thing about a court system, to me, is that it is simple, clear-cut, understandable—and most of all, fair. It is neither antilabor nor antimanagement, but rather is pro-everybody. Our courts have long been admired as symbols of impartial justice, and I believe that the labor courts would soon likewise become such symbols.

QUESTIONS AND PROBLEMS

1. Indicate the machinery that may be set in motion when the President finds that a threatened or actual strike or lockout imperils the national health and safety.

2. On what grounds do the Democratic Senators on the Joint Committee on Labor-Management Relations criticize the national-emergency provisions of the Taft-Hartley Act?

3. Why do you agree or disagree with the appraisal of the Democratic Senators in question 2?

4. Why does Gregory hold that it would be "dangerous" and "foolish" to repress strikes by making them illegal, assuming it were possible?

5. According to Gregory, does anybody—including the labor relations experts—have a *sure* alternative to complete license or complete repression in national-emergency bargaining conflicts? Why or why not?

6. First state and then criticize Gregory's proposal for government seizure.

7. Why does Senator Ferguson feel that labor disputes should be settled in court?

8. Describe and then evaluate Senator Ferguson's plan for labor courts.

9. Discuss these additional suggestions for coping with national-emergency disputes: (*a*) government ownership of key industries; (*b*) compulsory arbitration by a special governmental commission; (*c*) application of the Sherman Antitrust Act to strikes and lockouts imperiling the national health and safety; (*d*) prohibition of industry-wide bargaining; (*e*) stipulation that disputes jeopardizing national health and safety be treated as an unfair labor practice under the Taft-Hartley Act.

10. In the light of your reading, experience, and deliberation how would *you* propose that labor-management disputes that threaten the national health, safety, and welfare be handled?

SELECT BIBLIOGRAPHY

Bakke, E. Wight: *Mutual Survival: The Goal of Unions and Management* (New York: Harper, 1947). Maintains that free unions, free management, free enterprise, and free society will survive or go under together.

Carmell, Daniel D.: "Ban Industry-wide Strikes under Antitrust Laws?" *Modern Industry*, Vol. 15 (Apr. 15, 1948), pp. 104*ff*. Cannot ban industry-wide strikes without banning necessary industry-wide bargaining. Holds real bargaining, not banning, is answer.

Hartley, Fred A., Jr.: "Ban Industry-wide Strikes under Antitrust Laws? *Modern Industry*, Vol. 15 (Apr. 15, 1948), pp. 104*ff*. Urges ban on industry-wide bargaining to eliminate dangerous labor monopoly and to stave off undesired compulsory arbitration which will be used unless nation attains labor peace.

Legislative History of the Labor Management Relations Act, 1947 (Washington: National Labor Relations Board, Government Printing Office, 2 vols., 1948). A handy compilation of the basic bills, reports, and pertinent congressional proceedings. Does not include congressional hearings and drafts of all related bills. Excellently indexed. Explains why more stringent national emergency measures were not adopted.

Marceau, Le Roy, and Richard A. Musgrave: "Strikes in Essential Industries: A Way Out," *Harvard Business Review*, Vol. 27 (May, 1949), pp. 286–292. Suggests ingenious technique of "statutory strike." Would not permit regular work stoppage but would subject both parties to economic burdens comparable to that of regular strike as inducement to voluntary settlement.

Metz, Harold W., and Meyer Jacobstein: *A National Labor Policy* (Washington: Brookings, 1947). Recommends application of antitrust laws to certain monopolistic union activities. Would prohibit certification of bargaining units that include employees of more than one employee.

Riemer, Neal: *Labor Legislation and the Legislative Process: The Formation of the Taft-Hartley Act* (Harvard University: unpublished doctoral dissertation, 1948). A case study in the formation of a controversial public policy.

Rossiter, Clinton L.: "The President and Labor Disputes," *The Presidency in Transition* (Gainesville, Fla.: Kallman Publishing Co., 1949). Reprinted in *Journal of Politics*, Vol. 11 (February, 1949). A broad and illuminating examination of the President's emergency powers in major labor disputes. A relatively favorable appraisal of the national-emergency provisions of the Taft-Hartley Act.

Slichter, Sumner H.: *The Challenge of Industrial Relations* (Ithaca, N.Y.: Cornell University Press, 1947). Argues that in critical labor-management areas government should either have special emergency powers to deal with work stoppages or should give employees in these industries special status and privileges but impose an obligation to refrain from striking.

Slichter, Sumner H.: *The American Economy: Its Problems and Prospects* (New York: Knopf, 1948). If voluntary settlement fails, recommends limited trial by parties of decision reached by impartial but compulsory arbitration.

Simons, Henry C.: *Economic Policy for a Free Society* (Chicago: University of Chicago Press, 1948). Urges elimination of concentration of economic power in the labor union or in industrial units. See especially Chap. 6 for his questioning of the virtues of organized labor. Advocates a positive laissez-faire program.

United States House of Representatives, Committee on Education and Labor: *Amendments to the National Labor Relations Act, Hearings*, 80th Cong., 1st sess., 1947, 6 vols.

United States Senate, Committee on Labor and Public Welfare: *Reducing Industrial Strife in the United States, Hearings* 80th Cong., 1st sess., 1947,

2 vols. Contains, along with hearings in House, mine of information and divergent points of view. Must be winnowed with patience and discrimination.

United States Senate, *Reports of Joint Committee on Labor-Management Relations*, Senate Report 986 (5 Pts), 80th Cong., 2d sess. 1948; Senate Report 374, 81st Cong., 1st sess., 1949. Essentially politically partisan documents. Valuable as comprehensive statements of views of leading congressional champions and opponents of operation of Taft-Hartley Act.

AGRICULTURE

What Kind of Price Support Program, If Any, Should We Adopt?

Perhaps no governmental policy is so difficult for the layman to understand as the Federal government's price-support program for agriculture. Many farmers and nonfarmers may understand the importance of the varied governmental services that are extended to the farmer: from rural electrification to the Department of Agriculture's latest recipe for strawberry shortcake. But few understand the intricacies of "parity" and appreciate the complex apparatus in the Department of Agriculture that has been set up to "adjust" agriculture.

No pretense is made in this chapter of providing the "key" which unlocks the complexities of modern price-support policy. The following selections, however, may serve to introduce the student to the philosophies that lie behind a few approaches to the question of price supports.

Secretary of Agriculture Brannan, for example, sets forth a justification of a sound farm program. Such a program must serve the farmer without discriminating against any group. It must be efficient and, within the frame of its objectives, as economical as possible. It must also serve the objectives of peace and prosperity. Such a program can serve the interests of all the people by preventing depression, encouraging bigger industrial markets and optimum employment, sustaining high-level production of farm commodities, conserving natural resources, maintaining reserves for national security, and strengthening the rural economy.

Many—including the other contributors to this chapter—might agree with most, or all, of Mr. Brannan's ends without accepting his specific means. Brannan's most controversial proposal is for a "production payment" by the government to producers selling perishable commodities, such as whole milk, eggs, chickens, hogs, beef cattle, lambs, fruits, and vegetables. This payment—the difference between a calculated support standard for those commodities and their market price—is intended to encourage high production, consumption at lower retail prices, while providing a fair income for the farmer.

Allan Kline expounds the views of the American Farm Bureau Federation, the most powerful farm pressure group in the country. He accepts price-support legislation—with reservations. He also argues that Secretary Brannan's suggested plan would be expensive, would reduce farm efficiency and regiment the farmer. A flexible, nonrigid, price-support program should be considered as a form of insurance against drastic price declines and should be keyed to the major farm producers, not to the subsistence farmers. A price-support program should not be a method by which the government guarantees profitable prices to farmers.

Fortune Magazine contributes to this chapter a sharp critique of our price-support program as of January, 1950, attacking both Mr. Brannan and Mr. Kline by implication. *Fortune* claims that our farm policy causes farmers to produce wildly in excess and is expensive, inflationary, and inequitable. It has created a paradoxical embarrassment of riches in the form of unmarketable farm surpluses. *Fortune* holds that we need a radically new agricultural act "that will gradually ease the price-control falsework from under the farm economy, [and] expose it to the genuine incentives of the open market. . . ."

In reading the *Fortune* article the student must ask himself whether changing national and world conditions alter the validity of *Fortune's* article; and, if so, whether the argument is still sound for "normal" times.

The concluding selection in this chapter is a total attack on agricultural price supports and subsidies. Such legislation, writes H. M. Griffith, the author of this article, injures the farmer, impoverishes the nonagricultural population, and vitiates the entire economy. The Brannan plan is a fraud and illusion. Griffith maintains that we must return to an economy governed by the immutable law of supply and demand before social and economic disaster overtakes us.

These conflicting arguments may wax stronger or weaker, depending upon whether we are operating under a truly peacetime economy, a war economy, or a "cold" or "lukewarm" war economy. These views should stimulate the student to develop a reasoned and factual defense of what public policy should be on the question of a price-support program.

Should we adopt the Brannan Plan? Should we accept our present price-support program, while continually pressing for its improvement? Should we adopt a "sensible, honest, radically new agricultural act" unlike the Brannan Plan or the present act? Or should we oppose agricultural subsidies of any kind and return to the "immutable law of supply and demand"?

THE BRANNAN PLAN IS A FARM POLICY
IN THE PUBLIC INTEREST

BY CHARLES F. BRANNAN*

[Charles Francis Brannan has been with the Department of Agriculture since 1935. During that time he served in its Resettlement Administration, as a regional attorney, and in its Farm Security Administration. Assistant Secretary of Agriculture from 1944 to 1948, he has been Secretary since 1948. EDITOR.]

[The "heart of our farm policy"] . . . concerns our effort to assist farmers to maintain a reasonably stable income at a fair level—a level which is equitable to farmers and in the best interest of the other economic groups within our population.

The principal device authorized by the Congress for this purpose is commonly referred to as agricultural price support. It is, in my opinion, the most effective method yet suggested and must remain an integral part of our national economy until and unless a better method is suggested.

Some differences of opinion have developed about the exact formula and manner under which agricultural price supports should be made available. This is healthy and can only result in improvement if we all apply ourselves forthrightly to a solution to the issues. . . .

In view of the problems we face, I am thankful that we have had a great deal of excellent legislation and much good experience on which to base an effective farm program. We can learn much of great value from the farm legislation and experience of the last two decades.

. . . Throughout this experience, we have seen that the measures dealing with the selling prices of farm products and the incomes of producers are the keys to a successful program.

. . . From our experience, we can set up realistic criteria by which

* From testimony Apr. 7, 1949, before United States House of Representatives, Committee on Agriculture, *General Farm Program, Hearings*, Pt. 2, Serial P, 81st Cong., 1st sess., 1949, pp. 138–149 *passim*.

to judge and by which to guide our program. Prominent among the criteria and requirements will be the following:

First. The program must effectively serve the farmer and his family. As an isolated individual, the farmer has no control over the prices he will receive, and no adequate way of adjusting the total market volume of his commodities to the changing demand. After he has planted a crop, he is at the mercy of weather, price, and many other forces with which he is powerless to cope. On many occasions in the past, he has labored all season and produced a good crop only to find that, because of circumstances beyond his control, his labor will go uncompensated and sometimes his cash investment in seed, fertilizer, and other operating costs will be only partially recovered. A program to help him meet those basic difficulties is the very minimum for which we should strive.

Second. In serving the farmer the program must not discriminate unfairly against any group. It should be fair to consumers and business people. The customers of agriculture want plentiful and steady supplies, and they have a right to expect that a program supported by the public will help meet this need. Farmers want to furnish plentiful supplies regularly.

Third. The program must be efficiently operated and the cost must be commensurate with the benefits to the Nation.

Fourth. It must serve general policy objectives, including national security, the maintenance of high-level employment, and cooperation with other nations in the interests of peace and prosperity. It can do this by conserving and strengthening our basic productive resources, providing reserves against national emergencies, and encouraging free-flowing world trade by reasonably assuring sufficient products for export.

In short, the farm program must serve the best interests of all our people, and in my opinion that is the only kind of program the farm people want or expect.

Unfortunately, too many people still think of a farm program as some kind of class legislation. There is too little appreciation of the direct and definite ways in which it can benefit all the people and can help make this the kind of a country they want it to be.

Therefore, I want to list several ways in which we can expect effective farm-production and price-stabilization programs to serve the interests of all the people.

1. It can help to prevent depression. Most depressions have been farm-led and farm-fed. Farm prices traditionally go down before, faster, and farther than other prices. On the down swing of the business cycle, farm people are the major early victims of a squeeze. As their income and, therefore, purchasing power is cut by low prices or production failure,

industrial producers find a contracting market for their production. This throws workers out of jobs. They in turn spend less for farm products, which in turn further forces down farm prices, and farm purchasing power is further cut.

I don't mean to say that declines in farm prices are the sole cause of depressions, but they certainly contribute greatly and would do so more now than in the past because agriculture has become a bigger customer of industry.

Farm price supports cannot substitute for good markets that come with full employment and foreign demand, and, I believe, almost every farmer now understands the importance and relationship to farm prosperity of good wages for city and industrial workers. Supports are no substitute for city markets, but they can at least slow down declines in farm prices and provide stopping points so as to keep our fluid farm prices from going rapidly into a worse and worse relationship with nonfarm prices.

2. A farm production and price-adjustment program can help build markets for industrial goods and help maintain employment for labor. . . .

It is important to all of us to maintain balance between farm and industrial prices. A program that helps to stabilize farm prices and incomes will help to stabilize markets for factory goods and will keep thousands and thousands of "Main Streets" busy.

3. Stable farm prices and incomes encourage high-level production with the greatest assurance of reasonable prices to consumers. . . . Farmers, like manufacturers, want to produce what their customers want. But usually it is only with advance knowledge of minimum prices that small, individual producers, planning separately, can unify their efforts efficiently to increase the total supply of a particular commodity. . . .

Price supports should be available at all times to assure the maintenance of this supply. If prices are allowed to remain too low too long farmers are unable to buy the machinery, fertilizer, and other materials which they must have to maintain high-level production.

4. A program that helps maintain farm income helps to maintain agricultural resources. . . .

Obviously, conservation depends on something more than good farm prices. On the other hand, resources can be conserved and improved only if they are used profitably. . . .

Price supports can aid conservation in at least two ways: (a) By bringing additional stability into the farm business so that farm people can enjoy a good standard of living without mining their resources and (b) by directly encouraging types of farming which naturally conserve resources.

It is generally believed that, for the sake of keeping our resources permanently productive as well as to meet consumer needs, livestock production should be made a more important part of our agriculture. I agree with this. I also think the shift is not likely to take place as promptly and as fully as necessary without the assistance of a well-adapted production and price-adjustment program.

5. An effective farm program is essential to our national security, will provide a reservoir of goods which protects the Nation against crop failure, and will assure supplies for an even flow of world trade. . . .

It should also be remembered that a democracy with reserves and great productive power is a great comfort to nations fearing either famine or foreign aggression. Our practical ability to serve as a friend in need will determine how well we can meet our responsibilities of leadership—how well we can serve the cause of world peace and democracy.

Reserves of storable commodities are a natural adjunct of price supports. They are an aim as well as a result of the farm program. They represent an important part of the insurance which the public buys with the funds it invests in maintaining a healthy agriculture.

6. A price-support program which safeguards our rural economic strength can help stabilize the rural community and help maintain individual opportunity in our free-enterprise system.

One bulwark of democracy may be found in the prosperous rural community mainly composed of economically strong families farming in the traditional American pattern. It is an ever-present answer to communism.

We should be aware that for many years there has been a steady increase in the number of large-scale, industrialized type of farming unit[s]. Many of these are absentee and corporate owned. According to the 1945 census, about 100,000 of the largest units—fewer than 2 percent of all farms—are selling products valued at nearly one-fourth of all the farm products marketed in this country. This is more than is sold in total by two-thirds of all our farms, including half of our family farms.

If we are to have stable and prosperous rural communities with schools, churches, health services, and other facilities, it is plain that many farm people need greater economic security and opportunity.

Price supports are the farmer's equivalent of the laboring man's minimum wage, social security, and collective-bargaining agreements.

Of course, price support does not meet the fundamental problem of the operator who cannot produce a large enough volume to make a good return at any price. But it does help on the price side of the farm income equation. There are a great many farmers on the economic border line— they can make a fairly good living when prices are in reasonable balance, but a small drop cuts sharply into the income they have available for living expense and leaves only operating expenses or less. These people are a very considerable percentage of all the independent producers in our entire free-enterprise system. While price supports alone will not solve their problem, I see no reason to think it can be solved without some kind of a sound and effective program for maintaining stable and reasonable prices for the goods they produce. . . .

A program that will meet the test I have outlined will cost money, and the returns will have to justify the cost. We may not be able to set up a balance sheet in terms of dollars and balance it every year. But then, that is not the way we have measured the public cost and the returns from the tariffs which we have used to protect various industries, the value of less-than-cost postal rates, and the public cost and returns—investment and returns—from railroads, merchant marine, and air lines, and the public cost and returns from the minimum-wage law and social security.

We do know that agriculture is a basic segment of the economy. It must be highly productive and permanently so. It must contribute to the prosperity of the Nation, and in turn those engaged in agriculture must be able to share equitably in that prosperity.

I believe we can have that kind of agriculture if we really want it. We won't get it easily or automatically. We won't get it all of a sudden. But we have already made great progress toward it, and if we will work together we can make more progress.

In my opinion, production and price adjustment with a definite income objective must be the core of our united effort. . . .

Recommendations: Condensed into the fewest words possible, here are the proposals. . . .

Objective: The recommended program is intended to assure a volume of farm income and purchasing power which it is in the public interest to maintain for the reasons which have just been discussed.

The standard of support has been established with reference to income criteria rather than price criteria. A recent 10-year period has been selected as the base. Simplicity of computation and application has been a constant aim.

The recommended price-support standard for any specific commodity does not represent a parity price nor does the composite average represent parity income as those terms are now statutorily defined or commonly understood. This income standard simply represents a realistic minimum below which it is not in the interest of farmers or consumers to allow farm prices to fall and above which I would hope to find most farm prices most of the time. It is the minimum level from which we would be working toward narrowing, and eventually closing, the historical gap between farm and nonfarm income.

Formulas: As the start for our moving base, we have taken the average annual purchasing power of cash receipts from farm marketings for the years 1939 through 1948. From that, with the aid of the old parity index, we have moved first to an income-support standard and then to a specific price-support standard for the individual commodities.

Application of support: Loans, purchase agreements, production payments, and direct purchases should be available for use. These several methods would be used singly or in combination as experience and prevailing circumstances warrant.

Commodity loans and purchase agreements are probably the most effective and efficient methods for the commodities which do not appreciably deteriorate in storage and for those which should be held in reserve in appreciable quantities for production stability or against national emergencies.

Production payments, on the other hand, seem more adaptable as a method for supporting highly perishable commodities and those for which storage is too costly.

In the case of both perishables and storables, it may sometimes be desirable to remove surpluses or to obtain supplies for storage or collateral programs by purchasing directly from producers or intermediate processors.

Conditions of support: The availability of price support cannot be separated from the acceptance by farmers of reasonable undertakings to advance or accomplish the over-all objectives of a sound farm program in the interests of the public and their fellow farmers, such as (*a*) the observance of minimum and sound soil-conservation practices; (*b*) compliance with or adoption of whatever programs are found necessary to curtail wasteful production or disorderly marketing (such measures as acreage allotments, marketing quotas, and marketing agreements which may be adopted from time to time through referendums or by the authority of the Secretary under terms of specific legislation such as is now on the statute books); (*c*) the limitation of eligibility for price support to a defined volume of production on each farm—a volume high enough to benefit most farms but one which will not encourage the development of extremely large, industrialized farming.

These are my recommendations in brief. . . .

Price support methods: Commodity loans and purchase agreements are methods well adapted to the support of storable commodities which can be carried over without processing for a number of marketing years, if necessary. Storables account for roughly 25 percent of our annual cash receipts from farm marketings and include cotton, corn, wheat and other grains, tobacco, the oilseed crops, dry beans and peas, wool, and peanuts. These are not all equally storable, but experience has shown that loans and purchase agreements are effective for all the commodities on this list. Nevertheless, it would be desirable to have available, as a supplementary method, the authority to make production payments under certain circumstances.

The nonstorables—products which are either highly perishable or which can be stored only at heavy expense—include fruits, vegetables, meat animals, milk, butterfat, poultry, and eggs, and account for roughly 75 percent of cash farm receipts. Production of these commodities is geared largely to domestic demand and this demand fluctuates with employment, wages, and other factors which change mass purchasing power. We can hope to increase per capita consumption of all or most of these products in a healthy economic climate.

When it is necessary to apply supports to any of these nonstorable commodities, I recommend that we rely mainly upon production payments.

The term "production payment" means exactly what it says—a payment to the farmer to go on producing to meet genuine consumer needs, rather than restricting output short of that need.

Under this system the farmer would be paid in cash the difference between the support standard for commodities which he produced and the average selling price for those commodities in the market place. Because the payment would go directly to the farmer it would be an efficient support operation.

Another big advantage is that the system would induce efficient production and marketing, because any farmer who could exceed the average market price by quality of product or good bargaining would benefit to the extent that his selling price exceeded the average market price.

A third advantage of this system is that it would allow farm income to remain at a high level to sustain abundant production while retail prices sought their supply and demand level in the market place. This level is bound to be reasonable for consumers because of the larger supplies brought out.

It is obvious, of course, that the use of production payments must be qualified in such a manner as to avoid extremely depressed prices in the market place or a wasteful use of soil resources.

The payment method is not new. It has been used for various purposes before and during the war, and we know it is administratively feasible. We know it is a method which not only protects the farmers but gives consumers a real break.

THE FARM BUREAU SUPPORTS A MODERATE, FLEXIBLE FARM PROGRAM

BY ALLAN B. KLINE*

[Allan Blair Kline has a varied background in farming, farm business, and insurance. He is a director of the Federal Reserve Bank of Chicago. A long-time member of the American Farm Bureau, he has been its President since 1947. EDITOR.]

I intend to discuss government farm programs here, but only incidentally, and principally to illustrate major trends now operating in a much larger field. Solutions in this broader area, the national and world economy, are of more importance to the farmer than any price-support methods or any other specific agricultural measures which may be adopted.

The welfare of agriculture, the prosperity of farm people, depends on achievement of certain goals throughout our economy. Chief among them are high per capita production and well-distributed real income outside agriculture; a high per capita production within agriculture; a more stable general price level; the effective curbing of monopoly in all segments of the economy; and an adequate, healthy international trade.

If all these things were accomplished facts, we would not need government farm price programs. But they are not accomplished facts, and we must recognize present realities. . . .

Here it is well to note the difficulties which arise when those who discuss national farm policy fail to realize that the problems of that half of our farmers who produce most of the agricultural commodities that move in trade are quite different from the problems of the other half of agriculture. In the other half, there are many people who are no special problem. There are part-time farmers with good jobs; there are retired and semi-retired people who farm, but not extensively; and there are a considerable number of others who get into agricultural statistics, as far as the census is concerned, because the places where they live fit the census definition of a farm.

Then, there are a million and a quarter to a million and half of these farmers who are primarily subsistence farmers. Their problem is not a price problem. It is a problem of opportunity.

Unfortunately, many of those who deal in public policy fail to divide

* "Government and Agriculture," *Proceedings of the Academy of Political Science*, Vol. 24 (May, 1950), pp. 78–87 *passim*. By permission of the publisher.

this problem. Even many of those who think seriously about it and do have understanding of it insist on discussing the problem of the subsistence farmers every time agricultural price problems are discussed, thus adding to the public confusion on the subject.

Let us just see what the application of "guaranteed" prices does to the farmer who needs land and machinery and opportunity, say one who gets $750 gross in an average year. Some of you may say, well we do not have such farmers. Oh yes, we have; many, many thousands of them. They may get a higher price than before but, of course, they have to be content with less production. We must, to be sure, have controls to make such guaranteed prices effective. This leaves them about the same income, or at the very best, and if we exempt them from the controls, only a very little more. This is not good enough for America. These people need a progressive society most of all—new capital, education, better health, new opportunity. Also, they need industries in which some of them may find more profitable and useful employment. It is unnecessary in this country to stabilize and perpetuate poverty thus, and it is cruelly dishonest to hold out price guarantees to these farmers as an answer to their problem. We must and we can, working together, expand creative opportunity. This way lie progress, prosperity, personal liberty. . . .

It is scarcely necessary to say that the American Farm Bureau Federation believes in farm price programs. They are needed because agricultural prices rise and fall much more sharply than do prices of nonfarm goods. Farm production generally remains high even when prices decline steeply. These sudden declines in agricultural prices are not matched by similar declines in prices of things farmers buy. Outside agriculture, prices tend to remain stable, while production fluctuates widely. From the spring of 1948 to the fall of 1948, the cash price of corn was more than cut in two. The price of tractors was stable and freight rates actually rose. Costs in agriculture are "sticky." They are tied to certain costs which neither business nor labor can easily get away from under present circumstances, the most demonstrable of which is the hourly rate of pay.

However, we consider farm price-support programs as a form of insurance against drastic price declines, rather than as a method by which government guarantees profitable prices to farmers. We believe that the prosperity of the individual farmer, like that of the individual business man or the individual worker, should depend on his ability to produce efficiently and economically the commodities which consumers want and need.

Support prices should be flexible, geared to the supply of each commodity supported. This reduces the danger of accumulating unwanted surpluses, and permits the market to remain an accurate guide to intelligent production. Experience has clearly demonstrated that high and rigid support prices result in piling up surpluses which hang over the market until they are absorbed, somehow, in some channels of consumption. Unwarrantably high support levels can do no more than postpone the problems; they cannot solve it.

Price supports at any level are not, in themselves, an answer to the farm problem. They are not even the major part of any adequate "farm program." In the past fifty years, research and education have certainly been a number one farm program. To be of value on a long-range basis, a farm program must make provisions for soil conservation and improved farming methods, better marketing practices, and encouragement of adjustments in farm operations to produce more of the foods needed in improved human diets. Farmers must share the responsibility for, and be tuned in on the benefits of, over-all national progress.

These are the essentials of the Farm Bureau's program, a program designed to fit into our free-choice economy, consistent with the American tradition, and which does not place the individual farm family in a position of permanent dependence on the federal treasury.

The highly publicized Brannan plan represents the opposite philosophy on farm programs. It also typifies the thinking of those who would trade our American system for something quite different—a system in which the individual relinquishes to government much of the control over his own destiny.

If we are to consider the Brannan plan at all, we must take it either as political hokum—an offer of cheap food to win consumer votes and an offer of high farm prices to win farm votes—or we must consider it as a serious proposal, embodying the various features outlined in the mimeographed copies of Secretary Brannan's presentation made to Congress a year ago this month. I prefer to deal with it on the latter basis, assuming that it was seriously and honestly proposed.

Briefly, the plan would set up an income standard. This standard, however, is used only to calculate supports on specific commodities. It is reflected in the highest level of price supports ever seriously suggested. This, of course, means greater regimentation and control by government. It would permit commodities to clear the market at any price they would bring. Farmers are asked to believe that they would be paid directly from the United States Treasury the difference between the market price and the price reflecting the income standard. . . .

The notion that the Brannan plan would mean cheap food is an obvious fallacy. Not only is it more expensive to pay for groceries by way of Washington, but the effect on American agriculture would be to reduce the general standard of efficiency, thus increasing costs.

The plan would put government in the position of guaranteeing profitable farm prices. Inevitably it would have the responsibility of dividing the privilege of producing at these guaranteed prices. Again, of necessity, a democratic government would increasingly divide this privilege among farmers "equitably" (on a political basis, one vote, one share). Efficient producers are squeezed, and inefficient production is continued and expanded. This is bound to be the case in any high, guaranteed price program necessitating a comprehensive system of production and marketing controls.

The tendency would be toward standardizing agricultural production on a relatively low level of efficiency, and toward discouraging individual initiative on the part of the farmer. The result would be more expensive, not cheaper, farm products. (Incidentally, notwithstanding the impression one gets from statements by officials of the Department of Agriculture, the American consumer now can buy more and better food for the money earned with an hour's work than can the consumer in any other major country in the world.) . . .

The Agricultural Act of 1949 is not perfect. However, we consider it preferable to the Brannan plan or any similar scheme which would place the farmer at the mercy of the government for a major part of his income. The philosophy back of our program is that of a free-choice system. Mistakes we have made can be corrected by using the traditional democratic processes, which, on balance, have been dramatically successful.

Farm programs should be consistent with a dynamic, free-choice economy. The farmer should be given maximum opportunity to make his own decisions on production and marketing. These requirements the 1949 Act fulfills reasonably well. It provides for the flexibility in price supports necessary to keep the market a reliable guide to production and utilization of farm products. Unfortunately, however, it postpones application of this flexibility, and contains certain other features which make for a higher and more rigid price-support structure than the Farm Bureau considers consistent with the best interests of farmers and consumers.

We intend to use the Act, meanwhile doing the other things which make for prosperity. We shall recommend such changes in the law as experience indicates, in order to make it more consistent with full opportunity for farmers to benefit from an expanding economy.

OUR FARM PRICE-SUPPORT PROGRAM IS A FALSEWORK OF BOGUS VALUES

From Fortune Magazine*

The time has come for a sensible, honest, radically new agricultural act. The government's farm price-support program, seventeen years after Congress passed the original Agricultural Adjustment Act enabling the government to support the prices of basic farm products at "parity" by "lending" on those products or buying them outright, is coming full circle to its logical, preposterous conclusion. The program has erected a falsework of bogus values under the whole farm economy, which would collapse into ruin if the support were suddenly removed. It is forcing farmers to produce wildly in excess of any reasonable American capacity to consume. It is responsible for a major leak in the national budget. . . . It is one of the most potent of inflationary influences.

The program is also perhaps the world's most flagrant example of what happens when the government helps a group maintain or increase its share of the national income regardless of the group's contribution to that income. John L. Lewis, it is true, is trying to do the same thing for the coal-mining industry. But at least Lewis hasn't forced the government to support the price of coal, and to buy up surplus coal and give it away as railway ballast or burn it up in great bonfires. His exactions, inordinate as they are in their way, are modest compared to those of the farm pressure groups and their representatives and friends in government.

Almost everybody has heard or read stories of how the government lost $204 million by destroying potatoes or selling them for less than the price of their bags and thus enriched potato growers in Aroostook County and other places, how it fed millions of dollars worth of California raisins to hogs, how it bought tung oil that nobody can ever get rid of, how it kept the country saddled with flaxseed supports that resulted in an output more than twice its needs. Such incidents may sometimes be exaggerated, but they are not fictitious. They are a fair illustration of what happens when the government becomes the largest purchaser and warehouser of commodities in all history.

The government's Commodity Credit Corporation has a current investment of close to $3 billion in loans, in products acquired when loans were called, in purchases, and in agreements to purchase. Last year [1949] it actually took over 21 per cent of the wheat and 26 per cent of the cotton

* "Farmers vs. the People," *Fortune Magazine*, Vol. 41 (January, 1950), pp. 63–65 *passim*. By permission of the publisher.

crops. It has managed to dispose of only relatively small amounts, mostly to occupied countries, ECA, charitable outfits, and organizations furnishing free lunches for school children. Thus, besides its loans, it is left with a fantastic $2-billion inventory. The major items in which it is interested may no longer faze the experts, who think in terms of world consumption and are obsessed with the droughts of the 1930's, but they surely are impressive to the average man. . . .

. . . This immense store [of cotton, wheat, corn, dried eggs, butter, dried milk, dried fruit, wool, turkeys, and peanuts—among others] could obviously supply food and clothing for millions of poor people, were it not that CCC is forced by statute to price them so high that the poor cannot possibly buy them.

There is little hope, furthermore, that CCC's colossal inventory will melt away. On the contrary, present farm policies are bound to increase it. . . .

What does the government propose to do? Or to put the question more realistically, what can it do under the present law? The government *is* worried, not only by the sheer size and cost of the inventory, but by the lack of storage space. Commodities are being stored in oil tanks, hangars, gymnasiums, schoolrooms, and laid-up ships. This fiscal year at least $80 million is being invested in additional space, and storage expenses already run to $250,000 a day.

The Department of Agriculture recently released a book with more than seventy recipes using dried milk, but would doubtless admit even this will not solve the problem. The planners talk of selling the surplus cheap—i.e., of dumping it abroad at a loss. They can do some dumping under ECA, and they are considering accepting foreign currencies, cutting prices in the open markets (the complaint of competitors and trade policy of the State Department notwithstanding), or bartering their surplus for foreign strategic products (already sanctioned to some degree by law). The only sizable deal in sight, however, is a scheme whereby the U.S. would advance India a million tons of wheat against future delivery of strategic materials like mica and manganese. But even this Himalaya of wheat amounts to less than 10 per cent of CCC's interest—and India seems to feel CCC's terms are not too favorable.

The Department of Agriculture's other solution is to limit output by withholding price supports from crops that do not go along with output limitations—to impose in a loose way the rigorous acreage control it already exercise in the tobacco-growing business. The department has asked farmers to cut *acreage* of wheat, cotton, potatoes, peanuts, and tobacco, but whether this will cut production is another thing. Better seed and more fertilizer may well maintain output despite somewhat smaller acreage. And acreage taken out of restricted crops will be shifted to other crops, causing new gluts, new purchase and price pegs.

And even if acreage controls could restrict output considerably they would probably restrict it the wrong way. If there is one thing every so-called expert is agreed on, it is that production should be shifted somewhat from cereals and grain to livestock, that no fewer than 35 million acres now planted in wheat, cotton, and perhaps corn should be converted to hay and pasture. The domestic market for grain is strictly limited; that for *competitively* priced livestock and dairy products is immensely expansible. But politics will not let the Department of Agriculture allow commodities to find their own prices. Instead, it is pegging prices high by restricting production.

The Anderson-Gore Act of 1949, passed in the last days of the first session of Truman's Eighty-first Congress, was in fact in many ways a worse law than the egregiously inadequate Aiken-Hope law of 1948, whose main achievement was to promote production for federal loan rather than for market demand. In justice to Senator Anderson, his aim, when he introduced the act, was to correct some of the defects of the Aiken-Hope Act and give higher supports to meat and milk than to grain and cotton, and to eliminate the practice of supporting prices rigidly. But his sound intentions went for naught. The House lobbies rigged up their own act, the Gore bill. In the compromise between the two the large surplus crops came out with as rigid supports as ever for at least five years, and livestock products came out with lower supports or no guaranteed supports at all. Farmers still have almost every incentive to go on planting and growing all the potatoes, wheat, cotton, and corn they can.

The time has come, to repeat, for a radically new act that will gradually ease the price-control falsework from under the farm economy, expose it to the genuine incentives of the open market, and get rid of the growing multitude of experts, bureaucrats, and hangers-on in the government. The prospects for this are not so bad as they may seem. The notion that the government should maintain or increase the farmer's share of the national income regardless of his contribution to that income is fortunately running into trouble. The reason was once put rather cruelly but with a certain accuracy by H. L. Mencken. Speaking as a newspaper editor, he remarked that it is a terrific job to ram even the most elemental ideas into the average man but it is always easy to scare him. For the best part of fifteen years the injustices and absurdities of price support were expounded and criticized by the experts and the press. But they were necessarily expounded in theory. The average taxpayer, far from being alarmed, was bored if not mystified by the intricacies of the arguments, and gave them hardly a second thought. He also suffered from the notion that all farmers were as poor as a few once were. Thus the only real pressure on Congress was the pressure of the farmers, who knew what they wanted. And just when the government began to spend money on farm support at a rate that might have alarmed the average taxpayer (in 1937, it owned or had money out against nearly six million bales of cotton), the war came along and enabled the Commodity Credit Corporation to dispose of its surpluses at elegant profits.

In the past year, surpluses have grown so fast, the payments so large, the prospects of disposing of excess products so dim, and the possibilities for dramatizing and exploiting them in the press so palpable, that even the most indifferent citizen would have to be a dunce indeed not to be excited and even alarmed. The time has plainly come for the politicans to pay attention not only to the bureaucrats and to the farm organizations but to the rest of the people as well.

WE MUST OPPOSE AGRICULTURAL SUBSIDIES OF ANY KIND

BY H. M. GRIFFITH*

[Dr. H. M. Griffith is Vice President of the National Economic Council. EDITOR.]

The National Economic Council is fundamentally opposed to the so-called Brannan plan for American agriculture, or to any similar legislation. It is further opposed to any continuation of agricultural subsidies of any kind. All are plainly nothing better than economic quackery and political fakery. Designed as special-interest legislation to favor one part of the population at the expense of the rest, they actually do no good to anybody except the bureaucrats who dispense the benefits. In the long run they injure the farmer, impoverish the nonagricultural population, and vitiate the entire economy. Nobody with more than a smattering of sound economics would vote for them unless outside pressures made him think it necessary. It is time for statesmanship to take over from politics and have done with economic imbecility. . . .

As economics, and considered as economics only, the whole ideology of price supports and subsidies is a fraud upon everybody concerned. The Brannan plan gives to the consumer the illusion of low prices—but

* Written statement filed with United States Senate, Subcommittee of the Committee on Agriculture and Forestry, *Agricultural Adjustment Act of 1949, Hearings* . . . 81st Cong., 1st sess., 1949, pp. 371–372 *passim.*

the illusion only. Everybody knows that the subsidies to be paid to farmers would come out of general taxation. Some of it would come from the farmers themselves, and to that extent they are among the deceived. But most of it would come from the nonagricultural consumers and the prices they would actually pay, counting in the extra tax burden, would be greater than the law of supply and demand would fix both by the amount of subsidies paid the farmers and the political brokerage which is sometimes called the cost of administration.

By selecting one particular economic and political interest for this favoritism, such legislation, instead of balancing the whole economy, will throw the total economy out of balance, with ruinous effects for everyone. For only an economy which governs its free activity by the immutable law of supply and demand can long endure. That law cannot be repealed by any Congress. It exists in the nature of all economic life. It is the prime cause of efficiency, of production for real use in response to real demand (which alone can result in real profits), and it operates to promote the general welfare by the elimination of economic services and products which consumers do not desire. It would be better to play football with an atom bomb than with the law of supply and demand. For a while, politicians may think they are getting away with kicking the law around, but eventually it explodes in their face. The pity is, that when it explodes not merely the players but the spectators of this madness—the public—will be economically vaporized along with the team. That it has not yet happened in all its fury is no reason to imagine that it will not happen. The longer it is delayed, and the more the law is tampered with, the greater the economic and social disaster will be.

QUESTIONS AND PROBLEMS

1. Utilizing (a) your text or (b) U.S. Statutes at Large (for text of farm price-support legislation) or (c) the Congressional Record (for debate and text) or (d) the informational releases of the Department of Agriculture or (e) the files of a good newspaper, summarize the main features of present price-support legislation. (What crops are supported at what levels? What conditions must be fulfilled before price supports become operative? Etc.)

2. Compare and contrast the present price-support program with (a) the Brannan Plan; (b) the views of the American Farm Bureau Federation.

3. State why and wherein you and the other contributors to this chapter would agree or disagree with Secretary Brannan's criteria of a sound farm program and his view of the ways in which such a program can serve the interests of all the people.

4. Evaluate Secretary Brannan's recommendations extracted in this chapter,

laying greatest emphasis on his price-support proposals. Does the actuality of defense mobilization and the possibility of greater inflation strengthen or weaken Brannan's price-support proposals?

5. On what grounds does Farm Bureau President Kline attack Brannan's plan?

6. State and then appraise the criticism that *Fortune* makes of our price-support program. Be sure to consider the impact of changing world conditions on this criticism.

7. What position do Brannan and *Fortune* take on the question of a greater shift to livestock production? Why have their views not prevailed?

8. Assuming you agree with *Fortune's* criticism in question 6, what would be the specific content of the "radically new act that will gradually ease the price-control falsework from under the farm economy, [and] expose it to the genuine incentives of the open market . . . "?

9. How would Brannan and Kline answer the arguments of Mr. Griffith?

10. State and then defend your own views on a price-support program in peace and war.

SELECT BIBLIOGRAPHY

Anderson, Clinton P.: Democratic Senator from New Mexico and former Secretary of Agriculture. Led Senate fight for Agriculture Act of 1949. Consult *Congressional Record* for his position.

Business Week, "Still Needed: A Farm Price Program," Nov. 19, 1949, pp. 46*ff*.; "A Workable Basis for Farm Policy," May 6, 1950, p. 132. Reviews and attacks legislation of 1948 and 1949. Suggests shift to livestock products to eliminate embarrassing surpluses. Urges government to protect farmer against price falls only during hard times.

"Congress Explores the Brannan Plan," *Congressional Digest*, Vol. 29 (March, 1950), pp. 69–96. Contains background information, summary and explanation of Agricultural Act of 1949 and Brannan Plan, and a pro and con debate on Brannan Plan.

Congressional Record, 81st Cong., 1st sess., Vol. 96 (Oct. 19, 1949), pp. 14993–15005, 15007–15008, and 15055–15077 for concluding debate in Senate and House on Agricultural Act of 1949. Contains final bill.

Davis, J. S.: *On Agricultural Policy, 1926–1938* (Stanford University, Food Research Institute, 1939). A collection of articles and addresses on farm policy, frequently hostile to New Deal legislation. Provides basis for contrast with wartime and current legislation.

McCune, Wesley: *The Farm Bloc* (Garden City, N.Y.: Doubleday, 1943). A journalistic account of farm policy and the organizations and leaders who shape policy. Readable although somewhat dated.

Nation's Agriculture. Monthly mouthpiece of American Farm Bureau Federation. Read for Bureau's current position.

National Grange. Monthly organ of another major farm organization.

Shultz, Theodore: *Production and Welfare of Agriculture* (New York: Macmillan, 1950). A recent critical appraisal by an agricultural economist. Of greatest use to advanced students with background in both agriculture and economics. Deals with Brannan's approach on pp. 176–187.

United States Commission on the Executive Branch of the Government ("Hoover Commission"): *Department of Agriculture; Task Force Report on Agricultural Activities* (Washington: Government Printing Office, 1949). Reveals the complex organization behind our total farm program.

U.S. Department of Agriculture. Churns out a stream of material on all phases of the farm problem. Check current issues in government's monthly index to its publications.

Wilcox, Walter W.: *Alternative Policies for American Agriculture* (Washington: United States Library of Congress Reference Service, Public Affairs Bulletin No. 67, 1949). Reviews basic reasons for agricultural price legislation and major proposals, pro and con, on price supports. Written before acts of 1948 and 1949.

GOVERNMENT, THE ECONOMY, AND SOCIAL WELFARE

The Welfare State: Reactionary Bugaboo or Socialist Menace?

The current debate on the over-all domestic policy of the national government is reflected, in very interesting fashion, in the titles, sub-titles, and catch phrases of the books, articles, and speeches that have flooded our avenues of communication since 1933.

On the one hand, opponents of the New Deal saw it as a "Challenge to Liberty." They branded the New Deal as "Democratic Despotism." Planning jeopardized our "Good Society." Planning would put us on the "Road to Serfdom," would create "Omnipotent Government," and would produce "Planned Chaos." We must beware of "statism." We must not temporize with "collectivism" in any form. The Fair Deal is castigated as "creeping socialism" and condemned as "America's Creeping Revolution."

On the other hand, defenders of the New Deal still assert that "the only thing we have to fear is fear itself." We must still concern ourselves with the ill-housed, ill-fed, ill-clothed, ill-educated, and ill-treated "one-third of a nation." We must still maintain our democratic "new instruments of public power" against the "economic autocrats." We can, they insist, make ours "the century of the common man." Those who attack and reject democratic planning are on the "Road to Reaction." "Freedom Under Planning" is possible. Our government must be run by the "party of the people" and not by the "party of the privileged few."

Out of the welter of words, of glittering generalities, of catchy book titles, and of propagandistic clap-trap, the central questions of this debate emerge. What *is* our government now doing? What *should* be the role of government in the twentieth century? How do we assess the expansion of government into the fields of banking and credit, electric power, housing, agriculture, business, education, and medicine? How far can government go in "serving" its people without, consciously or unconsciously, enslaving them?

Understandably but unfortunately, passion and prejudice dominate too much of this debate, warping the facts, and coloring the conclusions of the participants. Thus it is extremely difficult for the objective observer to form a clear, accurate, and understanding picture of what is going on. It becomes the trying task of the student of political science to sift fact from falsehood, to analyze with discrimination the values of the interested parties, and carefully to scrutinize the logic of the debaters. To this task he must bring the highest kind of critical intelligence.

Lincoln once wrote: "If we could first know where we are and whither we are tending, we could better judge what to do, and how to do it." The selections in this chapter present varied answers to the questions: Where are we? Whither are we tending? What must we do? And how must we do it?

The first selection is an expression of the American socialist point of view by American socialists. The socialists highlight their view of the crisis of our modern world. They condemn capitalism and its spokesmen in both the Democratic and Republican parties for producing depression and war. Similarly, they condemn Fascism and Communism for producing economic slavery and dictatorship. Only democratic socialism can produce peace and prosperity. They deplore the fact that we have not yet achieved socialism in the United States.

Senator Harry F. Byrd of Virginia maintains that we are rushing headlong down the road to collectivism or socialism. This has been the trend for the past 15 or more years. It is traceable to the excessive taxing-spending-regulatory policies of the Federal government which are hostile to free enterprise. The Fair Deal is merely the capstone of previous policies. A drastic reversal in Federal policy is necessary if we are to preserve the American free-enterprise system and thus freedom and democracy in the world.

John T. Flynn, in the third article in this chapter, emphasizes that our chief enemy in this country is not the Communist, nor even the Socialist, but the Socialist Planner who denies that he is a Socialist. The Socialist Planners have infiltrated everywhere and are in the process of transforming our capitalistic society into a socialistic one. We must, he pleads, take vigorous measures to halt our march on the road to socialism.

Senator Paul H. Douglas of Illinois, in the last article extracted herein, denies we are headed toward "collectivism." He maintains that the welfare functions of the government fulfill, in an even-handed fashion, the purposes of our Constitution. Our huge government debt and expenditures, he argues, must be attributed to the "warfare world" and not to the "welfare state." Great savings can be achieved and free enterprise preserved, he insists, without cutting the heart out of present social and economic policies.

Briefly stated, these men are concerned with the following questions:

Is democratic socialism the proper alternative to the evils of capitalism, fascism, and communism? Is our American system being destroyed by our drift toward socialism? Or is the United States fulfilling the objectives of the preamble to the Constitution within the framework of a free-enterprise economy?

AMERICA NEEDS DEMOCRATIC SOCIALISM

FROM THE NATIONAL PLATFORM OF THE UNITED STATES SOCIALIST PARTY*

Mankind is haunted by new fears. In the crowded metropolis and on the distant farm, men ask themselves whether, under freedom, depression can be avoided, poverty vanquished and war uprooted.

Starvation stalks much of the world, and in our own land men dread the insecurity that tomorrow may bring. While millions go in rags, the world's looms are again knitting the uniforms that will shroud new victims to be offered on the alters of nationalism, imperialism and tyranny.

We face the elemental question of survival. The atomic revolution has burst upon the world and a new unity has been forged among the human race: men who have refused to be brothers one of another may now become children of a common doom.

[We face the elemental question of survival:]

. . . Unless we learn to reorganize our society for survival and not for mutual extinction;

---

* "National Platform of the Socialist Party adopted at the May 7–8–9 [1948] National Convention at Reading, Pennsylvania."

[Selections used are taken from the Platform's "Preamble" and "Basic Socialist Demands." A more detailed domestic program is spelled out in the rest of the Platform. EDITOR.]

. . . Unless we learn new techniques of cooperation to replace the old policies of competition;

. . . Unless we move rapidly toward socialization by which alone the individual can be preserved in the interdependent world of the turbine, the plane, the steel mill and the uranium pile;

. . . Unless we move rapidly to a world order without greed, profit and hate.

The American people, because of the accidents of geography, will make the decision for mankind. Our mines and factories were not devastated by the physical havoc of the last war. For America, and consequently the world, it is not too late.

Three forces today are competing for the loyalty of men. And in this race, the stakes are the survival of mankind.

On the one hand, an economic system calling itself "free enterprise" asserts that it can lead to the salvation of humanity. It has brought us repeatedly to depressions and wars, yet its spokesmen in the Democratic and Republican Parties still pretend they have solutions.

They have, in fact, betrayed the promises with which they woo the American people every four years. They offered prosperity and delivered depression. They pledged peace and delivered war. They promised to increase our standard of living and are now raising the cost of living. They promised freedom to organized labor and hobbled it with new bonds.

They have sought partisan advantage and jeopardized national welfare. The dominant wings in their parties have combined to destroy price control and give us inflation, to undermine restraints on greed and give us shortage, to favor the rich and deny the poor, to cut the taxes of the wealthy and insult the common man with a crumb.

There is a second force in the world—which promises security and speaks of freedom but delivers only economic bondage and dictatorship. It is the force of totalitarianism. Yesterday its most sinister front was Fascism; today it is Communism. . . .

As against these forces, the Socialist Party of the United States speaks for the Third Force—democratic socialism, the principles of democratic planning and international order. This socialist program for the United States today includes these major goals:

1. The natural resources of the nation—minerals, oil, electric and atomic power—are the property of the people. Their preservation for future generations and their management by the people for social purposes can be achieved democratically under socialism.

2. The basic industries, public utilities, banking and credit institutions —all the economic facilities needed for the satisfaction of the fundamental

requirements of the people—must be socially owned and democratically managed.

3. Socialism will democratize the economic life of the nation by the joint representation of workers, the working management and the consuming public, in the management of socialized enterprises; by the guarantee of popular control of enterprise through the maximum decentralization economically feasible and the use of various types of organization, particularly the public corporation and the voluntary cooperative; and by the preservation of the freedom of labor organization and of consumer choice.

With such control we can have democratic planning. The lessons of the last war have taught that only by planning, by large-scale government investment, by decisive national action, can production be increased to meet the goals set by the nation. In place of the destructive ends sought in wartime, the nation must now fix its peacetime goals—food for the ill-fed, clothing for the ill-clothed, homes for the ill-housed.

A nation that could fill the skies with planes and the oceans with warships can fill its streets and avenues with homes, schools and hospitals; swell its granaries and store-houses; bring jobs to its peoples and the world.

WE'RE RUSHING HEADLONG DOWN THE ROAD TO SOCIALISM

BY SENATOR HARRY F. BYRD*

[Harry Flood Byrd, Democratic Senator from Virginia, has represented the Old Dominion in the United States Senate since 1933. Before that he served as his state's governor for four years. Newspaper publisher, farmer, and apple grower, Senator Byrd is a severe critic of many Fair Deal policies. EDITOR.]

Collectivism is a system of government which subordinates individual freedom and initiative to an all-powerful state in which the government supports the people rather than the people the government. But for the sake of those who wish to be academic, the Library of Congress has supplied this definition of collectivism:

"A political or economic doctrine which maintains that ownership of property, especially land and capital, should reside in the community as

* "Are We Headed toward 'Collectivism'?" *The New York Times Magazine*, Dec. 18, 1949, pp. 7ff. *passim*. By permission of *The New York Times* and Senator Byrd.

a whole or in the state as the designated agent of the people. Collectivism is a broader term than communism in that revolutionary methods are not necessarily advocated. Moreover, the term is to be distinguished from socialism in its advocacy of broader controls over property rights."

. . . It is my belief that we are rushing headlong down the road to collectivism or socialism much in the manner of Great Britain. The foundation stone of democracy, indeed of all our liberties, is the free enterprise system; we cannot long enjoy political and religious liberty unless we likewise possess economic liberty. But the free enterprise system is being dealt savage blows—and if the trend is too long continued will be destroyed—by (1) excessive Federal spending; (2) excessive taxation; (3) excessive government regulation; (4) excessive government competition with private business. . . .

The American people never will knowingly and voluntarily give up their liberties, but the entire trend of government during the past fifteen or more years has been gradually and definitely toward a highly regimented state with personal liberty subordinated to bureaucratic control. Those who have determined the course of government during these years have proceeded on the theory that the Government knows best, and that the Government should determine when its citizens should reap and when they should sow. Planned economy has been the fashion, and planned economy, in its ultimate form, is collectivism. . . .

Presidential proposals . . . [in the year 1949] included these:

Authority to control prices, wages and employment practices; commodity control allocations; extended authority over consumer credit and bank reserve requirements; extended Federalized power developments through public works; expanded Federalized insurance; socialization of agriculture (which turned out to be the Brannan Plan); Federalized urban redevelopment, housing and farm housing; Federally aided education and socialized medicine, the latter being the most costly and far-reaching Federal program yet proposed. Adoption of a Fair Employment Practices Commission, recommended by the President, would empower the Federal Government to enter every private business and say who should be hired or promoted.

Such proposals, if adopted, would expand nearly 100 different programs already spreading out like tentacles from among the sixty principal Federal departments and agencies which extend Federal administration through financial aids, grants, subsidies and benefits; payrolls, pensions, payments and virtually every other form of government advance and contribution. It is my firm belief—and this is buttressed by history—that the people cannot surrender such vast power without eventually sacrificing basic individual freedoms.

Congress has so far defeated or resisted many of these new recommendations for extending Government control over individual citizens and embarking on new ventures of huge and unpredictable costs. But I say advisedly that if and when these proposals which the President is . . . urging upon Congress are enacted into law, then we shall have irrevocably committed ourselves to a socialistic state from which there can be no retreat. . . .

I say there is literally nothing in the world today so important as to preserve the solvency of the American dollar and the American free enterprise system.

This free enterprise system supports the Government of this nation in its present form and no other economic system can do that.

If the free enterprise system falls the Federal Government of the United States as it is known to the world also will fall.

If the American system and the American Government fall, so will the last hope for the preservation of freedom and democracy in the world.

I would begin [to change our present course] by eliminating the incompetence and extravagance that permeate virtually every branch of the Federal service. By this means, and notably by the dismissal of all unnecessary Government personnel, Federal spending could be drastically reduced. I would balance the budget . . . on a basis of sound fiscal policies. I would abolish functions of government that are too costly and infringe upon the economic freedoms of our people. The exhaustive Hoover Commission report shows—and my own careful and exhaustive research over a period of fifteen years confirms—that the Federal budget could be drastically slashed without any decrease in essential services.

I would change the present trend to collectivism by eliminating from high council those who distrust the people and feel that the people are not capable of handling their own affairs with an absolute minimum of Government interference.

I would reverse our present trend by appointing to administrative positions persons who recognize that the free enterprise system is the foundation stone upon which this nation was built, and that its maintenance is essential to the preservation of individual liberty and to the advancement of economic, political, scientific and human progress.

I would reverse the trend also by demanding that government administrators heed an economic truism: that excessive Federal spending necessarily must lead to excessive taxation or national bankruptcy; and that free enterprise cannot expand under long-continued oppressive taxation. Insolvency is the only alternative, but if insolvency comes in, freedom must go out.

An essential ingredient in reversing the trend toward collectivism is not new restrictive laws and oppressive regulations, but rather a desire and a determination on the part of those in authority to preserve our free enterprise system and the principles of government that have made us great.

Many civilizations which have entered the domain of history seem to present two evolutionary periods. The first period is that in which the individual seeks to safeguard himself against the excesses of arbitrary power by exacting guarantees from those trusted to rule. The second is that in which these guarantees are gradually surrendered to the collective power of the mass.

Let us always remember that human freedom is not a gift to man. It is an achievement by man, and, as it was gained by vigilance and struggle, so it may be lost by indifference and supineness.

BEWARE THE SOCIALIST PLANNER

BY JOHN T. FLYNN*

[John Thomas Flynn has been associated with the old *New York Globe, New Republic,* and *Collier's.* He has been adviser to a Senate committee investigating the stock exchange and to one investigating munitions. He is the author of *Country Squire in the White House, Meet Your Congress,* and *Epic of Freedom.* EDITOR.]

. . . Our American system is being destroyed not merely by Communist conspirators, but by all those groups united in the design of luring this country into a Socialist system on the British model. The Communist would like to ruin the American system by clubbing it over the head. The Socialist Planner would like to do it by slow poison. Both types of assassin are at work on it now. For the moment we have limited a little the energies of the assassin with the club. But we must not make the mistake of taking to our bosom the assassin with the poison bottle. Russian communism is merely a more extreme form of socialism than British Fabianism [the name frequently given to British evolutionary socialism]. Russian communism is the grand terminal. British Fabianism is merely a station on the line. The Communist will aid the Planner to get him to that first stop. Those who oppose taking the journey at all must understand the characters and techniques of both groups of schemers.

. . . As the British Socialists operated behind a mask called the Labor

* *The Road Ahead* (New York: Devin-Adair, 1949), pp. 126–129, 136–137, 146–147 *passim.* By permission of the publisher.

Party, so the new-style American Socialist operates behind the mask of
Economic Planning.

. . . In Britain . . . socialism did not mean State operation of every
enterprise. But it did mean socialization of everything—a part through
State ownership and the other part, left in private hands, through State
planning and control.

The British Socialists moved one step at a time and our American Planners are doing the same thing, always avoiding and even disclaiming the
word socialism. The British Socialists used the apparatus of the labor
unions and the American Planners have successfully imitated this procedure. The British Fabians moved into the Liberal Party, slowly corrupted
it, made it a prisoner because it became utterly dependent on Labor support for success, drove out the orthodox Liberals and ultimately put the
Liberal Party out of business, supplanting it with the Labor Party. Here
the American Fabians—the Socialist Planners—have moved into the Democratic Party, have made it their helpless tool and are driving out of it the
orthodox Democrats. It is merely a question of time when the Democratic
Party will go out of business or become absolutely the party of the
Planners.

As in England the Fabian Socialists captured the apparatus of great
church organizations and infiltrated the organs and instruments of opinion,
so the American Planners are performing the same operation here.

We must now ask ourselves how far the Planners have advanced their
program for socializing the American society. . . .

The depression which began in 1929 produced a deeply questioning
mood in the American mind. It seemed to furnish proof that the radical
revolutionists were right in their insistence that capitalism was on its last
legs. As the depression deepened the mood of frustration grew darker.
Meantime, we were being treated to radiant accounts of Russia's five-year
plans as distinguished from the planless wilderness of America. By 1933 we
moved into the first stage of the Fabian revolution—the Welfare State. . . .

. . . In 1938 when the mere social welfare schemes of the government
had failed to promote an enduring recovery, we began to hear that something more than mere welfare expenditures was needed. We were then
told that the economic system, disorderly and planless, must now be subjected to intelligent and central State planning. Oh, of course, we were
not going to scrap the Capitalist system. But we must understand that it
must be planned—and planned in the interest of "the people," the "little
fellow," the "common man," instead of the big corporations. And this
planning must be done under the auspices of the government, which was
the agent of the people. . . .

Do we want a Socialist society or not? The movements for these plans
go on, but never do the advocates use the word socialism. What we hear

about is power for the farmer, credit for the farmer and the "little fellow," power for your state and my state, business for the cement man and the steel man and the building industry, houses for all, floods of money for everything, jobs for all, security for all, a society planned and running smoothly on a program emerging from the "Brain" in Washington, money for the farmers, jobs for the workers, something for everybody. No one thing is called socialism. But when it is all put together the completed structure will be a Socialist state. . . .

From . . . [the Federal invasion of banking and credit, federal invasion of power, from Federal authority to take over the nation's mines and railroads during emergencies, from announced wishes to build additional steel mills to supplement the private steel industry, from proposals for socialized medicine, from the Brannan Plan, and from other bills relating to government powers over industry] emerges the spectacle of a society in which the government makes itself responsible for the security of every citizen from the cradle to the grave and for the continuous operation of the entire machinery of business and farming. The ultimate aim is to control banks, transportation, power, mines and the basic metal industries and, I am quite sure, the entire business of life insurance, fire insurance and other forms of insurance. The rest of the industrial system will be operated by private owners but under plans to be made by the President under broad powers and through a multitude of planning and enforcement bureaus. The farms will be brought under the wing of the government through production quotas, subsidies, allocations and priorities.

This corresponds in every essential respect to the system now in operation in England. And this is what we will have here if the men now in power in our government are permitted to have their way. . . .

This, then, is the road we are traveling. It is the road to socialism. And we will continue to travel it until the masses of Americans who still cherish the tradition of a free society understand where they are traveling, and take vigorous measures first to halt the journey and then to reverse it.

THE UNITED STATES FOLLOWS A SOUND
CONSTITUTIONAL PATH

BY SENATOR PAUL H. DOUGLAS*

[Democratic Senator Paul H. Douglas was elected to the United States Senate in 1948. A Professor of Economics at the University of Chicago, he is a past President of the American Economic

---

* "Are We Headed toward 'Collectivism'?" *The New York Times Magazine*, Dec. 18, 1949, pp. 7ff. *passim*. By permission of *The New York Times* and Senator Douglas.

Association and author of *Social Security in the United States*. Twice wounded during World War II and a recipient of the Bronze Star, he rose from Private to Lieutenant Colonel in the Marines. EDITOR.]

Collectivism is the public ownership of the means of production and distribution. Under it, the state would own and operate the railroads, mines, manufacturing establishments, banks, and insurance companies. Under the most sweeping definition of collectivism the state would also own and operate farms, retail stores and wholesale establishments; and virtually all members of the professions, such as doctors, dentists, teachers, and journalists, would also be employed by the state.

In the light of my definition, it is obvious that, far from traveling a dangerous road to "collectivism," the United States is continuing to follow a sound constitutional path. Our industries are privately owned and operated, with the exception of the roads, the schools and a small portion of electrical power. No responsible person proposes that this be altered. We all want to make the system of so-called free enterprise work.

But there are certain public functions directly confided to the national Government by the Constitution. The preamble to that document states very explicitly that in addition to forming a "more perfect Union," there were four specific ends which the new Government was to further. These were: to "establish justice, insure domestic tranquillity, provide for the common defense, promote the general welfare. . . . "

That this was not a slip of the pen is clearly shown by the fact that in Article I, Section 8, in enumerating the powers of Congress, the Constitution again states that "the Congress shall have power . . . to provide for the common defense and general welfare of the United States. . . .[1]

The duty of providing for all these purposes (including the general welfare) was thus made part of the basic obligation of the Government. It is our task to see what those basic purposes require today and how these requirements are being fulfilled.

The establishment of justice involves more than the mere creation of courts and the machinery of civil and criminal justice. It is something that must be established in our material affairs—in the market place, the bank and the factory; on the railroads and over the air waves. And justice must be sought as much in advance of grievances as after the occurrence of wrong.

Thus we have an Interstate Commerce Commission, which seeks to

---

[1] The words omitted after "power" ("to lay and collect taxes, duties, imposts, and excises, to pay the debts and") indicate that Congress can tax and spend *in order to* provide for the general welfare. EDITOR.

protect shippers and common carriers; a Federal Trade Commission, which stands guard against unfair trade practices and seeks to stimulate competition in order that we may have a free society. The Food and Drug Administration tries to protect consumers from injurious or spurious products. The Federal Communications Commission protects public rights in and over the air waves. The Securities and Exchange Commission seeks to safeguard the investor and the National Labor Relations Board substitutes the principle of collective bargaining for that of all-out industrial warfare. Further means by which justice is established in this country could be adduced almost endlessly.

The insurance of domestic tranquillity no longer means the use of Federal troops to put down a bloody strike. We, in this country, have learned from the events of the depression the relationship existing between internal order and the degree to which individuals may satisfy their basic wants. It was to insure our domestic tranquillity that a series of stabilizing actions were undertaken by the Roosevelt and Truman Administrations—and these in the face of bitter Republican and conservative opposition.

I need only recall the unemployment insurance programs, designed to take the terror out of joblessness and help maintain purchasing power during recession or depression; the guarantee of bank deposits to protect individual savings, at the same time permitting banks to follow more liberal credit policies in periods of stress. There are the Federal Housing Administration guarantees in the field of private housing which have provided the strongest stimulus in our history to the building of homes and have been greatly beneficial, both economically and spiritually. Again, the protection given farm prices has prevented a downward plummeting at crucial points, has given the farmer an incentive to produce and has prevented a breakdown of farm purchasing power. . . .

We live in a "warfare world," so to speak, rather than in a "welfare state." Like Senator Byrd, [one of the foremost advocates of economy in government expenditures] I deplore such huge expenditures, but they were created neither by President Roosevelt nor President Truman. To the degree that personal guilt is involved we should charge them up to Kaiser Wilhelm, Adolf Hitler, Karl Marx and Joseph Stalin.

In listening to attacks upon the so-called "welfare state," I have been struck by the derisive manner in which these words are employed. The way these words are commonly hissed out shows an ignorance of the Constitution, which told our lawmakers to provide for the general welfare. No such derisive overtones were heard when the Federal Government made lavish grants of land to build railroads or to encourage the marvelous growth of state universities. Nor could they be detected when the Federal Government took the lead in the construction of roads, in soil conservation and protection from forest fires; in flood control, the dredging of rivers and harbors and the building of levees; or the furnishing of vital information to business and agriculture.

Why, then, after 150 years should an honorable word like "welfare" suddenly become a synonym for the devil? The answer is a simple one. As long as it was the welfare of the propertied classes that was being advanced, the word stood as Holy Writ. But the horrors of the "welfare state" were shouted from the rooftops when the Federal Government began to spend money to aid the great groups in our society that had little or no property. The total cost of welfare items in the . . . year [1950] amounts to only $2.2 billion—about 5 per cent of the total Federal budget and about 1 per cent of the net national income.

Senator Byrd has said frequently that our budget, debt and taxes are enormous. But, as I have pointed out, our expenditures are primarily large because we live in what I have termed a "warfare world." I agree with him that there is waste in government. But where I differ from the Senator is that I believe the greatest waste lies in the administrative costs of government.

It is here that I would save, while Senator Byrd would, I believe, like to extend his concept of "waste" to cover the heart of social programs that are actually being administered. I have argued in the Senate that even without the elaborate reorganization plans recommended by the Hoover Commission, we could save nearly $2 billion annually. We could do this through better purchasing, more careful use of Government supplies and by cutting the staffs of our bureaus—by at least 7 per cent in nearly all instances, and by 10 per cent in most—without reducing the scope of the programs carried out by those bureaus.

I also believe that we should cut down our appropriations for rivers and harbors, which still constitute a form of "pork barrel." We should revise personnel practices and reduce the present $550 million deficit in the Post Office by increasing operating efficiency and by upping the rates on second, third and fourth class matter which are now carried at a tremendous loss. These latter losses constitute, indeed, a subsidy of about $400 million a year to the newspapers, magazines, advertisers, mail-order houses, etc., of the country.

It would be very heartening if all of these groups which believe so strongly in economy and which are opposed to subsidies would come forward with the fruits of their belief in the form of a voluntary offer to have their postal rates raised to meet the real cost of the services provided. This would be a mighty reinforcement to those of us who are trying to cut costs but who are checkmated because everyone wants the economies made at someone else's expense.

The opponents of so-called "statism" would bar the Government from any economic activity which competes directly or indirectly with private business. To that in general, a double amen. Neither I nor my party wants any concentration of economic power in either Big Government or Big Business. We want such power diffused and we want competition restored.

But in this struggle we get little help from the most vocal advocates of so-called "free enterprise." They seem, instead, to be using the language of free competition as a means for strengthening their beloved private monopolies. When we try to strengthen the anti-trust laws, for example, most of the vociferous advocates of "free enterprise" line up on the other side. It so happens that the only field in which there is any real degree of Government competition with private enterprise is that of electric power. And yet, even here, Federal projects generate only about 14 per cent of the nation's power. Government's investment is $2 billion as contrasted with private capital's stake of $32 billion.

There is no need to recite the reasons why the Government was forced to enter the field of generating and transmitting hydro-electric power in certain regions. Nor is there any need to recite the many benefits which have come both to individuals and to private utilities. Cause and effect are known to every schoolboy. Certainly Mr. Hoover knows them—else, if he disapproved, would he not want the name of Hoover Dam changed back to Boulder Dam?

I repeat: We continue to follow the sound Constitutional path laid down as a means of achieving a "more perfect union." And I shall persist in this belief until I can see a bit more flesh on the ghosts that seem to terrorize others of a different view.

QUESTIONS AND PROBLEMS

1. How do the contributors to this chapter define the following key and controversial words: "democracy," "socialism," "capitalism," "collectivism," "free enterprise," "planning," "Socialist Planner," "democratic planning," "welfare," "welfare state," "justice," "opportunity," "liberty"? Why is it so important to discover how these words are used?

2. How would *you* define the key words in question 1?

3. To what extent *does* the national government now perform functions and services once handled either by private business enterprise, private philanthropy, or state and local government?

4. What three forces do the socialists see competing for the loyalty of men? On what grounds do Byrd, Flynn, and Douglas agree or disagree with this socialist analysis?

5. Is the New Deal–Fair Deal the savior or destroyer of American Democracy? Of American capitalism? What evidence do Byrd, Flynn, and Douglas

present to buttress their answers to these questions? What case would you present in answering the same questions?

6. According to Flynn, how have the "Socialist Planners" been operating in this country? Do you agree or disagree with Flynn's acount? Why or why not?

7. What reasons does Senator Douglas advance to explain why after 150 years an "honorable word like 'welfare'" suddenly becomes "a synonym for the devil"?

8. Exemplify as fully as possible the factors that Senator Byrd feels will, if long continued, destroy the free-enterprise system.

9. How does Senator Douglas justify past and present governmental policies in terms of the intent of the Preamble of the Constitution that government "establish justice insure domestic tranquillity, provide for the common defense, [and] promote the general welfare?"

10. Is the demand of the American people for "welfare" a justifiable demand, or is it merely the irresponsible clamor of the mob for bread and circuses? How would the contributors to this chapter answer this question? How would you answer it? Why would you answer it the way you do? If it is a justifiable demand, consonant with the necessities of social evolution, is there any way to satisfy it without recourse to the authoritarian state? Explain.

11. What future course of action is demanded, either specifically or by implication, by the socialists, and by Byrd, Flynn, and Douglas? What course of action do *you* think should be taken?

SELECT BIBLIOGRAPHY

Davenport, Russell W.: "The Greatest Opportunity on Earth," *Fortune Magazine*, Vol. 40 (October, 1949), pp. 65–69. Asserts that American business, in American tradition, can provide realistic alternative to welfare state. Holds free business enterprise must implement American concept of economic rights.

Finer, Herman: *Road to Reaction* (Boston: Little, Brown, 1945). A rather hot-tempered answer to Hayek's *Road to Serfdom*. Denies impossibility of democratic socialism. Maintains that planning does not necessarily lead to fascism or communism.

Hansen, Alvin H.: *Economic Policy and Full Employment* (New York: McGraw-Hill, 1947). Favors properly timed and directed government spending to maintain and sustain high level of employment.

Hayek, Friedrich A.: *The Road to Serfdom* (Chicago: University of Chicago Press, 1944). A vigorous polemic against socialism. Opposes planning of the now competitive economy. Should be supplemented by his more recent *Individualism and the Economic Order* (1948).

Hoover, Herbert: *The Challenge to Liberty* (New York: Scribner, 1934). An early attack on the New Deal. Criticizes taxing, spending, and hostile business policies of the New Deal in many of the selections of his *Addresses upon the American Road,* covering period between 1933 and 1948, and published every few years.

Lauterbach, Albert: *Economic Security and Individual Freedom* (Ithaca, N.Y.: Cornell University Press, 1948). Seeks to demonstrate that democratic economic planning and individual freedom are compatible.

Lippmann, Walter: *An Inquiry into the Principles of the Good Society* (Boston: Little, Brown, 1937). Sees a struggle between true liberalism and collectivisms of left and right. Defends competitive economy against national planning.

Rauch, Basil: *The History of the New Deal, 1933–1938* (New York: Creative Age Press, 1944). One of best studies of New Deal. Should be supplemented by other histories, until time and perspective permit writing of definitive story.

Roosevelt, Franklin D.: *The Public Papers of Franklin D. Roosevelt, 1928–1945* (New York: Random House, 13 vols., 1938–1950). Invaluable for judging the expressed views of the symbolic leader of the New Deal.

Taft, Robert S.: "Is President Truman Taking Us Down the British Road?" *Collier's,* Vol. 125 (Apr. 8, 1950), pp. 13, 46–47. Argues that the Truman administration's policies parallel British socialist program which brought Britain to state of economic regimentation and misery.

Truman, Harry S.: *Truman Program: Addresses and Messages* (Washington: Public Affairs Press, 1948). A good summary and forecast of the Fair Deal. Has spelled out Fair Deal in more detail in more recent messages. Sees fulfillment, not destruction, of free enterprise and individual freedom in Fair Deal.

Wallace, Henry A.: *The Century of the Common Man* (New York: Reynal & Hitchcock, 1943). The New Deal vision of the post-World War II world by the then Vice President of the United States.

Wooton, Barbara: *Freedom under Planning* (Chapel Hill, N.C.: University of North Carolina Press, 1945). Examines how the varying freedoms of a democratic society may be preserved under democratic planning.

FOREIGN AFFAIRS

How Should We Deal with the Soviet Union?

" . . . A war of extermination, in which the process of annihilation would strike at both parties, and likewise at all Right at the same time, would reach Perpetual Peace only on the final Golgotha of the human race." This quotation from Immanuel Kant's famous eighteenth-century essay on *Perpetual Peace* is more pertinent today than when it was first written. Like the sword of Damocles, the possibility of World War III hangs over the head of twentieth-century mankind. Ominous and evil, modern warfare threatens to destroy man and his civilization, either through the catastrophic destruction of atomic weapons or through the protracted, but nonetheless deadly, struggle of "conventional" armaments.

Few nations seek war. Most violently condemn it. Yet the possibility of war molds the policies of all modern nations, in large part because most governments privately consider war the ultimate arbiter of the conduct of "realistic" men and nations.

World War III threatens to break out in full intensity only a relatively few years since the end of another cataclysmic conflict, World War II, primarily because two great world powers, the United States of America and the Union of Soviet Socialist Republics, are at odds.

What is the source of their disagreement? Can the United States and the U.S.S.R.—and their allies—learn to live together peacefully? On what basis? Can all-out war be averted? At what price? These are the questions that challenge the intelligence and conscience of modern man.

It is a matter of historical record that the high hopes of many that the United States and the U.S.S.R. might live in the postwar world in friendship were not to be fulfilled. Even before the end of World War II relations had become strained. American policy shifted. The key premises of a reoriented United States foreign policy may perhaps be found in a now famous article by George F. Kennan, "The

Sources of Soviet Conduct," which appeared in the July, 1947, issue of *Foreign Affairs*.

Kennan wrote: "It is clear that the United States cannot expect in the forseeable future to enjoy political intimacy with the Soviet regime. It must continue to regard the Soviet Union as a rival, not a partner, in the political arena. It must continue to expect that Soviet policies will reflect no abstract love of peace and stability, no real faith in the possibility of a permanent happy coexistence of the Socialist [*i.e.*, Russian Communist] and capitalist worlds, but rather a cautious, persistent pressure toward the disruption and weakening of all rival influence and rival power." Kennan stated that "it is clear that the main element of any United States policy toward the Soviet Union must be that of a long-term, patient but firm and vigilant containment of Russian expansive tendencies. . . . The Soviet pressure against the free institutions of the western world is something that can be contained by the adroit and vigilant application of counterforce at a series of constantly shifting geographical and political points, corresponding to the shifts and manoeuvres of Soviet policy, but which cannot be charmed or talked out of existence."

The fuller policy of the United States government is summarized, in the first selection in this problem, by President Truman, who occupied the White House in the crucial years following World War II. Because of the world tension created by the armed strength of the Soviet camp, Communist imperialism, and Soviet obstruction in the United Nations, the free nations of the world must oppose strength with strength. The Soviet Union, however, can reduce world tension by genuine proof of its peaceful intentions. The United States will always support negotiations in good faith. War is not inevitable largely because the United Nations provides a forum for peaceful settlement of disputes, collective strength to defeat agression, and machinery to relieve the crushing burden of armaments. If unanimous agreement could be obtained on a foolproof plan for disarmament, including all weapons, the world could move toward the achievement of a truly prosperous and creative community of nations.

This foreign policy which evolved during the years 1945 to 1951 precipitated a series of "great" and "greater" debates in the United States. The heated controversies evoked in these debates perhaps reached a crescendo in the relief of General Douglas MacArthur and the congressional hearings held to probe his ouster and the whole conduct of our foreign policy.

At one extreme in this debate are the advocates of a "preventive war" against the Soviet Union. They urge us to wage a military war to prevent that Soviet aggression they foresee.

Another position is that taken by James Burnham in the second selection in this problem. Burnham contends that the coexistence of the United States and the Soviet Union is impossible. He argues that we are at war now—and it is not merely a cold war. He maintains that, if we are to achieve victory in this war with an enemy who seeks our destruction as a step toward world domination, we must really take the offensive with the objective of reducing Communism to impotence. In this war we must not be afraid to use bold and vigorous methods—economic, psychological, political, subversive, and military. At best, Burnham contends, we can defeat the Soviet Union without all-out war. At worst we achieve victory in the war that may come in spite of whatever policy we adopt.

Another alternative program is outlined by the American Friends Service Committee. In the light of certain basic considerations the Friends maintain that improved relations are possible. They suggest that the United States take the initiative in reducing East-West trade barriers, in seeking the creation of a united, peaceful, prosperous Germany, in strengthening the peacemaking (rather than the coercive) functions of the United Nations, in reducing the burden of armaments, and in developing a large-scale, international program of mutual aid to eliminate the roots of war. A new spirit of negotiation may achieve peace throughout the world.

Former President Herbert Hoover summarizes yet another approach to foreign policy in the fourth article extracted herein. He advocates United States air and naval rearmament as the primary protection for ourselves and our allies. He opposes sending United States land armies into the "quicksands" of either Europe or Asia. He urges retrenchment in domestic expenditure and a "second line of air and naval defense" to guard our Western Hemisphere Gibraltar in the event of the failure of our allies.

The outright pro-Soviet point of view is presented by Jessica Smith in the final selection in this problem. She holds that capitalism and communism can coexist peacefully, that it is the United States and not the Soviet Union which has turned its back on peaceful settlement, that the Soviets don't fight because they want peace, and that there is no proof of an over-all Soviet plan to dominate the world by force. The Soviet Union, she maintains, will continue to press the United States for a settlement which will end the threat of a new war.

The vital question to which the contributors to this problem address themselves—a question whose answer may lead to all-out war or peace—is this: *How should the United States deal with the Soviet Union?*

PEACE WITH JUSTICE THROUGH THE UNITED NATIONS AND A REARMED FREE WORLD

BY HARRY S. TRUMAN

The name "United Nations" was first used in the dark days of the Second World War by the countries then allied to put down . . . [the] aggression [of the "Axis" powers—Germany, Italy, and Japan.][1]

From that day until this, the cause of peace has been strengthened by an active policy of cooperation among the free nations. It is not by chance, but as a result of that steady policy, that 53 members of the United Nations rallied immediately to meet the unprovoked aggression against the Republic of Korea.

It has been as a part of that same policy and common purpose that we have joined during the past 5 years in building up the strength of the peace-loving forces of the world. We have contributed to this end through the Marshall Plan in Europe and through economic assistance in many other parts of the world. We have also contributed to this end through military aid to countries threatened by aggression. All around the world, the free nations have been gaining strength.

We have to recognize that, as we have moved steadily along in the post-war years, our policy of building a peaceful world has met constant opposition from the Soviet Union.

Here, in San Francisco 5 years ago [in 1945], we hoped that the Soviet Union would cooperate in this effort to build a lasting peace.

But Communist imperialism would not have it so. Instead of working with other governments in mutual respect and cooperation, the Soviet Union attempted to extend its control over other peoples. It embarked upon a new colonialism—Soviet style. This new colonialism has already

[1] "Partnership of World Peace," *Bulletin of the Department of State*, Vol. 23 (Oct. 30, 1950), pp. 684–686 *passim*. Address delivered at San Francisco, Calif., Oct. 17, 1950.

brought under its complete control and exploitation many countries which used to be free. Moreover, the Soviet Union has refused to cooperate and has not allowed its satellites to cooperate with those nations it could not control.

In the United Nations, the Soviet Union has persisted in obstruction. It has refused to share in activities devoted to the great economic, social, and spiritual causes recognized in the United Nations Charter. For months on end, it even boycotted the Security Council.

These tactics of the Soviet Union have imposed an increasingly greater strain upon the fabric of world peace. Aggression and threats of aggression, aided and abetted by obstructionism in the United Nations, have caused grave concern among the nations which are honestly seeking peace. The response of the free world to the aggression in Korea has given those nations new confidence. But events in Korea have also made it more apparent than ever that the evil spirit of aggression is still abroad in the world. So long as this is true, we are all faced with a clear and present danger.

Today, we face a violent and cynical attack upon our democratic faith, upon every hope of a decent and free life—indeed, upon every concept of human dignity. Those who support this evil purpose are prepared to back it to the limit with every device, including military force.

The Soviet Union and its colonial satellites are maintaining armed forces of great size and strength. In both Europe and Asia, their vast armies pose a constant threat to world peace. So long as they persist in maintaining these forces and in using them to intimidate other countries, the free men of the world have but one choice if they are to remain free. They must oppose strength with strength.

This is not a task for the United States alone. It is a task for free nations to undertake together. And the free nations are undertaking it together.

In the United Nations, Secretary of State Acheson has proposed a plan for "Uniting for Peace," to make it possible for the General Assembly to act quickly and effectively in case of any further outbreak of aggression.

In our own country, and in cooperation with other countries, we are continuing to build armed forces strong enough to make it clear that aggression will not pay.

Our military establishment moved the necessary men and supplies into Korea, 5,000 miles away, in an amazingly brief period of time. This remarkable accomplishment should not delude us into any false sense of security. We must be better armed and equipped than we are today if we are to be protected from the dangers which still face us.

We must continue to increase our production for military purposes. We must continue to increase the strength of our armed forces—Army, Navy, and Air Force. We must devote more of our resources to military purposes, and less to civilian consumption.

All this will be difficult, and it will exact many sacrifices. But we are aware of the dangers we face. We are going to be prepared to meet them. Let no aggressor make any mistake about that. We value our independence and our free way of life in this country and we will give all that we have to preserve them. We are going ahead in dead earnest to build up our defenses. . . .

As we go forward, let us remember that we are not increasing our armed strength because we want to. We are increasing our armed strength because Soviet policies leave us no other choice. The Soviet Union can change this situation. It has only to give concrete and positive proof of its intention to work for peace. If the Soviet Union really wants peace, it must prove it—not by glittering promises and false propaganda, but by living up to the principles of the United Nations Charter.

If the Soviet Union really wants peace, it can prove it—and could have proved it on any day since . . . June 25th [1950]—by joining the rest of the United Nations, in calling upon the North Koreans to lay down their arms at once.

If the Soviet Union really wants peace, it can prove it by lifting the iron curtain and permitting the free exchange of information and ideas. If the Soviet Union really wants peace, it can prove it by joining in the efforts of the United Nations to establish a workable system of collective security—a system which will permit the elimination of the atomic bomb and the drastic reduction and regulation of all other arms and armed forces.

But until the Soviet Union does these things, until it gives real proof of peaceful intentions, we are determined to build up the common defensive strength of the free world. This is the choice we have made. We have made it firmly and resolutely. But it is not a choice we have made gladly. We are not a militaristic nation. We have no desire for conquest or military glory.

Our national history began with a revolutionary idea—the idea of human freedom and political equality. We have been guided by the light of that idea down to this day. The forces of Communist imperialism dread this revolutionary idea because it produces an intolerable contrast to their own system. They know that our strength comes from the freedom and the well-being of our citizens. We are strong because we never stop working for better education for all our people, for fair wages and better living conditions, for more opportunities for business, and better lives for our farmers. We are strong because of our social security system, because of our labor unions, because of our agricultural program. We are strong because we use our democratic institutions continually to achieve a better life for all the people of our country.

This is the source of our strength. And this idea—this endlessly revolutionary idea of human freedom and political equality— is what we held out to all nations as the answer to the tyranny of international communism. We

have seen this idea work in our own country. We know that it acknowl-
edges no barriers of race, or nation, or creed. We know that it means
progress for all men.

The international Communist movement, far from being revolutionary,
is the most reactionary movement in the world today. It is violently
opposed to the freedom of the individual because, in that Communist
system, the state is supreme. It is equally opposed to the freedom of other
nations because, in that Communist system, it is Soviet Russia which must
be supreme. . . .

. . . As your President, I realize what it means to the homes of America
to have the youth of our land called to meet aggression. These are the most
solemn decisions and impose the heaviest responsibility upon those who
must make them. I have told you tonight why we must do what we are
doing. We hate war, but we love our liberties. We will not see them destroyed. We want peace, but it must be a peace founded upon justice. That
American policy is as old as our Republic, and it is stronger today than
ever before in our history. We intend to keep it that way.

. . . At the present time the fear of another great international war over-
shadows all the hopes of mankind.[2] This fear arises from the tensions between nations and from the recent outbreak of open aggression in Korea.
We in the United States believe that such a war can be prevented. We do
not believe that war is inevitable. One of the strongest reasons for this belief is our faith in the United Nations.

The United Nations has three great roles to play in preventing wars.

First: it provides a way for negotiation and the settlement of disputes
among nations by peaceful means.

Second: it provides a way of utilizing the collective strength of member
nations, under the Charter, to prevent aggression.

Third: it provides a way through which, once the danger of aggression
is reduced, the nations can be relieved of the burden of armaments.

All of us must help the United Nations to be effective in performing
these functions. . . .

We believe that negotiation is an essential part of this peaceful process.
The United States, as one of the members of the United Nations, is prepared now, as always, to enter into negotiations. We insist only that negotiations must be entered into in good faith and be governed throughout by
a spirit of willingness to reach proper solutions.

While we will continue to take advantage of every opportunity—here
in the United Nations and elsewhere—to settle differences by peaceful

[2] "A New Page in History," *Bulletin of the Department of State*, Vol. 23 (Nov. 6,
1950), pp. 720–722 *passim.* Delivered before the United Nations General Assembly,
Oct. 24, 1950.

means, we have learned from hard experience that we cannot rely upon negotiation alone to preserve the peace.

Five years ago, after the bloodshed and destruction of World War II, many of us hoped that all nations would work together to make sure that war could never happen again. We hoped that international cooperation, supported by the strength and moral authority of the United Nations, would be sufficient to prevent aggression.

But this was not to be the case.

Although many countries promptly disbanded their wartime armies, other countries continued to maintain forces so large that they posed a constant threat of aggression. And this year [1950] the invasion of Korea has shown that there are some who will resort to outright war, contrary to the principles of the Charter, if it suits their ends.

In these circumstances the United Nations, if it is to be an effective instrument for keeping the peace, has no choice except to use the collective strength of its members to curb aggression.

To do so, the United Nations must be prepared to use force. The United Nations did use force to curb aggression in Korea and by so doing has greatly strengthened the cause of peace. I am glad that additional steps are being taken at this session to prepare for quick and effective action in any future case of aggression.

The Resolution on United Action for Peace . . . [which was supported by the United States and approved by the General Assembly of the United Nations] recognizes three important principles:

To maintain the peace, the United Nations must be able to learn the facts about any threat of aggression. Next, it must be able to call quickly upon the member nations to act if the threat becomes serious.

Above all, the peace-loving nations must have the military strength available, when called upon, to act decisively to put down aggression.

The peace-loving nations are building that strength.

However much they may regret the necessity, they will continue to build up their strength until they have created forces strong enough to preserve peace under the United Nations. They will do all that is required to provide a defense against aggression. They will do that because, under the conditions which now exist in the world, it is the only way to maintain peace.

We intend to build up strength for peace as long as that is necessary. But at the same time we must continue to strive, through the United Nations, to achieve international control of atomic energy and the reduction of armaments and armed forces. Cooperative and effective disarmament would make the danger of war remote. It would be a way of achieving the high purposes of the United Nations without the tremendous expenditures for armaments which conditions in the world today make imperative.

Disarmament is the course which the United States would prefer to take. It is the course which most nations would like to adopt. It is the course which the United Nations from its earliest beginnings has been seeking to follow.

For nearly five years, two commissions of the United Nations have been working on the problem of disarmament. One commission has been concerned with the elimination of atomic weapons and the other with the reduction of other types of armaments and of armed forces. Thus far, these commissions have not been successful in obtaining agreement among all the major powers. Nevertheless, these years of effort have served to bring to the attention of all nations the three basic principles upon which any successful plan of disarmament must rest.

First, the plan must include all kinds of weapons. Outlawing any particular kind of weapon is not enough. The conflict in Korea bears tragic witness to the fact that aggression, whatever the weapons used, brings frightful destruction.

Second, the plan must be based on unanimous agreement. A majority of nations is not enough. No plan of disarmament can work unless it includes every nation having substantial armed forces. One-sided disarmament is a sure invitation to aggression.

Third, the plan must be foolproof. Paper promises are not enough. Disarmament must be based on safeguards which will insure the compliance of all nations. The safeguards must be adequate to give immediate warning of any threatened violation. Disarmament must be policed continuously and thoroughly. It must be founded upon free and open interchange of information across national borders.

These are simple, practical principles. If they were accepted and carried out genuine disarmament would be possible. . . .

If real disarmament were achieved, the nations of the world, acting through the United Nations, could join in a greatly enlarged program of mutual aid. As the cost of maintaining armaments decreased, every nation could greatly increase its contributions to advancing human welfare. All of us could then pool even greater resources to support the United Nations in its war against want.

In this way, our armaments would be transformed into foods, medicine, tools for use in underdeveloped areas, and into other aids for human advancement. The latest discoveries of science could be made available to men all over the globe. Thus we could give real meaning to the old promise that swords shall be beaten into plowshares and that the nations shall not learn war any more.

Then man can turn his great inventiveness, his tremedous energies, and the resources with which he has been blessed to creative efforts. Then we shall be able to realize the kind of world which has been the vision of man for centuries.

This is the goal which we must keep before us—and the vision in which we must never lose faith. This will be our inspiration, and with God's help, we shall attain our goal.

THE UNITED STATES MUST TAKE THE OFFENSIVE IN THE WAR AGAINST COMMUNISM

BY JAMES BURNHAM*

[James Burnham, Professor of Philosophy at New York University, is the author of a number of controversial books, including *The Managerial Revolution*, *The Machiavellians*, *The Struggle for the World*, and *The Coming Defeat of Communism*. EDITOR.]

. . . If a retreat to appeasement is one direction that our policy can take, after we complete the present turn, there is another. This other is an advance to the offensive. The necessity and meaning of the turn to the offensive is the subject of my new book. . . . The title that I have used, *The Coming Defeat of Communism*, expresses my conviction that with whatever delays this turn will be made. As in all struggles, the offensive and only the offensive can win.

To make the turn to the offensive means first of all to recognize the truth about the situation in which we now find ourselves. The truth is simply this: We are at war. We are not confronted with the possibility of a war sometime in the future, but we are at war now. And we are whether we admit it to ourselves or not, because our enemy is at war with us, and it takes only one to make a war. Until we recognize this fundamental truth we have both hands tied behind our back. Our enemy fights for his strategic objectives with all those means that he considers appropriate. We restrain our actions because of empty legal and moral formulas which have no relevance to the real situation. And we must recognize the further truth that our enemy has clearly established the objective of his war: World domination, with the destruction of the United States the principal step in attaining that objective.

But the turn to the offensive means, perhaps above all, a radical change

* "How Communism Will Be Defeated: An Offensive Attitude and Strategy," *Vital Speeches*, Vol. 16 (June 15, 1950), pp. 520–521 *passim*. Originally delivered before the Economic Club of Detroit, Feb. 20, 1950. By permission of the publisher.

in our outlook and attitude, in will and in resolution. Since we are in a war we must be in it to win, and we are going to win.

I do not want in any way to minimize the gravity of the present crisis, or its urgency. Nevertheless, I believe that many of us and many of our political leaders in Washington tend now to over-estimate the capabilities of the Soviet Union as much as many under-estimated those capabilities in 1941. . . .

It is fatal, true enough, to be complacent, but why should we lack confidence? We have reason for confidence if we act; but if we fail to act it will be we who disintegrate. Our enemy, with time allowed him, will make good his deficiencies and will relentlessly shift the balance against us.

The turn to the offensive, then, means recognizing the truth about the situation itself, about the war, the enemy, his objective, his strength, and his weakness. Since that is the truth, the turn to the offensive must mean also a decision on our part to meet the demands of the situation. This decision, granted the truth, can only be the defeat of the enemy: that is, the reduction of Communism to impotence. That, then, is our objective.

The steps, the methods, whereby to attain the objective must naturally be adjusted to the given stage of the struggle, while at the same time we prepare for succeeding stages.

The present stage is not that of all-out fighting by all military arms, though it is a mistake to think of this present stage as merely a cold war. It has not been so cold in Greece, China, Indonesia and Indo-China. But the present stage is primarily one where the struggle takes place in terms of economic, psychological, political and subversive methods. All of these may perhaps be summed up, with the help of a word that became known during recent years, as "Resistance" methods. We must build a world-wide anti-Communist Resistance.

Our task then is, in terms of an offensive attitude and strategy, to aim at our ultimate objective, and to carry through appropriate measures in these various fields, supplementing them where necessary by military measures.

. . . We can, for example, strengthen the economic basis of our allies and potential allies, and we have been doing so, though not always in the most intelligent and fruitful manner. In this field we must make more certain that we are getting something worthwhile for our money. And we can do much more than we yet have to block the economic consolidation of the Soviet sphere. The inability of the Communists to solve the economic problem is one of their key weaknesses. It would be an immense error if through sentimentality or a short-sighted wish for profits we solved it for them.

By psychological warfare, material aid and intelligent cooperation we can win the labor movement of the world from Communist control. The importance of this task has been clearly recognized by the best of our own labor leaders. They recently took the initiative in launching the new democratic and anti-Communist world federation. But to keep world labor on our side we must prove in action, as well as in propaganda, that both freedom and a decent and expanding standard of life and livelihood are to be found on our side, not on the side of Moscow.

By facing and telling the truth we can break the hold which Communist ideas have on so many of the world's intellectuals. By psychological and subversive methods we could undermine the Communist regimes in the satellite nations and within the Soviet Union itself. The subjects of the Communist tyranny hate their present masters, and long for liberation. We must make clear to them that we are their allies against a common enemy, and that we seek to free, not to destroy, them.

We can today, if we make the necessary decisions, begin the building of an anti-Communist resistance movement which would draw forces from the vast exile groups and would extend directly into and through the Soviet sphere. . . . These exiles [from the Soviet Empire] today are an anti-Communist force of almost unlimited potential, but we have hardly begun to use or even understand that potential.

We must bear in mind that a conventional, purely military, strategy cannot in all probability defeat the Soviet Union. The purely military problem for both sides seems almost insoluble. The Soviet power will have to be destroyed at least in part from within, by the will and action of its own subjects. And it will be if our decision gives the necessary leadership. If we so decide, if we abandon both passivity and defeatism, we can look confidently toward much more striking operations than those that I have so far listed.

. . . [Formosa should not only be held] but used as a base for a counter-offensive to harry the Communists on the mainland by air and commando methods, by psychological and guerrilla methods, and to keep alive on the mainland a spreading Chinese anti-Communist resistance that will some day roll the Communists back and out. . . .

Why should Stalin be allowed to keep his untenable Mediterranean position in Albania? Are a few thousand Moscow agents plus a handful of native Communists enough to hold, if we decide to push, and to give the anti-Communist population of Albania a chance to re-assert its freedom? And if we clear Albania, then Bulgaria, and after it the rest of the Balkans would begin to crumble. This, by the way, the crumbling of the Communist position in Eastern Europe, would be a far better protection for France and Italy and Britain than anything that can be expected for many years from the Atlantic Pact and the program of West European Rearmament.

As soon as we adopt the offensive point of view, basing it on a true estimate of the real situation, dozens of specific proposals come at once to mind. It is no longer a question of reacting feebly and too late by hasty and ill-considered improvisations to moves of the enemy, but of seizing the initiative and by a whole series of actions on a world scale throwing him off balance.

But we must conceive our plans, not in a flea-biting, grudging, kibitzing sort of way. They must be massive, bold, audacious.

Such in outline is the other direction that the present turn in United States policy can take. Appeasement or the offensive. It is now to be one or the other.

If we accept the offensive, what may we expect? At the maximum we can attain our objective, the defeat of Soviet-based Communism, without all-out war. If the rigid totalitarian structure of Communism once starts to crack, it may well split wide open. At the worst we will improve our political and strategic position. We will seize the initiative and timing from the Kremlin, and prepare the basis not only for more certain victory in the all-out war that may come in spite of whatever policy we may adopt, but also for the more fruitful exploitation of that victory.

The choice between appeasement and the offensive in completing the turn from containment is in short the choice between defeat and victory. The making of this choice may be delayed and prolonged. Unfortunately, every week's delay has a heavy cost. But no one who knows our history and our people can doubt the final outcome.

THE QUAKER ALTERNATIVE: REAL NEGOTIATION THROUGH THE UNITED NATIONS, INTERNATIONAL DISARMAMENT, AND A WORLD AID PROGRAM

A REPORT PREPARED FOR THE
AMERICAN FRIENDS SERVICE COMMITTEE

This report[1] has attempted to indicate reasons for believing that improvement is possible in the relationship between the United States and

[1] *The United States and the Soviet Union: Some Quaker Proposals for Peace* (New Haven: Yale University Press, 1949), pp. 38–39. By permission of the publisher.

The members who prepared this report, between March and September, 1949, for the American Friends Service Committee included the following: Gilbert F. White, Chairman; Elmore Jackson, Secretary; Frank Aydelotte; Stephen G. Cary; William Edgerton; Thomas B. Harvey; Philip Jacob; Cornelius Kruse; Griffith G. Levering; Ray Newton; Theodore Paullin; James M. Read; Frederick B. Tolles; Richard R. Wood; D. Robert Yarnall; and Robert W. Frase, who served until May 1, 1949. EDITOR.

the Soviet Union. It has suggested certain policies in connection with economic relations, Germany, and the United Nations which we believe would lessen tension and improve relations between the two countries. The basic considerations and the specific policies are intended to give reality to our conviction that the world can be so ordered as to eliminate war, or the threat of war, as an instrument of national policy.

The basic considerations leading to our belief that improved relations are possible between the United States and the Soviet Union include the following:

1. The fact that there is a widespread and sincere desire for peace.

2. The conviction that both the Soviet social organization and the type of social organization prevailing in the western world are likely to persist for some time and that attention should be directed to their coexistence rather than to the victory of either over the other.

3. The conclusion that, while there are drastic differences in the methods of the two systems and some differences in their aims, both systems attempt to promote the general welfare, while defining it differently.

4. The belief that there is the possibility of sufficient accommodation between the two systems, as evidenced by changes that have occurred in both, to permit them to coexist and to compete peacefully in the same world.

5. The probability that much of the present tension between the United States and the Soviet Union reflects the mutual fear felt by each of attack by the other.

6. The improbability of overcoming this fear and attaining either the impression or the fact of security by arms competition.

7. The desirability of reducing armaments and the reliance on military weapons before the burdens of an arms competition weaken democratic institutions.

8. The likelihood that neither the United States nor the Soviet Union intends at the present time to promote its foreign policy by means of direct military aggression.

The economic policy suggested is one of increasing the welfare of East and West by opening up the channels of trade and encouraging in particular the constructive personal contacts made possible by increased trade between the United States and the U.S.S.R.

It is suggested that the United States continue to seek the restoration of a united Germany to a place in the community of nations, under conditions of international supervision which will effectively prevent the development of German industrial potential into an eventual instrument of military power and which will provide access for all nations, including the Soviet Union, to the benefits of trade with Germany.

Since a large part of the tension between the United States and the

U.S.S.R. appears to be due to the attempts of each to attain security, the report suggests steps for developing and strengthening the United Nations as an instrument for settling disputes and for reducing the economic and emotional burden of armaments—including atomic weapons. The modern scene offers what seems to us conclusive evidence that armaments competition and national preparations for war provide no practical solution to the problems of achieving national and international security. We are convinced that effective means for achieving security lie at hand in the economic and political fields. We have suggested certain measures which would, we believe, not only serve to relax present tensions but give substantial support to mankind's efforts to attain a greater measure of freedom and economic well-being. If the United States could, in a spirit of reasonable good will, persist in seeking agreements along the lines here suggested, we believe it would lead to the mutual concessions which are necessary if peace is to be made secure.
. . .

We recognize that we shall be criticized for suggesting that there is an approach to world problems that emphasizes something other than national military power.[2] "The Quakers mean well," people will say, "but they don't recognize the nature of the evil which the world faces." We believe we do recognize the nature of the evil we face. We have been out in the troubled places of the world trying to meet evil head-on, and we have found that reconciliation is possible in most unpromising situations. For ten years we have worked in China on both sides of the civil war. We think we do know something about evil in China—and goodness as well. We have seen Communism, for we have lived and worked in several Communist states. We have felt its terror and its ruthlessness, but we have also seen its strength grow because of needed reforms made and new hopes kindled. We may be mistaken in our specific recommendations, but we believe we are aware of the nature of the problem. . . .

An Alternative Program: New Initiative for Peaceful Settlements

. . . The attempt of the United States to limit the expansion of Soviet Communism by force has not only failed to advance our ultimate pur-

[2] *Steps to Peace: A Quaker View of U.S. Foreign Policy* (American Friends Service Committee, 1951), pp. 4–5, 31–63 *passim*. By permission. Copies of the complete report are available upon request.

This report, which supplements the Committee's earlier one, was prepared by the following: Stephen G. Cary, Chairman; Julia E. Branson; William B. Edgerton; Harrop A. Freeman; Corrinne Hardesty; Thomas B. Harvey; Lewis M. Hoskins; William R. Huntington; Elmore Jackson; Philip E. Jacob; W. Rhoads Murphey; Theodore Paullin; Clarence E. Pickett; Gilbert F. White; and Richard R. Wood, Secretary. EDITOR.

poses, but has tended to alienate our friends and increase the risk of all-out war. . . . The only alternative to attempting to reach a decision by force is to attempt to reach one by negotiation and diplomacy. . . .

1. *Negotiation requires a flexible attitude.*

Two conflicting points of view must be reconciled, and this can only happen if both sides are prepared to give up non-essentials for the sake of agreement on essentials. Basic principles must not be compromised, but give-and-take is at the very heart of the whole process, and negotiators must be free to alter their first suggestions as the explorations of conflicting points of view proceeds. It is important to avoid taking a "final" position from which there can be no retreat, for that means the failure of the negotiation effort unless this "final" position is acceptable to the other party. . . .

. . . The United States could well have encouraged negotiations with regard to a Korean settlement when its armies were first approaching the 38th parallel, or again, when the narrow "waist" of North Korea was reached. Similarly the Chinese government could have negotiated when its armies were throwing back the U.N. forces in December [1950]. Both have had positions of strength in the course of the struggle, but neither has been disposed to negotiate at such times because it seemed that much more could be achieved through the total military decision that appeared on the verge of attainment.

2. *Negotiation requires an open mind.*

Each side must be prepared to examine the proposals of the other on their merits. Flexibility on one's own position must be matched by a willingness to try to understand other points of view. This requires that neither side assume its opinion to be clothed in moral infallibility.

. . . India made one notable attempt to break this pattern [of stubbornness] last fall [1950] when her U.N. delegation suggested that since the American and Russian resolutions on Korea had a number of points in common, both should be studied carefully to see if the basis for a common resolution could be found. This step was in accord with good negotiation procedure, but unfortunately, the Indian resolution was defeated as a result of American pressure against it. . . .

3. *Negotiation requires privacy.*

It is important to maintain an atmosphere in which either side can make concessions without embarrassment. This suggests that negotiation cannot always be carried on in a goldfish bowl, a fact industrial negotiators have long been aware of. When differences are under discussion, the representatives of labor and management closet themselves without benefit of press or public. Only the results become public property, to be either accepted or rejected as the constituencies see fit. This technique might well be called one of "open covenants secretly arrived at." . . .

4. *Negotiation requires persistence.*

There may come a time when fundamental disagreement on matters of genuine principle force negotiations to be broken off, but no termination should ever be regarded as permanent, for new developments may serve at any time to break an apparent deadlock. If negotiators become discouraged or exhausted, they should be replaced. . . .

To what extent can new negotiations with the Soviet Union succeed? No one knows. Suspicion and lack of confidence in mutual good faith have grown so great that negotiation on any basis is difficult. Moreover, even if the United States were to make a fresh start, it will still require a new approach on the part of the Russians, whose conduct at the negotiating table has contributed to the present impasse. Patience and rigid adherence on our part to the best traditions of negotiation may yet bring an end to the Soviet habit of using conferences as a forum for ideological statements. In any event, we have the responsibility of making the record clear as regards our own conduct. A new spirit in diplomacy by this country undoubtedly would have a greater chance of eliciting more constructive responses from Soviet representatives than have past tactics. . . .

THE ESSENTIAL ROLE OF THE UNITED NATIONS

How is it possible, during . . . [the] period previous to general disarmament agreements, to strengthen the United Nations peacemaking functions? We believe the following suggestions are worth careful study.

1. Move immediately to admit all applicants who express the willingness to accept the responsibilities of membership.

2. Avoid exerting pressure on other countries to accept the position being taken by the United States Government. . . .

3. Renew efforts to settle the Korean conflict by negotiation. . . .

4. Emphasize and develop the Security Council and General Assembly in their peace-making functions. . . .

DISARMAMENT AND INTERNATIONAL CONTROL OF ARMS

. . . As long as individual nations engage in a race for armed preparedness, efforts to negotiate and to develop the peace-making machinery of the United Nations will be lost in the mounting fear and suspicion that an arms race is bound to produce. The writers have already rejected the concept that a high level of armament will produce an atmosphere more conducive to the solution of international problems. It follows that real progress toward laying the foundations of a peaceful world requires a new effort to achieve true disarmament. . . .

The chief disagreements between the United States and the Soviet Union regarding control of atomic weapons were originally over four issues: (*a*) the Soviet Union has insisted and the United States refused to agree that present atomic weapons be destroyed before a control system comes into effect; (*b*) the United States has asserted and the Soviet Union denied the necessity of international ownership and operation of all plants for producing and using atomic energy; (*c*) the United States has insisted on continuous and thorough inspection, and the Soviet Union on periodic inspection, supplemented by additional inspection on suspicion; (*d*) the United States has insisted on punishment of violators by majority vote in the Security Council, whereas the Soviet Union has insisted on the retention of the veto with respect to sanctions. . . .

It . . . appears [after a brief review of new scientific and political developments, including shifts by both sides on some of the four points of disagreement] that there are sufficient possibilities in the political area to justify serious new efforts in the field of disarmament as it relates to atomic energy.

Agreements as to timetable, inspection, management, and sanctions—the four controversial areas—do not appear entirely beyond the realm of possibility. The rewards of success are so great, and the costs of continued deadlock so high, that the United States should make vigorous and continuing efforts to explore every possible avenue for agreement. . . .

[The Committee also urges support of a "control plan for conventional arms."]

DEVELOPMENT OF LARGE-SCALE PROGRAMS OF MUTUAL AID

. . . We should help create the conditions under which the nations of the world can work together to help themselves in the struggle for food and freedom, justice and security. In some parts of the world, such as the densely populated sections of Asia, the struggle centers on health and improved methods of production, particularly of food. In other parts of the world, such as western Europe, where the arms burden is increasingly heavy, the problem is that of converting the large productive capacity from an arms economy to a peace economy, and thus avoid the depressing and disastrous effects of an armaments race. . . .

The present writers consider a world-wide program of **mutual aid,** properly conceived and excuted, as one momentous answer to . . . [the] problem of violent versus peaceful change. We feel that it is practicable. Wisely conceived within the framework of the United Nations, it might enforce and accelerate the profound social revolution now in progress in the world in such a fashion that arms and the threat of arms would become insignificant. . . .

Any alternative, however, must be an inclusive one. Half-way measures will not suffice; indeed, they might well make matters worse. Disarmament cannot be undertaken without a concurrent development of the United Nations into an organization having the confidence of all its members and the ability to carry out its inspection function. On the other hand, there can be no effective development of the United Nations as long as individual nation states engage in a competitive arms race that means international anarchy. Moreover, neither the elimination of arms nor the building of a strong world organization is likely so long as the basic causes of strife are allowed to continue unchecked. This means that a world-wide attack on proverty, disease, hunger, and outworn social and economic patterns must be launched simultaneously with renewed efforts toward disarmament and the establishment of world law. There is, of course, a vital economic relation between mutual aid and disarmament, both in freeing resources and in taking up the slack that would result from checking the arms race. Finally, and fundamental to the whole process, is the development of new faith and new reliance upon negotiation as a technique in international relations. Progress in any area, whether it be toward transforming the United Nations, ending the arms race, or raising standards of living, will be dependent on long and difficult negotiations. Unless Americans can overcome their emotional distaste for negotiation, there is no hope for reaching the objectives that they have set for their foreign policy.

Will this kind of vigorous alternative bring the peace and security and freedom that all men long for? We believe that it would. It provides a vigorous answer to the economic challenge of communism, without opening any nation to charges of imperialism. It tests the Soviet claim of interest in general disarmament and points a way out from the crushing burden of arms. By making the United Nations the focal point through which the entire program is carried forward, it greatly strengthens the position of the world organization and opens the way for its development into an effective instrument of world law. It puts us squarely in favor of a major peace offensive and makes clear our willingness to sacrifice and accept the risks that inevitably accompany a bold and uncharted step. The world longs for this kind of moral leadership from America, and we cannot afford to leave anyone in doubt about what we stand for.

UNITED STATES NAVAL AND AIR POWER WILL PROTECT OUR WESTERN HEMISPHERE GIBRALTAR

BY HERBERT HOOVER*

[Former President Herbert Hoover has an outstanding record as a public servent. During World War I he served as chairman of the Commission for Relief in Belgium and as United States Food Administrator. Under Presidents Harding and Coolidge he held the post of Secretary of Commerce. Recently he served as chairman of the Commission on Organization of the Executive Branch of the Government. A long-time foe of the New Deal, he has also been an outspoken critic of United States foreign policy. EDITOR.]

In order to reach any conclusions as to the wise course for America to pursue in the critical issues which confront us we must again and again appraise the constantly-shifting forces moving in the world. . . .

LAND WAR STRENGTHS

The Kremlin-directed horde has under arms and in reserves probably 300 combat divisions, with 30,000 tanks. I am now told they have over 20,000 mostly tactical planes and they have with their satellites fifty million men available for cannon fodder.

In World War II, when Russia was without the satellites, the Germans failed with 240 well equipped divisions to overcome her. With her allies of Gen. Man Power, Gen. Space, Gen. Winter and Gen. Scorched Earth, she had stopped the Germans even before lend-lease had reached her.

The nations of Europe in the Atlantic pact have at the present moment less than twenty equipped and trained combat divisions available for European action.

There is here a stark reality upon which our foreign policies must be based. With any seeable land forces from non-Communist nations, even including the United States, a land offensive against the Communist could bring no military victory, no political conclusion. But that does not mean that there are no other methods of stopping the Kremlin's ambitions.

THE DEFENSE OF THE AMERICAN PEOPLE AND THE WESTERN HEMISPHERE

The second stark realism upon which our foreign policies must be based is the defense of the Western Hemisphere. Its defense is not only in our interests but in the interests of free men everywhere. . . .

* *The New York Times*, Feb. 10, 1951, p. 4.

I may say at once that with proper economic action this hemisphere can be made self-contained in critical raw materials. . . .

Further, unless we so dissipate our strength as to become a beaten and crushed people, we will be able to keep sea lanes open.

Moreover, this hemisphere can be defended from Communist armies come what will. It is still surrounded with a great moat. To transport such invading armies either 3,000 miles across the Atlantic or 6,000 miles across the Pacific would require transport ships and naval protection which the Russians do not possess and could not build or seize, no matter what further countries they occupy. If we have a proper naval and air strength we could sink them in mid-ocean. With somewhat more atten-tion paid to our defense, this would apply to invasion via the Bearing Straits. Hitler could not even cross the English Channel. Atomic bombs do not transport troops over the ocean. Communist armies can no more get to Washington than any Allied armies can get to Moscow. . . .

The American people should not be frightened into rash action by fear that we cannot survive. I am not advocating isolationism. But if other nations should fail, we may be isolated by circumstances and against our will.

We might go into a period hard to endure, but this nation can stick it out.

Our Economic-Capacity Over a Long Period

The third stark realism upon which our policies must be built is our economic capacity. The bleak outlook of the world may well last more than a decade—possibly two of them.

The new budget calls for Federal spending of over $71.6 billion. This $71 billions alone, plus state and local expenditures, is about 37 per cent of our national income.

That is beyond the long endurance of any nation and fatal to the preser-vation of a system of free men. . . .

. . . We simply cannot carry this expenditure or such tax load [called for by such expenditure] for long. . . .

The United Nations

The fourth focal point of our thinking must be the United Nations.

Our stark reality here is the lack of cohesion and unity in the free nations. Even some of our European allies are anxious to appease the Chinese branch of the Kremlin on policies of the United Nations.

Despite this, we must not forget that the aspiration of mankind for over a century has been to find peace by collective action against aggressors. The United Nations was built on this same central idea as the concert of

Europe and the League of Nations. Halting and faulty as it may be, we cannot abandon this idea and this hope.

But it must be clear that the U.N. for the present will not be a substantial protection from Communist aggression.

OUR POLICIES IN THE FAR EAST

Our men are holding heroically to the mission assigned us by the United Nations in Korea. . . . But were we to drive all the enemy out of Korea, how much of our armies must remain there to protect it?

Japan, Formosa and the Philippines are vital links in our national security. This must not be minimized by nations anxious to direct our energies to Europe. We will need [to] retain much military strength in the Pacific to protect those areas.

Certainly there is little stark reality in talking about American ground divisions in Europe in view of our involvement in Asia.

THE NORTH ATLANTIC MILITARY ALLIANCE

The sixth consideration in our decisions revolves around the North Atlantic pact and the proposals to start another American expeditionary land army to Europe.

Current statistics stretch this pact far beyond its text. The pact provides that the nations shall aid each other in case of attack. There has been no attack.

Moreover, at the time of ratification of that alliance the administration, through the Secretary of State and the chairman of the Foreign Relations Committee, gave positive assurances that under the pact no expeditions of American ground troops would be sent to Europe. That certainly meant no forces to Europe prior to attack. Our participation, prior to an attack, was to be limited to munitions. The pact being the will of the American people through the Congress, and in the faith of the text and those assurances, I supported the alliance.

But last fall [1950] it became evident that the Administration was contemplating sending ground troops to Europe. It was also evident that after years of gigantic American subsidies, the European Atlantic pact nations had done nothing of consequence toward their own defense. Former Prime Minister Churchill had repeatedly and forthrightly stated this fact—the last occasion being only a few weeks ago. . . .

Then General Eisenhower was appointed to organize their military strength. And the general has become the potent symbol of the policy of at once sending American ground troops to Europe. . . .

But his appointment does not commit the American people as to policy. The stark reality in Western Continental Europe are their large Com-

munist parties and the disunities which gnaw at their vitals. Their prejudices prevent taking Spain into the alliance with twenty divisions and the
most defensible area in Europe. For some reason Turkey and Greece are
excluded from the alliance.

Equally vital is the fact that there is little hope of adequate land defense
of Europe without West German participation. . . .

From press reports based on information from European officials and
from Gen. Eisenhower's statements, it would appear that his army, including the two American divisions now in Germany, will start with nine
or ten divisions; by the end of two years, including American divisions,
it would seem to be thirty-five or forty divisions.

The stark reality is that such an army is small compared to the strength
of the enemy.

America is at present the major deterrent to the Kremlin's ambitions
of world conquest. There is nothing that Stalin would like more than to
get the United States into his clutches by fighting us on the ground in
Europe. There lies his overwhelming strength.

Disaster could thus come to the American Hemisphere with no salvation
to Europe. . . .

Despite all these stark realities and these problems, I have believed there
is a way to at least an uneasy peace for the world. . . .

I can most clearly state the points of foreign policies in which many of
us believe at this time by summarizing a program. No program can be
perfect—none without risk. For the present I suggest:

1. We should devote our overwhelming productive power to air and
naval strength and supply of munitions.

2. If the Europeans are attacked, we should be prepared and use such
overwhelming air and naval power to the limit and keep it up until they
have had enough. The Kremlin knows that we are committed by the
Congress to do so. I believe that reserve, if large enough, is Europe's real
protection.

3. We should supply munitions to nations doing their utmost to defend
themselves.

4. From the stark realistic, economic, political and military reasons
which I have given you, my personal conviction is that we should not
create land armies for expeditions into the quicksands of either Europe
or China. I do not want to even start on the road to another Korea.

5. There are those who think we should send more divisions to Europe
for their encouragement even before there is an attack. To them, I urge
watchful waiting until much more military strength has been developed
by Europe itself and there is more evidence they have resolved their disunities.

6. We must reduce our national expenditure to a level we can carry over a long term of years, and at the same time avoid economic disaster which can destroy freedom in America.

Sen. Byrd estimates that $8.6 billion of proposed non-defense expenditures in the budget could be reduced or postponed. We should spend all we can afford on air, navy and munitions rather than large armies.

7. We can and must defend Formosa, the Philippines and Japan. We can do it by naval and air forces.

As to Korea, we should demand of the United Nations that they call for a stop of supplies to Communist China by the non-Communist nations.

Since Red China is making war on our American armies, we should free Chiang Kai-shek to do what he wishes in China and furnish him munitions.

8. I proposed three years ago that we should give full independence to Japan and Western Germany under representative governments. During 100 years these nations were the great dams against these Russian-controlled hordes. In the last war we may have been engaged in a great crusade for freedom of mankind, but we certainly destroyed these two dams. The sooner they are given their independence the sooner, for their own security, they will resume their ancient role.

9. Recently I proposed that if the nations of Europe failed we should, as a prudent nation, have in mind a second line of air and naval defense based upon the foreign shores of the Pacific and Atlantic Oceans, both North and South, and I may add the Mediterranean and Indian Ocean.

10. Congress should recover its constitutional authority over starting wars. It could certainly do so through its power over the purse.

I have proposed no retreat, no withdrawal. I have proposed no repudiation of treaties or obligations. Rather I have proposed that the pledges to the Congress and the American people be kept. I have proposed that we stop, look and listen before we start on a road of land war that risks the loss of all civilization.

PEACE IS THE KEY TO SOVIET FOREIGN POLICY

BY JESSICA SMITH*

[Jessica Smith has been editor of *Soviet Russia Today* since 1936. To this editor's knowledge this magazine is rarely, if ever, adversely critical of the Soviet Union. An organizer and speaker

* "The Soviet Struggle for Peace, 1917–1950," *Soviet Russia Today*, Vol. 18 (November, 1950), pp. 4–7 *passim*. By permission of the publisher and Miss Smith.

in the woman's suffrage movement in the United States, Jessica Smith did famine relief work in the U.S.S.R. in 1922–1924. She is the author of *Woman in Soviet Russia* and *People Come First*. EDITOR.]

The search for peace is the key to Soviet foreign policy today as it has been from the first day of its existence.

Lenin's idea that socialism could be built in one country alone, or in several countries, triumphed over Trotsky's idea that socialism could never win anywhere until it won everywhere, and so had to be imposed on the world through continuing wars and revolutions.

The very concept of building socialism in one country presupposed the peaceful co-existence of the socialist and capitalist worlds which has been the chief aim of Stalin's foreign policy. For this reason Stalin and the other Soviet leaders have always sought to keep the peace by conciliation and agreement, and continue to do so today. . . .

In contrast to this attitude . . . it is worth recalling that on February 8 of . . . [1950] Secretary Acheson enunciated very bluntly what had already been clearly manifested as the foreign policy of the Truman Administration, and has since been confirmed by events in Korea and the Far East. Secretary Acheson stated that our country had abandoned all efforts to reach agreement with the Soviet Union by negotiation and that henceforth our sole reliance must be on superior force. He sought to justify this on the ground that no agreement with the Soviet Union is possible, because the Soviet Government does not keep its agreements and is pursuing an imperialistic, aggressive program incompatible with peace and national independence.

Having built up this bogey of Soviet expansionism, imperialism, aggression, reliance-on-force-and-violence, etc., the administration is hard put to it today to explain the absence of a single Soviet move that fits into this picture, or of a single Russian soldier in any of the postwar armed conflicts. Since the USSR refused to oblige by any single aggressive incident the new myth has been created of "indirect aggression," "war by proxy," etc. But this hasn't worked either, because all of this of course had to be part of an overall Soviet plan "to dominate the world by force." And now the moment has come when the Soviet Union might be expected to cash in on the results of all its indirect aggression and openly to launch direct aggression to achieve world domination. But still it makes no move.

The military experts point out that the time for the Soviet Union to launch its long planned aggressive war is now, when the West is demonstrably at a disadvantage. They point out that the Western powers dispose a bare fifteen divisions in Western Europe, while the USSR has ready and waiting at least eight times that many who could over-run Europe within a few days. They point to the lessons of Korea, where the U.S. has had to utilize most of its available land power, as well as whatever it could collect from Allied powers against "the weakest of the Soviet Satellites," representing about one per cent of the total military power at the disposition by the USSR and the socialist sector of the world. They point out how different would have been the outcome if the joint power of the Soviet Union and China had been thrown into the struggle, and ponder why they lost the chance of doing this when just a few Soviet airplanes might have broken the back of U.S. armed power in Korea, and thrown U.S. forces into the sea.

Why didn't the USSR take this opportunity? Why don't they take advantage of obvious present Western weakness, scatter their opponent's power by starting aggression all around the world, against Western Germany, against Yugoslavia, against Turkey, against Iran, get into the fray in Korea, and plunge the world now into the world war that, it has charged, they have so long been planning, now when it is so clear they could win, when time will only give the West the opportunity to complete its rearming of Germany and Japan, build up its fifty or more divisions in Europe, pile up more troops and armaments everywhere, stockpile more and better A-bombs, and perhaps H-bombs too?

Why don't they fight?

Because . . . the Soviet Union wants peace. Because it is engaged in the biggest peacetime construction projects ever launched by man which can be completed only under peaceful conditions. Because they mean what they say. It is as simple as that.

This is the plain, obvious, incontrovertible, unalterable fact. It does not mean that they will not fight when attacked, as they demonstrated when they were far weaker and had far fewer allies than they have today. It does mean that they will not start a war, and that they will do absolutely everything possible to avoid being provoked into war, to avoid the outbreak of a new world holocaust.

This, and no trickery, is behind all their policies. This and only this explains every word and deed of the Soviet leaders. This explains their wholehearted backing of the World Peace Petition for the outlawry of atomic warfare and the branding as a war criminal of the first country that will resort to it. No country, planning war, would go to such lengths to mobilize the desires of its own people and the world for peace. No country, planning to use the atom bomb, would take such pains to insure in advance that it would be branded as a criminal by the whole world in so doing.

On June 25 [1950], when the Administration plunged into its military adventure in Korea, pulling the UN in after it, without any attempt to reach a peaceful solution through negotiation, and in the succeeding months during which it has rejected all efforts at mediation and conciliation from whatever quarter, it demonstrated its determination to avoid all moves toward negotiations, even to the ultimate risk of a new world war.

The Soviet Union has never abandoned its efforts for peaceful coexistence through negotiations and agreement, whether on a bilateral basis, through the Foreign Ministers' Council or through the United Nations. The Soviet Union has not violated its agreements, but on the contrary has an unexcelled record of faithful adherence to its international obligations.

And today, true to its consistent and unswerving policy of peace, and despite all provocations, the Soviet Union continues unceasingly to press the United States and the other Western powers to join with it in new efforts to end the threat of new war and to settle all differences by peaceful means.

QUESTIONS AND PROBLEMS

1. Indicate, and then appraise, the action taken by the United States, within and outside of the United Nations, in connection with (a) peaceful settlement of disputes, (b) collective action to defeat aggression, (c) relief of the burden of armament?

2. Why does Burnham maintain that the United States must take the offensive in the current international crisis? How does Burnham's position differ from that of Mr. Truman's?

3. Indicate, in detail, what measures Burnham recommends to execute his offensive strategy? Why do you believe that these measures are or are not carefully calculated risks?

4. State and then criticize each of the basic considerations that lead the authors of the first Quaker Report to the conviction that war, or the threat of war, can be eliminated as an instrument of national policy.

5. Evaluate the alternative program for foreign policy sketched in the second Quaker Report?

6. Appraise Mr. Hoover's ten-point Foreign Policy Program in terms of his (a) confidence in air and naval strength; (b) lack of confidence in (1) United States land expeditionary forces to Europe or Asia, (2) the United Nations, (3) our European allies; (c) emphasis on a second line of American defense; (d) belief that his program is "a way to at least an uneasy peace for the world."

7. Evaluate the arguments that Miss Smith presents in her defense of the Soviet Union in light of what has happened since she wrote and what you think may happen in the future.

8. How does one reconcile the sometimes conflicting viewpoints expressed by the contributors to this chapter on the following points: (*a*) possibility of peaceful co-existence of the United States and the Soviet Union; (*b*) confidence in the United Nations; (*c*) causes of the present impasse in international affairs; (*d*) proof of peaceful intent and good faith; (*e*) attitudes of the United States and the Soviet Union toward peaceful negotiation, disarmament, and the meaning of democracy; and (*f*) strategy and tactics that have been used, are being used, or should be used by the United States and the Soviet Union in executing their respective foreign policies?

9. How *should* the United States deal with the Soviet Union? In answering this question be sure to make explicit the basic value judgments and premises with which you start and the factual evidence that you utilize to buttress the logical presentation of your answer.

SELECT BIBLIOGRAPHY

FOREIGN POLICY ALTERNATIVES

Bulletin of the Department of State (Washington: Government Printing Office, weekly). Handy source of official statements and documents on American foreign relations. Presents the State Department point of view.

Burnham, James: *The Coming Defeat of Communism* (New York: John Day, 1950). Contains fuller exposition of thesis that United States must take the offensive in war now upon us.

Current Digest of the Soviet Press. Published weekly by Joint Committee on Slavic Studies appointed by American Council of Learned Societies and Social Science Research Council. Indispensable and comprehensive coverage of Soviet publications.

Hazard, John N.: "The United States and the Soviet Union," in *A Foreign Policy for the United States,* edited by Quincy Wright (Chicago: University of Chicago Press, 1947), pp. 25–33. Notes Soviet suspicion of foreign world and lack of Soviet desire to conquer the world. Urges United States to reduce and ultimately eliminate suspicions of United States aggression, while yet preserving power of self-defense and resisting aggression.

Hoover, Herbert: "Reorganizing United Nations without Russia," *The New York Times,* Apr. 28, 1950, p. 13. Reviews with misgivings United States experience with Russia. Urges moral and spiritual cooperation of God-fearing, free nations. Other Hoover speeches may also be consulted.

Kennan, George F.: "The Sources of Soviet Conduct," *Foreign Affairs* (July, 1947). Analyzes Soviet power in terms of Communist ideology and Soviet history. Contains the now classical exposition of the policy of containment. Subsequent articles may also be reviewed.

Lippmann, Walter: *The Cold War: A Study of U.S. Foreign Policy* (New York: Harper, 1947). A sharp critique of the policy of containment as strategically unsound, unworkable, and disastrous if attempted. His regular column in the *New York Herald Tribune* and other papers is a cogent and incisive presentation of Mr. Lippmann's foreign-policy views.

The Nation, Vol. 171 (Dec. 16, 1950). Devoted to question: "Peace with Russia—Can It Be Negotiated?" Stimulating group of critical essays, many of which are written from the "left-of-center" viewpoint.

Patterson, Ernest M. (ed.): "World Government," *Annals of the American Academy of Political and Social Science*, Vol. 264 (July, 1949). Contains recent discussion of world government as solution of problem of war and peace.

Streit, Clarence K.: *Union Now* (New York: Harper, 1949). Latest edition of pioneer plea for federal union of democracies.

BACKGROUND ON CURRENT FOREIGN POLICY

The Brookings Institution: *Major Problems of United States Foreign Policy* (Washington: Brookings, yearly).

Council of Foreign Affairs: *The United States and World Affairs* (New York: Harper, yearly). Problem papers on policy alternatives of particular interest.

Foreign Policy Reports. Published semimonthly except July and August by Foreign Policy Association.

Padelford, Norman J. (ed.): *Contemporary International Relations, 1949–1950* (Cambridge, Mass.: Harvard University Press, 1949). First of an annual series. Current collection of reading materials.

United Nations Bulletin. Published monthly by the United Nations department of public information. Indispensable summary of and guide to United Nation affairs.

United States House of Representatives, Committee on Foreign Affairs: *Background Information on the Soviet Union in International Relations*, House Report 3135, 81st Cong., 2d sess., 1950. Treats Soviet treaty violations, territorial expansion, obstructionism in United Nation and in international affairs, and United States efforts to cooperate with Soviet Union.

OF SPECIAL INTEREST

The student should also consult the record of the voluminous Senate hearings held in 1951 to investigate the relief of General Douglas MacArthur.

RANGER JUNIOR COLLEGE LIBRARY

Date Due

NO 1'55			
APR 14 '84			
APR 26 '84			